Living on the Edge of Chaos

Also available from ASQ Quality Press:

Thinking Tools for Kids: An Activity Book for Classroom Learning, Revised Edition
Sally J. Duncan and Barbara A. Cleary

Permission to Forget: And Nine Other Root Causes of America's Frustration with Education
Lee Jenkins

Transformation to Performance Excellence: Baldrige Education Leaders Speak Out
Sandra Cokeley, Margaret A. Byrnes, Geri Markley, and Suzanne Keely, editors

Charting Your Course: Lessons Learned During the Journey Toward Performance Excellence
Robert Ewy and John G. Conyers

The Quality Rubric: A Systematic Approach for Implementing Quality Principles and Tools in Classrooms and Schools
Steve Benjamin

Boot Camp for Leaders in K–12 Education: Continuous Improvement
Lee Jenkins, Lloyd O. Roettger, and Caroline Roettger

The Principal's Leadership Counts!: Launch a Baldrige-Based Quality School
Margaret A. Byrnes, with Jeanne C. Baxter

Improving Student Learning: Applying Deming's Quality Principles in the Classroom, Second Edition
Lee Jenkins

Quality Across the Curriculum: Integrating Quality Tools and PDSA with Standards
Jay Marino and Ann Haggerty Raines

Smart Teaching: Using Brain Research and Data to Continuously Improve Learning
Ronald J. Fitzgerald

There Is Another Way!: Launch a Baldrige-Based Quality Classroom
Margaret A. Byrnes with Jeanne C. Baxter

Futuring Tools for Strategic Quality Planning in Education
William F. Alexander and Richard W. Serfass

The Quality Toolbox, Second Edition
Nancy R. Tague

To request a complimentary catalog of ASQ Quality Press publications, call 800-248-1946, or visit our Web site at http://www.asq.org/quality-press.

Living on the Edge of Chaos

Leading Schools into the Global Age

Second Edition

Karolyn J. Snyder, Ed.D.

Michele Acker-Hocevar, Ph.D.

Kristen M. Snyder, Ph.D.

ASQ Quality Press
Milwaukee, Wisconsin

American Society for Quality, Quality Press, Milwaukee 53203
© 2008 American Society for Quality
All rights reserved. Published 2008
Printed in the United States of America

12 11 10 09 08   5 4 3 2 1

Library of Congress Cataloging-in-Publication Data
Snyder, Karolyn J.
 Living on the edge of chaos : leading schools into the global age / Karolyn J. Snyder, Michele Acker-Hocevar, Kristen M. Snyder.—2nd ed.
     p. cm.
 Includes bibliographical references and index.
 ISBN 978-0-87389-741-9 (casebound : alk. paper)
 1. School management and organization—United States—Case studies. 2. Total quality management—United States—Case studies. 3. Educational change—United States—Case studies. I. Acker-Hocevar, Michele, 1948- II. Snyder, Kristen M., 1964- III. Title.

 LB2806.S585 2009
 371.200973--dc22

                    2008013088

ISBN: 978–0-87389–741-9

Publisher: William A. Tony
Acquisitions Editor: Matt Meinholz
Project Editor: Paul O'Mara
Production Administrator: Randall Benson

ASQ Mission: The American Society for Quality advances individual, organizational, and community excellence worldwide through learning, quality improvement, and knowledge exchange.

Attention Bookstores, Wholesalers, Schools, and Corporations: ASQ Quality Press books, videotapes, audiotapes, and software are available at quantity discounts with bulk purchases for business, educational, or instructional use. For information, please contact ASQ Quality Press at 800–248–1946, or write to ASQ Quality Press, P.O. Box 3005, Milwaukee, WI 53201-3005.

Quality Press
600 N. Plankinton Avenue
Milwaukee, Wisconsin 53203
Call toll free 800-248-1946
Fax 414-272-1734
www.asq.org
http://www.asq.org/quality-press
http://standardsgroup.asq.org
E-mail: authors@asq.org

To place orders or to request a free copy of the ASQ Quality Press Publications Catalog, including ASQ membership information, call 800-248-1946. Visit our Web site at www.asq.org or http://www.asq.org/quality-press.

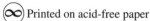 Printed on acid-free paper

Special Thanks . . .

For this second edition of *Living on the Edge of Chaos,* we want to thank our friends and partners around the world for the opportunities you gave us to learn about local living conditions, both good and poor, as well as the schooling challenges you face each day. We have found everywhere that great opportunities exist for educators and students who venture out onto the global stage. Your contributions to our lives have made this new work possible. The ideas from systems, chaos, and complexity theories continue to be the foundation for living and working in this dynamic and challenging global age. And many of you gave us examples of how these theories play out in practice as we journeyed through your schools and your lives and learned to live together in digital cultures. The stories of your school's global mindset, new images of power relationships, and the power of social networks provide a pathway to the future for many. To the international directors, board members, officers, hub coordinators, and Principals' Council members of the International School Connection, we are grateful for the special journey we have had together over the last decade as we explored options and found pathways to the future for twenty-first-century schools.

We want to give special thanks to several individuals who have made a difference for this second edition. To Professor Xinmin Sang and Professor Shuhua Li (who wrote the introduction to this book) for showing us the unique gifts to the world from the Chinese culture and its rich traditions. While Eastern and Western cultures are very different, we learned that we shared common views of the opportunities for educators to learn and work together across regions of the world. As such, your contribution to this work is important. To our colleagues and friends in the Pasco County School District in Florida, USA, who, after 20-plus years of working together, recently gave us a new challenge: *to design a training system to prepare school- and district-based leaders for building and leading sustainable school development for this global age of living.* The stories about the cutting-edge work of Pasco County School District that filtered through the first edition have provoked new thinking and action for many educators around the world. It is our hope that the new story of the last several years will once again inspire leaders to consider the importance of preparing their leaders with a systemic world-view, digital cultures, and a global context for school development.

A special thanks is given to Dr. Elaine Sullivan, our colleague in the International School Connection, who carefully edited and redirected our thinking about the new Chapter 1. To Dr. John Fitzgerald, also our colleague in the International School Connection, special thanks for your perspective, recommendations, and careful consideration of the intent of the final chapter in this book. Your perspectives mattered. And a special salute to Bob Anderson, our faithful (great) editor friend, who lived with us through the birth of this work in the woods of Maine one summer and who helped us craft each chapter in both the first and second editions. We are grateful!

Karolyn J. Snyder, Michele Acker-Hocevar, and Kristen M. Snyder
2008

Table of Contents

Tables and Figures

About the Authors

Karolyn J. Snyder, EdD, is President of a non-profit global organization called the International School Connection (ISC), which represents a global learning network of educational leaders and youth leaders who are building schools as global learning centers. Snyder retired as a Professor of Educational Leadership at the University of South Florida in 2002 to assume responsibility for the ISC. Snyder has six book publications, and over 250 journal publications on a systemic approach to school development. Her work on Systems Thinking and Living on the Edge of Chaos has taken her to over 40 countries around the world, with several diagnostic instruments on school culture and benchmarking quality systems translated into many languages. Her training program from the 1980s and 1990s in systemic school leadership, *Managing Productive Schools,* has recently been updated for the global context of schooling, and is called *Leadership for Sustainable School Development.*

Michele Acker-Hocevar, PhD, is a professor in Educational Leadership at Florida Atlantic University where she conducts research and works in the principal preparation program and also the doctoral program preparing future educational leaders and scholars. Her areas of teaching and research interests include school and leadership development, especially in regard to schools that are high poverty and serve students of color. Dr. Acker-Hocevar (2007) has recently finished an edited book on the study of the superintendency. The book, entitled, "Successful School Board Leadership: Lessons from Superintendents" is a national study of over 100 superintendents and their candid sharing of what works and what does not, particularly in their partnerships with school boards. The book, intended for school boards, shows the importance of superintendents and boards working collaboratively to achieve the vision and mission of their school district. Dr. Acker-Hocevar has published more than 30 articles that address her research on high poverty schools, school development and change, and building partnerships around shared power and a common vision. Her combined work experiences in education as a teacher and a school administrator, along with her work in business, and now at the university, provide her with a broad lens to study school reform and building community with strong partnerships that build the capacity to address tenacious issues like poverty and other inequities impacting our educational and social systems. She is a strong advocate of working collegially to identify common ground that builds connections within a concerned community. She believes that learning is a collective endeavor in which everyone's voice matters and that by working together, great things can happen.

Kristen Snyder, Ph.D., is a Senior Lecturer at Mid Sweden University in Sweden. Originally from the United States, Kristen has worked as a researcher and program developer for many years in both countries. Through her different academic positions and vantage points she has explored educational development, incorporating both global policy and local contexts for schooling. As a researcher over the years, Kristen has studied both schools and social organizations such as health, mental health, juvenile justice, and substance abuse programming for youth. At the heart of her focus has been organizational communication culture and leadership to support organizational development. In more recent years, with the development of globalization, her research focus has expanded to include networks and digital communication technologies and the impact that they have on organizing, communication, and leading.

As part of her contribution to the book, Kristen offers an exploration of the possibilities that now exist for education and learning as a result of advances in technology that promote what she considers the digital culture of living, learning, and working. In addition to her research focus, Snyder has also developed a repertoire of tools and knowledge regarding benchmarking and its application to whole school development. In her work with benchmarking she has participated in shaping two tools: The Education Quality Benchmark System, and the European Education Quality Benchmark System, the latter of which is a web-based tool that integrates dialogue processes for school connection and partnership learning. Moreover, Snyder has participated in leadership training programs for school districts and for government agencies regarding benchmarking, distributed team and organizational development, and whole school development for schools of diversity. As well, she is the Vice President for Research and Publications for the International School Connection, Inc. and Editor in Chief of the electronic journal WINGSPAN.

Introduction: Co-Creating Educational Wisdom For the Global Age of Living

Xinmin Sang

Professor of Education, Founding Director of Institute for Digital Learning and Management,
Dept. of Educational Sciences and Administration, Nanjing University, Nanjing China

Shuhua Li

Professor of Philosophy, Dept. of Philosophy, Nanjing University,
Nanjing, China

When we stood at the door of the twenty-first century, people held hopes for the future. However, when we entered this new century, we faced both hope and despair. We must examine the roots of these challenges from the perspective of social cultural psychology, and thereby promote discourse and understanding of different cultural traditions. Educators all over the world need to learn how to walk and work together for the future of the global human community. We must find ways to avoid disaster and embrace prosperity in this rapidly changing and highly competitive world. To find the answers to these challenges, we need the wisdom from politics, economics, and technology, and even more wisdom from understanding culture and education. The important mission of education now is to replace the outdated educational cultures from the industrial period. During the last 300 years, the industrial civilization created miracles for social development, and at the same time it fostered alienation from society, education, schools, and even from one another. In the first decade of the twenty-first century, we find that information technology is a double-edged sword that aggravates alienation on the one hand and that provides opportunities to solve many problems and re-energize society and education on the other.

With the tide of globalization advancing across the world, educators everywhere are challenged to enter the global stage and build more connections with each other in order to give shape to emerging systems of living and learning. In this book, the authors summarize their rich experiences from the past three decades and establish an important theoretical and methodological foundation for the transformation of schooling from an industrial age to a global and digital era of living. Their argument is to link schools together across the world to learn with and from one another, and to influence the preparation of youth for emerging local and global conditions.

To achieve this ambitious goal of creating a global context for learning, this second edition presents a striking portrait of both current global conditions and development opportunities, which offers a dynamic context for school learning today. An argument is set forth for developing digital cultures in which much of school learning can occur, not only by accessing the abundance of Web site resources, but also by students connecting with each other and with experts all over the world. They project that social networks of teachers and students will become the strategy for acquiring twenty-first-century knowledge and skills. The authors' new work on the issues of poverty and race presents the stark realities of cultural differences that are found within nations, which call for educators to develop a mindset for creating access to learning for all young people locally. A partnership model of power is necessary now for shared leadership and accountability, one that distributes resources and decision making among all role groups in education for transforming the lives of many students.

The emergence of systems science, the foundation for this book, marks the biggest revolution in Western science and has special significance for educational change. Education systems are not only living systems, but they are also complex systems, and as such they enable people to inherit the legacies of the past while adapting to current conditions for raising a new generation. At the beginning of the twenty-first century, an urgent task is to abandon mechanistic ideas about how institutions grow and to develop capacities to evolve active, responsive, and creative learning environments that prepare students for their future. However, it is an arduous task to apply systems science, especially emerging science, into practice. It is very exciting to read the book of Snyder, Acker-Hocevar, and Snyder, for they seem to understand the emergent nature of change in education as it adapts to changing world conditions. Even more important is their promotion of cross-cultural educational exchanges and cooperation to develop schools as global learning centers.

Three years ago, we met the authors and have communicated since through various means of technology, and also by visiting each other's countries. In the process we became acquainted with their work in the International School Connection (ISC), which was written about briefly in the first edition of this book. This context for their work provides a living laboratory for learning the lessons from chaos theory. As a systems scientist, Li has studied the new sciences for many years, and as an educator with a background in philosophy believes that this second edition provides a bridge for conversations about educational development around the world, for the sciences are based neither on nation nor culture. This chaos book provides a medium for both practical and academic conversation in a global and flat world of living and working.

The authors seem to enjoy the state of disequilibrium that is found at the edge of chaos, for in the development of the ISC they are living the theory: "Life is an emergent phenomenon, which thrives at the edge of chaos" (2000, 73); "Disequilibrium rather than equilibrium is the condition in which they are most alive, vital, responsive, and creative. Life at its best exists at the edge of chaos between order and surprise" (68). The theory of emergence provides them with wisdom and sensitivity for these times. "If we are sincere in becoming proactive for all student populations, new knowledge about the growth of natural systems will enable us to create a mental and spiritual shift that can breed success for all student populations" (70). "We can play a major role in guiding the emergence of new habits. This is the dance of life, which holds opportunity now. Information is the virtual lifeline for an organization's catalyzing" (2). They continue to argue that we have to "replace a machine metaphor for schools with that of a living organism" and "that the essential problem in changing the traditions of schooling is largely a matter of leader perception about the emergence of social systems" (55).

The ISC is becoming a powerful global network for educational leaders who want to address the realities of globalization and who are co-creating educational theories and practices through their international experiences, social networking, and digital cultures. Today, the ISC fosters global learning centers and partnerships among its member schools and colleges across the continents to promote school development that is grounded in the systemic theories that are presented in this book. Through the distributed ISC network of hubs, their members are using cost-effective cross-cultural communication systems with the help of information communication technology.

The ISC offers a living global learning laboratory of the new sciences world wide. In addition to creating a digital culture among educators, the ISC sponsors annual global summits in different parts of the world to provide a global platform for its members to learn and to share their valuable ideas and experiences relevant to sustainable school development. In October 2007, we hosted the third ISC Annual Global Summit in Beijing at the world-famous Beijing 101 Middle School. Educators and students learned together about educational change in China, heard about change initiatives in other ISC hubs around the world, and celebrated the first school in the world to be credentialed as an ISC Global Learning Center: A. Y. Jackson Secondary School in Ottawa, Canada. In our view, the ISC is a sustainable international educational organization because of its grounding in research and the new sciences and because of its promotion of international connections among educators and students. A new platform for education emerging from their work breaks the constraints of space and time, crosses cultures, and increases the influence of outstanding schools from around the world.

Educators who are building schools from a global mindset are the pioneers today. Frederick Engels (1940, 2) commented in his uncompleted work, *Dialectics of Nature,* that the Renaissance was "a time which called for giants and produced giants." Today calls for giants and should produce giants, for we are faced with intense competition and huge change. During the Renaissance, giants were personal, but conditions today require collective action. And now we need the collective wisdom that crosses borders and cultures. We propose the following four ways to develop educational wisdom for the global age: (1) renew the philosophy of learning and develop the wisdom of learning; (2) reinvent the philosophy of instruction and build the wisdom of teaching; (3) update the philosophy of schooling and generate the wisdom of school development; and, (4) promote educators to work together globally and gather their collective wisdom.

In this digital age, the serious challenges that schools face are similar. We propose the following three principles for developing wisdom for sustainable school development in the digital age: (1) Schools need the wisdom to learn both individually and organizationally to free the creativity of teachers and students who will fashion schools as learning organizations; (2) schools need wisdom to collaborate with one another and share what they are learning beyond their immediate obligations and interests to embrace win-win games; and (3) schools need wisdom to create new paradigms for culture and education, making full use of information communication technology and enabling everyone to break the constraints of space and time in order to connect with partner schools, families, and communities.

Educators need wisdom to understand each other through dialogue across cultures, to share and collaborate, and to transcend and enjoy co-creating the future of schools for our times. Virtual environments developed by information technology are attractive but dangerous for students to some extent. Improving the educational functions of the Internet, and reducing its potential risks, should become a priority to expand the globalization of schooling. Digitalization, digital cultures, and learning across borders free educators to imagine more possibilities for co-creating the future of school learning.

We plan to introduce the second edition of this chaos book to educators in China. The emerging science encourages diverse systems to self-organize, self-adapt, self-adjust, and self-learn,—for the connections that exist among diverse nations and cultures enable people to move beyond limitations and adapt to this changing world. "Simple systems do not evolve in isolation but are part of a complex web of co-evolution, and the web of co-evolution has taken the education enterprise quite naturally to the dawn of a new century" (2000, 70). Schooling practices that build on principles found in the new sciences free educators to take advantage of global resources and opportunities for themselves and for their students. The essential ideas in the emerging science are compatible with the idea of *emergence* in Chinese traditional culture. At the ISC 2007 Annual Global Summit in Beijing, we compared the ideas of this chaos book with that of *I Ching: Book of Changes,* and many participants were interested in this topic. We hope educators will want to learn from one another across Eastern and Western worlds to create more flexible conditions for developing a new course for education.

Let us together build unprecedented classrooms, schools, families, and educational communities across various cultures by breaking the constraints of space, time, and culture. Let us design global-age curricula, textbooks, teaching methods, learning environments, and resources. We are working together with students, teachers, parents, principals, superintendents, and other educational leaders who are living in this global context; let us stimulate in our education institutions global social networking for all role groups. We can fashion unprecedented international relationships among students, teachers, parents, and superintendents, and among different regions and nations. For the sustainable development of education, let us increase our capacities to be open to new possibilities while we overcome obstacles. In the last chapter of this second edition, the authors propose new educational leadership capacities for creating and sustaining dynamic learning organizations that will prepare students for this new global/local era. Stories of high-performing schools and their leaders, found on many continents, offer a glimpse of the global models for social networking and building schools for our times, with insights into the new leadership capacities in practice.

Both of us believe the second edition of this chaos book will certainly help disseminate new ideas and methodologies of education all over the world and connect educators across borders to develop the educational wisdom that is needed in this dynamic and challenging global age of living and learning. This is our challenge and opportunity, one that is complex, emergent, and vital to the human community.

REFERENCES

Engels, F. (1940). *Dialectics of Nature.* New York: International Publishers.
Snyder, K. J., Acker-Hocevar, M., & Snyder, K. (2000). *Living on the Edge of Chaos: Leading Schools into the Global Age.* Milwaukee, Wis.: ASQ Quality Press.

Part 1

Shifting Paradigms of Educational Change

Part I explores the challenges of adapting schooling to the great transformations of our times. In developing world-class schools, leaders are faced with a new century of global life while the problems with at-risk youth, families, communities, and social systems continue to mount. The greatest challenge of all for leaders is to know how to think about the paradoxes and contradictions as they refashion schooling for a new era. Our assumptions about schools and how they develop over time will determine the future of schooling as a social institution. This part begins with the global conditions as a new context for school learning in the twenty-first century. To stimulate a mindshift for educators, this part highlights key principles from physics for adapting schools to the local and global conditions that are changing our lives. By developing a fresh lens for viewing education in a global era, leaders can achieve great success as they adapt schooling to the times.

Chapter 1, Reinventing Schooling for a Global Age of Living, provides a range of perspectives for the development of youth today. The mission of schools in this global age changes in fundamental ways, for technology opens the windows of the world to teachers and their students. Some nations are realizing greater success in adapting to this new age than others. New achievement benchmarks are emerging to guide every nation in its school development process. The reality and presence of global trends and their dynamics are creating a new era of work that is more collegial and entrepreneurial than in the twentieth century, and within international work teams and markets. The human condition, however is reaching new highs as well as lows, where building bridges to prosperity is now one of the moral issues of our times, in which schools can play an important role. In the process of changing our concept of schools, educators are finding that networking is becoming a key professional capacity for building schools as global learning centers, and students as both local and global citizens.

Chapter 2, A Mechanical View of Change, represents the static machine laws of Newtonian physics and their application to a mechanistic way of leading members within organizations. Values of fragmentation, segmentation, and disconnection assume organizational life is unchanging, static, and predictable. The central tenets of Newtonian physics gave the world bureaucratic systems of work that are controlled through laws, policies, and evaluation systems. These traditions that stimulated phenomenal growth in the twentieth century must now give way to more responsive and adaptive approaches to organizational life.

Chapter 3, An Organic View of Change, illustrates how the laws of quantum physics, which emerged at the end of the nineteenth century, provide a foundation for changing the machine model of organizations to an organic model. Some essential principles of new physics offer clues for shifting from a static view of organizations to one that is organic and grounded in open-systems theory and that builds on the new features of wholeness, interdependence, and energy development. This chapter ends with a basic set of principles for organizational growth developed from quantum physics and systems theory to provide the reader with a firm foundation for fashioning new prototypes of schooling.

Chapter 4, An Emergent View of Change, develops new understandings of change within natural systems. The historical development of chaos and complexity theories offers a backdrop for understanding the commonalties of change within all kinds of social and behavioral environments. This chapter presents the challenge of *living on the edge of chaos,* accepting the conditions of change, and living with ever-present contradictions and ambiguity. The new principles of emergent change enable leaders to move away from incremental change to responding within a rapidly moving and shifting environment.

1

Reinventing Schooling
for a Global Age of Living

In the last decade it has become increasingly clear that life today is global on many levels, both personally and professionally, and that the twenty-first century will indeed be earmarked as the first age of global living for the masses. It is within this context that the second edition of this book has been prepared. Our obligation now as educators is to prepare students to function as global citizens, to work and live with people from other cultures, and to learn within the multiple forms of technology. Having an online virtual life every day in school must become a norm if students are to grow up with the rapidly changing speed of human exchange and learning in virtual environments. Our belief as authors is that creating new approaches to schooling represents a departure from the school improvement agenda of past decades. Educators need a new mindset to lead them to a new paradigm of schooling, with a new curriculum called *life.*

Education throughout human history has sought to prepare young people to contribute to the sustainability of their social context and times. Schooling in the twentieth century prepared young people for industrial realities of punctuality, predesigned work, performance monitoring, assessment, and then promotion. Schooling for the twenty-first century will continue to promote healthy work habits, as well as entrepreneurial living, exploration, projections, and teamwork across borders and age groups. Today the capacities that are required for success are seeing the big picture, crossing boundaries, and being able to combine disparate pieces in a new whole (Pink, 2006). Young people in time will also work in virtual environments in school with people across continents, time zones, and languages to achieve common purposes.

In this chapter attention is given to perspectives on the global community and the transformations in our lives. Comparisons of national education systems offer glimpses of who is adapting to emerging world standards of student success and social equity. The new forms of global work will provide direction for reshaping learning environments for world citizens and leaders. Human challenges around the world are the centerpieces of the school's new curriculum if educators and others are to prepare the next generation to address the remaining and emerging crises. Conditions in one part of the world affect all other parts at an increasing rate because of the global systems of communication now in place. Attention must be given to networking as a new life skill for educational leaders, for building resourceful networks of influences and learning will make a difference to their success. In the end we provide benchmarks for schools as Global Learning Centers, which evolved as educators worked together in the International School Connection's global learning network. The intention of this chapter is to stimulate a mindshift toward what it means to be a twenty-first-century educational leader who prepares students for an era of local and global living.

PERSPECTIVES ON THE NEW MISSION OF EDUCATION

Let us consider the purposes of education in the twenty-first century. Already we know that the transmission of knowledge, along with compliance, repetition, certainty, and an emphasis on time clocks, will no longer prepare youth for the dynamic age of exploration. Dealing with complexity and pursuing entrepreneurship is likely to provide the most promising opportunities for the next generation. "Right answers" have given way to multiple perspectives that require exploration and creativity within global and local networks of workers with different skills and orientations. Educators will need to make tough choices in the days ahead as they shed the outdated systems of schooling from an industrial era. In the process, it seems necessary to evaluate such twentieth-century devices as multiple-choice tests with supposed right answers. There are none! How ready are current education systems to adapt to uncertainty, ambiguity, and the enormous possibilities of life today?

When the first edition of this book was written, we as authors believed that schools could adapt better to emerging global working and living conditions if they were free of bureaucratic thinking and instead held systemic thinking as a mindset. While the systemic mindset continues to be vital for creating a good future of schooling, we now perceive that a much sharper focus is needed: *developing schools as global learning centers that prepare students now to be competent and caring global citizens.* It is within the global context of living that the mission of schools needs to change course so that students, at every age, can become citizens who are both knowledgeable and skillful and who care about the human community and its sustainability.

In their book *Wikinomics: How Mass Collaboration Changes Everything* (2007), Tapscott and Williams write about how traditional forms of collaboration in meeting rooms, classrooms, conference calls, and convention centers are giving way to a new form, which is shaping twenty-first-century systems of learning and work. People are participating in co-creating goods and services rather than focusing on just the end product. Mass collaboration across organizations, nations, and time zones is fast replacing individual- and company-developed products for purchase. It seems that the world of work has turned upside down, as have the rules of how organizations work. Classrooms of the world will reflect many changes if we are to be successful in preparing future generations for continuous development of the human community.

At the same time that this mass revolution is taking place in work, the challenges of human health, safety, and wealth will demand the attention of the developed world as never before. Not only will the twenty-first-century quest be one of keeping up with the rapid transformation of work, but the sustainability of the world community, all of it, also will be vulnerable and must be addressed through a caring and passionate citizenry. A new report on top corporations in the world reveals that world-class companies with an orientation to both profit and passion are outstripping others (Sisodia, Wolfe, and Sheth, 2007). Work alone is inadequate to motivate people to achieve greatness, for love, joy, authenticity, and soul are now identified as business values that matter. Emotional, experiential, social, and financial features of work will be the pathways to long-term competitive advantage.

In this century we must prepare young people not only for success in the world of work and careers, but also to be passionate about making a difference in altering the life-success potential for all. New world-class job requirements need to become the foundations of learning, while the new content of learning will revolve around global sustainability issues. Our moral obligation as educators is to prepare competent global citizens who care about the human community and its sustainability and who find an important role for making a contribution to the world.

Transforming the purpose and nature of schooling for twenty-first-century conditions will require us, at the most basic levels, to shed bureaucratic thinking, to revise rules and regulations, and to adopt an entrepreneurial mindset with habits of systemic thinking and continuous emergence. The old rules of the game will not lead schools to a global future, for new habits of mind for a global age will require continuous adaptation, exploration, imagination, creativity, caring, and bold action from leaders. Emerging trends and *new resources already exist in abundance for engaging students of all ages in the drama being played on the global stage.* We need only to explore our opportunities, for the YouTube generation already experiences this phenomenon. They are advancing their social networks on a global scale.

The Beijing Summer Olympics of 2008 promoted the theme *One World, One Dream.* The message is timely not only for international athletic competition, but for education as well. For more than 100 years the world of sports has operated within emerging world standards of many particular specializations. During the last century many other people across sectors and regions created global systems of business, medical care, finance, trade, and so on to bring forth this new global moment in which many global systems can connect people instantly. It is time to reshape school learning environments to prepare youth for active participation in the global community with its challenges and opportunities and to raise the human condition to more sustainable levels.

COMPARING NATIONS ON EDUCATIONAL PERFORMANCE

In 2000 the Organization for Economic Co-operation and Development (OECD) reported its first set of findings from a multinational effort to compare national education systems around the world. They found that countries are seeking to learn from one another about the best approaches to schooling to prepare their young people for success in a knowledge society, and they recognize the need to manage teaching and learning that promotes learning throughout life. OECD's Program for International Student Assessment, which is referred to as PISA (OECD, 2000, 2003), resulted from the work of scientists and educators in participating OECD countries as they worked to establish an international reference for the quality of national education. PISA aims to provide a new basis for policy dialogue and collaboration in improving the outcomes of education. The first test administration took place in 1999, followed by a second in 2003, and a third in 2006. National trends in the highest-performing nations have helped those in lower-performing countries improve their national educational practices. The reports contain evidence on the performance of 15-year-olds in reading, mathematics, and science literacy and in conditions of social equity. The analyses of test results provide insights into the factors that influence the development of competence at home and at school, which have implications for national policy development.

What does PISA measure? PISA is concerned with the capacity of students to apply knowledge and skills and to analyze, reason, and communicate effectively as they pose, solve, and interpret problems (OECD, 2004). The concept of achieving literacy in PISA is broad, for it emphasizes a range of competencies and assumes that literacy is a lifelong process. PISA assesses the ability to complete tasks relating to real life, rather than to subject-specific knowledge. Literacy is measured in terms of the content or structure of knowledge in math, reading, and science, and also the processes that need to be performed in situations where the student will encounter problems.

As a result of the 2003 PISA Report, where for the second time Finland was identified as the #1 country in student performance and social equity, educators at the National Board of Education and Helsinki City Schools became inundated with a stream of visitors from every part of the world seeking to understand the

Finnish education system. Other countries in the top PISA quartiles included Hong Kong–China, South Korea, Canada, Sweden, New Zealand, Australia, Austria, Macao-China, and Iceland in the second round of testing. Poland made the greatest gains in the world on its student performance. The United States was in the lowest quartile on academic performance and social equity.

In November 2007 the results of the third administration of the PISA examinations were reported on mathematics literacy and science literacy. Tests were administered to both OECD and non-OECD Countries, and the highest scores were found in both groups of nations. In science literacy, Finland again came out on top, followed by Canada, Japan, Hong Kong–China, Chinese Taipei, Japan, New Zealand, and Estonia. U.S. student scores were lower than the average of other OECD countries. In mathematics literacy, Finland, Chinese Taipei and Hong Kong–China emerged as the highest performing countries, along with South Korea, The Netherlands, Switzerland, Canada, and Japan. The performance of U.S. students in mathematics was lower than the OECD average, scoring lower than its peers in 23 OECD countries. (www.ed.gov.org; www.ies.ed.gov.org)

The PISA international analysis of student performance provides a larger context in which to interpret national testing results and inspires new policy for the development of systems of learning. The test results provide international perspectives on schooling trends and their impact on young people. What emerges from the international standards and national examinations suggests that significant changes are needed in the processes of educating young people.

Although the People's Republic of China is not included in the PISA test administration, its story of modernizing education provides an example for the rest of the world to consider. In the last several decades China has infused an educational digital information infrastructure throughout the country, laying the technological foundation for development (Sang, 2006). This infrastructure has prepared a contingent of teachers and students who can understand, adapt to, and participate in "cyber-culture," all of which has led to historic changes in the idea, the model, and the system of education in China. The reality, Sang notes, is that all countries have great needs and strong desires to communicate and cooperate, which provides a stimulus to move beyond any obstacles there may be. Technology will play an increasingly important role and completely transform education for all, Sang notes, from the old model of lectures and cramming information to cross cultural communication and information sharing.

GLOBAL TRENDS AND DYNAMICS

In the 1990s the advance of computers and common systems of international communication led to new economic and social possibilities on a grand scale. Volumes have been written about globalization and its influence in many sectors: economics, politics, culture, technology, and the environment (Snyder, 2005).

These trends are commonly known today, but they are not necessarily what matters now. The key force in globalization of the 1990s was economics and the opening up of international markets. By 2000, it had become apparent that economic globalization was leaving many parts of the world behind, although it had raised the standard of living for some (Stiglitz, 2006). The World Trade Organization (WTO) was born in 1995 to bring some rule of law to new levels of international commerce and free trade. However, Stiglitz, who was the former chief economist for the WTO, points out that its policies actually prevented developing nations from moving ahead. Poverty in the developing world has increased in the past two decades, with over 40 percent of the world living in poverty. The problem is political, he argues, and one that can be corrected with a new democratic body to govern the WTO, which seeks to create more fair systems for developing nations.

In response to growing evidence of global poverty and its impact everywhere, the United Nations established Millennium Goals for 2015 to significantly reduce extreme poverty and also create sustainable development in education, food, water, equity, child mortality, combating HIV/AIDS, improving the environment, and creating global partnerships that bridge the cultural divide (www.un.org). The Group of 8G8 leaders of the developed world made commitments in 2007 to prepare an agreement on global warming, missile defense systems, and enlarging the G8 institution. The leaders also pledged assistance for Africa and emerging economies, and they sought to dialogue with Brazil, China, India, Mexico, and South Africa (U.S. Department of State, www.state.gov). However, while the G8 addresses major issues of the globe, protests against the G8 continue because of unfulfilled promises to cancel national debts. The G8 members are indeed a major source of international influence on how global problems are addressed, but they are also viewed by many as protectors of inequities. (Countries that are G8 members include Canada, France, Germany, Italy, Japan, Russia, the United Kingdom, and the United States.)

The balances of power are shifting as the global dance plays out. Goldman Sachs Investment Bank leaders recently put forth an argument that the BRIC nations—Brazil, Russia, India, and China—are expected to become the four dominant economies by 2050 (www.wikipedia.org/wiki/BRIC). China and India will become the major suppliers of manufactured goods and services, while Brazil and Russia will supply raw materials. Brazil is dominant in soy products and iron ore; Russia supplies oil and natural gas. Nothing seems to link the four nations to one another, for two are manufacturing-based economies and big importers and two are exporters of natural resources. Two have growing populations (Brazil and India) and two are shrinking (Russia and China). What is missing in this picture is the involvement of the current G8 nations, except for Russia. How might this dramatic shift in global power affect the world economies as well as the life styles of both the haves and have-nots?

As many critics of globalization argue, globalization has been mismanaged; there are too many losers. At an international level, democratic political institutions have not emerged yet to address the challenges, which will be required if we are to make globalization work (Stiglitz, 2006, 276). Stiglitz calls for an international economic regime in which the well-being of the developed and developing countries is in better balance: a new global social contract (285). A democratic decision-making system is required for a more balanced global community to connect with anyone, anywhere, anytime.

Many of us are only beginning to learn that the great democracies of the world at times are anything but honorable in their efforts to help developing nations. The new flat world enabled us not only to achieve beyond our imaginations, but the plight of women around the world, starving peoples in Africa, and the widening gap between the haves and have-nots in South America also have raised our awareness of the complex problems in this new global age. And the power of global terrorist networks is a bold new reality. The media keep it all in front of us daily. Decades ago, prior to cable, television news was fairly brief and delivered once or twice a day. Now the news is 24/7/365. How are we to cope? What must our education programs become to prepare the next generations to re-balance life on the planet?

NEW GLOBAL FORMS OF WORK

Let us look now at one global dynamic: the emerging world of work. Within the global dynamics of shifting economic powers, Thomas Friedman's book *The World Is Flat* (2006) has created excitement around the world because of its breakthrough synthesis on the global world of work that has evolved because of a common computer language and systems and the Internet. His book was a wake-up call, especially for educators, for it documented how a service empire had been created and managed by India, and how China almost overnight has become the manufacturing center of the world. What is emerging is a picture of global cooperation, rather than competition, with many of the major players being new to the global scene.

The new forms of work that Friedman brought to light provide clues to educators for redesigning educational work systems. As you read about a few of these forms below, consider how students might participate in a global learning project for each of these new work prototypes. How can these prototypes become learning systems for students who work in partnership projects with schools in other parts of the world?

• **Open-sourcing** is a form of global development that is open to anyone, anywhere, and any time, by connecting with someone who is willing to participate in this enterprise. Friedman (2006) calls open-sourcing communities of workers that pool their talents to create something new. Wikipedia (www.wikpedia.com) a collective online encyclopedia with more than two million English entries, is open to anyone, anywhere to add entries. The global community edits and controls its own collective work, which has now emerged as one of the most reliable sources of information on the planet.

• **Out-sourcing** is a form of distributing jobs elsewhere to add value to the completed work that needs to be achieved. India has become the world capital of outsourcing, with a trillion-dollar economy that has evolved because of its facility with the English language (*New York Times,* September 25, 2007). India provides services for the medical field, the travel industry, the manufacturing world, and other industries in western countries. Indians now translate doctors' client reports worldwide and send the transcriptions back by the next working day, a 24/7 workforce in operation. Airline reservations, an outsourced task for major airlines, are now made for people in the Western Hemisphere by workers in India. Because of its success, India is transferring its outsourcing volume to other countries around the world. Have you talked, for example, to someone recently by dialing for help and reaching people in Belarus, Egypt, Mexico, or the Philippines?

• **Offshoring** is the relocation of a business from one country to another for production, manufacturing, or service. In a sense it is the substitution of foreign for domestic labor in white-collar jobs. When China joined the World Trade Organization in 2001 and agreed to follow global rules governing imports and exports, the conditions were ripe in China to take advantage of cheap labor and open market regulations (Friedman, 2006). Microsoft has its own university in China; electronics components are made in Taiwan; and Hewlett Packard, IBM, Intel, and Cisco Systems have transplanted parts of their companies to other parts of the world.

• **Supply-chaining** is a form of worldwide distribution to provide a company with many outlets for supplying needed goods. Friedman (2006) calls this method of collaboration a horizontal strategy among suppliers, retailers, and customers to create value. For example, Wal-Mart has become the world's largest business because of the supply chain system it has created to keep Wal-Mart providing reliable goods everywhere on the planet at a low price. Dell Computers is another example. Parts of computers made in many places around the world are assembled in three locations to create personalized computers for clients anywhere.

So vast are systems of supply-chaining that colleges are offering graduate programs in supply-chain management. For example, Polk County Community College in Lakeland, Florida, offers a supply-chain management program through its e-Learning Center. Emphasis is given to students obtaining global partnerships with top companies and working on self-study courses to develop the new job skills. Programs are also offered in export management, global business communications, and international business and global trade. A new era has begun.

• **In-sourcing** is a service provided by one company within another large company. No longer only in the global mail delivery business, United Parcel Service (UPS) provides services for major companies, such as repairing Dell computers in airports around the United States (Friedman, 2005). In a form of supply-chain management, companies such as UPS move products, store merchandise, assemble products, repair goods, and even talk to customers of the client company. UPS services companies such as Nike, Toshiba Laptop, and Royal Canin (*Time,* November 21, 2007).

The challenge for educators is to consider how to prepare students for this global worklife of 24/7/365, working across time zones, cultures, and languages to provide service to the world community. Where does one begin? Perhaps the first step is to become knowledgeable about these new forms of work. Just Google any of these work systems to learn more about its function and operation and find ways to stimulate learning and engagement with students. Connect students across the world to work on projects within virtual environments, using these different collaborative systems. A new infrastructure is needed for all students, requiring at the very minimum their access to a personal computer. Students need to grow up working in the same environments as adults if they are to be ready for the next phases of innovation.

What Has Changed?

The August 27, 2007, issue of *BusinessWeek* featured many perspectives on the future of work. The issue begins with a series of articles whose authors argue that globalization and technology together are creating the potential for startling changes in how we do our jobs and determine the offices in which we work. Offshoring means that jobs can be broken into smaller tasks and redistributed around the world. Technology with its virtual offices is in many places, transforming what it means to "be at work." No longer representing the assembly-line factory with its mindless repetition, the modern workplace more often reflects the design studio, where the core values are collaboration and innovation (Mandel, 2007, 45). The offshoring trend means moving rapidly up the value chain to take advantage of new opportunities, or to become part of an international mobile labor force. What possibilities might exist for students to participate with others around the world in "learning work" within these new work systems?

The very idea of *company* is shifting away from a single unit with full-time employees and a recognizable hierarchy. It is more fluid now, within an ever-shifting network of suppliers and outsourcers (*BusinessWeek,* August 27, 2007, Engardio, 50). The hard part for multinationals is getting people to work well together, especially since day and night collaboration across the globe is growing. Such pressures on management require recruiting new staff who are globally minded from the outset and whose work norm is collaboration. Europe is developing a new generation as a mobile labor force, which bodes well (Ewing, 78).

Changing technology will alter how and where we labor, and it even can redefine the notion of an employer. With cell phones and laptops, people can work alone or together anywhere, anytime. Digital technology has allowed us to break up bundles of work and reassemble them into mass-customized jobs (Hooshmand, 2007, p. 83). These new developments raise questions about the ultimate impact of technology on workers and the companies they represent. Where is this trend heading? How are these trends influencing students as workers, in general? And, how are networks altering career preparation programs for youth?

The Changing World of Work for Graduates was a feature article in the April 2007 edition of *Educational Leadership.* In it, Stewart (8) argues that the future is here. It is multiethnic, multicultural, and multilingual. In short, she claims that high school graduates will:

- Sell to the world

- Buy from the world

- Work for international companies

- Manage employees from other cultures and countries

- Collaborate with people all over the world in joint ventures

- Compete with people on the other side of the world for jobs and markets

- Tackle global problems, such as AIDS, avian flu, pollution, and disaster recovery.

To prepare for local and global life, students need to develop their own personal world knowledge; acquire language skills in English, Chinese, Spanish, and Arabic; endorse civic values; make friends in other countries; and have many international experiences. In addition they need growing capacities, beginning now, for working in digital systems of all kinds, which is a new *content* for school learning. But, this is the age of complexity, and the playing field is not level. Let us also include in planning the unfavorable living conditions for almost half of the world's population, for this is part of the complex landscape of life that will shape the future for everyone on the planet. It is the new curriculum.

HUMAN CHALLENGES
IN THE GLOBAL COMMUNITY

The Copenhagen Consensus Project sought to identify the 10 most pressing economic challenges for the globe (Lomborg, 2004). After sorting through U.N. papers and publications, the project identified the most pressing problems:

climate change, communicable disease, conflicts and arms proliferation, access to education, financial instability, governance and corruption, malnutrition and hunger, migration, sanitation and access to clean water, and *subsidies trade barriers.* A renowned economics specialist within each field was invited to prepare a challenge paper. A panel of Nobel Prize laureates responded to the conclusions of each paper and offered additional perspectives, which are reported in the book by Lomborg (2004). These 10 world challenges can become the curriculum for every school, for students at any age, to learn about and also to participate in providing assistance or contributions to the development of global responses.

In the October 2007 issue of *Newsweek,* the feature article gave further perspective on many of these issues and offered others as well. Its headline was, "From hunger in Africa to pollution in China, there is no shortage of need in the world. To help solve the problems, in 2005 Americans gave $33.5 billion in donations to developing countries while the U.S. government aid totaled $27.6 billion." Their list of global challenges also includes the environment, natural disasters, human rights and religious freedom, economic development, and reproduction and child health. The authors argue that while funds will help, there is growing evidence that money by itself is not sufficient. There must be a human global will to alter the conditions of poverty and its accompanying problems if ever there will emerge a sustainable future for these regions of the world.

Let us consider a few of these challenges, while anticipating this question: *What can schools do now to promote learning, caring, and development for these major crises of the world community?*

1. Safe Water and Sanitation: Access to water supply and sanitation is a fundamental need and a human right. The World Health Organization (WHO) (www.who.int) estimated that in 2003 approximately 1.1 billion people had no access to safe water and 2.4 billion had no basic sanitation. Left unattended, current conditions lead to a wide range of diseases, such as cholera, typhoid, and malaria. Dirty water is often the cause of ordinary childhood diarrhea, a leading cause of death among African children. Malaria is Africa's leading killer of children under 5 years of age. The African Medical Research Foundation's goal is to ensure that communities have adequate capacity to develop, operate, and maintain their water sources, as well as to improve the health of all people (www.amref.org).

A new venture called *Engineers Without Borders* was recently launched by a group of Western engineers to provide projects that address identified community needs (PBS, *The News Hour with Jim Lehrer,* December 7, 2007). Engineers from developing countries are volunteering to build water systems for the poor in Africa, as an example. In the process the engineers were confronted with their own "engineer mindset" for solving problems. This experience of working with the poor has caused them to move from their computers to engage with the people in poor communities and bring their heart to the challenge of providing a service.

The Carter Center in Georgia has over the years dedicated its time and energy to providing services to poor nations. The center is now, for example, in its final phases of eradicating Guinea worm disease. Its malaria control program is monitoring the impact of 3 million insecticide-impregnated mosquito nets it distributed in Ethiopia in 2007. The goal is to fight against trachoma, river blindness, lymphatic filariasis, and other diseases that torment the world's poor (Carter Center Newsletter, December 2007).

2. World Hunger and Poverty: The World Health Organization estimates that one-third of the world is well fed, one-third is underfed, and one-third is starving (http://library.thinkquest.org.) The Indian subcontinent has nearly half the world's hungry people, with the rest in Africa, Asia, and Latin America. Lappe et al. (1998) project that there is an abundance of food resources in the world, even though millions are starving. Sending more food is not the sustainable response to this problem. The real problem, they suggests, is poverty, for economies fail to offer people opportunities to build their own sustainable systems of food supply. What is required is a political will to create sustainable systems for healthy living.

The *New York Times* on December 2, 2007, reported a story of hope for the rest of Africa. Malawi is ending its famine simply by ignoring the experts. Farmers explain Malawi's extraordinary turnaround with one word: fertilizer. President Mutharika declared, "Our people are poor because they lack the resources to use the soil and water we have." Over the years the World Bank pushed Malawi to eliminate its fertilizer subsidies. Through lobbying efforts, however, Malawi got deep fertilizer subsidies and lesser ones for seeds. Record crops of corn production have leaped from 1.2 billion in 2005 to 3.4 billion in 2007. Now Malawi is feeding many other countries because of the use of good seed and inorganic fertilizer.

3. Genocide in Darfur: In 2004 the U.S. House of Representatives labeled the killing in Darfur, Sudan, "a genocide." It is reported that pro-government Arab militias have forced more than one million black Africans from their homes and killed thousands of others (BBC News, July 2004). Drought, desertification, and overpopulation are among the causes of the Darfur conflict. Already over 200,000 people have died in Darfur; two million have been displaced; and 1500 villages have been destroyed because of the government's destructive policies. Three ethnic groups in Darfur have been targeted for genocide, with rape, burning of villages, and murder of tribes contributing to apparent national goals to eliminate some of its population (www.darfurgenocide.org). The U.N. Security Council has created several peacekeeping initiatives, but the condition of structural inequality helps to sustain the problem, causing the government to spread its violence on U.N. peacekeepers.

The *New York Times,* on November 20, 2007, reported that an area in Somalia, in the corridor between the market town of Afgooye and the capital of Mogadishu, is now worse than Darfur. United Nations officials report higher rates of malnutrition, more current bloodshed, and fewer aid workers than in Darfur. This situation has become the new priority for the U.N. peacekeepers.

4. Terrorism and Challenges in the Middle East: As terrorism escalates and with threats to global peace on the rise, the East and West are challenged as never before as a worldwide community to find ways to create sustainable pathways for the "have-nots." Many in the Arab world are building energy for maintaining a way of life that is built upon paternalism, terrorism, and illegal activity, while many others in Arab nations continue to fight for a developmental approach to life. What is needed is access to education and hope for a good life for young people everywhere. How can this evolve and turn the tide of terrorist activity? While ideology may inspire terrorists, scholars say, it takes intimate social forces to push people to action. Terrorism is really a collective decision, not an individual one, one expert says. The solution is about kinship and friendship (*New York Times Magazine,* November 25, 2007, p. 77).

5. Domestic Violence: Violence against women is now a global human rights scandal. According to Amnesty International (www.web.amnesty.org/ actforwomen), a growing global condition is met in many societies with governmental lack of interest, silence, or apathy. For countless women, home is not a refuge but a place of terror. Violence is seen as both physical and psychological, for sexual assaults on women are made by husbands, fathers, and other family members. SEDA (Center for Women's Development), a nongovernmental organization in Curacao, is conducting dialogue sessions in communities all over the island with parents, children, and educators. Dozens of projects have emerged to curb the patterns of domestic violence and build healthy communities and their families (www.5starcuracao.com). The Departments of Justice and Education, along with the business community, are now partners in building a violence-free island nation.

6. Crime and the Systems of Justice: [This section was prepared by T. Richard Snyder, whose work as a theologian led him to the problems of justice in America. After researching justice systems in South Africa, Sweden, and the United States, he began a project in Maine to create alternative and more humane approaches to justice (2001).]

According to the Bureau of Justice, violent crime in the United States has decreased by more than 50 percent in the last three decades (www.ojp.gov). Despite this, the rate of incarceration continues to rise dramatically, largely driven by sentencing for drug use. There are more than 2,250,000 adults in prisons or jails, and over 7 million persons (one out of every 31 adults) receive some form of correctional supervision, including prison, jail, probation, or parole (www .sentencingproject.org, December 2007). This is the highest per capita incarceration rate in the industrialized world.

In large measure this is due to a punitive response to crime that includes man-datory sentencing and the politics of getting "tough on crime." This approach ignores victims' needs, dehumanizes offenders, fails to rehabilitate, and results in a recidivism rate of more than 60 percent. To compound the tragedy, many schools are turning to punitive responses to disciplinary problems, relying heav-ily on suspensions and expulsions or instituting "zero-tolerance" policies that automatically result in referral to law enforcement.

The Restorative Justice movement offers an alternative that seeks to heal rather than to punish. It focuses on harms and needs, addresses accountabil-ity, involves all stakeholders, and uses inclusive collaborative processes (Zehr, 2002). This approach, which has its roots in Aboriginal, Native American, and First Nations people, is now being successfully used in the criminal justice and educational systems in New Zealand, Australia, Europe, Canada, and the United States.

One local project in Maine, The Restorative Justice Project of the Midcoast (RJP), has trained more than 60 volunteers who serve as mentors both with adult offenders recently released from jail or whose sentences have been deferred and with juvenile offenders who are referred to the program rather than to the court system. The results have been remarkable: Adult recidivism among par-ticipants has been reduced by more than 40 percent, and 45 of the 47 juvenile cases have been closed, eliminating the lifelong stigma of a criminal record. The jails, law enforcement, and courts in two counties are supporting this approach. In addition, a pilot program in Restorative School Practices was introduced in one middle school with the aim of creating greater accountability and reduc-ing detentions, suspensions, and expulsions. In its first full year of the program, detentions dropped by 40 percent and many students advocated using the process when an offense was committed. A number of other schools in the region are now exploring the restorative justice approach.

7. Human Trafficking: The Public Broadcasting Service (PBS) in 2007 re-leased a report on the global sex slave market. An undercover journalist followed a man determined to rescue his wife who had been kidnapped and sold into the global sex trade. He reported that over one million girls are sex slaves around the world, being trafficked across national borders and states. Johns, who are social predators, tend to be molesters, slavemasters, and pedophiles who use bribes and abuse and who appeal to impoverished families to sell their girls for brothels and street living. Girls are often sold by their parents for as little as $10. Ground zero for the sex slave business is southwest Asia, where 50 percent of the girls can't read and 75 percent can't write. Fifteen percent are boys who are sexually abused before age nine. It is estimated that 600,000 to 800,000 young people are traf-ficked across borders each year. What would happen if these children were read-ers and could envision a prosperous future in a growing society? This deplorable condition is maintained by a political desire to control citizens. The education of girls is the way out of poverty. Sex slaves are often women in poverty who have no hope and no pathways to another kind of future.

8. Environmental Clean-up: Much of the criticism leveled at globalization comes from ecologists concerned about the effects of rampant consumerism on the world's environment. Without global efforts to save the earth's natural resources, we could witness an end not only to globalization, but also to civilization as we know it. Multinational corporations are being called upon to stave off the depletion of the earth's resources. Critics, however, believe that these institutions are concerned only with the proliferation of the global market economy. A new international force is emerging to ensure the well-being of all people. The pollution from China's industrial empire is causing new concerns around the world, and the levels of waste in Western countries is prompting attention everywhere for the "greening" of the earth, a human responsibility. A predominant element is *global warming,* a label that has been given considerable attention lately, due in large measure to the global influence of Al Gore and his message in *An Inconvenient Truth* (2006). The movie won two U.S. Academy Awards in 2007, and it resulted in his receiving a share of the 2007 Nobel Peace Prize.

9. Education Gaps: The plight of education in the developing world, unless resolved, has serious implications for the prosperity of the entire human community. Life on any continent now affects life on all continents. The challenges below provide clues to the severity of the problems and to signs of hope.

- In a 2000 study, the UN reported that 70 percent of illiterate people came from three areas: Sub-Saharan Africa, South and West Asia, and the Arab States with North Africa. Illiteracy in Latin America and the Caribbean accounts for 11 percent of all illiterates. Sixty-four percent of the world's 78.1 million illiterate adults are women. The World Bank predicts that educating girls will yield a higher rate of return than any other investment available in the developing world (www .unicef.org).

- The United Nations sponsors an initiative called the *Global Youth Leadership Summit.* The focus for building world peace is sports, which holds promise as a tool to help overcome poverty, illiteracy, and disease, and for promoting understanding and respect for others (www.un.org/youthsummit).

- Oprah Winfrey opened a girls school, called Oprah Winfrey Leadership Academy, in South Africa. She says, "You change a girl's life and you start to change a family, a community, a nation, and yes, the face of Africa" (www.oprah.com).

- Nicholas Negroponte's famed $100 computer for third world children is now a reality. Called XO, the computer consumes two watts, which gives it a long battery life. The computer has a camera, communications ability, and a high-resolution screen. It is being offered today for $200 for the donor to keep one and the other goes to a child overseas (*New York Times,* April 8, 2007). This remarkable development identifies an overlooked two-billion-person market. Let's hope it makes it through the political and financial barriers that already exist for this computer.

- Greg Mortenson, the director of the Central Asia Institute, is a former mountaineer. While climbing some of the highest peaks in the world he determined to make a difference in the education of rural girls and boys in Pakistan. Living at almost the poverty level himself, he found the resources to fund and build 55 schools in remote villages. His work has spread to Afghanistan, working in Taliban terrain. His story, reported in the best-seller *Three Cups of Tea* (2006), reflects the power of the human spirit and what can happen with a vision and commitment to make a difference (www.threecupsoftea.com).

- Chinese education is becoming increasingly decentralized and learner centered, which is the opposite direction from recent U.S. reforms (Preus, 2007). Teacher education reform in China involves continuous professional development of both novice and experienced teachers, who conduct their own research regularly to improve their practice, share planning space and time, and observe each other's work in classrooms. A national digital network connects every teacher in China to new knowledge and skills, as well as to new training programs. The network of teacher development is strong and vital for China's education transformation.

10. Merging Eastern and Western Values: In our research on the connection between systems thinking/chaos theory/complexity theory and Eastern wisdom with the philosophies of the ancient Chinese, we recognize the strong similarity with the concepts of integration, interdependence, emergence, and holistic thinking. Modern science is now in sync with ancient Chinese philosophy and in sharp contrast to the Western practices of isolation, separation, "now-thinking," and "parts thinking." Because the authors of this book have been working in partnership with Professors Xinmin Sang and Shuhua Li at Nanjing University in China, we have come to realize that many of its ancient philosophies provide a foundation for Chinese life today, and these very principles of life are important, we believe, for the Western world (Li, 2002).

Xinmin Sang (2006) comments that China observed Western culture in order to launch its long march to educational modernization, having missed much of the industrial era of the twentieth century. Now the West is paying more attention to Eastern culture and its educational traditions in order to get over the *demerits* that industrial civilization brought about. These two very different habits of mind and spirit hold promise for a more integrated approach to development on a global scale: a yin and yang of life. Drawing upon her scholarship in both ancient Chinese philosophy and chaos theory, Shuhua Li shared in conversations with us that "yin" preserves, accumulates, sustains, and stabilizes the human system, while "yang" transforms the human system with negative information, which creates disruption to the system to stimulate creative and innovative responses. A yin-and-yang approach to developing educational systems might enable us to proceed with our current duties while we engage in entrepreneurial activity to shape the future. The two basic rhythms of life, the routine and the disrupted, are complementary and necessary for a sustainable future for the world community. We need to promote schools in the West to form partnership with schools in the East, so that our students can learn together and from each other about the desirable habits of life in yin-and-yang thinking. That's a beginning.

NETWORKING: THE NEW LEADERSHIP CAPACITY

A question many educators ponder is how to garner energy and support for transforming education systems for the global era. Networking, we believe, holds great promise for educational leaders to build energy systems to rebuild and sustain schools that prepare young people as global citizens. Knowledge about networks and how they grow enhances a leader's strategic thinking. Networking, as a personal capacity, gives energy and resources for the journey.

We believe that *networks are the new structures for the global age, and networking is fast becoming a primary leadership skill.* The very survival and growing strength of terrorist networks has convinced us of network strength and power to promote a purpose or cause. Manual Castells, an eminent Spanish sociologist, compiled an impressive three-volume work in the late 1990s and early 2000s under the general heading *The Information Age: Economy, Society and Culture.* The first volume, *The Rise of the Network Society,* was published first in 1996 and again in 2000. Castells documented the nature of the information technology revolution, the development of which contributed to the formation of the milieu of innovation in which discovery and applications would be tested, requiring the concentration of research centers, higher-education institutions, advanced-technology companies, a network of ancillary suppliers of goods and services, and business networks of venture capital to finance start-ups (2000, 65). This mix generated its own dynamic to attract knowledge, investment, and talent from around the world to form the networks of technological innovation.

Castells' conclusion is that the dominant functions and process in the information age are increasingly organized around networks, the new social morphology of our societies (2000, 500). A network-based social structure is a highly dynamic, open system organization for capital, management, and information, whose access to technological know-how is at the roots of productivity and competitiveness. Naturally this new network environment creates questions about power and power relationships. Who are the owners? Who are the producers? Who are the managers? Who are the workers? These traditional features of work have become increasingly blurred within the context of global teamwork, networking, outsourcing, and subcontracting. Networking has always been a tool for communities to form. The conscious act of building networks can lift the education enterprise to its rightful place as a useful social development agent.

If networking is the centerpiece of human activity at the dawn of the twenty-first century, what can we learn about networks and how they evolve? Networking science is a recent development, which builds upon the latest major development in *Physics: Complexity Theory* (Buchanan, 2002). Networking theory began in the 1960s around the concept of six degrees of separation between people in *random networks*. As scientists continued to study networks, they learned there is a more reliable structure to them in their origin and development; they are not random at all.

The concept of the *scale-free network* was born in the 1990s, after scholars studied the ways large computer networks and other human networks emerge. Lacking in a hierarchical function, scale-free networks are dominated by hubs that stimulate a network's growth. In time the strongest hubs influence the direction of the network as it serves a function for the whole.

The ideas below represent a distillation of central concepts to the development of networks, as reported by Barabasi in *Linked: How Everything is Connected to Everything Else and What It Means for Business, Science and Everyday Life* (2003).

The twenty-first century is likely to be the century of complexity and the network, with these characteristics:

1. A network is a rapidly evolving dynamic system of interconnectedness.

2. The scale-free network idea is built around hubs of interest.

3. Networks are self-organizing and based on the strength of hubs.

4. Hubs have many nodes and links internally.

5. Hubs connect to other hubs through weak links, forming the network.

6. Large hubs define the direction and shape of the network.

7. Two laws govern networks: growth and preferential attachment (Barabasi, 2003).

If the network pattern for work will become a dominant feature in the twenty-first century, what are the implications for management, for network development, and for institutions such as education?

Consider these basic shifts for which Barabosi argues (2003). The twenty-first-century business model will move from hierarchy to networks in the following ways:

1. All organizations need to shed hierarchical thinking and develop networking thinking patterns.

2. For the network to grow, hubs must get bigger and stronger and also connect with one another.

3. The shape of a network is governed by the biggest hubs, which keep the network together.

4. Strategic partnerships and alliances are the means of survival in development, training, service, and research.

5. Each hub must add value to the network to survive in it.

6. Products and ideas spread through hubs.

7. Real networks are self-organizing.

8. Three types of networks exist: centralized, decentralized, and distributed.

9. Multi-tasking is an inherent property of networking.

10. Clusters of workers develop parts of the system and its functions (Barabasi, 2003).

Karen Stephenson, a pioneer in social networks, has developed a mathematical process for identifying the networks that exist in organizations so that their leaders can provide leverage for moving ahead (Kleiner, 2003). Stephenson provides clarity by arguing that:

- Informal networks are not what you think they are.

- Knowledge networks are more powerful at any point than hierarchy.

- Networks are key to building trust and sustaining collaboration.

- Networks enable a group of organizations to act as one yet retain their uniqueness.

- *Netform Analysis,* her tool, can help for succession planning, leadership development, and retention and retraining strategies. (Check Stephenson's Web site for more information: www.netform.com).

By examining the existing networking patterns within organizations, leaders can leverage energy for development by using the natural forces at work, either to strengthen or eliminate them. If networks and networking are the new conditions for social and economic development, which networks will emerge to shape our future? Which networks will redefine and transform the preparation of youth to participate in and shape the future of the world community? What network of global pioneers will give shape to education for a united global community, one in which peoples of the earth have equal opportunity to thrive in its midst?

The questions surrounding educational innovation and networking are numerous. By drawing a picture of the networks in our own organization, I was able to understand better the energy patterns and influences on our work. This new kind of picture prompted me to act differently as a leader and to stimulate networking among our leaders to a greater extent. I then asked myself who was included in my own professional network, as it related to my leadership goals, and then who in my network had the strongest networks. With this picture I was able to see where my strategic energy might have the biggest payoff for achieving our goals. The natural and invisible set of relationships can become conscious and intentional for moving ahead, and it can reveal new prospects for moving ahead.

You might ask yourself a few questions: How big is my personal professional network? How strong is my network for the big areas of development that matter to me? Who are the strongest links in my network? What hubs do I belong to in other networks, and how does this influence my work? How strong is the network of individuals or organizations in my network? Are there potential resources for me in the network(s)? These questions are vital to understanding the natural dynamics within our organizations and help us make good use of natural connections in stimulating action and outcomes. This activity also highlights people who are unconnected to anyone, or a few, and prompts a different leadership strategy to stimulate their growth for the organization's sustainability.

Now consider your staff. How are they building networks as teams to advance their work? Are individual professionals connected to useful and strong professional networks? How about students? Are they actively building networks to stimulate their own understanding of this world? To promote their career goals? In other words, how connected are you and those with whom you work for achieving your professional and organizational purposes? Think about your network as a major resource, and strengthen its density and function for realizing your goals. Connections, strong connections, are vital for building the energy for the growth we want. Networks provide great promise for building strong connection systems.

Social Networking and the Youth Culture

Digital communication technology has enabled the youth of the world to engage in social networking at a rapid rate. Social networking has created new opportunities for them to connect with others around the world and share their lives in unprecedented ways. When will schools figure out how to capitalize on this phenomenon to advance academic learning and develop pathways for students to become competent and caring global citizens?

At age 19, Mark Zuckerman created a way for college students to connect with one another, which launched an online revolution (*Newsweek,* August 27, 2007). *Facebook,* now with 35 million off-campus users, has attracted a flood of interest in developing tools to stimulate profit. Microsoft purchased 1.6 percent of *Facebook* for $240 Million on October 24, 2007 (www.marketpilgrim .com/2007). Young people today are bypassing schoolwork to connect with others virtually anywhere. News reporting is open to anyone with a video camera or a phone camera. Consumers of news can now become the reporters of news as well. ABC News and Facebook announced a new partnership, which allows Facebook members to electronically follow ABC reporters, view reports and video, and participate in polls and debates (*New York Times,* Monday, November 26, 2007).

Jeff Bezos, who is CEO of Amazon.com, says that books are the last bastion of the analog era. In the November 26, 2007, issue of *Newsweek,* he announced the development of Kindle, an e-dedicated reading device, which operates independently of a computer. One can purchase a book and download it onto the Kindle, or buy a newspaper subscription, or search the web. The Kindle sells for a modest $399 and just might launch the potential demise of the printed book. Amazon.com offers this option on its Web site.

iPods have enabled people of all ages to download music and carry it with them anywhere and anytime. CNN integrated YouTube into the presidential debates in 2007, inviting people to ask questions of the candidates through televised connections. The iPhone has created excitement because of its Web browser, which may promote a sea change in the mobile phone business. Web 2.0 is here and bringing new systems for collaboration in writing documents, sharing photos and videos, engaging in chats without IM messaging, gaining greater access to Google Earth, and more (cmpnet.com). These new technologies have lifted individuals onto the global stage to participate personally in creating new futures for living and working. It's not only for the business world; it is for anyone anywhere. How can schools catch the wave to advance learning within these environments?

BENCHMARKS FOR A GLOBAL
LEARNING ENVIRONMENT

In 1992 in Berlin, educators from Sweden, the United States, Finland, and Russia met to explore opportunities to link school principals in common international experiences. There evolved over the next decade a multi-university cooperative from seven nations on four continents, called the International School Connection (ISC), whose mission has been to work with educational leaders to shape schools as Global Learning Centers that prepare young people for success in this global age of living and learning. A new mission of the ISC is to develop a network of youth leaders who will learn and work together to care about the future of our global community. To begin, the ISC provided professional development experiences for principals through a virtual community, online discussion rooms, annual meetings in one host city, and from online graduate degree programs called *Global Organizational Development.* Research conducted by Kristen Snyder (2002, 2003) highlighted the cross-border social networking of school leaders in a virtual networked environment, which led to an understanding of the concept of "digital culture" in schools and other organizations and paved the way to the next phase of ISC's development.

In 2002, the ISC initiative became a private nonprofit organization, with an international board of directors and officers, as well as a network with hubs of educators and their coordinators in ISC hot spots around the world. Ten benchmarks for schools as global learning centers emerged from the work of this global community in 2005 in an attempt to identify features that set some schools apart in preparing students as global citizens (Sullivan, 2006; Snyder, 2006). These are the characteristics of schools for this global age at the beginning of the twenty-first century. (The benchmarks are expanded upon in Chapter 14.)

Benchmarks for Schools as Global Learning Centers

1. The curriculum provides opportunities to learn about local and global forces that are influencing change.

2. The school as a growing system has a vision and a plan to provide opportunities to connect with the global community and its dynamic forces.

3. Educators participate in professional development activity in a global networked environment to promote learning and exchange.

4. Partnerships are formed with local, regional, and/or global businesses to enhance the direction of school development.

5. The school has achieved high student performance results using local, regional, and/or international measures.

Benchmarks for the Preparation of Students for Success in a Global Environment

6. Current knowledge about human learning guides learning practices throughout school life.

7. International projects are included in local curriculum to promote global learning opportunities for all students.

8. Students are developing capacities for success in the evolving global workforce, which includes emerging technologies.

9. Students in Global Learning Centers learn and use democratic decision-making processes, peace-building strategies, and practices for ethnocultural equity as guides and foundations for becoming global citizens.

10. Students demonstrate an orientation for caring about the global community and its sustainable development.

The mission of the ISC is to connect educators and students across borders and regions of the world to help them shape their schools as Global Learning Centers. Its leaders are promoting students as global citizens, educators as global leaders, schools as Global Learning Centers, and International School Partnerships.

The ISC works primarily with school leaders to fashion their schools as Global Learning Centers. University and college professors are now beginning to connect students on different continents with each other to explore the concept of "the global citizen". Its intent is to develop students during their education as the next generation of global leaders to:

- Work across borders and regions on common projects.

- Learn about global challenges.

- Learn about different cultures.

- Care about the human condition.

- Develop their own networks of friends and other connections.

- Make friends in other cultures and regions of the world.

- Develop skills with new communication technology.

- Advance local communities and support their integration into the global community.

- Develop tolerance and ethical values.

- Imagine new local and global futures.

- Address some of the major problems of the world.

To achieve these purposes, the ISC is developing a variety of opportunities for educational leaders. We:

- Manage a registry of schools that are seeking international partnerships.

- Develop hubs of educators in regions of the world.

- Provide a credentialing system for becoming an ISC Global Learning Center.

- Offer a virtual community space on the Web and through Homemeeting, a Web office environment.

- Develop an international principals' council to guide ISC development and its projects.

- Research ISC social networks, with their development and effects.

- Produce *Wingspan Journal* (www.iscweb.org).

- Organize annual global summits for educators and also for youth leaders from ISC hubs around the world.

How do the international board of directors and international leadership team function to achieve ISC goals? And how are they connected with hub coordinators around the world? The ISC, being a virtual organization, relies on many forms of communication for its daily work, which includes regular connections through e-mail; Skype, a computer telephone service; shipped CDs and DVDs; telephone; and fax. The HomeMeeting and Joinnet Web office environment was made available to us by an ISC board member, Professor Kai Sung, from National Central University in Taiwan. The ISC recently organized an international advisory board of business leaders, consultants, and agency leaders. In 2008 we launched an international Principals' Council to give shape to the next phase of ISC development. All ISC leadership groups will work in the multiple communication systems available.

Our board meetings occur in real time in one of our Homemeeting Web offices to follow a posted agenda on what is called the white board. Communication and dialogue occur through voice, video, internal e-mail exchanges, sharing of documents, voting processes, and connections to the Internet. For these periodic events, we schedule meetings for Tampa, Florida (USA) and Ottawa, Canada at 8 a.m.; Ostersund and Flen, Sweden at 2 p.m.; Sochi, Russia at 4 p.m.; and Chung-li Taiwan and Nanjng, China at 8 p.m. We are all together at our computers in real time. Members of the Leadership Team or Board of Directors meet regularly in pairs or four persons in Skype to talk, see video, and share documents and notes. When we are more than four persons we meet in HomeMeeting, which accommodates up to 20 computers. Documents are worked on virtually through e-mail and mailed CDs and memory sticks until we are satisfied and ready to go. Services to members are provided both virtually and locally or internationally among the Hubs. The strongest Hubs influence what happens in the ISC network, while we all work to improve existing Hubs and build new Hubs that will strengthen our community for the mission we hold dear. Knowing how networks evolve and grow has been instructive to us as we seek ways to expand the influence of the ISC as a global learning network.

CONCLUSION

What do all of these trends mean for guiding schools into the global age? Educators will necessarily push the boundaries of schooling and break barriers so that global opportunities and challenges can be pursued. In the process, educators are finding themselves *living on the edge of chaos,* a necessary condition for stimulating significant and enduring change. Networking is an important key to success for any person or enterprise in the twenty-first century. This is a big moment in the history of education, one that needs courageous people to imagine new schooling futures, those who find ways to link to the local and global business communities and also consult educators around the world who have a similar mission.

In his book *Tsunami: Building Organizations Capable of Prospering in Tidal Waves,* Victor Pinedo (2004) argues: "To survive, organizations must transform themselves into agile and responsive organisms, with the stamina of an adolescent and the abilities of a mature adult. They must discard the elitist hierarchy, undoing the myth that it is natural for all organizations to have superiors and inferiors. They must build a new organizational sailboat that allows them to sail through tsunamis." Pinedo's work with major business organizations around the world guides leaders in organic competencies that he calls "the Seven C's": Confidence, Commitment, Co-creation, Connection, Communication, Celebration and Course Correction, and Caring. There are the characteristics of mature organizations. They represent a course for us to pursue in developing schools as global learning centers.

Students are the explorers today in this new era of living, which is virtual, local, and global. Let's learn together about the trends and their impact by sharing our stories, learning about opportunities to participate globally, examine global problems, create novel learning programs, and continue to imagine better learning futures for our students. And, while we invent education that is fit for this new age, let us bury the mentality that gave us schooling for the industrial age. It is time to replace the Industrial Age mindset with a global mentality for education and lifelong learning.

2

A Mechanical View of Change

In recent decades, it has been broadly recognized that the traditional schooling practices of isolation, fragmentation, and fear have little potential for servicing the lifetime learning needs of students today. Yet, many schools remain virtually unchanged despite all the innovations that have been introduced and the financial resources that have been made available. *Why are so many schools and school districts virtually stuck today in what many informed critics consider an outdated and unworkable model of schooling and learning?* It is this question that this book addresses as we explore an alternative: *living on the edge of chaos.*

As educators move into the information age in a global village and are faced with the challenges of serving increasing at-risk student populations, schools will need to shed old control strategies and compliance expectations. Professional exploration and invention within and across institutions, communities, and nations will become the new work norm; the answers and programs of the past are no longer sufficient for the enormous social challenges we face today. Because the future is unknown and views about human needs are changing dramatically each day, schools need to prepare students to become competent dreamers and designers who can give shape to an increasingly complex world.

Our recent journey into the new sciences has given us fresh perspectives as to why schools seem to be stuck in the old paradigms of schooling. We are beginning to understand why change initiatives often have little impact on either the content and delivery of school services or on student performance patterns. In fact, so fundamental are the differences between the old and new scientific laws that leader decisions about the future can produce significantly different outcomes for their institutions. Change is inevitable, it seems, but progress is not, for progress depends on our assumptions and values and the choices we make. To guide successful change initiatives, we need to understand the nature and consequences of our choices, for their selection may well define the future of our schools.

Over the last century, educators have assumed that schools were rather simple systems that exhibited reliable characteristics within and across communities.

Student development was viewed as rather predictable, and so the established graded curriculum with its structures, programs, and school services seemed well suited to the achievement of desired learning levels. If problems arose, it was usually assumed that the school-based professionals were at fault. Centralized decision making relieved workers in schools from worrying about matters that seemed not to relate directly to their day-to-day jobs, while power was concentrated in the hands of a few to ensure that predetermined programs functioned in an efficient and predictable way. For those students who exhibited other than presumed normal abilities, alternative services were provided so that the mainstream programs and students could proceed without interruption. This was a rather simple system for giving a standard education to the masses.

A major flaw with a standard education today is that life no longer is either stable or simple at any level, for the exceptions now exceed the norm. All social systems, not only schools, have begun to burst through their established boundaries; and unless new mental models of institutional purpose and work cultures emerge, social agencies and work systems everywhere are at risk of not surviving. In response to the growing complexity of social organizations, multiple networks and partnerships have literally mushroomed so that professional educators can gain rapid access to the information, resources, and opportunities they need to do their jobs. Decision making has gradually been decentralized from the federal to state levels, from the state to school districts, from the district to schools, and now from schools to teaching teams. Adaptations and changes are happening at such a rapid pace that top-down management patterns are no longer fast enough or good enough to work.

The contradiction between the laws of change within Newtonian and quantum worldviews presents a central paradox for leaders today: the mechanical view is to fix the problem, whereas the *natural view is continuous development.* The differences are so vast that it seems virtually impossible to manage fundamental change while simultaneously exercising power over others to control what happens. A larger issue, we suspect, is whether there is a way to function within bureaucracies and yet stimulate an organization's natural growth process. We think there is, and we believe that understanding the paradoxes, the complexities, and the natural growth of living systems offers a path to an even more complex and yet more promising future, There is no choice but to function within legal parameters in public institutions, yet there are ways of thinking about constraints that will enable us to break through barriers and facilitate progress. By re-examining some of the outdated laws of science and their management derivatives and by becoming familiar with those that are more dynamic and responsive, we can rethink our own journey and become revitalized for managing the paradoxes and complexities in the decades ahead.

To begin our journey together, we will explore the foundations of twentieth-century schooling, which has its roots in the machine laws of Newtonian physics. We believe these laws continue to be useful for designing and building modern technology, but we question their utility for guiding change and growth within dynamic human organizations. It is our intent to explore the lessening relevance for social behavior of the machine model in a growing age of complexity and paradox. When we understand the foundations of our traditions more clearly, perhaps we can reduce the stranglehold of those that are inappropriate and move on to more promising ways of working together within and across institutions.

NEWTONIAN PHYSICS

The laws of a fixed, machine-like universe, which are grounded in Newtonian physics, functioned as a guide for early management theorists such as Max Weber and practitioners like Frederick Taylor. Their pioneering work led to the rigid structures, policies, and practices of the twentieth-century organizations, most of which were appropriate for managing unskilled laborers for production purposes a century ago. Tenets of the bureaucracy evolved to prevent any kind of fundamental change in work systems, for established practices are protected even today by the complex systems of control that have evolved over this century. Because of the strength of bureaucratic traditions, many public institutions today find it virtually impossible to sustain any kind of change in the basic systems of work and their services.

Let us now look more closely at the laws of physics that governed scientific thought and management action in the past to better understand our own history and its hold on leadership practices today. The roots of physics are found in the sixth century B.C. in Greece, where science, philosophy, and religion were all integrated, and where answers were sought to the meaning of life and to how things work in the universe (Capra, 1991). The Greeks speculated that beneath its varied appearances the world was composed of a single substance . . . all quantum stuff (Herbert, 1985, 40). *Physics,* a term coined by the Greeks, refers to the essential nature of things. During the fifth century B.C., Greek philosophers began to consider that *basic change in the universe was impossible,* which led to the *concept of indestructible substance* (Capra, 1991, 21). *The concept of a fixed universe eventually became the very cornerstone of Western thought, which was in stark contrast to the ecological worldview of Eastern philosophies and religions.*

Prior to A.D. 1500, the dominant worldview of Europe was organic, linking interdependently the spiritual and material phenomena (Capra, 1982, 53). Eastern philosophy stressed the organic unity of a universe with spiritual and physical dimensions. In time, however, Western thought began to embrace fragmentation as a principle, along with rationality, abstraction, and logic of the mind. Change during the Middle Ages was perceived as a mere illusion of the senses, and hence the idea of a static world emerged to govern thought for centuries. This fragmented view of the universe eventually separated Western scientific development from Eastern philosophy and religion.

It was Descartes who developed many of the techniques of modern mathematics and gave us the picture of the universe as a giant machine (Zukav, 1979, 50). Human identity was equated with the mind, rather than with the whole human organism and its physical and spiritual dimensions, which further separated the human experience from the world in which humans function (Zohar, 1990, 29, 136). Scientific reasoning took the form of mathematical descriptions of nature and thereafter spawned the scientific revolution. Scientists used this dichotomy to separate themselves (the mind) from the material world (matter) in pursuit of new knowledge. In time, the growing preeminence of scientific knowledge diminished the influences of both philosophy and religion in the Western world (Capra, 1982, 54).

It was within this context of identifying the fundamental fragmentation of matter and mind that Sir Isaac Newton constructed the laws of mechanics in classical physics, laws that have guided the work of scientists for centuries (Zohar, 1990, 69). Newton's time was one in which the dominance of religion was replaced by the authority of science. Classical physics established linear models of reasoning that were based on observable data and that led to precision in the sciences through language, then to greater abstractions through mathematics and eventually through statistics. Ambiguous words began to be replaced by more precise symbols, which were rigorously defined and enforced in scientific inquiry (Capra, 1991, 32).

By the nineteenth century, scientists believed that the universe was indeed a huge mechanical system running according to Newton's laws of motion, which firmly established the clockwork assumptions of the world that were characterized by repetition and predictability. For Francis Bacon, the goal of science, through the separation of mind and matter, was to dominate and control nature (Capra, 1982, 56). The classical principles of physics are still used today as a foundation for machines and technology, which are both static and controllable.

John Locke (Capra, 1982, 68, 69) used the machine principles in his atomistic view of society, in which the basic building block was not society but individuals. This new emphasis on the individual paved the way to modern economics and political thought, with a focus on individual property, rights, and responsibility. This value of the individual as the basic unit of society led to prevailing practices in twentieth-century schooling. Consider a few:

1. Classrooms have been regarded as collections of individual students and a teacher (rather than as a more natural social system).

2. Students have worked alone and been tested individually (rather than collectively).

3. Teachers have worked in isolation from their peers (rather than cooperatively) and have been judged by their individual superiors (rather than by their peers, students, and parents).

4. Principals and superintendents within the same district performed separate as well as independent functions.

If communities had been the social building block in the minds of early scientists, perhaps different forms of schooling would have evolved with enduring connections rather than the isolationism that persists today.

Basic Laws of the Mechanical View

Several basic principles in classical physics, which we call laws, now seem clear:

Law 1: *The scientific concepts of fixed time, space, and matter emphasize parts of a system and help establish predictable stability through mathematics and statistics.*

Schools have the traditional clock, which ticks on in 50-minute periods, with 6 different and isolated subjects a day, for 180 days a year, for 12 or 13 years. The graded curriculum, which is divided into separate subjects, is taught by teachers who work independently with the same students. Typically, the subjects have been unconnected to each other and also to the dreams and interests of students of any age. It has been presumed that success within fixed programs will enable students later to function as successful workers in their communities. This schooling formula is now out of touch with the human experience of growing into adulthood in a rapidly transforming global community. *The underlying Newtonian law is basically one of disconnection.* It should be no surprise that so many at-risk students fall through the cracks or drop out of school. Nor is it any wonder that many high schools today are at risk of not surviving as social institutions.

Law 2: *Predictability through mathematics and logic is a chief cornerstone in the formulation of knowledge, which also locks in a rational, empirical, and scientific tradition for establishing new truths.*

Knowledge is controlled through the separation of mind and spirit to ensure the predictable evolution of the self-regulating universe. This is not to say that mathematics and logic do not give us some useful form of truth, because they do. What appears to be at issue, however, is that truth and knowing can be derived in many other, and sometimes more reliable, ways. As Jaworski reflects on his work with leaders around the world, "People were suspicious of what could not be measured or quantified. I had come to see the immeasurable as precisely that which was most real, that which I cared most deeply about" (1996, 152).

Think for a moment about the knowing that it is possible to achieve after a few brief minutes in any school. All kinds of information bombard the senses and generate some relative truth about the quality of school life for adults and students. And yet the continued reliance on standardized test scores is becoming more pronounced today, even though educators have been protesting for decades about the false picture that is produced from such a limited method for establishing truth. We must acknowledge that real knowing is derived from multiple sources and that truth about the quality of schooling cannot be measured by statistics alone. The dynamics of the organization are far more influential on the success of students, whereas statistics only yield measures about the effects of these dynamics.

Law 3: *Rationalism and reductionism generate simple truths about harmony within the universe, for they emphasize what can be both observed and measured with relative certainty.*

Simple truths are typically affirmed through statistics with a reductionist approach to the analysis of data; a simple cause-and-effect relationship is said to exist between the parts of a system. In schools, we design curriculum and structures for learning and testing that emphasize individuals and their deficiencies, all of which is justified through the use of quantifiable data. In many schools, teachers are observed and evaluated in 30-minute segments to determine the numbers of predetermined desirable behaviors that exist, which yields a score of the teacher's relative worth.

The wide range of student abilities and competence is considered to be irrelevant to the "truth" being sought within the reductionist tradition of teaching. Teachers and principals have argued for years that teacher-evaluation systems, which typically are grounded in brief observations of prescribed teaching behaviors, yield only partial truths, at best. Far more information is needed to understand the complexities within which classroom observation data are generated and understood. In recent decades, leaders have begun to question the brief classroom observation as a defensible way of establishing a teacher's value. The lived experiences with teachers during the entire school year will surely generate more valid and reliable information about their professional worth to the school as a whole and to the students they serve.

We have been hooked on old scientific principles for centuries (Wheatley, 1992, 26):

We've held onto an intense belief in cause and effect. We've raised planning to the highest of priestcrafts and imbued numbers with absolute power. We look to numbers to describe our economic health, our productivity, and our physical well-being. We've developed graphs and charts and maps to take us into the future, revering them as ancient mariners did their chart books. Without them we'd be lost, adrift among the dragons. We have been, after all, no more than sorcerers, the master magicians of the late twentieth century.

As we continue our journey to examine the evolution of the machine model of life, it becomes clearer how Newtonian laws led to the design and evolution of modern institutions. These very traditions are creating the paralysis that now exists, which helps to explain why so many institutions are not able to adapt to the times. Innovators often discover that traditional institutional practices seem impossible to alter, for work systems are grounded so thoroughly in the machine view of the world, With assumptions about order and control and change initiatives that seek only improved compliance patterns, the natural process of change and emergence in institutions is often aborted. Let us consider the Newtonian roots of twentieth-century institutions, including schools.

THE MODERN BUREAUCRACY

By the dawn of the twentieth century, the laws of Newtonian physics had so permeated life around the world that its principles were employed to solve almost every type of social problem. Bureaucracies were evolving worldwide to provide some order for the masses who were working in urban factories at the dawn of the industrial age. To standardize the work of great numbers of unskilled laborers and to bring efficiency into the workplace, the emerging industrial context employed the fixed and stable laws of Newtonian physics. When the new class of managers was faced with large numbers of unskilled workers in their factories, the challenges of producing reliable products was met by employing the mechanical laws of science, a concept that launched the age of industrialization for the next century (Crozier, 1964).

Max Weber, who is generally recognized as the father of modern bureaucracy, was a German sociologist who became interested in the issues of social control and dominance within organizations (Kasler, 1988). He did not invent bureaucracy but gave definition to what already was flourishing; and, because of his scholarship in sociology, he provided a rationale for social control within organizations. Weber's foray into the world of bureaucracy was merely one of his many intellectual ventures (Mommsen, 1989). He lived with a paradox himself in believing that modern industrial societies would not survive without bureaucratic techniques of social organization, even though he feared that this very bureaucratized and collectivist society would reduce individuals to utter powerlessness (110, 111).

Although disturbed by the potential negative effects of modern bureaucracy, Weber perceived that the monocratic bureaucracy was superior to all other forms of administrative organization (Mommsen, 1989, 112). The hierarchical structure and the subjection of all operations to rational rules and regulations provided crucial advantages for precision, speed, unambiguity, knowledge, continuity, discretion, unity, strict subordination, and reduction of friction (113). The characteristics of a bureaucracy, as promulgated by Weber, evolved over time and remain in operation throughout the industrialized world.

Capitalism and bureaucratization, in Weber's opinion, were the two revolutionary forces that would replace all traditional forms of social organization throughout the world (Mommsen, 1989, 109). All operations were to be pursued according to formal-rational rules without regard for personal preferences or values and attitudes, and this was a pattern that precluded leadership development among members. Innovation and change were not in keeping with the concepts of regulation, and the pure type of bureaucratic social system became a legal institution of work, rather than an informal one. Eventually, the bureaucracy became a force for legitimate domination, which guaranteed a submissive mentality among workers (Weber, 1922). Such a static and unchanging view of work was promoted around the world, as were the functions of fear in the workplace and managerial control over workers. Weber accepted this paradox; yet, he feared that Western societies were doomed because of the irreversible advances of rationalization and devoted energy to mobilizing resistance to its spread. The bureaucracy was a necessary structure for work as society advanced through its stages.

Scientific Management

During the late nineteenth century, manager Frederick W. Taylor began his experiments to standardize work patterns by conducting a form of job analysis (Longenecker, 1964), His method was not based on a theory, but it was a practical solution for increasing the efficiency of workers, with emphasis placed on management planning, standardizing work, and improving the human effort (Kast and Rosenzweig, 1979). In the Midvale Steel Company, Taylor fashioned a science of shop management that was based on a scientific analysis of the job; later, also as a manager, he conducted experiments using his method at the Bethlehem Steel Company. He began with an analysis of the motions and steps of workers, which were first examined systematically in his famous *pig iron studies*. The application of Taylor's management process at Bethlehem Steel led to significant increases in daily worker output (Longenecker, 1964, 12, 13), which caught the attention of management everywhere. By the beginning decades of the twentieth century, Taylor's success spawned a worldwide movement to increase worker effectiveness and efficiency through scientific management within bureaucracies.

Taylor based his concepts of shop management on two observations he made over time: (1) a lack of uniformity in work, which was the challenge of management; and (2) the lack of an apparent relationship between good shop management and the payment of individuals (Taylor, 1912, 17). A strong work ethic prevailed in those years, for hard work from employees was prized and economic rationality and individualism were valued, both of these being dominant principles within Newtonian physics. A stable work environment was evolving as managers used scientific principles for planning large daily tasks for workers, providing standard conditions and equipment, and giving either high pay for success or loss of pay and benefits for failure in work (63, 64). The intent was for the unreliable judgment of individual workmen to be replaced by more reliable laws, rules, and principles; to be managed daily became the science of the job (Callahan, 1962, 27). The specific tasks of managers focused on conducting *time and motion studies* that gave them a basis for measuring the job. *Standardization* of the best and fastest way of doing the job helped managers *define the tasks* for each worker each day, in which managers taught workers new methods of work that were combined with a bonus plan (29–32).

The great mental revolution that Taylor promoted eventually resulted in several management principles: (1) replace rules of thumb with science, (2) obtain harmony in group action, (3) achieve cooperation among human beings, (4) work for maximum output, and (5) develop workers to their fullest potential (Taylor, 1912). The values of human cooperation and learning on the job were necessary in order for workers to acquire precise techniques, but somehow this part of Taylorism failed to carry forward through ensuing decades of management scholarship; this may account for some of the eventual failure of scientific management principles. Scientific job analysis and its management simply offer an incomplete picture of human productivity in the work environment. To illustrate his strong beliefs about harmony and group work, Taylor wrote in 1912 that the relations between employers and men form without question the most important part of management work (25).

SCHOOLING AS A BUSINESS

The widespread adoption of bureaucratic and scientific management principles influenced industrial and social institutions throughout the world. In time, educators adopted many of the same scientific practices for a rapidly growing population. The emergence of the school administrator as the educational efficiency expert during the first several decades of the twentieth century was to become one of the most significant movements in educational history (Callahan, 1962, 97). By 1925, the superintendency had more characteristics of a managerial job in business and industry than of one that was educational (148). Because the numbers of educational administrators were so large by then, and their management needs were so similar to those (including school hoard members) in the business world, business perspectives were adopted throughout the schooling enterprise.

Education systems therefore became streamlined, efficient, and standardized, but society has paid a heavy puce for adopting these mechanical principles for managing what are really "natural systems" in schools. Until recently, principals were preoccupied with such matters as the details of the school plant and equipment, warming and ventilating the building, and school seating and landscaping. Teachers, meanwhile, were given secretarial duties without any assistance and were forced to spend many hours on clerical work in addition to their full-time teaching responsibilities (Callahan, 1962, 108).

Additional bureaucratic features were developed early in the century to control the performance of teachers and students, as well as educational leaders. In 1913, the *American School Board Journal* published a report of teacher rating in Park City, Tennessee, which led to a national movement for principals to devise means of measuring teacher efficiency (Callahan, 1962, 105), In 1914, an efficiency-rating system was created for teachers, who were expected to increase the efficiency and product of the laborer (pupil) and to make good use of raw materials, such as textbooks and charts.

The final responsibility for efficient learning was placed on the pupil, with the teacher's rating of their performance as the ultimate control device (Callahan, 1962, 58). Even the classroom had become the focus for efficiency through student testing, record keeping, and teacher ratings (103). By 1913, several normed tests had been developed for use in schools (e.g., Thorndike and Ayres, or Thorndike and Hillegas), and gradually a testing industry emerged that would thereafter measure student knowledge. Questions about program value led quite naturally to scientific management in the budgetary process of schools. Dollar values were given priority over educational values, which paved the way to the now century-old practice of purchasing according to bids that are made on financial rather than educational grounds (73).

Referring to the concepts of scientific management and bureaucracy, English (1992, 39) shows how the classroom eventually resembled a manufacturing plant, for the job shop was similar to the classroom, and the production line was kin to the homogenous grouping of students. The mixed assembly line related to mainstreaming patterns, whereas the automated production line illustrated continuous education through the grades. *Rework* of employees, English notes, was similar to remediation for students, while inspection came through supervision and testing, and class performance was controlled through standardized tests. Work was designed scientifically, accomplished through graded structures, and monitored through administrator oversight, teacher and student supervision, and testing programs.

In time, the school survey was devised as part of a procedure for reporting to the school board on the community's financial investment (Callahan, 1962, 113). The issue before boards was generally one of getting greater returns on their investment. Hence, the dominating force in education continued to be economic rather than educational. Even information about students was limited largely to enrollment and promotion statistics. Superintendents spent much of their time on business matters and interpreted educational activity in business terms in order to survive. The challenge in preparing an annual report to the board of education was to justify expenditures and to educate the public about what funds were needed. In the end, Callahan charged, people in the United States got what they deserved by forcing their leaders to spend time on accounting rather than on educational concerns (120). How regrettably true this observation remains!

Bureaucracy has been the major influence on educational credentialing systems for all role specializations and on measuring the performance of teachers and pupils through standardized testing. Quality control of programs is maintained through fixed time parameters each year and each day for each subject. Data-processing systems account for human activity and levels of performance, and salaries are based on the amount of employee education combined with years of experience. Control over workers is maintained through employee contracts and appraisal systems that are built upon compliance values, while job descriptions control for work within allowable limits. Budget decisions are made by administrators, who place a certain amount of fear in workers, who have no sense of the big picture. Assignments are made by administrators, while workers at lower levels consider themselves fortunate to be employed at all. Table 2.1 summarizes a few essential principles of Newtonian physics, its effects on bureaucracy and scientific management, and the processes of traditional schooling.

Table 2.1. The roots of traditional schooling in the twentieth century and its effects

Mechanical Physics	Bureaucracy/Scientific Management	Traditional Schooling
Unchanging universe	Laws, regulation, policy, schedules	13 years/180-day school calendar
Precision through math	Annual reports, record keeping, budgets	Data processing, reports, budgets
Fixed time, space, matter	Standardized work and supervision	Graded curriculum/placement
Individual building block	Assembly line/managing individuals	Supervision of individual workers
Reductionism as truth	Performance evaluation	Teacher and student evaluation
Self-regulating universe	Work, pay, contracts, dismissal	Work, pay, contracts, retention, promotion

A rather simple view of schooling emerged in this century within a context of great political dialogue about economic and efficiency matters, and the rather rigid structures for work that evolved were to ensure that all U.S. youth received a standard education. *Times have changed, however, and very few of these bureaucratic rules and scientific management strategies seem to work now for the advantage of anyone, much less everyone.* The variation of pupils has become far too great for a graded structure to serve a useful purpose any longer. The knowledge explosion is making graded textbook learning and testing passé, and the public, now better educated, is demanding new kinds of standards for students and teachers, as well as for school leaders.

THE BREAKDOWN OF BUREAUCRATIC THINKING

The tension between control over work processes for standard programs and the freedom to respond to a changing environment is so strong today that educators at all levels are experiencing many new pressures and frustration. Some are leaving the profession altogether, because meeting needs seems almost impossible within the current legal and political context. We recognize that the social system of education is in a state of turbulence at all levels and in many dimensions, which is a condition in which most systems have broken down. It is the tension between control and freedom to act that we examine in the next several chapters. We believe that education as a social enterprise may not survive much longer unless the natural dynamics of institutions are freed to explore their potentialities for responding to our times.

There are no guarantees that schools will survive much longer in their present form. School systems have been around for only the last century or so, a small fraction of human experience. Already there are fears that public schooling might become extinct as a social institution unless it adapts quickly to rapidly changing global conditions. While many leaders continue to control for change within the traditional parameters of schooling, alternatives are appearing that break with those very traditions, such as private corporations managing large city school systems, and K–12 schools functioning within business environments.

The recent involvement of the business community in the problems of schooling has signaled broad concern for the economic well-being of our nation. A U.S. Department of Labor study of the basic requirements of the workplace today (SCANS, 1992) serves as a wake-up call to educators, for it emphasizes the vital link that exists between our nation's economic future as a world force and the quality of our schooling. In response to a groundswell of public concern, President Bill Clinton and many governors made education a top priority, noting that the quality of our way of life depends on how well prepared the workforce and the citizenry are to shape the future.

Although innovative responses to growing social needs keep coming along, many have been constructed with a mechanical view of change. At the same time, a political backlash protects conditions of an age gone by. In fact, so accustomed are educational leaders to controlling change agendas that many collaborative development systems that were designed as innovations have been co-opted as forms of control for compliance with the traditional forms of schooling. Consider a few:

1. *Clinical supervision,* which began as a peer-development process to help teachers develop team-teaching strategies, soon became a control system for teacher evaluation.

2. *Site-based management,* which was conceived as a structure for enabling school-level educators to respond to local conditions, has become a tool for getting teachers and parents to rubber stamp what principals have already decided.

3. *Cooperative learning,* which began as a process for students to help one another explore, discover, and produce new concepts and ideas, is now being used in many places as a strategy to ensure student achievement of traditional curriculum objectives.

4. *Total quality management,* which evolved worldwide as a philosophy of work to enable an organization to deliver what customers need or want, became a strategy for evaluating and controlling school performance by placing emphasis on statistical analyses.

5. *Benchmarking,* which is one of the latest innovations, is an evaluation typology designed for those inside an organization to assess their own work processes and systems against world-class standards and those of other high-performing organizations. This, too, is being co-opted in some places as a control system over teaching to ensure that all students, no matter their previous experiences, are expected to achieve age-graded standards.

However, several breakaway models of schooling show promise for meeting current human requirements; they include *schools of choice, charter schools, full-service schools,* and the rapid rise of *homeschooling.* While their ultimate value remains uncertain, they threaten the time-honored traditions of "one kind of schooling for all." Vocational/technical schools are becoming *technology centers* that are forming dynamic partnerships with the business community and with colleges and universities. Simultaneously, while schools are developing new pathways to their communities, some state officials continue to wage war against schools, usually in troubled neighborhoods, that fail to demonstrate normal levels of student achievement on age-graded and isolated curriculum variables. To raise achievement standards and tighten the control systems, many schools with large at-risk populations are being placed on state lists of "at-risk schools," even though they are often beacons of hope for their communities. Furthermore, within the current climate of focusing on at-risk youth, teachers and parents are worried about "normal" and "high-achieving" students who seem to be resistant learners; they too are becoming at risk for school failure. The traditional views of schooling and the power that continues to place a great emphasis on normal evaluation are simply out of sync with current social and economic conditions.

Clinchy (1998) argues that "educationally challenged school districts" are engaged in a factory-model approach to school system reform. It is not really a reform or restructuring movement at all, he argues, but a simple return to and a shoring up of the traditional, top-down, highly centralized, bureaucratic school system that we have had for a century. By continuing to apply the industrial model to public schools, efficiency and low cost become the order of the day. In this rigid factory model, everyone is treated as interchangeable parts of a production machine called education. Curriculum and testing are still standardized; content and grade-level standards are still taught and tested. School autonomy within this context is a myth, for the prototype of the factory model is guided by sleek, modern, downsized, technologically advanced orientations. This new system is intent upon producing dutiful young people who can become human resource capital for a savagely competitive global economy. The language, Clinchy observes, has become more sophisticated and up to date since Taylor's day, but the autocratic, antidemocratic, dehumanizing ideology of corporate domination and control is essentially unchanged.

Education is at a turning point, and the choices and decisions made in the next several decades could determine whether education survives or becomes extinct as a social institution. Examples exist in many places of an alternative view of school reform that is guided by the human spirit to explore and invent the future, a movement that follows in the Dewey tradition of progressive education, which surfaced at the turn of the twentieth century. It is time for political leaders from national to local levels to decide either to tighten controls, and thereby reinforce traditional programs and structures, or to free educators to invent more vital forms of schooling to match the conditions of our time. From our reading in the new sciences, we now perceive that the choices leaders make will send an organization either in the direction of extinction or toward survival and adaptation for changing times.

Few would argue that families function like machines that follow rules of control and predictability. We tend to nurture the family's growth through a wide array of behaviors and stages, doing whatever it takes at any point in time to help family members achieve success in the world. Yet, schools and other social institutions are governed as though they were reliable machines with predictable parts. Perhaps our traditions of bureaucratic thinking have so tainted our views of how social institutions work that it will be some time before we come to understand and facilitate their natural growth over time. If we could alter our assumptions about fixed time, space, and programs, along with predictable controls through statistics with its accompanying rationalism and reductionism, schooling might have the potential to serve a broader and more useful function for society.

Today, schools provide complex program offerings to meet a wide range of student needs. Credentialing systems seek to ensure that qualified educators provide schooling services. New programs and services have increased in number in recent decades, as have the laws that govern their operation. Laws, policy, job descriptions, evaluation systems, and financial parameters all are more ambitious and influential than ever before. Yet, as Hodgkinson wrote in 1991, "our house has a leaky roof." Even with tightened policy and control devices, and with increased funding, role specializations, and program options, far too many students are failing in school and dropping out, and in so doing are at risk of failing as citizens. *It is time to consider that our schools are at-risk social institutions.* It is time to explore new laws of change. It is time to recognize the implication of the information age and the global village and to invent altogether new systems of learning and schooling. It is time for local school systems, state bureaucracies that control them, and national policy makers to face up to the contradictions in current reform strategies and laws and to resolve the conflicts so that educational leaders can move ahead and respond to the natural challenges that are now apparent. Our survival as a nation may well depend on our educational responses to changing conditions, both individually and collectively. For leaders, it means engaging in a mind shift from control to emergence so that the natural evolution of schooling will be in sync with dramatic changes in the environment.

3

An Organic View of Change

A turning point in education, at the dawn of the twenty-first century, requires that leaders use unconventional approaches for redesigning schools and districts as organic and responsive systems while carrying the torch for emerging world-class standards. The problem with the mechanistic view of change (as discussed in Chapter 2) is that machines can only be designed, constructed, fixed, and, when they become out-of-date, tossed on the heap. Living organisms, however, grow and emerge through various stages during their life cycle and can address many new challenges in an effort to survive.

David Bohm (1995), a theoretical physicist who is one of the foremost scientific thinkers of the twentieth century, developed the concept of *wholeness* in quantum physics. He argues that fragmentation leads to confusion of the mind, for the notion that fragments are separate in their existence is an illusion that leads to endless conflict (1, 2). Fragmented thinking has led to pollution, destruction of the balance of nature, overpopulation, worldwide economic and political disorder, and the creation of an overall environment that is neither physically nor mentally healthy for most of the people who have to live in it (2). When we come to see the connections and the interdependence of everything, different values emerge, along with new priorities. Bohm contends that wholeness is what is real; the unbroken wholeness of the totality of existence is an undivided, flowing movement without borders (172).

Fragmentation has become such an art form in schools, with categorical funding requirements, laws, and regulations, that a movement toward holism as a way of life is likely to be filled with roadblocks, detours, and lawsuits. Yet, schooling problems now are so complex that the eventual demise of fragmented thinking and action is essential to the survival of schooling in any form. We cannot continue to blame students and teachers for the inadequacies of the education system. There are too many reasons for current dissatisfactions with schooling, and any substantive change in practice will require leaders to orchestrate a much more systemic and thorough change over time. The social conditions of the home and community are known to be probable predictors of a student's success in school. If schools are to become effective in equipping all students for success in life, then new ways must be found to link the family and community dynamically to the educational processes.

Fresh ways to think about the very social purpose and function of schooling are needed as we develop our communities and nations. Outdated models of change need to be tossed out and reimagined so leaders can adapt their institutions to current realities. We need not be fearful of the unknown but bring ourselves up to the challenge, for humans have an enormous capacity to adapt to changing environments through flexibility, self-organization, self-maintenance, and self-transformation (Capra, 1982, 285)!

RELATIVITY THEORY AND QUANTUM PHYSICS

Let us now explore laws within the new sciences of quantum physics. In his 1982 book, *The Turning Point,* Capra explains the major revolution of ideas that began in physics and eventually influenced most of the biological, social, and other natural sciences. He wrote, "The current crisis is not a crisis of individuals and governments, or of social institutions; it is a transition of planetary dimensions. *We are reaching a turning point*" (1982, 15, 16).

Einstein's theories of relativity and atomic phenomena precipitated a revolution in the classical sciences, for he advanced the breakthroughs of physicists in the late nineteenth century and the beginning of the twentieth century (Lindley, 1993, 65). For Einstein, reality was the real business of physics (Herbert, 1985, 4). Eventually, he made a revolutionary suggestion that gravity is not a force like other forces but is a consequence of space-time being curved (rather than flat) by the distribution in it of mass and energy (Hawkings, 1988). Einstein argued further that because there appears to be a dynamic relationship between time and space, they cannot be understood separately. Space-time is a single concept, he argues, and it is curved rather than flat.

An example of the relativity of space-time is found in our need to get away from home to have a restful and invigorating vacation. A two-week vacation at home typically is experienced differently from two weeks out of town. Even more pertinent is that teachers who work alone have a significantly different professional view of how much can be accomplished from that of those who work in teaching teams. Altering our views of space-time in some schools is already having a profound impact on professional work patterns and on the services provided to students.

Quantum theory evolved from initial studies of the atomic and subatomic world and gave us a completely new perspective on the natural order. Although space, time, and motion are relative concepts, Einstein insisted that physical quantities are absolute (Herbert, 1985, 7). For example, the speed of light is the same in all conditions; changes in space cancel out changes in time; and matter is made up of atoms (8). The small particles in atoms, which were first called *quanta* by Einstein, sometime are also waves. Mass is really energy in the form of electrons that move around the atom's nucleus and are bound by an electromagnetic field (Capra, 1991, 65–66). Herbert (1985, 63) suspects that everything in the world is pure quantum stuff, a physical union of particles and waves.

Nature does not show us its basic building blocks (that which we can see); rather, it reveals a complicated web of relationships in the form of energy (that which we experience). To illustrate this phenomenon of an energy field, we observe schools becoming dynamic energy systems when they link together their programs and services when students are organized in clusters of multiaged groupings. The relationships that emerge tend to generate new forms of energy, which alter working and learning patterns and their effects on everyone.

Because predictability and control are the two pillars of the scientific age, Newtonian physics was severely shaken with the discoveries of relativity and quantum uncertainty (Beavis, 1995). Quantum mechanics challenges the notion of linear chains of cause and effect, for systems are seen as whole, which may be differentiated into subsystems, but these are also wholes, so the emphasis is not on how they fit together but on how they relate to one another. The environment is the single most important condition for systems formation, for it is in the relationship that the system continues to evolve.

Quantum reality is not only a science of the material, physical world; Bohm (1995) argues that it embraces the unfolding of human consciousness as well. The order of consciousness is not distinct from matter, for there is an underlying unification of mind and body in quantum physics. If growth is discontinuous, as Bohm suggests, and dependent upon environmental conditions, then any natural condition within an organization can influence the changes made to systems of work. Likewise, if growth truly is an unfolding of life that connects experience to conscious thought, then the transformation of schooling may be more akin to metamorphosis (a new form) than to a restructuring of traditional practices.

In the quantum worldview, nature cannot be understood at all by dissecting it into parts, for nature does not present itself in separate parts (e.g., a person's intelligence, goals, integrity, physical health, or drive). Nature is a rather complicated, dynamic web of relations among all the parts (e.g., a certain 10-year-old girl who is an award-winning swimmer, or a particular middle school and urban community endangered by crime and drugs). *The scientific shift from a study of separate, observable objects to one of relationships and connections is central to our understanding of the dynamics of natural systems in schools as they grow or decline over time.* The universe, as it turns out, is essentially an interconnected web of relations, which is intrinsically dynamic and can either be enhanced or destroyed (Capra, 1982, 87). *This implies that each school's web of relations becomes the center of attention for educators, students, parents, and the community as they adapt their schools to changing conditions.*

David Bohm's theory (1995) went beyond the concept of interdependence to establish the idea that wholeness is the essence of quantum physics and is a more pervasive understanding of *how life works* in its natural unfolding. Reality is based on the interconnections, interrelationships, and interdependencies of life, which are constantly changing. And energy is produced by the connection of atoms, which at times are particles and at other times are waves, depending on the context. *Stability within nature then is one of dynamic balance within* what Capra (1996) calls *the web of life,* a concept that is similar to Bohm's wholeness. *The emerging central concept is that the total human-energy system that exists in a particular school influences the success of each student, whose progress depends on the strength of human caring and assistance, rather than on prescribed programs.*

To illustrate: We have observed over the years that teaching teams or departments transform their work cultures quite naturally when they are given the combination of time, space, and programs to arrange and adapt to their students' needs. It is almost impossible to become an energy system as a team within the traditional structure of six or seven disconnected 50-minute periods a day, for that structure ensures the isolation of time, space, programs, and teachers. It is *the dynamic organic features of school life that hold the greatest transforming potential, rather than new programs or materials.* Although redesigning curriculum and services is also a major part of the work, such activity will alter human experiences only if active connections among professionals and others are able to generate energy for a particular purpose and, in the process, become a positive influence in the lives of students.

It Is a Matter of Energy

Early in the twentieth century, the question of energy became a curiosity to quantum scientists, who examined it in many forms; motion, heat, gravity, electricity, chemistry, and so on. They learned that these energy sources are each transformed by subatomic particles colliding in what the scientists call the *dance of life* (attraction) *and death* (repulsion) (Capra, 1982). Not only are the basic patterns of the universe dynamic, but they also exist in stages of constant flow, transformation, and change. The quantum field of light and waves in nature, which is changed through conditions and connections, is what scientists today believe to be the only reality that exists.

Many educators now believe that school learning cannot be influenced through test scores alone, curriculum revisions, or new teacher evaluation systems. It is the interdependency among these and other revised systems that creates each school's *dance of life and death.* Many traditional practices will quite naturally fade from use in favor of those that are more responsive. In this sense, a classroom or school cannot be understood only in terms of statistics, Scores on *normed* tests provide information about the effects of services, but the dynamic interaction between school services, home conditions, the needs and aspirations of students, and the response of professionals is the dance of life that matters in the long run. It is the interaction of all these variables that determines the quality of education (the life in a particular school) for each student, not the isolation of any one feature.

Student success in school each quarter, each year, and over 13 years is due to more than passing courses and grade levels and having good attendance. Success depends on the totality of human attention given to each student and his or her interests along the way and, most importantly, to the connections that are built around life issues with peers and with adults in preparation for significant success as an adult. *The dynamic nature of the connection systems in a school is what matters.* It is the *school's* dance of life that needs to be studied, understood, and enhanced, a dance that reflects the perceptions and energy of all professionals, their programs and resources, and their use of space-time.

Not all connections build to the same extent, however; nor do they all become equally powerful in facilitating continuous growth (Capra, 1991). Where there are no exchanges, there is neither any energy nor any vital signs of life. Where there is negative energy, growth of any kind is stunted. While all positive interactions promote growth, they do not create the same energy force and result. Scientists now perceive that *the stronger the interaction system* (its density), *the stronger is the resulting force* (between people, programs, and institutions) (Capra, 1991, 228–230).

Consider the scientifically established four-stage hierarchy of interactions (Hawkings, 1988, 69). *Strong interactions* (1) hold protons and neutrons together in a "continuous dance" around an atomic nucleus, and their strength is so great that they can build a nuclear force. Because of a confinement property, particles are bound together into a new entity, which prevents the isolated elements from being recognized. *Weak interactions* (2), if strengthened, have the potential to become strong interactions that produce their own energy. *Electromagnetic interactions* (3), result from the attraction between negatively charged and positively charged particles. *Gravitational interactions* (4) are so weak between particles that they cannot be detected at all in experiments. Nevertheless, because of its mass, gravity is the dominating natural force in the universe.

Consider for a moment how this energy hierarchy helps us understand organizations and how they grow at varying rates. In schools, for example, *strong learning communities (strong interactions)* are easily recognizable as "lighthouses" of success, for the educators within them are constantly responding, improving, modifying, discarding, inventing, and piloting programs and services. Individual workers, students, and programs do not stand out, but the energy system and its effect is evident. Students and professionals thrive in these schools, for the energy system has broken the straitjacket of tradition and stimulates continuous learning and innovation. Professionals and students in such connection systems have become *learning communities* that build their own continuous energy flow for responding to life as it presents itself. In high-performing temporary systems, ad hoc work groups, committees, networks, and partnerships have the potential for evolving as strong interaction systems that function interdependently in random, complex, and nonlinear ways to keep the dance of life and death alive in the organization.

Even schools that have added only a few *ad hoc work teams or teaching teams (weak interactions)* are succeeding better than most. The regular exchanges generate significant energy to inspire some changes, although there are not as yet sufficient connections for these work units to jell as learning communities that have transformative potential. However, when the natural professional energy is nurtured, and if the connections become strong enough, these schools have the potential for becoming genuine learning organizations capable of adapting well to their changing environment.

Schools that add *a few new features, such as a school-improvement council,* create a negative and positive tension between the traditional structures of work and the work of an occasional improvement unit *(electromagnetic interactions)*. These forces often cancel each other out, as we observe in schools where school-improvement councils nurture little change. If the interaction systems are limited to one or two collaborative units where the normal work continues in isolation and independence, there simply is insufficient energy to overcome the gravitational pull of tradition, and nothing much happens that is new. When leaders understand that building a strong connection system is the objective for building learning organizations, observable change will result that affects students.

The strength of gravity and its mass can serve as a metaphor for schooling traditions (gravitational interactions). Little integration or few relationships exist between and among any part of the school's professionals and its services, even though state and district policy may require structures to support collaboration. Many professionals in these schools continue to favor tradition, resisting change to any extent. And, we observe that leaders in these schools make choices to retain basic traditions by controlling the extent of change initiatives.

In our research on involvement patterns in the school decision-making process, we found that the greater the density of professional involvement, the more the staff perceives that they are able to address challenges well together (Snyder, Snyder, and Acker-Hocevar, 1995). We observe that a continual flow of energy evolves in the best schools with *tendencies* and *possibilities,* rather than with *absolutes.* Within the natural rhythm of continual change, clear patterns emerge to pave the way to the future, for, as noted, *the quantum world is one of connections and relationships, not programs and services.* Awareness of these ideas provides us with a hopeful future for transforming schools. The trend to restructure schools often emphasizes changes in the calendars, clock, and location of work.

Consideration is seldom given to the processes of learning and working and to the dynamic that evolves from connecting students and educators. *The process of creating promising prototypes and destroying out-of-date, unworkable structures and services is the educational cosmic dance.* As Capra writes, "There is motion, but no moving objects; there is activity, but there are no actors; there are no dancers, there is only the dance!" (1982, 91).

PIONEERS OF A NEW WORK ORGANIZATION

Early in the twentieth century, while physicists were exploring curved space-time, energy, and the atomic world, similar kinds of changes evolved as well in the field of management science. Although there is little evidence that the new developments in relativity theory and quantum physics were an influence on management science, there was a trend to consider human factors in the workplace and their effects upon performance. Theories of motivation and leadership that emerged between 1920 and 1950 reflect the new laws of interactions, connections, energy, and curved space-time evolving in physics. Before we explore any further the relationship between the sciences and schooling, let us consider a few of the transition developments in management thinking that evolved early in this century.

Mary Parker Follett, who wrote about management in the 1920s and 1930s, was a transition scholar from scientific management, especially because her focus included both the psychological and the social aspects of the job. She viewed management as a social process that functions within the context of an organization's social system. This was a rather bold idea for the time (Merrill, 1970). Follett assumed that leaders are responsible for "getting the full power of the group to focus together, and for making them a team with a spirit of adventure that blazes trails" (300).

To some, these ideas seemed strange, for they were in sharp contrast with writings that reflected the tight management control and the predictability of work environments found in the early decades of the century. Yet, Follett's work heralded in the beginning of a new era in which the human element was considered a useful dynamic in the organization, an idea that evolved over the twentieth century (the power of connections!). In a 1995 book by Graham, *Mary Parker Follett: Prophet of Management,* Rosabeth Moss Kanter notes in the introduction that Follett sent one principle message to today's managers: Relationships matter, not just transactions. Follett wrote about how mutual influence makes things happen, no matter what formal authority may exist. She understood the basic principles of systems theory as well, arguing that nothing can be examined in isolation, for everything is a function of the organization's dynamics (xvi).

Elton Mayo's studies of worker productivity in the Hawthorn plant of the Western Electric Company between 1927 and 1932 actually launched the new management era, for he established through research the influence of the organizational context on variations in work performance (Kast and Rosenzweig, 1979). Mayo's studies signaled the importance of factors such as *belonging* and *recognition* in the workplace, and they spawned the theories of human motivation and leadership in organizations that evolved over the twentieth century.

Chester Barnard, the president of New Jersey Bell Telephone Company, was another pioneer. In 1938, he wrote what became a classic, *The Functions of the Executive,* in which Barnard emphasized the manager's responsibility for the psychosocial aspects of the organization, along with the technical and economic. Organizational growth involves both production and personal forces, he argued, and the function of management is to coordinate activity that creates equilibrium between the contributions of workers and their satisfaction.

Kurt Lewin was the first social scientist to explore the context of an individual's life space and the group's environment (1935, 1951). A person's growth can best be understood within his or her own historical life-space continuum. Over the next several decades, Lewin developed the concept of *field theory* from studying personality development and extended the ideas for understanding the dynamics of groups (1931). He was perhaps the first social scientist to examine the psychological dimension of the group context of work and its effect. Lewin's strategy for changing conditions in a person's life or in a group was known as *force field analysis,* a problem-solving strategy that is still in use today.

SYSTEMS THEORY

The influence of quantum physics expanded into the natural and social sciences, often with parts of the old physics still evident and with considerable confusion during the transition years. In 1968, Bertalanffy's major work, *general system theory,* documented 30 years of scientific inquiries into the understanding of quantum theory in biology, mathematics, physical systems, the sciences of man, psychology, and psychiatry. He is credited with the major translation of quantum principles to other natural sciences and with the introduction of the name *system theory* to the application of quantum physics in other natural sciences. System theory fostered a greater understanding of life within organizations. Understanding systems theory requires a shift in thinking from parts to wholes and requires attention to the dynamic interactions at play rather than to static features. The aims of general system theory (GST), according to Bertalanffy, were based on the assumption that systems are not understandable by investigating their parts in isolation; it is a science of wholeness.

The first principle in GST to be applied to organization theory was that *closed systems are isolated from their environment and have a tendency to move to a state of probable disorder and destruction.* The concept is that if a system is closed to its external environment, the original condition really determines the end state of the organization. For example, if a school is in a poor community whose school leaders attempt to educate its students, there is very little the school can do to offset the community decline and its effects on students without an engagement with the larger educational and social communities.

The second principle in GST is one of contrast to closed systems. *Open systems are integrated with their environment, building up and breaking down components with input and outflow, and these patterns have a tendency to move toward a steady state of dynamic equilibrium, a state of maximum health* (Bertalanffy, 1968, 39–41). In open systems, this final state can be reached from different initial conditions and in different ways. For example, schools that are vitally linked with their communities import all kinds of energy to offset the natural downward trend of the school and, in the process, evolve characteristics that distinguish them from other schools.

By the 1950s, various social and behavioral sciences had developed research agendas and new theories of life that built upon the foundations of systems theory. In 1951, Talcott Parsons' major work *The Social System* was published. Parsons' contribution to our understanding is in his declaration that existing equilibrium must be upset for the process of socialization to proceed further, a process that fosters the internalization of new value patterns (492). His concepts were directed toward the unfolding of the life cycle in social systems and toward the role of the action system in providing direction to social change. It is within a social context, Parsons argues, not a control position, that people become shapers of social systems.

Lilenfeld (1988) documents the adaptations of systems theory for the technological world and the advances that have been made in U.S. society as a result. He describes the development of cybernetics, information theory, artificial intelligence, operations research, systems analysis, economics, and the rise of the welfare of the state. To him, systems theory represents some kind of consensus of social contract or goals of society. In this context, systems theory is being used to control the forces of technological growth in society. One can easily see how systems theory facilitated the technological revolution and at the same time perpetuated the values of control and dominance.

There soon followed a split among scientists over which two distinct branches of systems theory evolved: (1) the technological world of systems, and (2) the natural world of social systems. The remainder of this book connects with the developments in natural social systems. Getzels and Guba (1957) were among the first to develop the idea of an organization as a social system. Two classes of phenomena were identified; they were (1) institutions (nomothetic) with certain roles and expectations that fulfill the goals of the system, and (2) individuals (ideographic) with certain personalities and needs/dispositions, whose interactions comprise social behavior. Social behavior results as individuals attempt to cope with the environment of expectations.

Cleland and King (1972) were among the earliest theorists to translate the concepts of systems theory into the processes of management. Their operational definition of *management* includes multiple features: (1) it is a process of organized activity where there is an objective, (2) objectives are achieved by establishing certain relationships among available resources, (3) authority is a legal right to direct activity, (4) objectives are achieved by work through others, and (5) it requires an active involvement of decisions within an environment of risk and uncertainty. The contribution of Cleland and King to systems theory was a viewpoint of an organization as a conglomerate of interrelated and interdependent parts, which requires an interaction (a dynamic) to produce desired effects over time. The task of management is to influence the quality of interactions in the organization for achieving these results. Tilles (1963) reinforced these new systems features by identifying the *management tasks* in organizations as (1) defining the company as a system, (2) establishing system objectives and performance criteria, (3) creating formal systems, and (4) managing the system's integration. The new science and knowledge about human organizations, Tilles noted, helped managers understand how the organization relates to its complex environment and perceive the relationship that exists between the whole of a company and its interdependent parts.

The basic parts of a system were identified in 1966 by Young and Summer in terms of its *inputs,* its *mediating variables* (processes and operations), and its *outputs;* this set of ideas paved the way for understanding the dynamic relationship between the organization and its internal environment. The role of management was to identify the organization's problem (input), manage the decision and work processes (mediating variables), and be responsible for its organizational solution (output). This rather linear view of systems wholeness (input/mediating variable/output) dominated scholarly thought and practice in organizational studies for the next quarter of the century.

In 1978, van Gigch published *Applied General Systems Theory,* a book about modern change and its management, in which a complementary linear model of systemic change was outlined. Managers were to identify the problem, observe conditions, compare actual with expected conditions, hypothesize reasons for the problem, and conclude how to solve the problem using information. This problem-solving approach, though somewhat linear, gave managers a process for meeting established goals. Assumptions of change were still based on the premises of predictability for the organization, even though emphasis was on the wholeness of the system; its controllability could be ensured through sound *system* management.

The landmark work of Kast and Rosenzweig, as presented in *Organization and Management: A Systems Approach* (1979), built upon these prior developments in systems theory and yet seemed less concerned with worker control and predictability issues and more focused on the interdependence of work subsystems for realizing the system's goals. Organizations essentially were viewed as goal-oriented living systems that were designed to serve humankind. This prototype of an organization was built upon the now-familiar systems principles of feedback, growth, stability, reproduction, decay, and open and closed loops. An organization and its subsystems were seen as functioning within an environmental suprasystem that included various subsystems: *goals and values* (people with a purpose); *technical* (using knowledge and equipment or technology); *managerial* (coordinates, plans, and controls); *structural* (working on integrated activity); and *psychosocial* (social relationships). Together these subsystems of work enabled the organization to function as a cohesive whole to accomplish its purpose. Their model of dynamic equilibrium became the prevailing model for managing change for decades and is still influential.

Senge (1990) writes that "systems thinking is a discipline of seeing the structures that underlie complex situations and for discerning high from low leverage change" (69). This new emphasis represents a mental shift from seeing the parts to seeing the whole and from seeing workers as helpless reactors to seeing them as active participants in shaping new realities (Capra, 1994). Capra further suggests that elements in systems theory are universal to all domains:

1. A shift from parts to whole

2. A shift from structure to process

3. A shift from objective to epistemic science

4. A shift from building to networking

5. A shift from truth to approximate description

Senge's concept of the *learning organization* (1990) makes an important extension of the concept of an organization as a system. He proposes that five dimensions of the learning organization nurture its growth: systems thinking, personal mastery, mental models, shared vision, and team learning. Throughout his writing, he places emphasis on the concepts of interdependence, work function, role relationships, and common goals.

Systems Theory for Schooling

Throughout the twentieth century, the field of educational administration followed primarily the traditions in classical, human relations, and organization and management theory. In the 1970s, Immegart and Pilecki (1973) introduced the concepts of systems theory to the work of educational administrators. They sought to address the unfolding of complex problems through systems thinking that offered an antidote *to putting out brush fires*. Rather than presenting a theory, however, the authors offered a cross-disciplinary way of thinking by focusing on a holistic view of a given context. For them, systems thinking is systematic and relational thought, which revolves around the application of systems theory in PERT (Program Evaluation and Review Technique) and PPBS (Program Planning and Budgeting Systems), which are planning, budgeting, and cost benefit and analysis systems. Their approach to a systems analysis was logical and rational and functioned to help administrators gain control of work life in their institutions.

One of the few major works in education to use systems theory as an organic approach to developing the culture of work was *Managing Productive Schools (MPS): Toward an Ecology* by Snyder and Anderson (1986). This volume was heavily influenced by the work of Kast and Rosenzweig (1979), and it formulated a theory of change management in schools that is grounded in systems theory. Ten dimensions of the work culture are identified for school leaders to oversee, and these function within six interdependent subsystems to influence student success patterns. These are the *goal subsystem, the organization subsystem, the performance subsystem, the program subsystem, the management subsystem,* and *the leadership subsystem.*

School leaders around the world have been so receptive to the natural systems approach for guiding school change that in the last decade more than 200 publications have emerged to advance the MPS version of systems thinking. Included in these publications are research studies, books, chapters, edited journals, articles, doctoral dissertations, and masters theses. In addition, the *School Work Culture Profile* (a diagnostic instrument published in six languages), was developed and validated, the *Education Quality Benchmark System* was designed and validated (see Chapter 9), and more than 60 training programs evolved for central-office leaders and school-based leaders.

In 1992, the team of Snyder, Acker-Hocevar, and Snyder launched a study of 28 schools, K–12, whose principals were grounded in a systems approach to change. The research was reported initially in 1994, and it has since been shared in numerous ways through publications in various international literatures, seminars, and speeches. The principals in our study had all completed the MPS training program and had also served as trainers of their peers in the same 25-day/2-year program. Change in these schools, no matter the level, condition, or community type, was regarded to be successful and systemic and often quite dramatic. Because we had observed so little fundamental change occurring in more traditional site-based managed schools, we were eager to learn what was making the difference in the MPS schools, especially because their principals were grounded in systems theory.

The most striking feature we found from our study was the sense that each school was a growing and dynamic system that was continuously learning how to respond to its students, its community, and to the emerging demands that were placed on the school. These principals have a strong belief that their staff can learn how to design more responsive programs together and help all students become successful. Over time, other evidence accumulated to document the gradual commitment of the faculty to continuous renewal, as successes and failures became the learning ground for the work ahead.

The formation of interdependent linkages and connections within schools, with their communities, and with their feeder schools happened naturally in all 28 schools and increased in quantity and quality over time. The concept of *the school as a system of change* guided daily choices that were made to move the school forward, progressing toward greater integration of services and programs to help more students succeed. Assumptions about *the school as a whole unit of influence* enabled principals to build smaller learning communities of varying strengths that could respond to changing conditions. Psychological barriers gradually were diminished for many educators as their successes and risk taking lead to new learning patterns of success for themselves and their students. From the data collected in these 28 schools, it became clear that *strong interaction systems* were the central feature of the school's professional energy, which enabled them to respond collectively in bold new ways to their challenges.

QUALITY MANAGEMENT

Having its roots during the scientific management era, quality management evolved over the twentieth century as an organizational restructuring phenomenon around the world. Before the word *quality* came into use in the management literature, early proponents focused mostly on statistical procedures for measuring the effects of work in industry. Early writers on quality (Deming, 1986; Juran, 1988, 1992; Ishikawa, 1985) demonstrated the power of information and statistical analyses for refining products, services, and programs to meet quality standards and to also enhance marketplace value. The limitations of statistical tools, however, eventually led away from only statistic control to the broader concept of quality control, which became a human and organizational concern.

During the earlier decades of the twentieth century, it was assumed that any error in performance was due to the individual worker. Supervisors emerged to oversee the quality of work, often by using sampling techniques for observing performance and gathering data that were then interpreted statistically. By midcentury, leaders had come to understand that improving the quality of the product went well beyond examining the daily performance of individual workers, for work patterns and improvements became an organizational issue

(Ishikawa, 1985). Quality assurance teams from multiple disciplines and role groups evolved within the workplace to examine each organizational problem and its potential solution from collective perspectives. The focus for problem solving and improvement therefore became the organization (the system) as a unit, rather than the worker. As the decades advanced, it became increasingly clear that producing a quality product or service derives less from expecting the individual worker to do things right and more from an organization improving its systems of work.

In the 1980s, customers and their needs became the focus for problem solving within quality organizations and gave birth to new work systems and patterns around the world. At the dawn of a new century, quality management centers organizational attention on the customer(s) being served and on information systems that help in the continuous improvement of work systems. Not only are quantitative data useful in charting progress, but qualitative data also are valued for understanding the dynamics within the system. By the late 1990s, leaders at all levels of organization hierarchies, as well as researchers, have come to value both quantitative and qualitative data, for each generates different kinds of information about the effects of work systems and the degree to which customers are satisfied (its quality and its value).

Since the late 1980s, the international quality movement has gained momentum for virtually all types of organizations in public and private sectors (Morgan and Murgatroyd, 1994). Educators began to explore the potential for schools in making the same dramatic gains that have been made in business. New professional associations in quality management, along with several new publishing houses such as ASQ Quality Press and the Malcolm Baldrige National Quality Award along with its derivatives, have heralded a dynamic new movement to revitalize institutions of all types. In our reading of the quality literature for developing the *Education Quality Benchmark System,* we soon realized that the very foundation of quality management that has transformative potential is *systems theory.* Quality management is a way of life, as systems of work are aligned around the needs of customers. We have observed, however, that unless top administrators are grounded in systems theory (or naturally understand its laws), a school or school district often uses quality management tools and its language to improve only the efficiency of the bureaucratic system.

In a more thorough analysis of more than 50 books on quality management, six themes emerged that provide a beginning framework for becoming "quality driven" (Snyder, 1994):

1. *Client satisfaction* is the proper focus for work within the entire organization.

2. *Top-level leadership* for quality drives organizational change.

3. *Systems thinking* and recognizing the interdependence of functions, programs, and services enables the organization to respond quickly to needs.

4. *Strategic planning* is essential for improving quality, a practice that concentrates on a few big new directions and changes to adapt to fluctuations in the environment.

5. *Continuous training* in collaboration and in the use of data systems enables workers and leaders to meet challenges routinely.

6. *Continuous improvement* toward quality, as viewed by the customer, becomes a way of life (through numerous data-gathering and analysis strategies).

One of the leading quality school districts in the United States is Pinellas County in Florida. This school district won the Florida Sterling Quality Award in its first year of recognizing businesses and agencies within Florida. In the early 1990s, James Shipley, the director of the Pinellas County Quality initiative, was instrumental in shaping our thinking about a quality system and participated in the development of the *Education Quality Benchmark System,* which is presented in this book. The quality system, which began as a measure of school development, has since been translated for use in classrooms throughout the district. Shipley now is working with school districts throughout the United States as they develop their own quality systems. Pinellas County is continuing to refine its system and now offers training in *quality implementation* to educational leaders in many school districts, universities, and social agencies. Its work serves as a national prototype of a quality school district.

In our view, very little fundamental change has occurred in most schools and districts that have attempted to use quality management principles. The missing piece seems to be an understanding and commitment to systems thinking (the interdependence of everything within the life of an organization around the needs of students and communities). Where the systems of work and services for students have been transformed to influence success patterns, however, systems thinking has provided the theoretical foundation, whether at a conscious level or not. Where this foundation is absent, on the other hand, the deep work culture and its traditions cannot be understood because there is no vital connection system (energy) to stimulate life and its continuation. The question of *quality of life* in the organization comes from connections and interdependence and their effect upon the whole.

4

An Emergent Theory of Change

Is there hope for creating fundamentally new forms of schooling that correspond with social challenges in the age of globalization? We believe there is, and we are encouraged by the fact that our study of 28 schools, whose change efforts are grounded in systems theory, are showing remarkable gains. Pasco County in Florida, one of the most successful school districts in our study, has operationalized systems theory in all the major dimensions of its work for over two decades. Its leaders have been persistently and successfully redesigning and reshaping an entire 76-school district, with over 65,000 students, in the last several decades.

We are convinced that the essential problem in changing the traditions of schooling is largely a matter of leader perception about the emergence of social systems and not a matter of laws, policy, compliance patterns, or funding. When leaders replace a *machine metaphor* for schools with that of *a living organism* and shift their management and leadership behaviors to facilitating growth instead of compliance, successful change occurs in a natural way, although this happens in uneven patterns. In the Pasco County School District and in many lighthouse schools in Hillsborough County Public Schools in Florida, we have observed success with change initiatives as school and district leaders shift their thinking from compliance to development to organic views of schooling, where everyone is involved in the renovation task.

CHAOS AND COMPLEXITY THEORIES

Chaos theory, which builds upon the foundations of quantum theory, offers bold new ways to think about the change process in institutions and helps us understand that *natural evolution is a force that is continuously emergent*. All of us have observed the magical process through which babies emerge into adults. We have seen how young families grow up and create new generations. We have seen how a single tree joins with others to become a forest and how a rainstorm can become a hurricane. This *phenomenon of emergence* provides a new perspective on change within social organizations and offers guideposts for leaders as they facilitate the growth and evolution of social institutions. *The matter before us is the essential nature of emergence and how it can best be facilitated in institutions, for we need to find new ways to dream!*

Chaos and complexity theories are said to be among the great achievements of natural sciences in the twentieth century (Peitgen, 1990), and their laws for natural systems give us hope for creating more dynamic and effective working and learning environments in educational institutions (Holte, 1990). Natural systems include not only geology, biology, the weather, and mathematics but also the social sciences of families, work organizations, social services, governments, communities, nations, and other human networks. Hence, schools and school districts fall within the category of the natural social sciences. In the latter part of the twentieth century, systems theory became a framework for studying and understanding the dynamics of social institutions, within which are included those concerned with education.

The term *chaos* appears to have been appropriated by Li and Yorke in 1975 to describe the dynamic behavior in natural systems, which now appears to be more complicated than the familiar *steady state* or *cyclic pattern* described by early quantum theorists (Holte, 1990, vii–viii). Since about 1970, the principles of chaotic dynamic systems have been given definition by scientists, and these principles were eventually brought to public attention by Gleick (1987) in his landmark book, *Chaos: Making a New Science*. In addition, new laws have been constructed about the emerging complexity of natural systems, such as economic, political, and social systems. These laws are rooted in chaos theory, and they explain much of what we experience naturally in our personal lives. However, the natural ebb and flow of life, with its emergent dimensions, tends to be thwarted in organizations that are still governed by the machine metaphor. The lessons from chaos and complexity theories can help us shed what we now recognize as unnatural assumptions (which perhaps remain useful for machines and technology) and embrace their natural principles for managing our own lives and our social institutions.

Quantum scientists who study the stars, mathematics, zoology, and the weather have been exploring changes in these dynamic systems over the twentieth century (Gleick, 1987). They have observed, for example, that the state of chaos (rather than a state of stasis) stimulates the most noticeable kinds of growth and adaptation. Things do not fall apart in a state of chaos unless the system goes over the edge into a destructive state of turbulence, in which everything is out of control. Scientists have found that within naturally dynamic systems, order and stability emerge from within as the system adjusts to changing conditions; order is not superimposed. *This basic concept of "self-organization" is significant for redirecting our thinking about facilitating change in institutions,* for it refutes many of our cherished beliefs and gives us hope for unleashing more natural impulses and facilitating (not directing) their emergence as responsive systems.

Chaos? Complexity? Dynamic natural systems? How do these concepts relate to the work of educational leaders? Mary Giella (1996), one of the chief architects of change in the Pasco County School District over the last three decades, prepared a handbook for new superintendents, under the sponsorship of the Florida Association of District School Superintendents. In it she argues, "Schools and districts are not laboratories where clinical conditions exist. They are sociological and political in nature. Conditions change, evolve, and move; they are not controllable. Leaders are to navigate their schools or districts through the ocean of change, toward school improvement or school transformation. They need a compass, a vision to guide them, flexible plans to structure what can be, and wisdom and experience to feel and think their way through" (43).

If the old assumptions of control and order no longer are viable, how does one navigate within the complexity of schools and districts? There are some clear guideposts and patterns that can be derived from the newest sciences, and in this chapter we provide a foundation for a few "new anchors." It was Feigenbaum (1990) who reported the regularity that underlies chaotic behaviors, for he observed that things start out not being chaotic and end up so and somehow pass from one state to the next. *The basic principle is that the natural order in biological or social systems is based on connections and dynamics and on emergence within the system over time that is irregular, discontinuous, erratic, and complex, and yet it is also stable and structured.*

This complex condition of change, a seeming paradox, helps explain why many of our notions of control and predictability within human organizations are obsolete. The classical laws of order and logical progression are virtually out of sync with how social systems actually function. *The new laws that have potential for social institutions include self-organization, possibility, and emergence.* We use many of the principles of self-organization quite naturally in our daily lives, for example, when dealing with our personal health and physicians, our own finances and banking institutions, and our own role in the political environments that surround us. We recognize and are at ease with normal fluctuations, randomness, contradictions, and variability in human systems, as well as with the structures and stability that exist to control for growth. And yet public institutions such as schools are still governed to a great extent by outdated assumptions about controllability and the lockstep path to success. As it turns out, the survival of our social systems actually depends on the capacity of leaders to adapt to complexity and to rapid, discontinuous change in the environment.

We must face the truth! The machine model of organizations that shaped "bureaucracy" fails to explain or anticipate the natural dynamics within and across units and time and the unexpected occurrences that evolve along the way. It disregards the vital connections that nurture human curiosity, dreaming, growth, and creativity. The machine model also fails to explain what happens in organizations when professional groups launch cooperative ventures. We have observed that when the natural emergence of groups is facilitated within and across schools and districts, special networks and partnerships quite naturally evolve to explore new possibilities. No one seems to be telling anyone what to do or holding anyone accountable for preconceived outcomes in these ventures. Networks just emerge and work naturally when the major players facilitate rather than control. However, these structures also break down when any one party grabs control and tries to exercise power over the process and the content. Emergence happens naturally when old concepts of change have been shed and when the natural dynamics are encouraged.

Chaos Theory and the Early Years

The actual beginnings of chaos theory are difficult to determine. Many writers identify Henri Poincare's work as seminal (1892/1962/1990). He found that observable energy is formed by two elements: *kinetic energy* of the units involved and *potential energy* that corresponds to their interactions and resonances (Prigogine, 1990, 58). This new concept envisioned energy within a dynamic, rather than a static, universe, which paved the way for scientists to examine anew fundamental interactions and their dynamics throughout nature.

Most writers of chaos and complexity theory point to the Santa Fe Institute in Los Alamos, New Mexico, as a beginning site for the research on dynamic and nonlinear systems. Originally the location for J. Robert Oppenheimer's 1940s atomic bomb project, Los Alamos became the place where more than 100 scientists and mathematicians were funded to explore the edges of their sciences (Gleick, 1987). The advent of the computer enabled these and other scientists to explore the irregular side of nature, the discontinuous and erratic, which they believed to be mathematically accessible (3). So *chaos* has evolved into a science of the global nature of systems, *a science of process rather than of state* (Gleick, 1987, 5). The early scientists had an interest in the seeming randomness and complexity they observed, where jagged edges and sudden leaps appeared to be quite normal. While in search of wholes that accounted for irregularity, scientists found that order arises spontaneously and is bound inseparably with chaos. Natural systems, they observed, have the innate capacity to learn and to adapt to changing conditions in the environment.

What Is Chaos Theory?

Scientists who study chaotic and complex systems and the transitions of these over time focus on nonlinear relationships (Begun, 1994). Turbulence is quite different from chaos, however; turbulence is an unstable mess of disorder at all scales that drains energy and creates drag and in which motion breaks all the rules and becomes random (Gleick, 1987). Systemic change within chaos can be rapid, radical, self-generating, and skipping stages; and, in the process, it can develop its capacity for self-renewal and self-organization. Hence, *randomness* eventually was relabeled *chaos* (Peitgen, 1990, 37).

Scientists who study nonlinear relationships in complex systems focus on dynamic patterns rather than stable ones. Mandlebrot (1990), a mathematician who developed a language for the study of chaotic systems, claims that *nonlinearity* is central to the new meaning of chaos, whereas *randomness* is the key to chaos in the old sense of the word. Nonlinear systems are essentially unpredictable and yet contain patterns of regularity. As systems organize themselves, learn and remember, evolve and adapt, common patterns and fundamental principles of dynamic systems shape their behavior (Ruthen, 1993).

Most of reality is not orderly and stable but is bubbling processes of disorder, observes Nobel Prize winner Prigogine (1990). All systems contain subsystems that fluctuate, and at times small shifts can cause a reorganization of the total system in the unpredictable direction of either order or chaos. But order and organization, observe Prigogine and Stenger (1984), arise spontaneously out of disorder and chaos through the process of self-organization. And, they further observe, those systems far from equilibrium have the greatest potential for creating fresh order in social systems.

We live with and adjust to complexity daily, and we are not surprised with its irregularity or instability. We adjust to fluctuations and to crisis well when we permit the dynamics of self-organization to emerge within our environment. We continually observe this basic phenomenon of self-adaptation as we see businesses come and go, families flourish or disintegrate, and social agencies rise to meet new challenges or begin rapid dysfunction. Human organizations adapt to changing environments as a matter of choice, and the choices that are made have either extinction or continual emergence consequences.

When the natural laws of unpredictability actually replace the illusionary practices of total control, leaders in social institutions are able to explore dimensions of life, previously ignored, that hold promise for the responsive adaptations. These new laws of growth have direct bearing on how we envision the transformation of schooling, for *the dynamic that has enduring capacity is that which evolves from inside the organization as it selects ways to respond to changing conditions.* Complex systems, such as schools and districts, have the capacity themselves to carry out and coordinate the most complex behaviors.

The central message of chaos theory is that disorder is natural, and yet there are structures within randomness that are always the same (Feigenbaum, in Gleick, 1987, 183). Following are some of the basic claims of chaos theory as we have derived them from a number of scientists and their writings:

1. Natural relationships do not fit a linear model.

2. Within chaos there is randomness, and yet order and structure exist.

3. Natural dynamics within systems create growth, not stability.

4. The growth of natural systems is essentially unpredictable.

5. Self-renewal and self-organization exist in dynamic complex systems.

6. Change in systems can be rapid, radical, and self-generating.

7. Chaos conditions present a time of opportunity for a natural system.

What Is Complexity Theory?

A new science of complexity has emerged recently to explore the natural conditions of human life today (Coveney and Highfield, 1995; Casti, 1995). Conventional science, the authors suggest, is blind to the connections between and among complex phenomena; it sticks to a detailed study of one small aspect of a single subdiscipline. Yet the majority of real-world problems do not fit into neat boundaries; they are integrated in surprising ways. Two ingredients are necessary for complexity to emerge: *time* and *nonlinearity.*

Hidden regularities exist naturally in all kinds of complex systems, as is evident in stock markets, economic systems, climate and weather systems, populations, business cycles, markets, urban growth, and international security (Holte, 1990). To illustrate, the *weather* on any day depends on air temperature, air pressure, humidity, wind speed, and cloud cover. While the weather system in northern Sweden is predictably distinct from that in Florida, the actual daily weather in either location can be determined, at best, two to three weeks ahead. *Tides* depend on the shape of the coastline; the temperature of the sea and its salinity; air pressure; waves on the surface; and the position of the sun, moon, and stars. *School learning* depends in large measure on a student's physical and psychological health and readiness to learn, plus home and school environments that nurture successful experiences. *Complexity* is naturally all around us; it *is the dynamic of emergence that we live with daily* with all of its hidden regularities.

New understandings of life on earth cause us to see that radical change has been more the norm throughout the history of the earth than has continuous improvement over time. Scientists now estimate that between 99 percent and 99.9 percent of all species that once existed are now extinct, and extinction is forever. This view is in stark contrast to the Darwinian laws of continuous improvement over time. Rather than continuous improvement of species over time, scientists now perceive that each successive period of time following the Cambrian and Permian explosions was repopulated with new animals and plants that had different capacities for adapting to the new environment.

Kauffman (1995, 233) tells us that when one species is driven to extinction, the event may trigger a small or a large *extinction avalanche* that sweeps through some or all of the ecosystem. Consider a few events that can stimulate a rippling effect: *the election of a new mayor, the opening of a Wal-Mart in town, the death of parents, laws that launched welfare, a new principal at a school, an updated personal computer, an e-mail account, the World Wide Web in classrooms,* or *a new superintendent.* Each change may introduce a radical stimulus, which is followed by rapid change in the natural course of events.

We also adapt in our personal lives as we enter new phases of our lives or move to new locations and jobs. Living by an ocean or a large lake, we may establish traditions of boating on weekends and during summers. A change in location might find us learning different skills, such as horseback riding or cross-country skiing. Within human organizations, we see other trends in survival and extinction. One job might call for interactions with only a few workers and others in one town, whereas another job in the same field may create a work context of international flights and hotels as new connections are explored in locations around the world.

In our institutions, we observe that extreme innovations and programs get weeded out in the process of rebuilding new systems of work, for only a few of the new forms survive the tests of time. Subsequent innovation focuses on improving the few remaining prototypes (Lewin, 1993, 70). While innovations come and go, it seems that the pattern of innovation in complex adaptive systems is predictable to a degree, the environment always acting to diminish the stability of some attractors and to improve the stability of others (73). *What is required for innovations to survive over time are strong connections and interdependencies that are continuously responsive to changing conditions.* This kind of emerging response to life is the key to survival in an increasingly complex and rapidly changing environment.

The message for educators is that we are more powerful as participants in shaping complex schooling environments than as the *boss over.* We can play a major role in guiding the emergence of new systems by routinely gathering information and then orchestrating response systems within the organization. This is the dance of life that is our opportunity now. Information is the virtual lifeline for an organization's catalyzing, for it informs decisions about facilitating the emergence or extinction of natural social systems.

So crucial is information that the survival of any system depends on knowing about subtle shifts in the environment, whereas ignoring or being unaware of vital information has caused many businesses to fail. At the edge of chaos, the most complex responses emerge, notes Capra (1982, 87); and these responses are orderly enough to ensure stability and yet be full of flexibility and surprise. *Preparing and sustaining the capacity of the organization to respond to complexity is the new work of leaders.* The strength and health of random and complex interactions within and across institutions have transformative power.

Following are some basic claims of complexity theory that we have derived from the various authors already mentioned:

1. Complex systems cannot be controlled, but they can adapt to their environment.

2. Living systems are never in equilibrium; they are inherently unstable.

3. The creative principle of emergence is the deep mystery and property of complex dynamic systems.

4. The dynamics are from within the system, not from outside.

5. Increased complexity is a fundamental property of complex dynamic systems.

6. Survival of a system has to do with information that is gathered about the environment and its response.

7. The concept of *emergence from within* is central to understanding the whole of complex natural systems.

Based on the existence of both internal and external forces, this new theory claims that *an increase in complexity is a fundamental property of dynamic systems* (Holte, 1990). Things get more complex rather than simple, but growing complexity does not necessarily equate with progress; survival of the system has to do with the information it gathers about the environment and the ways in which the system responds to information. Chaos and complexity theories have only begun to emerge in the management literature as a frame for understanding growth processes of systems. Johnson and Burton (1994) perceive that we are still very early into this stage of organizational development to claim any explanations or even constructive interventions. We must let the natural course of events shape our thinking.

BASIC PRINCIPLES OF NATURAL SYSTEMS

The complexity of managing diverse student populations and their programs while at the same time preparing them for the unknown twenty-first century is a major concern to educators. The range in student readiness for school learning and the wide variations of intellectual, emotional, physical, social, and psychological characteristics of students within all age groups have precipitated multiple new school services that are managed by multiple role groups. To assist and to manage this array of services, the federal and state governments have allocated funds for a huge enterprise with many special programs, and accompanying those funds have been special policies for their use and accountability. Hence, part of the growing complexity of schooling today stems from the institutionalization of special programs for a growing, diverse student population. As Hillsborough County Superintendent of Schools Earl Lennard says, "It's like shoveling coal to keep the trains running while at the same time laying new train tracks for new destinations." How is this possible? Is this not the essence of the paradox of change in social institutions and the very context for complexity and chaos for "living on the edge of chaos"? "Life rolls on in an unending procession of change, with small and large bursts of life, small and large bursts of extinctions, ringing out the old and ringing in the new" (Kauffman, 1995, 14, 15).

We can experience this avalanche of creations and extinctions when a new national or state education agency official is appointed, one who has a different change agenda from previous years. The sudden redirection of change initiatives throughout the state may be followed by retirements of the old guard in the state office, which in turn precipitates mass retirements, reappointments, relocations, and new hires in key roles within universities, school districts, and service agencies. In time, the new force redirects collective energy for school reform initiatives. And so it goes. *Diversity drives the growth of complexity,* for once the diversity is activated, the system will keep on exploding in diversity (Kauffman, 1995, 296, 297).

When we consider the nature of postmodern forms of schooling in all their complexity, we see that the system of education has always responded in dramatic ways to changing environments. Schooling today is far more complex than it was a half century ago, as is evidenced by the numerous, varied programs for students who fall outside of some norm. However, the problem is that, as prototypes of isolated programs escalate, the structures and processes of learning have remained virtually the same for all other students. As schools respond to the shifting needs of students, the processes of teaching and learning must become as varied as the types of schooling services offered in response to the complexity issue. This suggests to us that the simple days of schooling, say, the 1950s, will never again appear, and the future of schooling is likely to be far more complex than it is today. Somehow we must develop human capacities in more natural ways and understand and facilitate the growth of schooling in directions that will enhance (not control) the human condition.

Self-Organizing Systems

The basic *principle of fractals* in chaos theory provides clues about the faulty nature of piecemeal and fragmented approaches to organizational change and can instruct our thinking about systemic change. In 1975, IBM mathematician Benoît Mandelbrot invented a way to study nonlinear geometry, which he called *fractals* (1990). He created a language and form to enable us to understand nature in new ways. "Fractals," says Mandelbrot, "are natural shapes whose roughness and fragmentation tend neither to vanish nor fluctuate up and down, but remain essentially unchanged as one zooms in on the smallest parts of the system" (10). *Fractal geometry* is a mathematical language for describing chaotic states in these nonlinear natural systems; it is the geometry not of straight lines, circles, and spheres of Euclidean geometry but of natural phenomena (Mandelbrot, 1990). The essential principle is that the structure of every piece of a system (like a single section of a cauliflower) holds the key to the whole structure (the cauliflower head), which he calls a *fractal dimension* (Lauwerier, 1987, 80).

When a fractal aggregate grows, its boundary is continually changed by the dynamics of the generating process, which eventually leads to an extraordinary structure (Mandelbrot, 1990, 30). A fractal aggregate is not predictable; rather, it is emergent, as in a storm, a forest, a family, or a learning community. The future shape and design of the fractal is determined not in some original design but in the process itself of growing the next iterations. Fractal shapes are created by repeated iterations of themselves and provide a glimpse of infinity that is well bounded, of complexity feeding back on itself to create beautiful complexity (Wheatley, 1992).

Do we not marvel at the sunset, at the changing colors of the sea throughout a day, or at what we see during a drive down a chilly Vermont country road in early October? Yet, within these emergent fractals, there is no ultimate surprise. The most minute part of a nonlinear system has the same characteristics as the whole, which means that a cauliflower will never evolve into broccoli, nor will a maple leaf evolve into an oak tree, and neither will a child turn into a fox. However, the development of each over time in overall shape and size is unpredictable.

What is important, Wheatley (1992) suggests, is the quality of the system of a particular fractal: its complexity and distinguishing shapes and how it differs from other fractals. To study the essence of complexity requires the use of qualitative as well as quantitative measures. It is the multiple dimensions and shape of the whole system—or the fractal—that matters and how it develops, changes, and compares to other systems. The emergent property of fractals provides clues to guide organizational growth over time. *The first clue is that it is necessary to concentrate on complete new systems,* working on all the parts simultaneously, for it is the interaction of all parts, not the adding up of, that creates the dynamic of the whole and determines its growth potential. *The second clue is that the shape of the system ultimately cannot be predicted.*

The emergence phenomenon of natural systems is filled with surprise as the internal dynamics play out within an organization's context. For example, teaching teams evolve in unexpected and sometimes surprising ways; partnerships and networks spawn innovations; cooperative learning creates unpredictable leaps in achievement. Self-organizing systems, Capra tells us (1982, 270, 271), have a high degree of stability, but stability in this context is dynamic rather than static and is not to be confused with equilibrium. Any natural system maintains its same overall structure in spite of ongoing changes. Teachers and principals need to be free to encourage the natural dynamics of schooling to play out in the emergence of new systems.

We have observed from our study of the change process in schools that when new expectations are given and when leaders gather information about environmental conditions that affect students, there are choices to be made about the future direction of a school. Schools whose professionals understand that their moral obligation is to the students tend to perform well in many ways, for they integrate new information into their decisions while they remain continuously flexible and open to the emergence process. In other schools, where district administrators or principals determine ahead of staff discussions what the responses will be to new information, professional work systems remain static and unresponsive at best. There is simply no way in this context for professionals to participate in shaping the natural course of life in a school. Teachers and principals together need to be free to respond naturally to their own dynamic processes and options. Capra (1982, 279) reports that studies of healthy ecosystems over time show that most dynamic relationships between living organisms are essentially cooperative ones characterized by coexistence, interdependence, and symbiosis.

Systems that are capable of managing complex behaviors have a decided survival advantage over others, for natural selection finds its role as the molder and shaper of the spontaneous order. This truth about emergence and the use of information helps explain why all natural systems do not evolve over time, nor are some capable of responding to their changing environment. Perhaps this is why so many schools continue to function as they did 40 or more years ago. *Only those systems that are able to organize themselves spontaneously may be able to evolve further.* Great organizations of all kinds, including social systems, emerge because leaders and workers figure out together how best to respond to changing conditions.

The evolution and emergence of natural systems, such as schools and school districts, occurs not because of the responsiveness of individuals but in direct relation to the networking capability of the system. Networks are clusters of similar organizations or role groups, and they are successful because of the energy that is generated through the connections across systems. As such, networks have their own unique growth dynamics and exist within one of three regimes (Kauffman, 1995, 103). (1) *Sparsely connected networks* exhibit internal order; (2) *densely connected ones* veer into chaos; and (3) *networks with a single connection* freeze into mindlessly dull behavior (87). Those networks that are poised between order and chaos, observes Kauffman, are best able to carry out ordered yet flexible behaviors.

Pasco County School District's success through the mid-1990s can be attributed to the strong connection over many decades of its top leadership team: Thomas Weightman, Mary Giella, John Long, and Myndall Stanfill. So powerful a force had their district become in Florida that Thomas Weightman was appointed executive director of the Florida Association of District Superintendents after 30 years as superintendent of schools, and John Long was then elected without opposition as Pasco County's new superintendent of schools. Long appointed three principals to form the district leadership (Sandy Ramos, Susan Rine, and Bob Dorn) with two former district leaders (Chuck Rushe and John Gains) for other leadership positions. Today those roles have changed again with retirements, and other leaders who were seasoned in the systemic culture of the district were appointed to key positions. The strong cohesive culture of Pasco County was able to survive the pressures from external forces, and today thrives under the leadership of Superintendent Heather Fiorentino. Strong connection systems were built over time in Pasco County among and across role groups, and those connections continue today because of the continuity in the quality of district leadership. These connections have spawned innovations that extend beyond the planned change initiatives, although each one that has evolved in some way supports the district's *strategic dance of connected schools.*

After a dozen or more years, the principles of networking in Pasco County had generated sufficient energy to turn the tide in the district's operation; and, by the end of the 1990s, the traditional (gravitational) forces were essentially overcome. Networking spawned the dynamic that was essential for building the district's energy system to transform all schools, although at very different rates. Schools now *know the direction,* and each year each school's comprehensive plan tells the ways in which it will move strategically toward the district's vision, a vision that everyone helped to shape. A major leap forward was made in 1996, by which time all secondary schools followed the patterns established by the elementary and middle schools. High schools piloted and gradually institutionalized nongraded structures, continuous progress systems of learning, and interdisciplinary instruction within learning communities. To achieve this landmark, secondary principals and teachers were involved in shaping and piloting initial features of the new system for many years while participating in prototypes with elementary and middle schools under the district's leadership.

The question that one ponders is whether a district change initiative of this kind can make a difference in student performance. What is the evidence? A Pasco County longitudinal study tracked 1000 students since 1994 in schools that adopted continuous progress (CP) systems, which is the centerpiece of the district's change process (*St. Petersburg Times,* April 4, 1999). Students in schools that embraced the school district changes showed greater gains in reading and math than those in schools where the reforms had not yet fermented. Over five years, CP students increased their reading scores by 57 percent, compared to an increase of 30 percent for students in traditional classes. In math, CP students increased their scores by 74 percent over five years, compared to the 56 percent increase posted by other students.

LIVING ON THE EDGE OF CHAOS

Over the past several years, we have shared the concepts of chaos theory with educational leaders around the world. There has been enthusiastic affirmation of the notion that the good life in schools today is one of *living on the edge of chaos,* and there seems to be a widespread recognition and acknowledgment of the natural laws of emergence. As we perceive it, leaders easily acknowledge the growing chaotic condition of schools, and, with relief, their discussions emerge quite spontaneously. An affirmation of their own experiences in managing an essentially uncontrollable environment seems to free educators to pursue more of their natural options.

To admit that schooling challenges now are beyond the capacity of human control and traditional work systems is the first step in rebuilding from the ground up. A question that is imminent in the minds of many is, "What kinds of systems have a greater payoff than those with which we have worked over the years?" In other words, will there be a sufficient trade-off for educators in exchanging the known for the unknown? We believe that when professionals perceive there is a way to maneuver through the mazes of complexity and chart a promising pathway to the future, a more promising path will always be selected, despite all of its unknown qualities.

A major discovery about natural dynamic systems is that disequilibrium rather than equilibrium is the condition in which they are most alive, vital, responsive, and creative. Life at its best exists at the edge of chaos between order and surprise (Kauffman, 1995). What is new in chaos theory is that, contrary to what was believed by early quantum theorists, equilibrium corresponds to death in nature. Our intuitions about the requirements for order have been wrong for millennia, for, as it turns out, our human creativity comes from addressing the extremely complex webs of interacting elements that appear to be connected; humans often figure out how to respond (Kauffman, 1995, 84). Prigogine (1990) tells us that life itself is an emergent phenomenon, primarily because diversity drives a system beyond its threshold and stimulates adjustments to the new condition (Kauffman, 1995, 21, 24). *Life emerges whole.*

Early quantum theorists found that natural systems are not static, as had been believed for centuries, but they are always in a dynamic state of equilibrium. Later, chaos theorists learned that even more dramatic and healthy change is created by disequilibrium, for disorder is useful as a source of new order. Natural, healthy systems tend more often to *let go* of their present forms in order to explore new ones that are more compatible with changing conditions. The state of disequilibrium is filled with masses of complex connections that provide strong and healthy energy for creating new order. Evolving systems learn how to respond to their own internal dynamics, which are often unpredictable. Handy (1994) suggests that *the edge of chaos exists somewhere between stability and turbulence and is the place where a complex system is the most spontaneous, adaptive, and alive.*

Why is it that things do not just fall apart with disequilibrium and its chaos? Scientists tell us that *systems far from equilibrium, in a state of disequilibrium, possess a dynamic of self-renewal and self-organization.* Systems that are poised at the edge of chaos were first called *dissipative structures* to emphasize that the origins of self-organization are far from equilibrium (Coveney and Highfield, 1995, 162). Wheatley notes that dissipative structures demonstrate that disorder can be a source of order and that growth is found in disequilibrium, not in balance (1992, 20). Scientists have learned that natural systems not only are most dynamic and energetic at the edge of chaos, but they also possess innate properties to reconfigure themselves to deal with new information because of the *self-organizing principle.*

Given these new basic principles of emergence in natural systems, the leadership challenge is to study the deeply rooted cultural patterns that exist within an organization, while being mindful of rapidly changing external pressures, and then become an internal force in giving shape to the natural growth process (Holte, 1990). Managing paradox and contradiction requires "listening to a different drummer," which means shifting the emphasis from external political pressures and administrative mandates to the internal needs of students and the professional systems that provide services to client groups.

On September 22, 1996, the television program *60 Minutes* aired a feature about the Franklin Douglas Academy, a public school in New York City that has made productive use of disequilibrium in the daily home lives of its students. With a student population of 80 percent African Americans and 20 percent Hispanics, these mostly poor and disadvantaged students were given a tough life challenge. The principal, Dr. Monroe, said that the school's mission was to get every kid into a prestigious college and for its students to become world leaders. Dressed in uniform, students were challenged repeatedly by Dr. Monroe: *It does not matter what your family problems are, nor the street problems and dangers, having no father or rarely seeing him, or the presence of drugs. You are not responsible for those conditions. But you are responsible for getting here on time so that we can work with you!* The kids somehow are able to put aside during school hours those disabling home and community conditions in their lives and to rise above it all and meet the challenge. The school raises a great deal of money to give their kids a social advantage. Students travel internationally so that they will have their own stories of experience other than those of the street to share with their peers in college. This approach is bold and daring, and it seems to be working for most students. Kids in the academy are beating the odds because they are being given a chance for a good life.

Our contention is that seeming irregularities in learning and schooling can be contemplated, sorted, measured, understood, and projected if we understand that nonlinear/natural systems can actually become self-organizing and self-regulating when sufficient pressure to change is applied. In other words, what is natural cannot be controlled, and what can be controlled is not natural (Prigogine, 1990). If we think about student learning as a process of emergence for an individual, then surely that process will be different for each person. Some learn through music, others through the arts, while some learn best in role play, in sports, or by creating a videotape on a topic. The new research on brain learning and its implications provides evidence for rethinking school learning. To continue expecting all student populations to achieve success only within narrow language-based prescriptions that are age and time bound will surely fail today. If we are sincere in becoming proactive for all student populations, new knowledge about the growth of natural systems will enable us to create a mental and spiritual shift that can breed success for all student populations. We need school environments that set professionals and students free to explore their own potentialities and capacities within multiple modes of learning and working.

How can systemic problems be addressed districtwide or schoolwide? A condition near the edge of chaos breeds disequilibrium, which provides the energy for change. Systemic change is never simple, but it involves many features in complex ways. Kauffman (1995, 240) explains that simple systems do not evolve in isolation but are a part of a complex web of coevolution. For example, using the horse as a means of travel launched the need for a buggy and whip, a smithy, saddlery, a harness maker, and so on. The car as a means of transportation spawned the oil and gasoline industry, service stations, motels and fast-food restaurants, paved roads, traffic courts, suburbs, and malls. The economic web leads to new jobs, tasks, functions, products, and consumption; and the web of technologies causes an avalanche of goods and services to become extinct and others to coevolve. The special services in school districts sometimes prompt new programs, new credentialling, new funding, and new aspects of accountability. And so it goes. The web of coevolution has taken the education enterprise quite naturally to the dawn of a new century.

Systemic disequilibrium, if it is examined through coinvolvement strategies up and down the hierarchy, will naturally lead to new systems of work at all levels and for all functions. To prepare for a new age of schooling in Pasco County, all principals, all directors, and many teachers were involved in reading and study groups for years before any formal action was taken, although many innovations naturally emerged. A *strategic dance* was orchestrated by assistant superintendents Mary Giella and Myndall Stanfill (1996). Within the context of districtwide, multiple role group study teams, plans began to take shape and pilot projects were tested for potentially useful systems of student work. The message was clear. Whatever evolved was to advance the district toward its long-term dream of continuous progress for students in a community of connected schools.

Eventually, design teams from all role groups used the best prototypes to create interdependent work systems. Multiaged continuous progress learning communities were formed in all schools, K–12. A continuous progress curriculum was developed for K–5, 6–8, and 9–12 age groups; and team teaching and cooperative learning systems were launched within learning communities of teachers and students. Pupil reporting systems and teacher accountability systems were also redesigned and then institutionalized. Training programs soon were offered for all role groups throughout the district in every dimension of the district's grand plan, with *systems thinking* as the foundation for development. Theirs has been a dynamic journey, a story about a strong connection system that has enabled them to build an infrastructure to support the community of 50 connected schools. While the transformation of all services and programs is not yet complete, each school and division is engaging in its own strategic dance, getting ready for a phased transition into the schooling pattern that everyone helped to create.

How has a districtwide collaborative venture such as Pasco County's been launched and sustained over time? In our view, the structure that was created to foster districtwide learning was as important as was the vision and the facilitation of the leadership team. A nested design of work contributed in the aggregate to the success of the overall change initiative. A steering committee assumed responsibility for the results of the four major committees and their numerous work teams. Through a structure of organized connections, the district was able to maintain momentum around the same focus for about a decade. All role-groups in every dimension of the district have participated in the design, the development, and the assessment of pilots. So central has been the nested structure to the district's successful transformation of all its work systems and services that we were eager to learn what might be the scientific principle.

An explanation for why this structure and others that are similar are found in cell biology and the basic scientific principles reinforces a continuation and expansion of *a nested group work system* as a way of life in postmodern institutions. Kauffman (1995) found from his studies of cell biology that a natural clustering among cells occurs when conditions increase in complexity. When the problem is filled with complexity and conflicting constraints and cells form *patches,* each patch is able to complete its own work in ways that help all patches to coevolve (262). When any cell system is broken into well-chosen patches, each adapts to conditions for its own benefit, and yet the patch makes a contribution *with a reasonable amount of energy* for its network of patches. Kauffman noticed that the reason small patches work in dealing with complexity is that they have freedom to explore options quickly, whereas large patches lack flexibility and tend to freeze into poor compromises. Patching works because of the internal stability and order that emerge as the cluster progresses quite naturally *near the edge of chaos*. The system becomes self-adapting and mutually accommodating for both the patch and the system of patches. Kauffman observes further that when properly parceled into the right-sized patches, complex problems can rapidly be brought to fruitful compromise solutions (266).

Patches can stimulate change faster and better than the traditional work hierarchy. However, structure without a vision and goals is inadequate. Leaders are needed to become locally wise in stimulating disequilibrium and in designing systems of work that facilitate natural emergence. Ultimately, the only choice leaders have is to act on their own stage to create the conditions that will promote flexibility and invention and to promote pilots that are examined and refined. This could be our finest hour, for evolving new forms of schooling is a marriage between spontaneous order and natural selection; we are part of the process of guiding and creating the emergence of schooling prototypes. As Kauffman salutes, "To the great nonlinear map in the sky!" (1995, 304)

PRINCIPLES OF EMERGENT CHANGE

As we review the new laws of emergence within natural systems, there seem to be a few basic principles for guiding change within schools and school districts and within all other forms of business and social institutions. Drawing from essential scientific principles, as gleaned from the many discussions of both chaos and complexity theories, we have developed the following guidelines that have potential for altering the course of change within organizations in ways that enable the system to survive and become increasingly responsive to changing environments:

1. Order and stability emerge from within a system as it adjusts to changing conditions.

2. The natural growth process is irregular, random, discontinuous, erratic, and complex; yet, it is also stable and structured.

3. Strong connections and interdependencies are essential to the survival of natural systems.

4. Information is the lifeline for a successful future and is the primary source of disequilibrium.

5. The most dynamic state in a natural system is life at the edge of chaos.

6. Disorder can be a source of new order.

7. As natural systems grow, their boundaries are continually changed by the dynamics of emergence.

8. Self-organization in natural systems is a prerequisite for evolvability.

9. Disequilibrium creates the best condition for growth in natural systems.

10. Life is an emergent phenomenon, which thrives *at the edge of chaos.*

Joseph Jaworski (1996, 2) suggests that the fundamental choice is to serve life: "My capacity as a leader comes from my choice to allow life to unfold through me." Progress depends on how we collectively shape our future. He goes on to say, "Successful leadership depends on fundamental shifts of being, including a deep commitment to the dream and a passion for serving versus being driven by the pursuit of status and power." Jaworski quotes Michado, a Spanish poet, who says, "Wanderer, there is no path. You lay the path in walking" (134). Ultimately, this is our life. What choices will each of us make to serve the improvement of the human condition?

Part 2

The New Mental Dance for Guiding Change

Networking, partnerships, and power are key elements in this global age of living and working. As educators shift to a global mindset for schooling, questions of energy, power, and resources will continue to preoccupy leaders, while the conditions of poverty and race will surface to challenge the bravest among us. The new skills of networking for these times are expanded into the idea of building social networks, which will offer the energy and resources for the major renovation tasks ahead. The issues of power must be addressed, for moving toward shared communities of power is the condition for success in most places today. With a co-involvement mindset educators will be able to address successfully the nagging problems of poverty and race, a necessity for stimulating a sustainable future for the human community.

Chapter 5, Living on the Edge of Chaos: A New Theory of Organizational Change, presents six dynamic behaviors found in natural systems, which we culled from the literature of chaos and complexity theories. These behaviors provide leaders with a systemic action framework for the survival and sustainable growth of their institutions. Together, these six lessons give readers fresh perspectives for responding to the paradoxes and complexities of life, as school work is an immediate reality yet requires dramatic new systems of learning.

Chapter 6, Confronting the Issues of Power, examines the historical and traditional definitions of *power over*. Past definitions of power within bureaucratic and dominator perspectives are contrasted with partnership power. Perspectives on organizational power offer options for shaping the transformation journey. Dominator and partnership alternatives offer clues for designing a pathway to the future.

Chapter 7, The Power River, offers a metaphor for depicting power differentials under distinct frameworks of bureaucratic and dominator power: *power over, power to, power with,* and *power through*. Findings from four studies on power and empowerment report how teachers' perspectives of power and empowerment reflect multiple contextual and relationship effects. Recommendations for change require alterations in hierarchical relationships of power and the adoption of more relational and collegial ways of working.

Chapter 8, Acting Locally and Thinking Globally about Poverty and Race, is a major educational challenge for this new century. The issues of poverty and race are global and now require an international response. Educators need to join with politicians and business leaders to forge social justice standards for everyone everywhere. Education for all is a chief element in creating a sustainable future for the human community. The challenges that were brought about by the "No Child Left Behind" legislation in the United States illustrate the important work ahead as educators develop communities of compassion and action both locally and globally.

5

Living on the Edge of Chaos: A New Theory of Organizational Change

We must face the likely extinction of schooling as a viable social institution if schools and school districts remain essentially unresponsive to the dramatic sea of change. We have the opportunity to fashion new forms of schooling that thrive on information and are responsive to emerging social functions. Facing the truth is ultimately a matter of choice, one that prompts action for the growth of schooling or for its eventual extinction. Put another way, *living on the edge of chaos is the survival choice;* anything less will surely lead to a dismal end.

To succeed as an educational leader in the next several decades will require an understanding of how social systems function within a complex and rapidly changing political and economic environment and also a belief that transformation is within the power of educators to facilitate. *Fuzzy thinking,* we are now being told, may be useful for moving ahead within random and nonlinear environments, which are increasingly complex. Kosko (1993), an expert in this new science of fuzzy thinking, claims that it addresses the essential grayness of nature and the multivalence we often experience involving three or more options instead of two extremes in an either-or world. In the past, Kosko observes, science treated facts as black-and-white, even though these were always vague or inexact (xv). At the core of fuzzy thinking is a shift from black-and-white to gray views of reality and from polar perspectives to multiple possibilities (xvi). We now consider normal such phenomena as multidisciplinary programs, multilingual persons, multicultural communities, and multitalented leaders, which calls for a growing understanding of the nonlinear and fuzzy social realities in our lives.

Fuzziness entered the scientific vocabulary about 40 years ago, having its roots in Asia, where Japanese managers emphasized practical engineering, South Korean scholars talked about a fuzzy society, and India and China produced fuzzy-oriented theorists. Kosko (1993) observes that fuzzy knowledge (the relativity of things) comes down to fuzzy rules in terms of conditional statements: If traffic is heavy, keep the green light on longer; if students need more resources and time to build their spaceship, give it to them. Fuzzy systems blend together all information and produce answers using terms such as *tend to, possibly,* and *anticipated.*

Kosko (1993) builds his arguments for fuzzy logic by noting that most math is really nonlinear; it never stops. Contrary to common perceptions, not many things in mathematics are certain, as computerized information tends to bear out in many natural sciences. It is within a natural environment of irregular shapes, patterns, and contradictions that leaders search for stability and facilitate self-organization. In order to renovate schooling, leaders will need to *trade in* some of the traditional rules of right and wrong, along with order and linearity, and embrace emergent structures and fuzzy logic. It is all a matter of how we see and process things. We are learning that leadership of natural social systems not only requires up-to-date assumptions about the dynamic nature of organizational growth and the advantages of *living on the edge of chaos,* but it also demands an extraordinary belief in the potential that exists in listening and responding to environmental shifts, while building human-energy systems that respond.

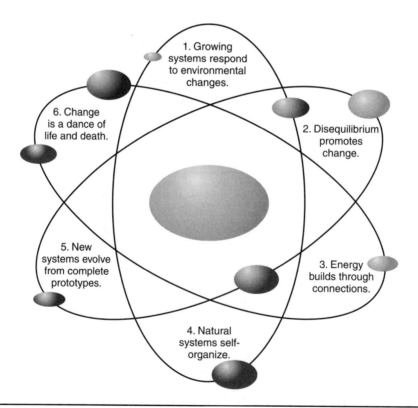

Figure 5.1 Living on the edge of chaos.

In the past several years, the enthusiastic reactions to the concepts of chaos theory from educational leaders around the globe have affirmed their relevance to us for guiding the great transitions in education. It seems there is indeed some profound truth in the new ways of thinking about how things work. Educators' reactions have given us insights into the potential of such thinking for facilitating the emergence of truly responsive institutions. As we began to filter these reactions through the various literature we continue to read, several principles of change have emerged as lessons.

What meaning is there in the principles of chaos and complexity theory for school leaders? Which new laws are vital to leading the emergence of new forms of schooling? The atomic model in Figure 5.1 resulted from many deliberations with school leaders and presents six lessons about *living on the edge of chaos.* In this chapter, we explore some of the features for each lesson and offer stories from leaders of many institutions who are thriving on chaos.

LESSON 1: GROWING SYSTEMS RESPOND TO ENVIRONMENTAL CHANGES

External forces that impact human organizations are always numerous and complex and will only increase over time in their complexity. The leadership function is to acknowledge both internal and external paradoxes and to become an influence on the external environment as well as on the organization's responses to changing conditions.

Acknowledging global paradoxes requires keeping current on changing trends and standards and making appropriate institutional responses. To promote systemic reform, many strong districts and their schools are finding ways to get around governmental rules and policies that inhibit growth. To keep current with the changing times and to prepare students for *the global village,* much of what we have been doing in schools will have to be tossed out and replaced almost simultaneously. If we face the current realities of life, the complexities of transforming schools will become both evident and overwhelming; we really have no other choice but to respond creatively if we want public education to survive.

A major question is whether or not public institutions can *live with the paradox of compliance with governing laws while they invent completely new forms of schooling.* Can educators break out of lockstep bureaucratic systems without breaking the law? Some states, such as Florida, have passed *forgiveness laws* that give schools permission to do for their students whatever is needed. For example, the Pasco County School District, one of the most innovative districts and one that is highly successful with its students, is granted 100 percent compliance on its annual state audits in recognition of its exemplary practices and policies. How is it able to be the most innovative and at the same time the most in compliance? Its leaders say it is a matter of knowing how to think about the paradoxes while keeping the real purpose of schooling in focus. Leaders center their attention on what they need to be doing for their students and then figure out how the new laws of each legislative session can be used to their advantage. This illustrates how *listening and responding systemically to global trends and external pressures are the essence of moving ahead to transform education institutions.*

Several of the paradoxes we face as a nation will continue to drive change initiatives for some time. For example, although the United States is considered a world superpower with one of the best education systems anywhere, many of our students perform at low levels on national and international tests. In the third International Mathematics and Science Study, which tested a half million students in 41 countries, U.S. eighth graders scored below the world average in math (*Newsweek,* December 2, 1996). In the 2003 administration of the TIMMS (Trends in International Mathematics and Science Studies), the United States scored above the average in math, with Singapore, Hong Kong, Japan, Chinese Taipai, Netherlands, Latvia, Lithuania, Russian Federation, England, and Hungary surpassing the United States In the 2003 administration of the science test, the U.S. scored above average, with Singapore, Hong Kong, Chinese Taipei, Japan, and England outperforming the United States (http://timss.bc.edu).

Students in the United States spend more time in class and have more homework than students in other countries, but the curriculum is less demanding and the teaching style is usually based on the lecture and practice, which is different from other countries in the study. While schools have made many changes in curriculum and instruction over the last few decades, the changes apparently have not been sufficient to offset the negative effects; change is happening more rapidly throughout the world than educators are able to handle.

Many educational traditions are tenacious, and exceptionally strong counterforces will be required to alter them to any extent. Per Dalin (1995) observes in a book published in Swedish about restructuring schools that the United States will have more difficulty than many other nations in transforming its schools because of the complex bureaucratic systems—with their legal parameters—that dominate the U.S. schooling environment. We are bound not only by our traditions but also by legal parameters within which schools seek to invent new forms of schooling. This presents a serious contradiction in practice. While other nations have adapted their schooling practices better to complex environments, many U.S. traditions continue to dominate practice in negative ways.

When educators have shifted their focus from traditional teaching and measuring the minute segments of isolated and graded subjects and have concentrated instead on real-life performance capabilities, they find themselves quite naturally reconfiguring the curriculum, instruction, learning, and leading. In so doing, they engage in the dance of life and death in the essential dimensions of schooling by tossing out inappropriate practices and rebuilding the school enterprise in desirable ways. Working toward the *new workplace standards and the dynamic global marketplace* will require something very different from the kind of schooling that was provided in the twentieth century.

Many schools need to be overhauled from the bottom to the top if they are to survive as useful social institutions. A report from the Secretary's Commission on Achieving Necessary Skills (SCANS, 1992) reveals that the essentials for success in adulthood are working interdependently with others; using a wide array of information, resources, and technology; and understanding systems and how they work. Therefore, the 13 years of schooling ought to concentrate on those same work patterns for every student all day and every day. Because technology drives the processes of work in the business world, technology should also permeate the learning environment of schools for every student every day all day. If U.S. students are not doing well on international achievement measures, educators need to analyze that information and respond. *The leadership challenge is to pay attention to the external pressures and then garner the resources and support for appropriate internal responses.* Not to respond is to encourage the eventual demise of public education.

A contradiction in schooling is the extent to which *telecommunications* have transformed daily life and the workplace around the globe versus the influence of telecommunications in classrooms. We perceive that students tend to spend, at best, a few minutes with technology during each school day, where the learning curve is steady but slow. However, when state-of-the-art technology permeates the learning environment, students are able to pursue their interests at any time and as they contact a universe of people, ideas, and resources. In technologically dense learning environments, students and their teachers no longer limit learning to their classrooms and schools, for through technology they are finding ways to connect with resources and peoples within their community and around the world. When schooling includes technology every day all day for every student, it has transformative power for their success and it prepares them for the future, which will surely become more complex and dominated by technology.

Schools as we knew them in the twentieth century will become obsolete as centers of learning due to advances in technology and the multiple forms of access to information and knowledge that are already available everywhere. The new schooling policies in Norway, where students enroll in industry or businesses for the last two years of high school, signal this major change. Schooling will shift away from a fixed location with specific hours toward a more fluid arrangement that includes a multitude of professional and technical fields with learning opportunities that include international connections. Shifting from *school* as a physical and operational phenomenon to something that operates within the framework of a global energy field is difficult to imagine today. If, as the scientists tell us, reality is not fixed in time and place, we will in all likelihood let go of the concept of school as a certain facility, certain schedules for local professionals and students, a standard curriculum, and 13 linear years of learning.

To illustrate: Within the past several years, we have become involved in graduate research projects of students in universities in other countries. It seems quite natural to participate in their research as an influence, especially when they are building on the work of *managing productive schools* (MPS) and its systems theory base. Students do not pay for our guidance, nor do our universities receive money for their "work." Yet this kind of professor/student relationship is growing, and we are finding ourselves connecting continuously in new ways with students and scholars all over the world as we develop new knowledge together. At times we teach courses in other countries, or students and professors visit our universities to work with us for a time. Typically there is no exchange of money. Over time, their work is shared with us through the fax machine, e-mail, and telephone. We return our feedback to these international students through the same complex systems of telecommunication, all of which seems more efficient than working with students on our own university campuses.

We are in the midst of new *sense making* as professors and developing prototypes of learning together that span locations and financial resources. Building natural connections with learners and ideas is joyous, while it engages us in continuous learning about schooling in other countries and for the applications of our work. The power of connections and influence is breaking down the barriers of time, space, credit, and resources as people pursue interests they have in common. Do we benefit from this kind of "work" when there is no fee involved? Yes, for what we continue to learn and how it causes us to stretch our understandings of issues and concepts we care about can never be put in financial terms. We are experiencing life in a wide range of new connections, each adding value to our lives as lifelong learners. What greater joy is there for a professional educator?

To prepare students for the current realities of the workplace, much of the time spent in school learning ought to relate to or even replicate the world of work, for this not only stimulates personal development but it also enhances curiosity and a desire for lifelong learning. Fortunately, many schools are simply abandoning the single text/single subject approach to learning and are promoting more complex avenues for pupil engagement in real-life issues, using real-life skills and work habits. When we visited the Stickjo school in Sundsvall, Sweden, in 1995, we learned that the entire curriculum for the entire school for several years had been built around the dying pond on the school's property. Lena Heniksson, the principal, reported that not only were students studying the water itself through samples, but they were also inserting interventions with potential into the death process of the pond and studying their effects. In the process, students became actively involved in the town's political process as they gathered support and resources for cleaning up the pond. All their communications activity and math involved real issues in rebuilding the ecology of the pond. All students of all ages were engaged in special work projects that were interdependent and important to everyone as learners and as citizens of the school community. The school has became a force for progress in the town as its students learn about social and physical conditions and develop many lifelong skills and capacities.

If we fail to acknowledge the complex context of schools today, the quality of the other major decisions we make will not matter, for they will only perpetuate schooling for an age gone by, which may in the end fail society. Not only will individual students lose over a lifetime, but so will their communities and the nation. It is time to open school doors to the world and see what happens. We are confident that school professionals can figure out how to organize themselves. Students will probably adjust quite well, for the most part, although the same may not be true for habit-ridden educators. The risk should be worth whatever temporary negative effect and fallout there may be. In fact, the future will depend on how rapidly and how well we are able to connect schools with the processes of the rapidly changing systems of the globe. Let us involve students in reshaping our schools. Is this not their preparation for life in a complex age? Will they not be working in a world without answers, only possibilities?

Who among us would knowingly go to a dentist whose practice is wholly guided by the 1950s science of dentistry? Who would trust a physician, or an auto mechanic, or a plumber, or a lawyer with out-of-date professional capacities? Many school leaders worry about how to deal with parents who want outdated forms of schooling for their children. Such attitudes reflect the parents' limited knowledge about schooling and how it seeks to keep up with changing times, and educators must therefore endeavor to help parents value a more modern and essential definition of education. The same marketing practices that cause us to buy new cars, new clothes, new appliances, and new technology may be useful as principles for marketing more modern approaches to schooling.

Listening goes both ways; at times the community needs to listen to the changes and needs within schools and districts. Because of its population explosion in recent years, the Hillsborough County School District in Florida (now the eighth largest school district in the United States) was in desperate need of a bond issue for the construction of many schools. In 1994, the bond issue failed. The voters did not approve of the half-cent sales tax referendum that was attached to the issue. Bewildered, the school board initially blamed its own strategic plan for the bond failure. In 1996, a few months after Earl Lennard was sworn in as school superintendent, the referendum was again on the ballot. This time, Lennard launched a campaign to provide information to voters about the needs by working through each school's PTA and within local networks. The bond issue was passed on its second attempt due to the influence of information made available through the district's system of networks. Building connections for listening to what schools need is another major leadership challenge today.

LESSON 2: DISEQUILIBRIUM PROMOTES CHANGE

Disequilibrium rather than stability stimulates the system to respond in the most dynamic, fundamental, and noticeable ways. The leadership task is to use information to stimulate disequilibrium, which provides the energy for change.

Chaos theory suggests that any lasting change is built from within the organization and is driven by identified needs and internal forces calling for change. This translates for schools into high-energy work cultures that have the vision and strength to offset the power of tradition. Yet, this is really nothing new, for Glen Heathers wrote as far back as 1972 that when there are failures in an innovation, weak or inadequate linkages are found between aims, means, and accomplishments, these being primarily human factors that integrate all dimensions of the change initiative. Why is the human linkage factor so often ignored? Why do leaders still issue edicts with the fear of punishment attached and expect that wonderful things will happen? We have known since the 1940s and 1950s that workers need to be involved in shaping their organizations. Yet, for whatever reasons, change remains one of the most elusive properties of organizational life today (Dubinskas, 1994).

Recent large-scale and well-funded change projects have been such disasters that serious questions now are being raised about the feasibility of traditional models of planned change. One example is a $40 million grant from the Annie E. Casey Foundation that was given to four cities to alter the life chances of at-risk youth. This project required that all social agencies in the city work together with schools to transform the quality and effects of their services (Welhage, Smith, and Lipham, 1992). After three years of cross-agency activity, a study was conducted by the University of Wisconsin to determine the effects of the new structures, programs, and services on the city's youth. The researchers concluded that no fundamental change of any kind had occurred within any social agency, including schools, in any city and that no evidence exists of visionary leadership for the targeted youth. More money to accompany a plan, they reported, is not the answer.

Another example is the $1.2 million federal NASDC (New America Schools Development Corporation) grant given to the Bensenville community in Illinois to invent a twenty-first-century systemic approach to schooling (Mirel, 1994). Before the project had even completed its planning year, however, the teachers' union stopped all work, which ended community dreams about the schools as well as future government funding. The reasons for union actions are unclear from Mirel's report, but the fact remains that good ideas (enough to acquire the highly competitive funding), lots of money, and a strategic plan proved to be insufficient elements in transforming the traditions of schooling. Another mental model of change might have yielded more promising results.

For many years, scientists failed to notice the roles of positive feedback and disequilibrium in moving a system forward. Prigogine received a Nobel Prize in chemistry in 1977 for his work on *dissipative structures* (Wheatley, 1992, 10). He demonstrated the capacity of living systems to respond to disorder with renewed life, and, in fact, he learned that disorder plays a critical role in giving birth to new, higher forms of life (Prigogine, 1990). "The world around us," he said, "involves instabilities and chaos, and this requires a drastic revision of some of the basic concepts of physics" (82). For example, dynamics in the environment play a crucial role in creating new structures. Environmental changes provoke responses, and, when they grow to significant levels of disturbance, the system can no longer be ignored (Wheatley, 1992, 19). The response to disturbance often is to self-organize in ways that integrate new information, for open systems use disequilibrium to avoid deterioration and to continue growing. Disequilibrium is a leverage point for change!

The implications of Prigogine's work are simple and clear. As Wheatley (1992) urges, we must invent organizations in which process is allowed its varied tempo and dance, in which structures come and go, and where form arises to support necessary relationships. Change is seldom significant under stable conditions; rather, it requires the density of connections that emerge into states of disequilibrium (strong and dense connections are everything!). In a crisis, which creates a highly charged environment with multitudes of interactions, the condition is ripe for long-lasting and complex change. The challenge for leaders, however, is not so much to make things happen as to *create the conditions under which change will naturally occur, to manage changeability* (Hurst and Zimmerman, 1994). Our attention shifts from simple systems and steady states to complexity and change over time. Begun (1994) argues that complex relationships cannot fit linear models, for chaotic systems will learn how to respond spontaneously to unpredictable shifts.

Organizations that develop and apply these new concepts about the energy for change and the vitality that is found in states of disequilibrium will gain a competitive advantage, for the radically changing environment demands radically changing (responsive) organizations (Nadler et al., 1995). Some changes are rather simple, while others are more dramatic and influence all parts of the system. Nadler and his colleagues found four types of change in organizations, each of which requires different leadership strategies and worker responses: (1) *incremental change* occurs within existing patterns of work or frames; (2) *discontinuous change* is that which alters the frame; (3) *framebending change* modifies and reshapes work; and (4) *framebreaking and rebuilding change* involves the destruction of existing elements within the system, followed by massive redesign of all structures, processes, and services.

With respect to *incremental change,* Nadler and his colleagues observe that a linear change process works when conditions are low in both complexity and intensity. An example might be to introduce a new reading series throughout a school to heighten student comprehension. The second type of change, which they call *discontinuous change,* accounts for growth spurts and pauses, such as launching cooperative learning systems in classrooms. *Framebending change* considers new rules to govern what occurs, such as shedding the practice of expecting that all students learn a specific skill within prescribed time limits and from the same processes. These three rather simple approaches to change involve responsibilities that can be delegated to others, such as ordering new instructional materials, training and coaching teachers in cooperative learning, or encouraging teachers to think about allowing three years rather than nine months for students to master certain skills.

Framebreaking change is more radical, for many former systems of work probably will cease to exist and be replaced with new ones that correspond to needs. This radical kind of change is what is occurring in many school districts today, which is far beyond the empowerment of one role group. When we consider altering the time constraints of learning for all students and providing students with interdisciplinary programs within continuous progress systems, we realize that such an approach to change is far beyond the capability of one or even several teachers to manage. The basic systems of work in an organization require top leadership to engineer and to manage the development of complex redesign initiatives. This approach to change is systemic, where an integration of change in all systems is necessary. All four types of change can be found in highly innovative institutions. however, and the selection of an approach depends upon the needs. The more simple approaches to change are used in low overall performance requirements. Change is a different phenomenon in different places and at different times (Hurst and Zimmerman, 1994). It is sometimes continuous or smooth, almost linear, and occurring at various paces; and it is sometimes discontinuous, relatively stable, rapid, and nonlinear. It requires destruction and always includes self-organization as an underlying principle.

In writing about discontinuous change, Nadler and his colleagues (1995) observe that large-scale *efforts inevitably include resisters* who need to be moderated if the change effort is to succeed. In our study of 28 schools, those with high-involvement work cultures had all somehow taken care of the resisters, whereas in the lower-involvement schools pockets of resistance still existed. This condition dramatically affected the quality and sustainability of change initiatives in these schools. The responsiveness of the system as a whole directly related to the strength of its positive connection systems in using information. The *transitions need to be controlled* as managers communicate clear images of the future, use multiple leverage points, organize for the transition, and build feedback mechanisms into the process. Information about the conditions for learning creates the strongest form of disequilibrium when it is accompanied with clear intentions of a response.

The key dynamic at work is *disequilibrium,* which creates both the energy and the direction for systemic change, for it simultaneously and radically shifts roles, work cultures, power relationships, and the design of services and programs. It provides insufficient energy to offset stable patterns and move the system forward. By contrast, when the human connections are complex, strong, dynamic, and even close to turbulent, there is sufficient energy and power to disturb the routines and to transform the old organization into a prototype. *Living on the edge of chaos is where transformational change happens; the leaders of tomorrow will need to be those who thrive in its context and demonstrate confidence in facilitating the direction and quality of change.*

LESSON 3: ENERGY BUILDS THROUGH CONNECTIONS

The stronger the internal web of interactions, the stronger the force and human energy for change. The leadership function is to develop professional capacities and networks that respond to emerging challenges in the system.

To transform the traditions of isolation and irrelevant practices and programs, the strength of new connection systems will need to be sufficiently powerful to redirect their course. We recognize the energy that emerges from collaborations and partnerships; connections enable the natural energy to nurture the unfolding of promising new ideas and relationships.

There is a sense of urgency for developing strong internal connection systems; many organizations, through routine work teams, are doing so by nurturing multirole task forces, multidisciplinary project teams, networks, and partnerships with external groups. Professional development for cooperative work requires not only permission but also a mix of tools and technologies for collaborative ventures, as well as emerging knowledge for specific projects. More often today, the greatest learning happens on the job as multidisciplinary teams use established, observed, and personal knowledge to tackle problems together and invent prototypes.

A few years ago, a nuclear scientist shared information about a 50-year-long international project to create an unlimited supply of energy through a form of energy called *fusion.* At the time he talked with us, over $5 billion had been spent by the United States, Japan, Russia, and European nations. Because coal and oil are being depleted as energy sources, the goal is to develop new global energy options for the twenty-first century. The research team is working toward producing machines of vast complexity to produce hydroenergy, which will be clean, cheap, and inexhaustible.

Fission, the scientist explained, is a form of energy with which we are more familiar, for it creates nuclear energy. To create fission, an external force is used to split atoms. Energy is released when a neutron splits the nucleus of a heavy atom to create two smaller nuclei, thereby creating energy from costly fuels such as uranium. External forces are needed to create fission, which depletes our natural resources in the process. In so doing, there is a negative fallout as well as debris that creates new problems for the environment.

Fusion, the new approach, occurs as energy is released from the nuclei of two small atoms that combine to form a larger nucleus. Hydrogen atoms are superheated, enabling them to strike one another with such force that they fuse together; in the process, the energy released is clean, safe, and in limitless supply. The main fuels are tritium and deuterium, which are extracted from the oceans of the world (a neverending source for energy) and when combined form helium. The process is neither polluting nor dangerous.

To create this complex form of energy, international multidisciplinary teams of scientists will work together for the next five decades. When we inquired about how scientists learn what is needed for their task, the response was somewhat surprising. By studying the developments as they unfold and using established knowledge along with their collective, creative problem-solving capacities, scientists expect to find new products and processes. It is a story of professionals using knowledge to create the future and inventing knowledge as they face fresh dilemmas.

A few days later, headlines all over the world announced that after a half century of work and billions of dollars, scientists from 14 European countries had created two seconds of fusion. This development created 1.7 megawatts of energy, which is enough to light 17,000 one-hundred-watt lightbulbs (*USA Today* and *The New York Times,* November 12, 1991). The U.S. Department of Energy predicts that by the middle of the century they will be able to bring fusion power to the grid (www.ofes.fusion.doe.gov/performancetargets.shtml).

There are two points of interest in this story. The first is the difference in the two energy-producing processes. For *fission* (nuclear energy) to occur, external forces must be used on atoms to cause a split. The use of uranium over time depletes the world resource. We are mindful of the Three Mile Island and Chernobyl disasters and of the actual dangers to the natural environment from this form of energy. The process of creating fission is destructive both to atoms and to nature, and it uses up a world supply of fuel. *Fusion* (hydroenergy), on the other hand, occurs as two forces are combined to create heat, a process that produces no negative side effects and leaves no fallout. Also, in the fusion process, energy re-creates itself; it will be unending. To summarize the essential concepts, fission is externally produced, has a limited life, depends on external energy, and has a negative fallout. *Fusion* derives from internal connections of atoms found within a limitless supply of the earth's water, generates more energy, and has no negative fallout.

It occurred to us that perhaps our school-improvement initiatives over the years have been based on the *fission approach* to creating energy. An example is the new state law in Florida that requires all schools to show evidence of normal gains in achievement for all student populations within a school year. In response, some schools have virtually stopped working on relationships with families and community agencies as they gear up for tough drills in basic subjects. In contrast, others are responding differently by using the *fusion approach* to change. Continuous progress programs continue to expand and are linked with team teaching, cooperative learning, and non-graded structures. Natural connection systems become self-sustaining and energy producing.

The second element of interest to us in the fission/fusion story relates to the professional development of the scientific teams that seek to create a new energy supply. The team of *international scientists is* essentially *multidisciplinary,* and its members work together in many phases of the project's development over decades. The plan is for at least 10 teams of scientists to work on the project, each for about a decade, before the world supply of energy will be ready; those who begin the project will not actually be those who eventually *produce fusion.* There are not even two kinds of scientists who know all that is necessary for creating the new energy form. Progress is contingent upon the *next-phase problems* being addressed through multidisciplinary perspectives. When we asked about the continuous professional development of these teams, we learned that because selected scientists are creating something new and because there is no training in any field that would be of use, professional development occurs daily as the teams use existing knowledge to invent the long-term global energy source.

We have in this story an analogy to both bureaucratic and systems approaches to enhancing organizational life, do we not? In the last four decades, professional-development programs in education have been largely externally driven, designed, and delivered, and only a very few add value to the daily problem-solving capacities of professionals. In other words, the basic principles that create fission have driven professional-development practice. Now it is clear that a different and more long-lasting approach to increasing the school's energy systems will be needed to sustain continuous development as an organizational task.

Some would argue, as does Lewis Rhodes (in a 1996 paper he wrote for a study group at Wingspread, which is a conference center in Wisconsin), that schools do not have the capacity to fix themselves. The traditions of isolation and fragmentation have created conditions of unsustainable change, even though multiple kinds of innovative programs may exist. Without a capacity for continual on-the-job training and problem solving, the survival of schools seems hopeless. Rhodes calls for school systems to become collaborative knowledge-building communities that function within a well-designed collaborative infrastructure.

After all school- and district-based leaders had completed *managing productive schools* training in systems thinking, Pasco County school district decided to form a districtwide movement to alter the dropout rates. At first the effort was called *graduation enhancement,* and it involved all principals and district leaders in a two-year learning initiative. Hundreds of people were organized into elementary-school, middle-school, high-school, and promotion/retention study groups, in which participants read and discussed the current literature on school reform and related fields. No strategic plans were made, no new projects were launched, and no major policy decisions were made during this knowledge-infusion time. The guiding assumption of district leaders was this: "If their leaders knew how to think differently, schools would become different, and more students would choose to remain in school."

This strategy demonstrated what has been called *the butterfly effect* in chaos theory, for unplanned change initiatives began to emerge simultaneously all over the district. The strategy of *learning together first* was so powerful that principals decided to launch the same process with their own professional staff. After years of learning together across role groups and working together as leadership teams, the district greatly reduced the dropout condition; what also evolved was a K–12, multidisciplinary, continuous progress curriculum with portfolio assessment systems at all levels, and all teachers work in learning communities with nongraded groups of students. Pilots of the prototypes exist at all levels, with second- and third-generation efforts now in place. This school district became a large and cohesive learning community, and, as a result, was able to overhaul many major learning and work systems for students and professionals. Most importantly, it has created a movement (based on fusion principles) that has sustainability.

Building the internal energy for change includes virtually flooding the intellectual work environment with books, audiotapes, and videotapes, as well as journals and papers on change, systems thinking, and major innovations, so that daily professional dialogue and problem solving reflect the best that is known. Professional team members are encouraged to visit schools, districts, and other innovative organizations of all kinds, engaging in continuous learning through observation and dialogue with other professionals. Through continuous study of the literature, through site visitations, and through gathering information continuously from within the school, each school's professional staff becomes a quality learning community that over time is able to address complex problems routinely. Through the use of many forms of self-examination, the response capacities of the staff become stronger as time goes on.

A school or any other organization will be as useful to its clients as is the capacity of its professionals to respond to changing conditions and needs. *Building a self-sustaining connection system that responds to a changing environment is the core of emergence leadership* and is well within our reach when we embrace the new laws of change in natural systems.

LESSON 4: NATURAL SYSTEMS SELF-ORGANIZE

Natural systems have a strong capacity to respond to both external and internal forces, to self-organize, and to become self-determining. The leadership function is to respond to and develop the organization's internal readiness and dynamics for change.

Professional resistance to change is one of the major forces holding schools hostage while the rest of society moves along. Most of these reactions to a changing environment are normally defensible. Yet, some leaders continue pretending that things are not so bad, while the complexity of neighborhoods increases and international telecommunications spin their own webs of rapid change. Chaos theory suggests that *growing* systems respond quite naturally to environmental information when they are free to do so. That is how they survive. The school leader's job is to listen to the internal needs as well as to the internal dynamics and capacities for change, while building a professional learning community that explores and responds to changing conditions. Responses are internally driven in growing organizations, however, rather than externally directed. We need the courage to abandon many of the old ways of thinking and to abandon old assumptions about what does and does not work. We need to take a fresh approach and nurture the *deep culture* of the organization and its fresh emergence.

Part of the paradox is that responding to internal needs is not always valued as a strategy for student success; the habits of control are still very powerful and pervasive. In Florida in 1995, the state commissioner of education published a list of low-performing schools in all of the state's newspapers. These schools, with the help of their school districts, were required to show gains on state standardized tests within a short time period or the superintendent had to explain the lack of progress to the state. Not surprising, the failing schools were located in low socioeconomic communities. This new state policy created pervasive professional fear, and yet it offered the necessary disequilibrium to promote change and growth for students.

In some cases, Florida schools had already been reaching out to parents and students, and yet the attention on test scores prompted some schools to drop the new innovations and return to *the basics*. Their successful strategies were of little or no interest to state officials in the face of low test scores. Consequently, new forms of resistance emerged as others gave up hope in their profession altogether. A few principals retired, and some were transferred to other schools. Teachers also retired, and a few left at-risk schools for higher socioeconomic communities where the demands for student success were less complex and challenging. Principals who remained in the low-performing schools told news reporters how they had to eliminate many of the extra *caring* strategies and replace them with a tightening-of-the-belt response to learning the *basics*. For a few of the schools, however, the challenges the staff faced with their student population provided the energy and direction that was needed to respond in ways that helped students. For example, Cleveland Elementary in Tampa raised its student performance significantly and was eliminated from the state's list of critically low schools (*St. Petersburg Times,* May 11, 1996).

For the first time in Florida, the success of all students became public. Schools whose students fail to achieve certain levels of academic performance on state tests become the target for continuous supervision by the state until acceptable levels of achievement are realized. On November 26, 1996, both the *Tampa Tribune* and the *St. Petersburg Times* reported that 93 schools had been removed from the state's list of critically low schools, for they had demonstrated significant gains in student achievement in reading, writing, and math. Those that remain on the state list were in jeopardy of state interference into school district governance, for districts ultimately are accountable to the state for the performance of their schools. The expectation is right: Schools should be held accountable for demonstrating increases in student achievement routinely, for many schools in low socioeconomic communities have achieved beyond what might be expected for years. What can be disputed, however, is the time frame for demonstrating growth, especially in schools with large migrant populations that have as much as 100 percent student turnover every year. Perhaps the next major challenge is to achieve the success-for-all expectations within school environments that nurture the human spirit while advancing learning.

The very survival of an organization and its value to society depend on how well it responds to information about changing conditions. As scientists report, 99 percent of all species that ever lived are now extinct. This information has a number of practical implications for organizations. The survival of schooling as a social function is likely to cease unless we figure out how to respond to changing environmental conditions. In most communities, we can look around at shops and industries that once thrived but are now gone. Some of these enterprises chose to ignore certain vital signs about their environment or the changing market. Consider, for example, those companies that were at one time engaged in a certain business but are now engaged in another. Fifty years ago, the Singer Company was a world leader in sewing machines, but as more women bought ready-made garments for their families, they had less need to sew at home. Singer changed its mission and survived by becoming an aerospace company. Sears Roebuck and Co. provides another example of survivability through adaptation: At one time the company sold only merchandise; now it sells multiple kinds of products and services for a changing marketplace.

Public education is not immune to potential extinction. Cities such as Baltimore, Milwaukee, and Minneapolis have handed over some or all of their schools to private companies. It remains to be seen how successful this trend will be, but it could well be that private companies have greater response capacities than do governmental agencies such as schools and districts. The private companies argue that public agencies need not become crippled by the tough challenges of responding to changing environments while complying with the law. The charter school movement may also become a prototype of schooling. The idea seems to be at least worth exploring: set a few schools free from established policy and watch what happens. We could all learn from the initial trials about what is possible on a broader scale.

We have observed from our research that successful change happens in schools where principals build strong connections and networks with and among students, staff, parents, and the community. Both the content and the intensity of change strategies at any moment depend on the staff's readiness to learn and to explore options. Many principals report that, when given new perspectives and skills, most teachers want to help create programs. But adding only a few programs here and there to traditional systems has little or no power to alter classroom or schooling effects significantly; virtually rebuilding the foundations for school learning and working has become the professional challenge. Success becomes a matter of redirecting energy. The gravitational pull that comes from tradition requires a strong energy system, a learning community, and external networks and partnerships to offset tradition and its effects.

Several years ago, Susan Rine, who at the time was the principal of a continuous progress demonstration school in Pasco County, Florida, shared with us the story of developing her school. It took five years of training, coaching, and achieving many small successes from collaborative ventures, she said, before the staff was ready to tackle the tougher problems of at-risk populations. When the staff felt confident with collaborative work systems, it decided to pursue non-graded/team teaching structures for students, along with continuous progress instructional programs, which provided a context for their rebuilding efforts. These innovations did not provide the solution to the problems, but they provided a context within which they could explore their options over time.

If *listening and responding* are important new leadership requirements, how is this accomplished in ways that differ from those in bureaucratic systems? Many writers about chaos theory claim that *information is the most fundamental ingredient for a constantly evolving, dynamic system.* Without information, the system might change, but it could very well change in a wrong direction. With lots of information, on the other hand, the organization's members will know what kinds of responses need to be made and which hold the greatest promise. It is a matter of choice: Use information and survive, or ignore it and become extinct. Wheatley (1992) calls information the *fuel of life,* something that disturbs the comfortable peace. Schools are now beginning to explore the utility of multiple forms of information, which becomes the *solar energy* of the organization. But for it to flow, Wheatley argues, we must abandon control and learn to trust the principles of self-organization. Information is the organization's source of nourishment, and it provides critical signs of the organization's health. We must become hungry for information, the density of which will help us to act with courage and confidence.

The extent to which some principals ignore information is surprising, and change sometimes seems to be the last thing on their agenda. Each semester, our university graduate students conduct case studies in their own school or district unit about some dimension of schooling (reform, culture, motivation, organization, leadership, strategic planning, and so on). In the process, faculty members and administrators in their schools are invited to participate. Most principals support the study; there are always some, however, who seek assurance that no one but the professor will see the results. In these schools, principals seem to want nothing to upset the status quo; they like things the way they are. Others seem fearful of reprimand from the central office if the results are not glowing. Ironically, most of these change-resisting schools call themselves *site-base managed* and have school-improvement councils. Other data the students gather verify that any kind of change is unlikely under the current leadership in these change-resistant schools.

Some graduate students report a very different story, however, for they work in schools where principals and teachers are eager to hear what the researcher has learned. The students are typically invited to report the findings of their case study at a faculty meeting. Such presentations, with handouts and transparency projections of the findings, lead naturally to discussion and almost always to some form of action. Other data about these schools show that learning together is regarded as a collective job, for they understand the function of information for change and they earnestly seek to further the well-being of students in their school.

When district leaders are serious about building successful schools, they select and develop principals who seem to have a passion for the school renewal process. Vigorous and demanding systems of principal selection, development, appraisal, and compensation can govern new district standards and set the tone for becoming *world-class schools.* In these dynamic districts, human-resource-development systems weed out principals who cannot or will not face the need for continuous school renewal and attract a new breed of educational leader. Ensuring that principals are facilitators of a new order is a major task of district leaders, for their schools' success depends on it. *It is time for zero tolerance of school leaders who are not facilitators of natural change in the school's work systems and culture; our nation's survival may depend on such change.*

Self-renewing structures have the capacity to self-organize, as do chameleons, to fit the moment (Wheatley, 1992, 90). Fluid structures, such as task forces, temporary work teams, and focus groups, develop flexibility as professionals gain access to new information about external factors, internal conditions, and resources. As an organization matures and stabilizes in its new conditions, it becomes more efficient and establishes a basic structure to support the system's development. High levels of autonomy and identity emerge within and across work teams as they stay open to information from the outside and use information to adapt services and programs. In the self-renewing process, boundaries develop naturally and change constantly.

Kanter (1995) says that being world class calls for reflecting the highest standards that exist anywhere for growing, for competing, and for commanding resources to operate beyond borders and across territories. This tells us that not only do our schools need to change but the standards for their performance must be raised considerably. An organization grows in proportion to the amount of information it absorbs about external conditions and in proportion to responses in the form of new structures, processes, and systems. Perhaps it is time to become clear and tough about creating the conditions for internal growth and about raising the standards and expectations for change. Unless this happens, tinkering with the systems will continue to produce few noticeable results. But where the standards have been raised and the school becomes an energetic learning center, miracles happen almost daily. Are not the current imperfect schooling conditions, then, a matter of human choice and will? We either can respond adequately to new information and challenges, ensuring a chance at survival for a while longer, or we can ignore the vital signs and muddle our way toward extinction.

LESSON 5: NEW SYSTEMS EVOLVE FROM COMPLETE PROTOTYPES

Building prototypes eventually leads to total systems that are composed of multiples of those prototypes. The leadership task is to sponsor development of all parts of complete new forms of schooling; the entire system of services and practices is to become transformed.

School-based management (SBM) was expected to be the answer to breaking through the barriers to improve schools. But the literature is filled with stories of how the bureaucratic decisions were only shifted from one location (central office) to another (the school site), and questions about student success still were not addressed. The research projects of our graduate students tell the same story semester after semester: SBM in many schools is all about improving compliance patterns rather than sponsoring innovation to help more students succeed. Teachers in these schools report that seldom are the deep structures of school examined or altered, and the learning patterns remain the same, even though teachers, parents, and members of the business community become involved in discussions and planning.

A useful way of thinking about the cluster of innovations that are emerging in high-involvement schools is to imagine the school as a web of connections.

The creation or extinction of one practice can create an avalanche of extinction or invention (Kauffman, 1995, 292–294). The web itself drives the way the web transforms. A basic principle is that diversity begets diversity, which begets growth. As diversity increases, the system explodes with a diversity of products, one example being the mushrooming of services for special student populations in schools. As we consider the web of diverse needs and services that will be required of schools, we need to work with an interdependent cluster of innovations and their natural emergence over time if they are to show promise for yielding new forms of schooling.

Sture Norlin (1996) developed a twenty-first-century prototype school in the early 1990s when he was a principal in Sundsvall. Located in an old school facility, this community-oriented school was transformed into one that is an excellent example of systems thinking. The entire staff and many parents were involved from the ground up in inventing a new form of schooling. What emerged from the planning phase included major changes in the physical plant, along with the integration of curriculum and organization into nongraded learning communities of teachers and students. To actually launch the prototype, the physical spaces, as well as learning and working systems, were all redesigned and piloted by one team of students and teachers at a time. With each pilot, all teachers in the school studied and learned from the experience of a few, which helped to shape the next iteration of the model. There were no failures, only learning opportunities, as the prototype was refined and spread gradually throughout the entire school. As a result, the concept of an innovation cluster has now spread to many other schools.

What does a cluster of innovations look like in schools? In all 28 schools in our study, we found that a common evolution of innovations occurred in varying orders and stages of development. In each case, the innovation cluster that eventually emerged included *continuous progress programs and nongraded structures, team teaching, integrated curriculum,* and *portfolio assessment systems.* In every case, the school began with a pilot of one innovation, which led quite naturally to all other innovations, which remained connected. No complete prototype was copied, but the essential dimensions of each were integrated into the school's natural emergence.

Learning about world-class prototypes has utility in shaping the quality of local innovations and prototype clusters. The piloting approach to overhauling systems, structures, and services allows for major problems to be eliminated in the emergence process, which prevents many of the common failures of school reform. Piloting, which is more than trying out something new, requires adaptation to local conditions through continuous study.

The concept of fractals may be useful, for it confirms how complex change is at even the smallest levels, while it reinforces the idea of adapting innovations through piloting. A prototype approach to improving schools ensures that the complete prototype becomes the new form of schooling. We learn from fractals that a droplet of water will never become an elephant when it multiplies; a leaf will never become a mountain; and the seashore will never become a forest. Each replication of the prototype will remain true to the specifications in the system, although how it grows in shape and size depends on environmental conditions during the expansion process. Schooling prototypes will never become transportation systems or hospitals; they will remain true to natural definitions of school and in the process develop more prototypes.

LESSON 6: CHANGE IS A DANCE OF LIFE AND DEATH

The process of creation and destruction is the cosmic dance in natural systems, whereby energy patterns are dissolved and rearranged to fit emerging conditions. From this perspective, the leadership task is to promote both the end and the beginning of work systems, structures, and services.

One of the basic laws of natural systems is that a continuous dance of life and death exists in the evolution process, which is both dynamic and stable and is designed to weed out and to create. Schools are filled with many structures, systems, programs, and services that are simply out-of-date and unresponsive to needs; yet, schools tend to be impervious to most change initiatives. Schools in many places still function as they did years ago, while the world around them has been transformed in every dimension. Why do schools and districts cling so tenaciously to practices and structures that no longer help students, as well as to those that actually prevent student success?

Age-graded structures, for example, are fiercely guarded, yet we know that students learn at variable rates in varying degrees and from the diversity of others of all ages. We continue to offer an age-bound, segmented curriculum, yet we know that skills for life are complex and require the integration of knowledge and skills to solve problems. We offer programs with linear progressions of simple skills and argue that the mastery of each skill is essential for the next skill, yet we know that learning is not linear and that it is rarely predictable. For example, small children mysteriously teach computer skills to their teachers and parents. We continue to use competitive grading systems that rate and rank students, yet we know that everyone learns better in cooperative environments in which everyone helps everyone else succeed. We perpetuate fear as a motivator for students and professionals alike, though we know that nurturing environments, albeit with some disequilibrium, stimulate the greatest gains. One might argue about exceptions to all these conditions, but these are still the pervasive patterns. Schools and districts are filled with systems that are out of sync with our knowledge about learning and organizational vitality. We conserve what we have when what we need to do is rebuild the major systems of schooling from the bottom up.

To understand the dance of life and death for schooling purposes, it may be useful to consider the various stages of growth and death in the *ecocycle* of a forest, about which Hurst and Zimmerman have written in insightful ways (1994). They observe that the *birth of a forest,* phase one, is characterized by exploitation of available territory, along with growth within clusters. In this early phase, there is rapid colonization of available space, where equal access exists for energy and resources. In *protection of the forest,* phase two, conservation of existing energy and prototypes is the chief characteristic as the cycle of forest growth reaches a climax. The forest is dominated in phase two by large hierarchical structures that control niches beneath them in a steady state. Huge amounts of burnable materials accumulate, yet there is external pressure for humans to leave forests alone, which includes fire prevention. But fire is a necessary part of the growth cycle for the forest. *The forest fire,* phase three, can become a creative form of destruction in which parts of the forest are destroyed to make room for new growth. Rigid internal structures, debris, and weak systems are destroyed through the crisis that is created by this form of mass destruction. The *creation and generation of a new forest,* phase four, mobilizes surviving resources for renewal purposes. The landscape is flattened, but the soil is now fertile from the decay of the former forest; with a vast and weakly connected network of living elements, the stage is set for the forest to be rebuilt. Anything is possible at this stage, for the condition is now *far from equilibrium.* Energy has been stimulated for rebuilding and sustaining a new and more healthy forest, one that is more suited to the changing environment, while the conditions are conducive to self-organization and growth among the cluster of species that remain.

The external environment is a major influence upon the direction of natural change. Hence, a symbiotic relationship must necessarily exist between a school and its community, and it is in this context that continuous improvement of schooling is possible. There need to be benchmarks, or world-class standards of success, that indicate how well a school is growing and how nurturing the quality of life is for those who learn and work within. Rather than relying on traditional kinds of information that show statistical relationships between this and that, teachers, school leaders, district leaders, and school board members are learning how to listen to their students and each other and also to emerging global needs. Their multiple perspectives provide a more reliable rudder to influence the direction of change within the system. The challenge today is to gather multiple kinds of information so that greater understandings of schooling complexities are developed. Then, leaders and workers will know how to shape the environments for learning in response.

The central question is this: *What are the effects of the work culture on the performance patterns of students?* Information can be generated continuously to guide the adjustments made daily and provide direction for changes to the system. The effects of a school and its services upon students provide the direction for change in the vision, the strategic plan, the systems of work, the information system, the human resources plan, and the appraisal of the school's programs and services. The Education Quality Benchmark System (EQBS) is based on a philosophy of integrated and purposeful work, and the information that is generated from its use can guide the growth process in the right directions. In the process, outdated systems will naturally give way to those that are more dynamic and have greater potential for preparing students for the global village.

SUMMARY

The six lessons for living on the edge of chaos provide a way of thinking for guiding school emergence into the twenty-first century. Listening and responding to a changing environment are matters of choice and survivability. The disequilibrium that new information produces is a great stimulator of change. The energy for organizational change comes from strong connections that are formed over time. The organization has the internal capacity to respond because of the self-organizing principle in natural systems. Change occurs to natural systems through prototypes of systems and their emergence, and change is naturally characterized by the dance of life and death. To embrace the six principles is a matter of human choice, one which can lead an organization to survival and growth.

A condition for the success of any organization is changing the structure and function of power. Without the power of professionals to build prototype systems together, there will be no future of the schooling enterprise as we have known it in this century. In the next chapter, we explore with you the various dimensions of power and contemplate the function of power within bureaucratic systems, which have been the predominant model for over a century. Being successful as an organization today requires that many role groups from all units within the system perceive they have the power to contribute to the redesign and delivery of adaptive services and programs and to the work systems that are required. If the issues of power are resolved and become transformed as an enabling function, than schools and school districts have a chance to become more viable as social institutions.

6

Confronting the Issues of Power

Much of how we think about power is embedded in a mechanistic organization metaphor, which assumes an orderly, structured, and bureaucratic organization focused on the control of work and workers. Implicit in this metaphor is an unchangeable world; it is predetermined, hierarchical, and organized around an immutable environment in which power is a predictable game with set rules and players. Control, authority, and command over resources and people permeate this organizational view.

Chaos theory, in contrast, evolves around nonstatic, emergent, fluid, and organic metaphors, where workers respond to changing conditions. This metaphor presupposes a dynamic world, open and emergent, fluid in membership, and organized around a vision of inclusiveness. Collaborative relationships guide members' work together and shape their beliefs and values, encouraging expertise that is shared and applied to make decisions (McLagan and Nel, 1995; Seiling, 1997). High levels of commitment, responsibility, and accountability result; agreement is fostered around the prioritization of resources and how best to respond to emerging trends, with pilots for testing new programs and services to better meet customers' needs.

Power within this worldview is *building capacity for action* to enable individuals to perform in ways that make an impact; thus, individuals have agency, feel more efficacious, can better serve clients, and believe they can influence the vision of a better future. Using one's agency and expertise presupposes an organizational culture that supports ongoing learning, building capacities for action, problem solving, and responsiveness. Contrast this culture to one that silences and shames, reducing the probability of ongoing responsiveness to customers' needs. Thus, the extent to which power is freely given to its members *and* is accepted by its organizational members comprises the norms for collective action, responsibility, and accountability for results, not to mention ongoing learning.

Authority, entrusted to people within a framework of action and clear purposes, frees people to act powerfully, to address common concerns, and to make decisions to address systemic problems that benefit customers. Collective commitment and accountability decrease if access to power is denied or curtailed. Or, stated another way, involvement in decision making will be limited if the *boss* is given the credit for others' ideas and all legitimate ideas must be funneled through the *boss* for endorsement and sponsorship. Frequently, adults have been too dependent on the benevolence of their patrons for *granting them permission* to take action or be involved in decision making. Power in this context is limited by hierarchical relationships that foster cultures of inertia. Often it appears that a bureaucrat's work is designed to ensure that nothing happens.

This chapter is the first of a three-part exploration of power issues. In this chapter, we examine historical definitions of power and their effects on workers and organizations. Two differing frames of power are examined to set the stage for a new era: dominator and partnership. In the next chapter, we use the *power river* as a metaphor to explore the journey from dominator to partnership forms of power and, in the process, share our research on the evolution of power prototypes. The new forms of power offer frameworks for socially constructing different power relationships—ones that engender competence, sharing of expertise, and partnership practices. Rather than seeing power as a zero-sum game and the customer as self with winners and losers, we challenge traditional views of power relationships and discourage Machiavellian manipulation and unjust exploitation of others' ideas. The third chapter explores responding locally and globally to issues of poverty and race and challenges existing paradigms that have institutionalized power practices that benefit some while systematically excluding others.

PERSONAL POWER WITHIN OUR FAMILY OF ORIGIN

The *family metaphor* is instructive in understanding the shifts in power that are natural in the maturation of a human system. Suitable for our earliest relationships between two sets of actors—parents/guardians and their children—this analogy fails to take into account an adult view of power *through* shared expertise and action, or power *beyond* hierarchy and dependence. Our families of origin, however, are the first places we learn about power relations and thus are instructive to us. Many times we recreate family dynamics in other relationships, often ones that are unhealthy.

The family provides a way of defining relationships along a continuum of behaviors that psychologists label *from dysfunctional to functional*. Dysfunctional behaviors limit personal power, maintain helplessness, and have a negative impact on agency or our ability to act in adult ways that are efficacious. In families, we experience a continuum of power relationships, from dependency to independency, control to freedom, punishment to discipline, withdrawal to engagement, and judgment to acceptance. These variations shape how we think later about the use of personal power within other contexts and relationships. The more opportunities we have to access power resources such as knowledge and expertise, participation in decision making, and support, the greater potential we have for making an impact.

We might conclude that our earliest relationships influence relationships later with colleagues and authority figures. They provide us with our earliest access to power resources such as education and cultural enrichment. When we are born, we are totally dependent on our caregivers to nurture and support us; they have complete power *over* our very survival. As we mature, presumably our families assist us in developing personal skills and competencies to exercise choices beyond physical survival, and power *over* is transformed to power *to* develop into young adults. Our maturity, within certain norms, expectations, and boundaries, mirrors family beliefs and values and reflects our capacity to put our resources to work and gain the confidence of others to exercise choice. If we are viewed as responsible and trustworthy, we might be granted more autonomy, or freedom, within family norms and expectations.

There is no doubt that our guardians have the legal authority to make decisions presumed in our best interest, not theirs. Decisions that are discharged within a reasonable "ethic of care" (Noddings, 1993) signal a gradual shift from dependence to independence. As our internal drives for autonomy and independence grow, we naturally find that we are becoming more self-reliant and capable.

Our freedom to respond and grow is so basic to our survival that family structures that limit freedom to create healthy interdependencies are called dysfunctional. Dysfunctional practices in families thwart autonomy and invite powerlessness. This powerlessness, often masked by symptoms of helplessness, withdrawal, violence, anger, and even depression, can severely limit healthy responses in present and future relationships. Referred to as *learned helplessness, this* phenomenon limits confidence and optimism for attaining healthy, interdependent, adult relationships.

Interdependent relationships occur only where there are mature power exchanges. As children, our dependency on caregivers is necessary for our survival. As we gain skills to be independent, essential for the next set of power exchanges, we develop the readiness essential for interdependent relationships. Interdependency, then, is built over time and evolves in the presence of shared norms of reciprocity. Our capacity for being contributing members in a relationship or a community is contingent upon many factors, the least of which is our access to power resources that provide us with the readiness to engage in these relationships. Reciprocal power relations, then, require accepting mutual responsibility and accountability for achieving shared goals beyond *self-interest.* Equal access to power resources, such as information, knowledge, and expertise, levels the playing fields for increased participation and involvement (Toffler, 1990). Sharing power in our families engages us in a process where we might begin to acknowledge three things: (1) our dependency on others, (2) our simultaneous need to learn how to act independently to develop the readiness for interdependence, and (3) our recognition of how interdependence helps us achieve things greater than we could accomplish alone.

Although our families of origin shed some insights into our earliest experiences with power, our families also mirror the subcultures we are a part of and the structures of our time. As adults, we have many choices about how to expand our personal power bases to include interdependent relationships. As we mature, it is unnatural to have adult (boss) and child (worker) relationships that foster unhealthy dependencies. This type of organization metaphor seems to reduce the possibilities for growth and development among mature people working together. It is time to rethink this metaphor for organizations and use another one.

To make changes in our power relationships within organizations today, we suggest that members (1) understand traditions of power, (2) examine new frameworks of power, (3) share stories about power to seek hidden meanings about their complicity in maintaining present power relationships that engender unhealthy dependencies, and (4) move beyond family metaphors to systems of interdependent relationships among people.

MOVING BEYOND THE FAMILY METAPHOR

Early definitions of power failed to recognize our connections within systems of interdependent relationships. Unless we confront issues of normative power snared in bureaucratic and hierarchical power traps, our relationships will continue to reinforce norms of isolation and alienation, with boss-over-child-like relationships. Modern power arrangements exist to exert power *over* resources and limit access to information in schools, districts, state departments of education, educational agencies, and universities. Without access to information, our natural responses to act in meaningful and interdependent ways are discouraged.

The historical focus on *control over people and resources* suggests that natural responses for connections were replaced with unnatural systems of work, which either maintained silence or compliance within norms of fear, isolation, and dependence. These organizational prisons engendered powerlessness and alienation and thwarted learning. We see the effects of institutionalized helplessness as rising depression rates among our youth across all socioeconomic levels and increased acts of violence at all levels of society. The desire for human connections, handicapped by a marketplace mentality of social Darwinism (i.e., survival of the fittest), has led some of us to ask fundamentally different questions about existing power relationships—questions about how we engage in actions to promote facilitative and integrative power relationships that liberate the human spirit rather than attempting to control it (Nemerowicz and Rosi, 1997); questions about how we read signs of optimism for our society; and, finally, questions about how alternative models and frameworks for power beyond utopian dreams can enable us to create visions for better futures for all, rather than for a select few. Confronting *bureaucratic, dominator power* structures is a vigorous journey that should not be taken by the fainthearted. Rather, a deep spirit of resiliency and a thick-skinned determination are required for leading you to new places.

Taking on power is part of a trilogy. Power beliefs and practices reflect cultural norms visible in our structures (Bennett and Harris, 1997). Thus, power, culture, and structure become mutually reinforcing concepts. Changes in power relationships often fail because there is scant recognition of how these three areas are intertwined. To effect changes in power relationships, the deeper meanings about power relationships must be unlocked, and the underlying structures within present social, historical, political, and economic patterns must be examined. To confront issues of power requires coming face-to-face with orthodoxy and tradition. Transforming power relationships is nothing short of rejecting historical and traditional practices of power *over* and adopting systems of power *with/for/ through.* We can begin this by countering issues of power that are rooted in our organizational traditions.

HISTORICAL AND TRADITIONAL DEFINITIONS OF POWER

Past definitions of power are familiar to us and need little explanation. Hence, this section of the chapter lays the groundwork for why the bureaucratic traditions of power are counterproductive to a learning society. Prophetically, Weber envisioned bureaucratic power structures as *iron cages* that limit freedom and autonomy of action, but he saw no alternatives to these iron cages as we entered the industrial age (DiMaggio and Powell, 1983). Weber did not envision the professional and knowledge society looming on the horizon of the twenty-first century. Now, with revolutions in communication systems, increased globalization, and access to information, the momentum that is needed if we are to redefine traditional power relationships within our society appears to be here.

Reward systems that continue to foster compliance and guarantee the status quo work against creativity and innovation. Coercive tactics that instill fear and limit action thwart learning and adaptation. More integrative and interdependent forms of power require different leadership styles, styles that are facilitative and participatory and that acknowledge personal authority. Work cultures of fear, with psychological tactics that coerce others into compliance, work against interdependence and are increasingly viewed as archaic ways of being.

Briefly, we turn to Dunlap and Goldman (1991), who claim that writers about Western educational organizations use ideas from men such as Weber to explain how power operates in educational institutions. Authority and maintaining domination translate into formalized roles and rules predicated on structures and hierarchy and ascribed to the institutional norms within these power structures. Until recently, a leader's ethics, capacity for sharing power, and ability for building communities of action appear to be scarcely addressed in the organization literature. Recent frustrations with limited "participatory" decision-making processes, gross and inequitable access to resources, and resistance to organizational change have encouraged organizational theorists to question the viability of bureaucratic power structures today. The *we* against *them* set of power arrangements limits change and development over time and prevents organizational learning and adaptation.

Traditional definitions of power gave use to such theories as Antonio Gramsci's (1971) theory of *hegemony*. This concept of reality refers to how certain ways of life and thought dominate one concept of reality that becomes diffused throughout a society's economic and political institutions.

These dominant ideas are propagated through a privileged access to the primary ideological institutions of the society such as religion, culture, education, communication, and media. This involves "the ability to define the parameters of legitimate discussion and debate over alternative beliefs, values, and worldviews" (Sallach, 1974, 44).

Traditional definitions of power leave little hope for organizations to promote organizationwide learning. Power within norms of collegiality and collaboration requires a different type of power relationship from power *over.* Open communication, leadership around *big* issues, sharing information, relinquishing control over power resources, and inviting more participation and involvement from others promote personal agency and efficacy. Instead of one dominant cultural perspective, other perspectives are openly acknowledged and invited into the debate and exchange of ideas.

Next, we present two diametrically opposed perspectives of organizational power that are juxtaposed to illustrate the choices we can make regarding our future work together in organizations. The first form of power maintains bureaucratic and structural perspectives. The second acknowledges and builds power relationships from poststructural, postmodern, and social constructivist perspectives. Following these two perspectives, a framework of dominator and partnership power is compared and contrasted. We personally sought to understand our own experiences with power that often appeared invisible within these perspectives and frameworks.

TWO PERSPECTIVES ON ORGANIZATIONAL POWER

Bureaucratic and Structural Perspectives

Bureaucratic models are built, in part, on the epistemology of structuralism placed within the period of modernity. Structuralism and modernity are equated with a top-down, hierarchical worldview (Piaget, 1970), in which a particular institution and persons determine programs, services, and policies for the good of the whole. These structures are created by a few for the good of many. It is the responsibility of all players in this paradigm to maintain the highest governance over controlling forces in the system to attain stated goals (Parsons, 1966). The structuralist orientation in schools and government for the last century determines what federal policies and programs will be implemented nationwide and leaves the states and schools responsible for meeting the federal requirements. History has shown that structuralism is no longer a healthy approach to school governance or reform, as suggested by previously failed educational systems and reform movements (Sarason, 1996). The dependence on outside experts fails to build the capacity of learning in local educational leaders. Instead, educators prepare themselves for the next flurry of mandates and hunker down to resist substantive changes, because everyone knows there will be a new wave of changes with the next group elected to office. Passive resistance and the appearance of compliance become the norms in many workplaces.

A bureaucratic approach to program development and school operations is now recognized by many as obsolete. Workers and students are treated like machines, responsible for attaining high achievement scores to make the school and the district "look good" (Sarason, 1996). An emphasis on government policies rather than on healthy learning environments fosters competition instead of stimulating cooperation and collaboration. Lacking a systems perspective, reform efforts focus on isolated parts of a system.

The time has come to embrace a new paradigm for schooling, one that releases the volume of centralized decision making from the federal and state government to educators with legitimate and accountable authority to respond to the clients they serve to create better learning opportunities. When we think of schools as living organisms, shaped by those who work and learn in them, we realize that freeing people to respond to the conditions they face equips them with agency and action.

Poststructuralism, Postmodern, and Social Constructivist Perspectives

The historical era in which social constructivism rests moves poststructuralism away from the order and hierarchy of structuralism. Rather than accepting the conditions of an objective, value-free reality, postmodern analysts raise new questions and give new meanings to power relationships. They seek to *disturb* our understanding of knowledge and existence (Foucault, 1984) and open new doors for designing different, socially constructed programs and services. This approach attempts to help us better understand current practices in ways that move *beyond* the prison walls of modernism and bureaucratic power definitions. A postmodern lens turns schools upside down and asks risky questions to explore avenues that were heretofore forbidden.

The postmodern/poststructural condition is reflected by ambiguity and ambivalence, rather than continuity (Sarup, 1993); and chaos and difference are descriptive of the times (Derrida, 1976; Hargraves, 1994). There is no longer a universal knowledge for all humans based on reason, because there is no reason, only reasons. Boundaries of knowledge and truth become blurred as multiple ways of creating meaning take shape (Sarup, 1993). Personal narratives of conscious experience replace scientific proof or legitimizing knowledge. Metaphor becomes the prevailing mechanism for sharing meaning because it is complex and connotes nonlinear relationships.

For schools, the philosophy most associated with the postmodern/poststructural condition is the social constructivist paradigm, which places value on the shared human experience as the site of meaning making. There is no longer a belief in an outside authority who knows what is best for all teachers and students in all schools. Rather, the socially constructed reality of the organization is the center of truth. Decisions by members within the organization make sense because of their experiences and sharing of various perspectives within and across traditional hierarchical boundaries.

Social constructivism redefines the ways in which people interact and make decisions. It assumes that structures, programs, policies, roles, and relationships are given meaning together by all members in reference to the multiple variables that exist (Lincoln, 1990). Within this framework, educational reform is shaped collaboratively by schools, communities, states, local governments, and businesses (stakeholders). Through collaboration and collegiality, the stakeholders determine their own needs and the best means to attain them. At the heart of social constructivism is an emphasis on the whole of systems thinking. This emphasis raises the potential for all stakeholders to move toward wholeness, leaving behind the segmentation and the isolation of a fragmented bureaucratic model.

Systems proponents argue for a shift from the outdated worldview of scientific rationalism, bureaucracy, and machine metaphors to social constructivism, integrated thinking, and community metaphors. Capra (1994) summarizes this shift as "a social paradigm [that is embodied by] a constellation of concepts, values, perceptions, and practices shared by a community, which form a particular vision of reality that is the basis of the way a community organizes itself" (335). He goes on to point out that the receding social paradigm that dominated our worldview for centuries—valuing humans as machines, the universe as objective and mechanical, and competition as the way to promote growth—is outdated.

The paradigm shift now taking place is built on a philosophical foundation of sharing that fosters cyclical relationships. Capra summarizes this movement as emergent and holistic, stating that it "recognizes the fundamental interdependence of all phenomena and the embeddedness of individuals and societies in the cyclical process with nature" (355).

For schools, as well as other social institutions, this paradigm shift represents fundamentally different ways of relating and doing business. No longer are hierarchy and domination the prevailing structures. Rather, partnerships and shared decision making are the frame or action within democratic principles. Because of the shift in role relationships, along with inter- and intra-organizational power, a key influence of organizational decisions is redefined. Within the bureaucratic structural model, power is seen as *power over:* power in the hands of a few over the masses. With the elimination of hierarchies in some cases and the extreme reduction of hierarchies in others, *power over* loses its base. In its place emerges an orientation of *power with, power for,* and *power through;* power becomes an energy source rather than a corrupting force. *Power over* creates a forced dichotomy between those who have it and those who do not, those who own it and those who do not. *Power with/for/through* is viewed as energy that embraces a holistic orientation, building upon the existing natural relationships that nurture and enhance the organization and its stakeholders. It is an antidote to powerlessness and our disconnection with others; it promotes integration, interdependence, strong relationships, and linking.

It is little wonder that philosophers and scholars like Gramsci (1971), Freire (1973), Apple (1982), and Hooks (1995) speak of institutionalized hegemonic practices in modern organizational structures and domination as *isms* (e.g., racism, classism, and genderism). Our challenge is to confront these practices that are based on domination and embrace alternative ways of being, acting, and knowing. We found a possible prototype for adoption in Riane Eisler's (1987) *dominator-partnership model of cultural power.* Her model, consisting of two social and cultural paradigms, positions power within a historical dialectic of opposing ideologies, with implications for economic and political policies and practices. These two frames of dominator and partnership power open up the space for a dialogue of possibility; one that exposes the dominator ideology for its underlying values and introduces partnership power for its systems and integrative power perspectives.

TWO FRAMES OF POWER: DOMINATOR AND PARTNERSHIP

In our work with schools and districts, we have observed that the work culture conditions and change processes vary greatly across and within institutions. Often, the partnerships and the empowerment granted to produce new products and services evolve into power struggles to control personal and political agendas. This is due in part to the fact that power is granted and, as such, can be easily taken back at any time in the process. These surprising twists in partnership efforts often raise fundamental questions about the rhetoric of change and the potential that exists for transforming educational institutions. In reconstructing our own experiences and observations, we have come to appreciate more than ever before that change is seldom linear and that rarely does it occur according to the models we create. More often, change is weighted down with strongholds of power to control change efforts rather than to meet customers' needs, which results in rather unhealthy social systems and work environments.

Eisler's (1987) theory of dominator and partnership societies evolved over 30 years from her work as an historical anthropologist, which led to her major writing, *The Chalice and the Blade.* Findings from her historical research studies of cultural patterns and fundamental values held by cultures over the last 6000 years raise fundamental questions for us concerning our simplistic assumptions about change in education today. We propose Eisler's theory of power as an alternative to oversimplifying our situations in our current attempts to understand our history.

On one hand, Eisler (1987) sets forth a picture of *partnership cultures* (actualization power), which are characterized by patterns of linking (rather than ranking), cooperation, nurturance, participation, sharing, spirituality, the creative arts, and a balance of male and female roles. *Dominator cultures* (domination power), on the other hand, are characterized by the dominance of one sex over the other (in most countries, this is male dominance over females); institutionalized hierarchy and ranking of one role group over another; in-group versus out-group thinking; acquired wealth and resources, along with poverty; and institutionalized violence. Eisler's studies reveal that partnership societies thrived before the dawn of civilization, and only in the last 4000 to 3000 years of history have we witnessed an increased use of dominance as a way of life among nations throughout the world. And so it seems that the top-down organizational structures that we know today were honed only over the last 100 years but have firm roots in the ancient traditions of dominance.

This historical perspective, according to Eisler (1993, 1995), projects that conditions were ripe at the end of the twentieth century for there to be a reversal of dominator cultural patterns in favor of partnerships, with Norway and Sweden leading the way and being among the best examples. Many of the partnership's central features are on the increase worldwide, even though forms of domination are surfacing in new and sometimes terrorizing ways.

Dominator Cultures

The role of domination between nature and man finds its roots in the Enlightenment era, when the relationship between nature and humans became separated.

No longer were humans viewed as a part of nature. Philosophers and scientists such as Francis Bacon, Rene Descartes, and Isaac Newton argued that the universe was an objective, separate reality to be studied and explained by humans (Merchant, 1994). This belief in human power over nature became the prevailing paradigm, which continued into the industrial era and eventually became the foundation for bureaucracies and scientific rationalism or dominator power.

Consider the characteristics of dominator cultures that follow, where domination power guides organizational change (*identified by Eisler):

One sex over another*	Rigid boundaries
Ranking*	In-group and out-group thinking
Institutionalized hierarchy*	Binary thinking
Institutionalized violence*	Acquired wealth and resources

Within this view, only *some* will have the power to direct and affect change efforts, and these directions commonly are self-serving for persons in leadership positions. Growth is controlled within the allowable limits of the traditions that maintain existing power bases; any movement away from the centers of power is not tolerated. Without a shift in philosophical orientations, the dominator model still prevails in our social, political, and economic challenges, establishing programs that merely pacify, temporarily, structural issues, for they never address the deeper cultural, structural, and power relationships.

Nothing changes fundamentally within the dominator-oriented organization. The role of power in society remains a dialectic between boss over worker, politician over school employees, those who have over those who do not, and humans over nature. Schools engage in reform efforts to develop new programs to create an image of change for the *viewing public,* but they are faced with the continuous task of meeting political agendas. Statistical data collection remains the norm for assessment; decisions are made by a few; there exists a strong emphasis on self; and a fear of risk taking permeates the work culture. Control over resources creates competition, while coercion and co-optation manipulate compliance. Change within a dominator model turns into a political play using the rhetoric of change rather than a different language to redesign relationships, programs, and services for new outcomes. Nothing substantive happens that is new or alters the deep structures of domination.

Partnership Cultures

Power within the partnership model becomes *power with* and *power through* as role groups and relationships are redefined. Cooperation replaces coercion and co-optation as more and more persons become involved in the decisions of the organization. Concepts and uses of power shift from the Western view of domination to the Eastern focus of internal strength and linking with others. As such, each member understands internal power sources, energy is created as a collective whole and power becomes the energy for engaging in change. Further, people build upon one another's ideas as *power with* becomes *power through* synergistic and collective action.

The partnership model has been absent from many school reform initiatives. Schools are now faced with challenges for which they are ill prepared, such as at-risk populations that have become social, political, and economic problems. Unfortunately, schools are the social institution singled out by government and business to *clean up the mess.* If this is to happen, we need to address many questions that lay claim to fundamentally different models of operating, ones that link with systems and partnership paradigms so that schools can link naturally with other social agencies. No longer is it feasible to *rescue* victims of bureaucratic and dominator power structures, for the numbers are growing. We must go to the source of the problem and redefine power as a fountainhead for linking across our human connections. Recognizing that we have a system that was set up for winners and losers, which both victimizes and then revictimizes out-groups through labels (e.g., *at risk*), is critical for reshaping educational organizations.

Consider the alternative features of partnership cultures where actualization power guides growth and change (*identified by Eisler):

Linking*	Nurturance*
Participation*	Cooperation*
Spirituality*	Permeable boundaries
Balance among sex roles*	Systems thinking
Creative arts*	Involvement

The initial challenge for educators, then, is to recognize and understand the deeper cultural and structural meanings of language (e.g., labels such as *at risk*) for these connote deeper structural power agendas. Limerick and Cunnington (1993) propose that in the new organization, leaders will use action learning as a strategy to examine existing beliefs and invent new modes of thinking during periods of organizational change. Further, these authors maintain that today's workforce is primarily concerned with empowerment and meaningful work. Therefore, it seems more critical than ever that, before educational leaders attempt to *empower* workers, they help them *understand* the power, structural, and cultural assumptions that are embedded in present organizational practices. New skills and competencies will be required if we are to alter the ways we relate to one another.

Within new definitions of power and possible frameworks are different epistemologies and worldviews. New definitions of power counter values of exclusion, hierarchical relationships, and nonparticipation in schools and develop values that foster inclusion, collegial relationships, and participation. Through dialogue, educators can begin to build a new language that is both inclusive and supportive of multiple ways of knowing, being, and valuing (Cherryholmes, 1988; Senge, 1990). This language can be representative of multiple perspectives of power and can challenge the deeper cultural assumptions of domination and control of one group over another (Eisler, 1995).

CONCLUSIONS

There are four areas we encourage educators and the public to examine. First, the local, state, and national political cultures too often drive change through external directives rather than by looking for ways to foster internal growth and development. Second, we need leaders with ethical perspectives who promote tenets of emergent leadership and engender trust among people to begin the work of transforming power relationships. Together with members, they must examine what it will take to alter structural and cultural perspectives, address hegemonic power strongholds, and develop competencies and skills to transition to new systems. Third, a better understanding of micropolitical behavior is needed by leaders to minimize self-serving spheres of influence. Fourth, the time is ripe for transcending the rational constructions of bureaucratic and dominator models of power and challenging the political cultures and micropolitical practices that hold us captive. Our society hungers for more democratic and open systems of work around principles of shared power and democratic ideals. Emergent leadership and partnership power shifts the *me* orientation to a *we* philosophy, replacing the machine metaphor with a human, organic metaphor.

The quietest revolution in organizations today may be occurring within power relationships. *Empowerment* under a zero-sum power game with winners and losers is a tragic loss of human potential. Only the *privileged* can win at this game; losers are more often the norm. People are expendable in this power game. We have choices!

7

The Power River

This chapter introduces the *power river* as a metaphor for power. The river is a means for examining traditional views of bureaucratic and dominator power to adopt learning, partnership cultures. As schools and districts consider moving to quality work cultures, there are choices to be made about the *intended purposes* of power arrangements and relationships. Will these choices continue the power dichotomy of haves over have-nots, males over females, in-groups over out-groups, and the privileged over the less privileged? Or, will power and new work designs advance the success and satisfaction of all constituents under a broader vision of change? These questions and others are central to the debate over choices that lie ahead of us.

SCHOOLS AS PARTNERSHIP CULTURES

Choices of dominator or partnership perspectives, presented in the previous chapter, pose fundamentally different results for organizations. The dominator culture seeks to change people through external directives and uses statistical tools exclusively to measure change, usually in the form of standardized test scores. Often, politicians use fear to induce changes and are quick to engage in punishment and reward systems rather than professional development for growth purposes. Ranking schools with classifications, such as *failed* schools, or placing schools on *alert* status for possible state takeover uses schools as the political battleground to address societal ills.

The partnership culture shifts the *me* orientation to a *we* focus of broader community involvement. Changes are facilitated and stimulated daily through a belief in continuous improvement and the engagement of all constituents. Rather than foisting blame only on educators in the system, the schooling vision emphasizes success for life for students and includes the community in deciding how best to achieve this. Working together on how to address complex issues shifts accountability from educators to the wider community.

Historically, there exists a social outcry for a different way of life. Civil rights leaders call for equality among races; feminists demand greater gender equity; and policy analysts encourage schools to move beyond political rhetoric to embrace substantive changes. There is much work still to be done if we want to move to a learning society. The only option for schools that retain dominator practices is to increase their controls over people and ensure stagnation and decline.

Partnership power, in contrast, requires a fundamental mental shift from bureaucratic and dominator practices to learning and partnership values within systems thinking and social constructivist beliefs. Here, balance between personal and organizational power is viewed as transcending bureaucratic boundaries of dominator control to become transformative and facilitative power (Dunlap and Goldman, 1991; Wartenberg, 1990). Partnerships by their nature use the unique skills and talents of all individuals to achieve collective and organizational results; they engage others in making a commitment beyond self-interest to communal, mutual interests valued by all members.

Our interest in partnership power grew out of a shared experience we viewed as *failed partnership,* which is an oxymoron. We grappled with how to assist others with what we had learned. We devised a metaphor to situate people in organizations on their journeys to partnership power. Power, as an energy source, needs to reflect movement, potential sources of new energy, and places where power gets stuck. More often than not, we learned how to navigate around restrictive power places to connect with broader sources of power. The *power river* shows how various agencies and organizations might plan their journeys together as they shift from dominator to partnership forms of power. We cannot begin our journeys to partnership power unless we are willing to reinvent our roles and relationships with one another.

THE POWER RIVER

The *power river* (Figure 7.1) illustrates how present power relationships might appear under bureaucratic and dominator power practices. The first half of the river illustrates power as confined and controlled by a few people. The source of power represents *power over* resources and opportunities; it is a place where many members feel powerless to affect change. Oxbow lakes cut them off from the resources and opportunities found in the river. Often this is due to power resources that are withheld from people. As the bureaucratic organization attempts to move downriver, there are fresh ideas, symbolized by tributaries, to renew the river and bring energy. Tributaries depict how multiple energy sources unite forces to make the river a formidable force that is difficult to turn back.

As organizations attempt to adopt more involvement practices, the movement from power over to *power to,* within an optimistic view of a develop-

Figure 7.1 The power river.

mental journey, requires that *growth of worker skills be fostered to solicit their input.* Frequently, however, input from workers is devalued. Stories told by select teachers of the year from several of the 67 counties in Florida illustrate how involvement can become a waste of time for teachers and reflect cosmetic input. One such story is about a year's work by a committee of teachers who examined different curricula options. During the year, the committee gathered research, visited other school systems, and collected data on student outcomes regarding different approaches used in their school and others. At the end of the year, the committee made several recommendations to the principal. All of these suggestions were abruptly dismissed as causing too much work for the administrators. In one brief meeting, the work of an entire year was dismissed with a terse *No.* Rather than entertaining options, seeking additional information, or devising a feasible plan to pilot the recommendations, nothing came to fruition. The teachers, willing to do the work, soon became disillusioned with any future involvement on school committees. The administrators did not want to deal with any changes. This story is not about administrators pushing teachers to make changes, but about how people were involved in meaningless work because nothing happened. This was a culture where no action was taken on teacher work group recommendations.

Power relationships, under present bureaucratic and dominator power arrangements, may give an outer appearance of *relinquishing control* by soliciting input from teachers, but present practices in some schools tell a different story. As another teacher of the year relates,

> We get talked down to something terrible. If you have the nerve to speak out, to have a suggestion, to think of a better way, or think you might have something to add, and it does not go along with what is being pushed, then you either need to be re-educated, or ignored. And, if you keep opening your mouth, you are put down. And that is it—there is no room for debate!

This story and others like it suggest that if schools are aspiring to become learning and partnership places, they might tell different stories about how a caring, compassionate, and respectful leader helped them come to points of agreement. If educators are truly interested in moving toward learning and partnership practices, then dialogue concerning differences of opinion is foundational to listening to alternative perspectives. This requires a mental shift in the energy of the river to move toward partnership practices.

Swift currents, with drops in elevation, suggest that profound changes in power arrangements will be under way. Power now becomes transformative, as *power with* and *power through* are shared among members within the organization. Personal power expands organizationally as work is done collaboratively to solve organizationwide problems. New work processes support the intent of shared decision making and give individuals the internal motivation to commit to ongoing, continuous improvement. *Power through* frees people to make decisions within agreed-upon visions of mutual, community goals. Members' issues and concerns move beyond self-interest to broad-based community interests. Instead of blaming people as within dominator systems, new processes free people from unnecessary restraints. Trust, communication, and vision are the invisible currents that propel the river to the sea.

Our interest in power relationships and the metaphor of power as a river frame power relationships to build organizational capacities for people to act using the natural energy they possess to solve complex problems. This requires high levels of personal mastery (Senge, 1990) and organizational readiness to work collaboratively. As researchers, we were interested in how educators might describe present power arrangements in schools. We wanted a better understanding of teachers' perspectives about power. We found that the power river could be descriptive of various perspectives of partnership and dominator values. Our goal was to illuminate these perspectives so that educators might begin their journeys downriver to engage in substantive changes in institutional power practices. To move toward partnership power requires learning about where the whirlpools and eddies are that have kept us stuck or mired on sandbars. Two studies' findings are shared now to raise consciousness for actions to alter power arrangements in schools. The first study began as a pilot to understand the phenomenological aspects of power. These descriptive findings formed the basis for several surveys to construct a dimensional model of power (Acker-Hocevar, Bauch, and Berman, 1997; Acker-Hocevar and Bauch, 1998).

STUDIES OF TEACHERS' PERCEPTIONS OF POWER ARRANGEMENTS

The *first* study sought to gain an understanding of teachers' views about power through analyzing responses to nine items in an open-ended questionnaire. Approximately 100 teachers in several master's-level classes in educational administration completed the questionnaires. Findings reported female and male perceptions around common themes and patterns for each question (Acker-Hocevar, Touchton, and Zenz, 1995). Elementary-, middle-, and high-school teachers from their early 20s to late 50s, with teaching experience of from three to nine years, participated in the study in 1995. Respondents were 95 percent European American, with only a few Hispanic and African American teachers. Approximately two-thirds of the respondents were females and one-third were males (actually representing more males than typically associated with the 80 percent female and 20 percent male overall ratio in schools). Focus groups concurred with results, allowing us to trust the findings. The themes present gender perspectives about power relationships. Participants agreed that if results were interpreted holistically, both females and males could benefit from an integrated model of power. As you read, you can make your own linkages and conclusions. We suggest some conclusions at the end of the first study and at the end of the chapter.

The *first question* asked educators to *describe an empowered educator.* Females saw empowerment from decision-making structures that allowed them freedom and autonomy to make decisions. These female respondents defined decisions as *voice* and *direct involvement* in the decision-making processes that resulted in *implementation* of decisions. Females expressed that an empowered educator had authority to make decisions but needed administrative support to carry them out. Females elaborated that an empowered educator was able to use *good* communication skills, expertise, and influence to impact decision-making processes. Males described empowerment as knowledge of trends and changes in society with *freedom from* administrators to make changes. They wanted the capability to accomplish their work with minimal supervision to achieve educational outcomes.

The *second question* asked *how responsibility related to power.* Females saw responsibility directly relating to their willingness to assume more of it. The more responsibility they accepted, the more power they had. Therefore, power was a reciprocal process with acceptance of responsibility resulting in more power. Males, too, viewed responsibility and power as one and the same. Power was embedded in responsibility and responsibility in power. Males assumed that they had freedom to take on more responsibility and thus more power. Males and females equated responsibility to hierarchical power in regard to positional authority.

The *third question* asked educators to *describe accountability within the context of power.* Females and males described it as personal and organizational. Personal accountability for females had a moral aspect to it with obligations toward one another for acting in ethical ways. From an organizational perspective, females felt the acceptance of accountability implied the *granting of* more power to members within the organization. Within present reform contexts, however, many females felt administrators were fearful of risk taking due to stricter accountability measures under reform. Females viewed accountability as results achieved and meeting the needs of students. Some women expressed a pervasive sense of accountability for nearly everything.

Males defined accountability within the context of organizational practices that governed their behavior. Accountability was connected to laws, efficiency, and positions. They saw accountability as answering to those above them, not necessarily those below. They, too, equated accountability to an overall perspective of achieving results for improved student outcomes.

The *fourth question* asked educators to *describe a powerful educator.* No other question had such a clear distinction between male and female respondents. Although females *and* males mentioned that a powerful educator garnered respect, males mentioned this far more often than females. Males described respect as a working knowledge of the system and gaining influence within the system, while females viewed respect from a relational perspective of effective interpersonal skills such as being a *good listener, meeting the needs of others,* and *exuding confidence.* Males perceived respect and power as influence, while women perceived it as knowledge and effective communication skills.

Specifically, females defined a powerful educator as one who is knowledgeable, is educated, and has expertise. They viewed a powerful educator as one who earns respect through others by listening and meeting their needs; they felt that a powerful educator had connections to a greater whole and was interested in motivating others. Finally, females saw a powerful educator as fearless and heroic—a person who took risks. Males, in contrast, described a powerful educator as free—one who engendered respect, influenced others, knew how to operate within the system, shaped changes, cut through bureaucratic red tape, associated with the *right* people, and brought about changes. They viewed leadership as the leader's ability or charisma to influence others.

The *fifth question* asked educators to *describe power in their contexts and present positions.* Females saw power as professional power influencing changes in their classrooms through their teaching, choosing of curriculum, and selection of materials. They defined power as status in relation to the number of committees a teacher served on and their formal leadership positions in the school, such as team leader. About a quarter of the women defined power within the context of collegiality and shared decision-making practices. Males were in strong agreement with females on this question but did not mention power in relation to collegiality and shared decision making. In fact, males tended to see teachers as possessing little power due to their low status. Females and males, however, related power in terms of their accomplishments in their classrooms as a way to exercise greater influence.

The *sixth question* asked about *beliefs of power that existed in current educational practices.* Females saw beliefs as changing because of current reforms, particularly in regard to decision-making structures, shared power, and the connections of decisions to the overall vision of their schools. Males saw power as positional and in their associations with others. They did not mention seeing changes in power beliefs. Females and males overwhelmingly saw beliefs about power in relation to organizational positions held in schools.

The *seventh question* asked educators to *describe the relationship between power and resources.* Females stated that power was access to resources and discussed resources in terms of control, rewards, and remuneration. They viewed resources as emerging, such as technology, worker information, and knowledge. Interestingly, males assumed they had resources and discussed resource utilization as providing even greater opportunities for influence.

The *eighth* and *ninth questions* asked educators *how information was disseminated in their work/school setting* and *who currently held power in their work setting.* All respondents reported administrative control through written and oral correspondence. Administrators held the keys to power through communication and change agendas.

Overall conclusions about power perceptions suggest subtle differences in power relationships for males and females. Many of the differences were slight with notable similarities. Primarily, power was defined within present structures that reinforced hierarchical roles and relationships, which reinscribed gender perspectives of subordination and dominance. Teachers saw their spheres of influence mainly within the classrooms and with other colleagues. There were also differences. Females discussed *access* and *being allowed* to possess more power. They identified *moral aspects of accountability* and *empowering others.* Males tended to focus on empowerment as *freedom from* and *assumed utilization* of resources to take on more responsibility and thus gain more power. They viewed power and accountability within *hierarchical relationships;* although females viewed power within positions of hierarchy, too, females stressed connections within the system, while males emphasized associating with the *right* people to attain greater status.

The findings suggest how *gendered processes* in organizations are reinforced. Acker (1992) concludes that implicit and explicit structural and cultural properties continue to sustain acts of domination and subordination of males over females, either "concretely or symbolically" (463). She claims that power and gender are linked to structural and cultural properties that comprise different forms of participation at work and in many other locations and relationships in society. These gendered processes maintain differences through a cognitive set of principles reinforced as gendered ways of being and acting (i.e., attitudes and behaviors), whereby gender is seen as a "pervasive symbol of power" (463). Gendered ways of knowing influence how men and women understand, gain access to, and use different forms of power resources (Belenky, Clinchy, Goldberger, and Tarule, 1986; Gilligan, 1982; Shakeshaft, 1986). Rusch and Marshall (1997) believe that these gender constructions are *filters* that limit and restrain our ability to create what we want. They suggest that these filters can also silence and deny differences through minimizing the effects of gender in organizations.

One of the gender filters may be female availability and use of economic and political power resources in society and in organizations generally. Kanter (1977) identified this access to power resources as the acquisition of support, information, and supplies. She concluded that many women, particularly midlevel managers, lacked this access to power resources and were subsequently unable to act quickly enough when organization conditions required swift responses.

Until recently, few studies have examined how successful females negotiate political issues surrounding gender in education. Assuming Acker's (1992) assertion is correct and there are *gendered processes* in organizations, then the question of how males and females access circuits of power needs examination. Brunner (1993) describes this process in a community where a female is a successful superintendent. In her study, women define power as the ability to get things done through consensus, inclusion, and collaboration. The superintendent viewed power as residing in interaction with others. Males, in contrast, in Brunner's study, define power as getting into positions of influence and using their positions to exert authority over others. They view power as taking on more responsibility and using information and knowledge to convince others of their perspectives. Brunner reported that the superintendent in the study was "culturally bilingual" (198) in her understanding of male and female circuits of power (also see Clegg, 1989). Brunner concluded that successful women in education "are able to speak the language of those in the male circuit of power while remaining feminine" (198).

Tannen (1995) minimized the difference between females and males in her studies of gendered communication styles. She argued that both genders use a different language to describe a similar phenomenon of power, whether it is referred to as collegiality or status. The different language relates to how power relationships were initiated. She illustrated how women established meaningful bonds in relationships they called *connections,* while men referred to these same associations through *status.* Connections for females were developed through *cooperation,* while males maintained relationships through *clout* or exerting influence or authority over others.

Generally, females and males employ different political strategies to attain influence within the same systems. We might assume that the language of power is constitutive of gender differences and similarities. Given an opportunity, females might be more likely to negotiate collegial power relationships, whereas males might use authority to establish dominance. Power or empowerment could be viewed as relationship- and status-related in different contexts. The language of females suggests that domination and control are used over them (e.g., *access to, allowed, afforded*), while males assume they have control (e.g., *use, freedom to, resourceful,* and *exerting influence*).

JOURNEYING DOWNRIVER

Earlier in the chapter we presented the *power river* for seeing how systems represent different perspectives of power. Wheatley and Kellner-Rogers (1996) assert that we choose to use images to communicate our experiences because they "connect what we see" (12) in nonlinear, complex, unpredictable, and holistic ways. Rather than using language that is linear and less complex, images and metaphors depict nuances and subtleties that engage the reader in their own sense making.

Within the river metaphor, it is easy to imagine how the river responds to changes in water levels. Sometimes the banks of the river overflow; the river suddenly changes course as water finds alternative paths and continues to move downstream. Predictions of how the river will reshape its boundaries are less accurate than knowing it will. The past patterns suggest paths of least resistance for the water to flow. In schools, educators might look for patterns, observed over time, where they feel little or no resistance to change and can build connections, while recognizing how small differences might signify deep cultural and structural patterns that are significant, and more difficult to change. We can learn to be more alert and sensitive to places where these differences are small but symbolic of salient areas for deeper structural change. By recognizing these places and making them visible, we can begin to liberate ourselves from institutional dominator practices. Coercion is replaced with possibility, hope, and the ability to inspire a different way of being. Traveling to new places along the river enables us to explore together what community means at each turning point.

From Power Over to Power Through

In a study of more than 400 Alabama and Florida teachers, a survey was administered using a five-dimensional model of power: (1) autonomy, (2) responsibility and accountability, (3) resources, (4) hierarchical beliefs about power, and (5) political efficacy and expertise (Acker-Hocevar, MacGregor, and Touchton 1996; Acker-Hocevar, Bauch, and Berman, 1997; Acker-Hocevar and Bauch, 1998). Teachers were also asked to respond to three open-ended questions in which they described the *conditions* they believed supported empowerment. Answers such as the following clustered under *power over:*

Administrators willing to delegate

No feelings of hopelessness

Less emphasis on top-down power structures

Administrators that are more democratic than autocratic

Freedom to express opinions/desires without penalty

Feeling free to question or ask for clarity concerning situations

Power over human beings limits their potential for growth, openness, and learning. We see evidence of this type of school in descriptions of cold and forbidding places, promoting status differences, and excluding members from having a say in setting policies and rules. Lack of caring, status differences, and limited involvement make these schools difficult places to work. These dominator practices limit learning.

Teachers described the *behaviors* of empowered teachers. The following responses clustered under *power to:*

Confidence, open communication, freedom to do what is best in your class

Teachers trying innovative techniques

A warm rapport, open communication at all levels, and a desire to fulfill the philosophy of the school

Communication, cooperation, flexibility, setting of goals, and goal achievement

Feelings of respect, trust, and appreciation by the system of administrators and supervisors

Administrators willing to involve teachers in decision-making processes and teachers willing to take on leadership roles

A board that listens to teachers and respects teachers

Power to releases energy in organizations to promote change. The evidence is increased listening, support for change, respect, trust, acceptance, ongoing feedback, time for reflection, nurturance of self-knowledge, encouragement of risk taking, practice at problem solving, communication, conflict resolution, team building, and learning shared decision-making skills. Readiness for power *to be actualized* is cultivated. It is like stocking a river with fish that will grow and develop over time or planting seeds to be reaped and harvested later. Without organizational development, the river has not been cultivated for learning to take place.

Characteristics of peers, families, schools, and communities that foster resiliency include promoting close bonds and cultivating a culture that encourages cooperation, provides leadership, fosters decision making, and nurtures opportunities for meaningful participation. Resilient organizations grow the talents of each individual.

Power with is actualized power in an organization. This occurs when changes in relating are felt at the deepest structures of the organization—the cultural values and beliefs reflect this. The river makes a wide turn as it gathers support for this type of energy. Actualized power is power through people working together.

Teachers describe *how* empowered teachers act. The following responses were clustered under *power with:*

- Teachers are actively involved in making decisions that affect their students and school.

- Teachers try new ideas, give feedback to administration, and know ideas are heard and taken into consideration for possible change.

- Teachers learn and observe from peers what works and what does not.

- Teachers realize society benefits from their reinforcement of individual power.

- Teachers work with students to actively engage them in participating in their learning.

- Teachers meet and discuss and share ideas about learning.

- Teachers communicate and are involved in team work and decision making, with a freedom to discuss issues with an open administrator.

- Teachers work together to help students be successful.

Power with is a river impossible to turn back. People begin to feel the energy of working across traditional boundaries (e.g., isolated role groups and grade levels) and in teams (e.g., cross-functional and multiage learning cohorts). Learning is noncompetitive with a focus on real-life challenges. Schools are partners with their communities, working interdependently within them. Clear and high standards for performance guide actions. Discourse, inquiry, and learning are core values; people are not afraid their ideas will be stolen or discredited. Instead, they work together to connect their ideas into integrated innovations.

Goal setting and personal mastery encourage prosocial values like altruism. The organization appreciates the unique talents of each individual. Individuals have an internal locus of control, autonomy, and a positive view of their personal futures. They possess feelings of self-worth and self-confidence and have a capacity for connecting with others for learning.

Power through is exercised power in the form of seeing rich information networks, having relationships that foster *becoming,* acknowledging widely shared values, maintaining open communication, encouraging team learning from one another, having multiple sources of data and feedback, and supporting the flexibility of an adaptive system to respond to change. The community nourishes itself.

Teachers were asked to describe *who benefits from* empowering teachers. The following responses clustered under *power through:*

All school faculty, staff, students, parents, and administrators benefit because empowerment increases teacher productivity, creativity, acceptance, and responsibility. A certain vitality exists in a work environment where teachers truly believe they have the power.

Students, teachers, administrators, and the community benefit because if you have teachers who "take it and run," the entire learning environment and the community benefit because there are more opportunities that are available.

Administration, teachers, students, and parents benefit because everyone is working together with the same input into decision making, which creates a better environment for everyone.

Power through transforms power into something new. Information networks, relationships across traditional boundaries, shared resources, community concepts, informal learning, and exercising personal power are critical. The organization transcends past definitions of power that limit team learning, moving toward an ethical community, which places a high priority on continuous learning and adaptation.

CONCLUSIONS

Systems thinking is the backbone of organizational learning that facilitates the journey from *power over* to *power through*. Institutional, bureaucratic domination keeps the system fragmented, people isolated, and resources and opportunities in the hands of a few. Encouraging access, allocation, utilization, and prioritization of resources by the community where power elites are few and communal power is pervasive begins to shape a different future. Different questions are asked about priorities. Group dialogue, systems thinking, and mutual relationships form the basis for learning and living in organizations.

Developing vital learning communities within and across institutions requires mental models of change that allow us the possibility to confront institutional strongholds of dominance. Vital learning organizations build strong connection systems among work teams and role groups within and across organizations and also among partner programs and services to serve the needs of our students. A requirement for the survival of a learning community is the freedom to exercise power for/with/through opportunities and resources. Responses are crafted to fit changing conditions of work, drawing on learning partnership power. Communities develop strong listening and response systems, giving shape to a new century of human experience and hope.

Power is energy for making conscious choices to take action for improving student learning, to have open communication systems that engender trust, and to build capacity. If we know where we want to go on our journey, we can begin to move to new patterns of power. Anything short stunts organizational growth and essentially promotes its decline over time. This chapter has presented a way of thinking about the journey to transform traditional control-oriented patterns of power into those that facilitate the emergence over time of new work systems that enhance the success chances in life for all students.

8

Acting Locally and Thinking Globally about Poverty and Race

At the 2007 annual conference of the American Association for Educational Research (AERA), a sociologist showed that Jamaicans who immigrated to the United States outperformed their African American counterparts. This was especially interesting to those of us who had worked extensively in Jamaica over the previous five years. We had observed how Jamaican graduate students were not afraid to challenge a professor's assumptions or those of their peers. These Jamaican students expected critical feedback on their work and, sought ways to improve it, and were not content to meet only basic requirements.

Another exception to general trends of student performance relates to Hispanic student achievement. We found that in Miami–Dade County in Florida and along the Mexican border in Texas, students in several schools fared better than would be expected for their ethnicity and socioeconomic status. These two sites were bound by a common thread of a highly concentrated Hispanic culture in the schools.

Why were more elementary schools in Miami-Dade and schools along the border of Mexico and Texas able to defy the odds and demonstrate high student achievement by poor and Hispanic students? In both places (Miami and the Tex-Mex border), educators held prior knowledge and an appreciation of the cultural and social capital, which these students and their families brought to school. Many teachers and principals shared and understood the students and families and were bilingual. Educators' connections to these students and their families through shared language and a respect for their cultural traditions created conditions necessary for these students to feel valued, thus engendering a feeling of belonging. As a guidance counselor at one of the schools at the border shared, "These parents are admirable and noble. I have the utmost respect for them. They have left their homes in Mexico to offer their children a better life. They live in barrios on the border made out of cardboard and cook on open fires. They see education as the ticket out of poverty."

WHAT ARE THE CONNECTIONS AMONG POVERTY, RACE, AND VALUES?

Most Jamaicans do not have the financial or material luxuries of many Americans seeking advanced degrees, so we began to wonder how the Jamaican sense of self, or identity, had been constructed differently than those of many U.S. students, especially African Americans. Why did students in certain locations do better, such as the students in Miami-Dade and along the Tex-Mex border? How did the institutionalized practices of racism in the United States affect African American and Hispanic performance? How did the legacy of being from a black country (e.g., in charge of their own social, economic, and political systems) impact Jamaican blacks versus African Americans? How did the values in Jamaica affect students' attitudes regarding competence? How did schools where educators understood the background (e. g., social and cultural capital of their students) make a difference?

As we studied the relationship between variables of race, poverty (i.e., class), and the interaction of these variables with educators' values, we saw how each of these variables had the potential to interact with one another, with differential influences on identity formation and outcomes that affected student achievement.

Educators who disrupted the system of deeply ingrained racist and classist practices and beliefs seemed to foster positive self-concepts and improved student and overall school achievement. Educators who understood and, even better, were part of the culture that the students came from, created a culture and climate that built capacity for student success, not failure. Students who had constructed a strong sense of self before they came to the United States seemed to have a higher probability of success.

Their beliefs and practices created an invisible culture of either higher or lower expectations for why blacks and Hispanics, who are often poor, underperformed or performed as well as or even better than whites in schools. We wondered how educators could begin to make sense of what it would take to impact deeper and larger social and cultural values to foster student learning success and build capacity for all students. What underlying social values held oppressive systems in place? Why did the federal No Child Left Behind Act (2001) fail to grapple with deeper social and cultural issues that could affect learning in schools more positively than punitively?

It seems to us that as the United States has focused its gaze inward, rather than globally, practices that might be solutions, particularly with certain student subgroups, have been trumped with terms like the "achievement gap." Deeper questions were sidestepped by bureaucratic mandates for percentage increases on tests of all subgroups with little discussion as to the deeper systemic causes of these achievement disparities. The U.S. system labels schools with poor performance as failing schools. The hard work of addressing social injustices, discriminations, and inequities within the system requires a different mindset for school improvement—one that reaches outward to embrace the whole community and asks difficult questions.

While some countries are redefining the skill set for the twenty-first century, the unjustly harsh measures of U.S. policy create a testing culture and have taken a toll, particularly in states such as Florida, where educators complain that the curriculum is "teaching to the test."[1] In Europe, eight competencies have been developed by the European Union (EU) Commission on Education (2004). These are: communication in the mother tongue; communication in the foreign languages; mathematical competence and basic competencies in science and technology; digital competence; learning to learn; interpersonal, intercultural, and social competence and civic competence; entrepreneurship; and cultural expression. These eight competencies describe a framework for lifelong learning, with underlying principles. Notably,

> The terms **"competence"** and **"key competence"** are preferred to "basic skills," a term that was considered too restrictive as it was generally taken to refer primarily to basic literacy and numeracy and to what are known variously as "survival" or "life" skills. "Competence" is considered to refer to a **combination of skills, knowledge, aptitudes and attitudes,** and to include the disposition to learn in addition to know-how. A "key competence" is one crucial for three aspects of life:
>
> a. **personal fulfillment and development throughout life (cultural capital)** . . . ;
>
> b. **active citizenship and inclusion (social capital)** . . . ;
>
> c. **employability (human capital).** . . .

The difference between the EU language and the U.S. policy is noted in the words for building competence versus achieving basic skills. Moreover, the EU framework takes into account the personal fulfillment of one's life; it is not only about how to educate students to maintain economic competitiveness. There is a philosophical difference in looking forward that takes into account the quality of a life that cultivates fulfillment versus only having a job and being an instrument for economic prosperity.

LOOKING TO THE FUTURE

The question becomes how educators can reflect the future of what life can become in a global world when schools are held accountable for nineteenth-century bureaucratic rules, work, and micromanagement? What values do we want to underpin this life? Are the values humanistic, regenerative, and supportive of building capacity? In the United States, the focus is on basic skills, while the countries in the EU are building different forms of capital for competence. Daniel Pink (2005, 2006) emphasizes, "The future belongs to a very different kind of person with a very different kind of mind—*creators and empathizers, pattern recognizers, and meaning makers.* These people—*artists, inventors, designers, storytellers, caregivers, consolers, big picture thinkers*—will reap society's richest rewards and share its greatest joys" (1). Pink provides a chronology, beginning with the agricultural age, moving to the industrial age, the current information age, and ending with the dawning of the new "conceptual age of creators and empathizers" (49). In many of our schools, we are still in the industrial age while the digital age passes us by. Or, are we addressing only basic skills while other countries are building capacity?

As we examine schools today, can we actually see fodder for *creators* and *empathizers* to grow their competencies and talents? We suggest that dramatic changes are needed to restore balance to some of our nation's schools so students can experience the quality of education that Pink (2005, 2006) describes as foundational to this next era of human living. It is unjust that in many of our most vulnerable schools, students are being "clunked" over the head with daily doses of repetitive teaching that numbs their senses and dulls their minds, just so they can pass a test. We need a revolution of the mind! A revolution that not only reframes the purpose of an education, but that also looks at why certain students succeed and others do not and that asks how to broaden educational access globally (Sachs, 2005), while simultaneously changing issues locally. It is not an either/or—local or global. It is both!

PART I: GLOBAL PERSPECTIVES— LET THE REVOLUTION BEGIN!

Creating an Ethic of Living

We used to believe that if educators could only understand partnership power, they would shift to a different way of thinking about how to share resources and opportunities within and across cultures and borders. We were, in fact, naïve. We now realize that nothing short of a revolution of the mind that affects actions can change oppressive practices disguised as serving the good, such as the No Child Left Behind Act (NCLB), and institutions, such as the World Bank, that hold nations hostage to large debts. Why is this so? Perhaps it is because legislation like NCLB does not address the deeper social and cultural issues that have held things like the achievement gap in place. The World Bank does not help people build capacity (competence) to lift them out of poverty; it in fact makes countries dependent. In *The Measure of a Man: A Spiritual Autobiography,* Sidney Poitier (2000), a black actor who grew up in the Bahamas, states:

> Wherever there's a configuration in which there are the powerful and the powerless, the powerful, by and large, aren't going to feel much of anything about this imbalance. After a while the powerful become accustomed to experiencing the power to their benefit in ways that are painless. It's the air they breathe, the water they swim in. . . . However much prodding they get from the powerless or the disenfranchised or the slaves, those in power just aren't inclined toward introspection or remorse. (126)

Poitier goes on to argue that we must make an effort to build equality, to foster "the nurturing of a civilized, fair, principled, humane society" (128). He encourages compassion to extend to the powerless so that as society becomes more humane it can see how it has behaved inhumanely. Poitier helps us understand that violence and rage are built up with injustices. "This injustice of the world inspires a rage so intense that to express it fully would require homicidal action; it's self-destructive, destroy-the-world rage" (128). Like others, Poitier learned how to channel his rage and find positive ways to release his anger. Why would this be any different for nations that have felt they have been treated unjustly? Poitier believes, as does Desmond Tutu, that the outlet for rage is forgiveness.

In *No Future without Forgiveness,* Tutu (1999) chronicles the moral high road taken by South African leaders to establish South Africa's Truth and Reconciliation Commission. Tutu explains:

> In a real sense we might add that even the supporters of apartheid were victims of the vicious system which they implemented and which they supported so enthusiastically. This is not an example for the morally earnest of ethical indifferentism. No, it flows from our fundamental concept of *ubuntu.* Our humanity was intertwined. The humanity of the perpetrator of apartheid's atrocities was caught up and bound up in that of his victim whether he liked it or not. In the process of dehumanizing another, in inflicting untold harm and suffering, inexorably the perpetrator was being dehumanized as well. (103)

There is no doubt that the human abuses during apartheid were savage, cruel, and inhumane. This part of South Africa's history is indisputable. What is telling in reading Tutu's book is that the leaders made decisions to raise their consciousness, to encourage others to do so, and to forgive and reconcile and create a future together. In the belief that both perpetrators and victims were caught up in the same vicious cycle, the power of forgiveness was used to enable people to tell their stories and then move onto living. Telling their stories freed them of their heavy burdens and represented the "truth of wounded memories" (26). This was seen as the first time that many South Africans felt that the heavy burden of pain and suffering had been lifted from their shoulders.

South Africa was at a crossroads when its citizens chose to use their power to hear, to listen and affirm, rather than to punish. We can learn much from the ways that people deal with their pain and oppression. We too are at a crossroads, in education. The vulnerable are those among us who need a hand extended, need to have witnesses to their pain by telling their stories, and need to be granted forgiveness and to forgive others to go on in life. This is the empathy Pink (2005, 2006) discusses as a "skill for surviving the 21st-century. . . . It's an ethic for living. It's a means of understanding other human beings . . ." (165). It's an ethic of caring. It's about compassion within and across borders (see University Council of Educational Administration's annual conference theme, 2007). It is about providing people with the various forms of capital they need to invent better lives for themselves. It is about walking in someone else's shoes. As educators, the challenge that we are presented is how to show empathy and compassion for students whose lives may be so different from our own: to build capacity for change. How can we use ubuntu to make connections and changes? How can we build partnership power with others?

Invisible Communities

In many areas, poverty makes the community (or country) invisible, the town you bypass on your travels, the neighborhoods you avoid out of fear, the countries you never visit, and the bewilderment of the isolation that exists. As one principal shared with us, "Some of our students have not been to Disney World; they haven't left our city of Fort Lauderdale, which is only 125 miles away from Disney. In fact, some students have not been to the beach which is just five miles from where they live."

There is a tremendous need to lead a low-performing, high-poverty school differently from the ways most leaders are prepared (Acker-Hocevar and Cruz-Janzen, in press). Leaders in highly impoverished schools need a lot of mentoring and support. They must engage in networks that unite them with other successful leaders so they can share their stories. As Pink (2005, 2006) states, the power of the story is part of the Conceptual Age. These leaders must practice empathy and demonstrate caring. They must create opportunities for students to experience things that other students take for granted—such as visiting Disney World.

In the memoir and autobiography of Elva Trevino Hart (2000), who wrote *Barefoot Heart: Stories of a Migrant Child,* her prologue begins:

> I am nobody. And my story is the same as a million others. Poor Mexican American. Female child. We all look alike: dirty feet, brown skin, downcast eyes. (n. p.)

You have seen us if you have driven through south Texas on the way to Mexico. We are there—walking barefoot by the side of the road. During harvest time there are fewer of us—we are with our families in the fields (Hart, 2000).

In a later passage, Hart describes how the town in which she lived and went to high school was really like two towns; it was divided by the railroad tracks, which seemed like the Rio Grande. Teachers were portrayed as basically two types.

One was the out-of-town teachers, who frequently came only for a year and were never seen again. Most of the imports were just well-meaning teachers who couldn't find a job anywhere else. The other variety consisted of locals: farmers' wives, bankers' wives, and male teachers who had family in town. The great majority of the teachers were white; you did not need all the fingers on one hand to count the Mexican teachers in the **entire school system** [sic, bold]. (175)

Too often students who live on one side of town are never made to feel part of the mainstream. The social isolation is intertwined with poverty and social isolation—the haves versus the have-nots. The experiences of students of poverty are not the same as those of many of our more affluent families—experiences often taken for granted. Being invisible means these students find themselves and their communities not valued. The potential for resisting what others think is best for them can be their only way of being heard. This is also true for countries that have been invisible because of poverty, often resisting what others have decided is in their best interest.

Giving Poverty a Physical Exam: A More Global Perspective

Moving away from autobiographies, Jeffrey Sachs' (2005) *The End of Poverty: Economic Possibilities for Our Time* provides a seven-part diagnostic checklist to use as part of a "'physical exam' of any impoverished country" (83). The checklist for diagnosis is:

1. Poverty trap

2. Economic policy framework

3. Fiscal framework and fiscal trap

4. Physical geography

5. Governance patterns and failures

6. Cultural barriers

7. Geopolitics

Although each of these areas is useful in diagnosing the extent of help required to assist an impoverished country, we will focus on the poverty trap, cultural barriers, and geopolitics. In fighting the poverty trap, Sachs (2005) advises, the clinical economist should use information such as household surveys, geographic information systems data, and national income accounts. How is poverty distributed across the population? Sachs warns that in the course of mapping poverty, the key risk factors that may exacerbate poverty in the future should be identified. "What are the demographic trends (births, deaths, internal and international migration) that may affect the numbers and distribution of the extreme poor? What about environmental trends, climate shocks, disease, and commodity price fluctuations? What about spatial distribution of basic infrastructures such as power, roads, telecoms, water and sanitation?" (83). The poverty trap infers that people remain poor because of the lack of certain basic structures, such as roads, which can connect isolated groups with one another and create better access for the distribution of goods and services. Furthermore, the poverty trap can get worse through hegemonic, economic practices by institutions such as the World Bank. When the World Bank keeps countries economically enslaved, it maintains the poverty trap. These practices need to be put under a microscope, named, and ended! When educators hold biases against certain groups of students, they keep them in the poverty trap!

When cultural barriers that tear a society apart, such as racism, caste, class, ethnicity, religion, or gender inequities, are considered, the basic values and beliefs of a culture are examined. On the other hand, when geopolitics is assessed, Sachs (2005) says, "Many institutions, both within the low income countries and internationally, should cooperate to address these diagnostic issues" (88). What becomes relevant is that there is a host of agencies that need to partner in how they address poverty within a nation. When you examine geopolitics, the very location of a country and the countries that surround it are important.

Sachs (2005) identifies five development interventions that could make an immediate impact on places like Sauri, Kenya. These are agricultural inputs, investments in basic health, investments in education, and investments in power, transport, and communication services. According to Sachs, the extreme poor lack six kinds of capital: human, business, infrastructure, natural, public institutional, and knowledge capital. Sachs explains, "The poor start with a very low level of capital per person, and then find themselves trapped in poverty because the ratio of capital per person actually falls from generation to generation" (245). This is also known as the "Matthew effect," in which the poor get poorer and the rich get richer.

The same type of diagnosis could take place in our schools. What is our poverty trap? What are our cultural barriers? What partnerships can we form with others to address problems? What partnerships can we form across borders to address problems? How can we take an advocacy stance?

In September 2000, 147 heads of state and government went to New York to forge a compact addressing issues of global poverty. Of the eight millennial goals of the United Nations, the eighth goal is "developing a global partnership for development" (as cited in Sachs, 2005, 212). Interestingly, Sachs states that the way this partnership plays out is that countries *are told what they will get.* They are not asked what they need. Again, this goes back to an idea of vulnerability that is discussed in more depth. A helping hand with regard to a people's future can be extended that restores dignity and control over their personal and national decisions. Or they can be told what is in their best interest—a *power over* mind-set that undermines *partnership power* (see Chapter 6).

Helplessness (e.g., Vulnerability)

According to Hanushek, Kain, and Rivkin (2004), schools in urban areas serving the economically disadvantaged and students of color tend to be the most vulnerable to teacher turnover. From our own experiences with what it means to be vulnerable, it brings up feelings of fear, worry, anxiety, anger, and not feeling valued or respected. We literally are at the mercy of those over us and our caregivers. Fears, often deep-seated, about the loss of control and the fact that we are silenced, conjure up shame, disenfranchisement, and humiliation. These emotions stem from the basic need to survive, feel accepted for who we are, and to move past biases or prejudices that lower the expectations others hold for us and that we hold for ourselves.

Drawing on our personal experiences, at no time did one of the authors feel more vulnerable than when she was in a hospital's intensive care unit recovering from an infection contracted after brain surgery. Feeling despondent over her return to the hospital after she had been home for a week, she began to feel defeated.

During her first morning in intensive care, she was greeted cheerfully by her nurse, who said, "What would you like to accomplish today?" The author's first reaction was, "You have to be kidding!" Upon reflection, she realized that control over her life was being handed back to her; she became engaged. This experience made an indelible mark on how she thinks about people who are vulnerable, be it students who come to our schools with different languages and cultural experiences and backgrounds, or students who are disadvantaged and have had a series of teachers, each of whom has left the school—leaving them to wonder whether they should invest in any long term or meaningful relationships with adults. Or countries that are at the mercy of the generosity of other countries. Or countries we visit that have socially constructed different ways to have their voices heard. We all need to be given control over our lives and our futures and this means we need to listen with empathy.

When we are vulnerable, we depend on the empathy of others to help us "deal with" and get out of our current situation(s). According to Pink (2005,

2006), "The growing recognition of empathy's role in healing is one reason why nursing will be one of the key professions of the Conceptual Age" (171). Experiences with an empathetic nurse demonstrated how critical this attribute is to healing—not just the physical healing but the emotional healing as well that helps us move beyond the pain of loss and hurt and to take back control over decisions, spiriting a hopeful attitude again. We believe that this is also true for schools we studied. We saw how educators worked with one another and their communities to build on existing social, cultural, and intellectual capital—to build hope for the future, to value the students and parents as human beings with dignity, to offer choices to their students and parents that built capacity. We saw that with the Jamaican students who were willing to ask for more than just meeting the minimum requirements.

This was also true for the difference between the strong constructions of identity among Jamaican students contra African Americans for achieving success. Jamaican students did not experience a sense of helplessness in their system. They spoke with the confidence that they would be heard. As educators, we can learn what we can do to better assist those who need our aid, while at the same time ensuring that we provide the mechanisms for allowing them to have a voice, to take charge of their lives. Simultaneously, we must demonstrate how we have listened and what we have heard to make changes to existing practices and social systems that are unjust.

Small Investments Make a Difference!

Nowhere is the foregoing better illustrated than in the work of Muhammad Yunus (1999, 2003), who wrote *Banker to the Poor: Micro-lending and the Battle against World Poverty*. Yunus began his work with the Grameen, a bank he established to make minuscule loans to the poorest of Bangladesh. The idea of the Grameen Bank, born in 1976, occurred when Yunus lent $27 to 42 stool makers to buy raw materials. What happened was that these women were able to break the cycle of poverty in their lives with some knowledge and a helping hand. Yunus found that by assisting the women learn a few sound financial principles, they were able to aid themselves and their children. Currently, more than 250 institutions use the Grameen methodology in 100 countries to operate microcredit programs.

In a 1984 workshop in Joydevpur, 16 decisions were agreed upon to form the basis of the philosophy for what people agree to do with loans from the Grameen Bank:

1. We shall follow and advance the four principles of the Grameen Bank—discipline, unity, courage, and hard work—in all walks of our lives.

2. Prosperity we shall bring to our families.

3. We shall not live in a dilapidated house. We shall repair our houses and work toward constructing new homes at the earliest opportunity.

4. We shall grow vegetables all the year round. We shall eat plenty of them and sell the surplus.

5. During the plantation seasons, we shall plant as many seedlings as possible.

6. We shall plan to keep our families small. We shall minimize our expenditures. We shall look after our health.

7. We shall educate our children and ensure that we can pay for their education.

8. We shall keep our children and the environment clean.

9. We shall build and use pit latrines.

10. We shall drink water from tube wells. If they are not available, we shall boil water or use alum to purify it.

11. We shall not take any dowry at our sons' weddings; neither shall we give any dowry at our daughter's wedding. We shall keep the center free from the curse of dowry. We shall not practice child marriage.

12. We shall not commit any injustice, and we shall oppose any one who tries to do so.

13. We shall collectively undertake larger investments for higher incomes.

14. We shall always be ready to help each other. If anyone is in difficulty, we shall all help him or her.

15. If we come to know any breach of discipline in any center, we shall all go there and help restore discipline.

16. We shall introduce physical activity in all of our centers. We shall take part in all social activities collectively. (136–137)

Yunnus (1999) has put in place some ways of living that challenge the traditions of culture such as the dowry, while providing a framework for an ethic of living that builds competence and capacity; it is a regenerative set of principles that promotes sustainability. Moreover, within this philosophy, there is a perspective of helping others—of extending a helping hand. This notion of embedding values of integrity, justice, and caring within the philosophy creates the conditions for sustainable improvements, centered on values, beliefs, and practices that support an example of an ethic of living.

In Part II we bring together various scholars and writers, and weave their stories together to show how issues of poverty and race are played out on the global stage and the local one, underscoring values that underpin actions for responding to injustices and needs. The work of Yunnus is particularly important, for it shows us that offering people a means of transforming their lives can be a small investment toward a more hopeful future, with dramatic effects on the lives of children and the community. The challenge is to make changes locally while at the same time understanding the impact of these changes globally—not exclusively focusing the gaze internally so that there is little knowledge of what is happening globally to make connections.

The next part of the chapter highlights qualitative research in schools of poverty and color.

PART II: MAKING CONNECTIONS LOCALLY, RESEARCH ON HIGH- AND LOW-PERFORMING, HIGH-POVERTY SCHOOLS OF COLOR

Three studies in Part II are related. The first study was conducted in 10 high-poverty, low-performing schools as defined by the Florida Department of Education (Acker-Hocevar and Touchton, 2000a, b, and c) and was a qualitative and phenomenological study to better understand the lived experience within low-performing schools.

Schools in Florida, as in many other states in the United States, measure student performance against a set of criteria called standards and benchmarks. Until most recently, students' achievement of reading, writing, and mathematics were tested.[2] Student performance is reported by scores along a continuum from 1 to 5, with students who score 1 or 2 labeled as nonproficient. When a school has a majority of its students in the lower ranges of nonproficiency, they are classified as low performing. Students scoring 3 are considered to be proficient, and students with scores of 4 and 5 reflect high performance. High-performing schools are those with a majority of the students at proficiency while demonstrating learning gains even with the lowest achieving 25 percent of their students.

Making Connections to Students' Prior Knowledge and with Their Families

Research in low- and high-performing, high-poverty schools was conducted from 2000 to 2006 in Florida. Both the high- and low-performing schools had similar demographics and revealed fundamentally different connections between and among how educators in these two types of schools enacted beliefs of power: socially just versus unjust, in working with each other, their students, communities, and families of poverty and color (see Acker-Hocevar and Touchton, 2000a, b, and c; Acker-Hocevar, Cruz-Janzen, 2005/2006; Acker-Hocevar and Cruz-Janzen, in press).

An initial study of 10 low-performing schools found that overall:

1. Educators in these lower-performing and failing schools were not making the connections with students' prior knowledge and experiences, often negating students' social and cultural capital brought to school, and failing to value their backgrounds and lives.

2. Leaders' beliefs and attitudes about their students, families, and communities were manifested as biases against students and families of poverty, subtracting social and cultural capital from learning.

3. Teacher recruitment and retention in the low-performing and high-poverty schools resulted in high teacher turnover and a large number of inexperienced teachers working in these schools—creating a culture that lacked sustainability because the players changed often and educators were not committed to the deep changes required to make a sustainable difference. Rather, they were focused on "getting out" of the school as fast as possible and teaching to the test (Acker-Hocevar and Touchton, 2000a, b, and c).

All Students Are Expected to Show Learning Gains

This first study of the 10 low-performing schools shocked Acker-Hocevar and Touchton (2002a, b, and c) regarding the harmful effects of poverty on the attitudes and beliefs that teachers and leaders held and exhibited. These beliefs seemed to contribute to the weak connections between educators in the schools and the communities they served.

Interestingly, the effects of earlier research on poverty and learning marked the beginning of the Effective Schools Movement, which occurred about 40 years ago. Leaders who reversed predicable outcomes of low student achievement in this research within high-poverty schools and schools of color were represented as larger-than-life archetypes, heroic in nature. It was not until after the passage of No Child Left Behind Act that the "turnaround school leadership" (see Fullan, 2006) literature began to appear. A different picture emerged about what leaders do to increase student achievement. In this literature, leaders were not viewed as heroic but as leaders who understood systems theory and worked to build capacity within the school and community they served that were both poor and minority communities—these leaders did not work alone. Fullan asks this question:

> Why not use our human and social ingenuity to mobilize the million change agents that it will take to accomplish two giant things at once:

greater equality and multifaceted prosperity? This is education's true calling in the twenty-first century. It is a time to go far beyond turnaround schools and to tackle head-on the deep system transformation called for in order to reduce income and education gaps. The stakes have never been higher. (96)

Fullan (2006) identifies components of capacity building that are multifaceted. They change professional development practices to ones that are internal and ongoing, encourage reflection and dialogue within and across groups, and engage schools in studying their own practices. What is significant about this literature is that the focus is on broad-based leadership development for capacity building. It takes the whole community and ultimately the society to make deep changes.

Only Nine Schools!

The schools in the second study were chosen from the database of *all* elementary schools in Florida and were selected for their patterns of sustainable achievement (Acker-Hocevar, Cruz-Janzen et al., 2005/2006). Sadly, only nine elementary schools in the entire state met the criteria to be included in the study—the schools had to include a high percentage of disadvantaged students and English language learners (ELL), along with at least three years of sustainable high performance in reading and math. The second study sought to identify practices that leaders, teachers, and parents identified in relationship to a conceptual model used for the study called the systems alignment model (Wilson, Walker, Cruz-Janzen, Acker-Hocevar, and Schoon, 2005/2006).[3]

Interviews were conducted with administrators, and focus groups were held with teachers and parents. All the interviews were transcribed. Questions were organized around 10 variables using a standard interview protocol. Variables represented in a systems alignment model depicted five elements of standards-based reform (SBR) as organizing variables of accountability, instruction, resources, personnel, and information management. These five variables were further broken down into subareas. Additionally, the conceptual framework for this study identified five other variables that included the sustaining variables of leadership, communication, decision making, culture and climate, and parent and community involvement (see Wilson, Walker, et al., 2005/2006).

The major finding of this study was that a learning partnership emerged. It connected the variables and was illustrated as the Learning Partnership Tree (Acker-Hocevar, Cruz-Janzen, et al., 2005/2006). The canopy of the tree depicts the SBR variables and flourishes to the extent that the tree is fed by a healthy root system. The tap root is the culture and climate that connects the root system to the values and beliefs embedded within the sustaining variables to the organizing variables of SBR. A healthy tree reveals that the root system, or the practices that leaders engage with their teachers and community, such as shared decision making, sustains the healthy learning partnership. For example, these practices spill over into the culture and climate, the tap root or main root that nourishes the health of the school, impacting collaborative relationships within the learning community. If teachers leave one of these schools, it is often because they are promoted; the move is followed by genuine grieving over losing one of the family members. To recap, their connections with one another and others are so strong it created an energy system that could be described as partnership power—or as we later saw, the nucleus that sustained student learning within a partnership power paradigm that fosters organizational efficacy (see Figure 8.1).

Strong connections within and outside these nine schools and the collective power beliefs promoted shared leadership and accountability and distributed leadership theory. Put into action, these behaviors allowed principals to be honest about their individual strengths and weaknesses and to identify where to pool the collective expertise of their teachers to enhance organizational learning and impact learning. Their partnerships and networks brought in more resources from the community and created an added capacity to sustain the schools' success with parents as partners in learning. Their core beliefs and values *added* capital to what students brought to school. Their successes attracted others to invest resources, both human and financial, in schools visibly making a difference with populations that others were failing.

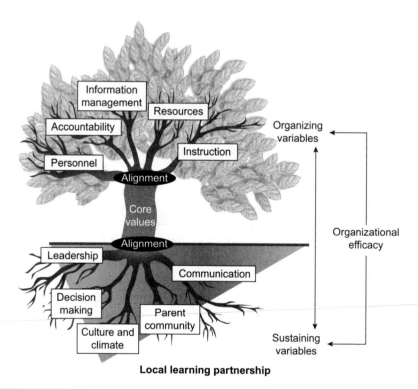

Local learning partnership

Figure 8.1   Local learning partnership: what nine schools did.

Parents reported that they trusted these educators. It appears that trust, which is central to how these schools garnered support within and across their communities, was built over time by all the educators in these schools. Eventually we came to realize that sustainable school improvement is neither a recipe for success nor a recipe for failure. What matters most is what happens in and at the school and is reflected in the core beliefs and values of its members. This is at ground zero of the school.

Study three sought to learn more about the values and beliefs that underpinned the work in three of the nine schools. Table 8.1 depicts the values that both principals and teachers held at three schools we revisited from the second study. We sought to learn more about the actual tasks that these educators did in relation to the learning partnership (Acker-Hocevar and Cruz-Janzen, in press). These values, extrapolated from the interviews and focus groups with principals and teachers, found that teacher and administrator values mirrored each other almost perfectly. The values and beliefs were named the humanistic philosophy and they sustained positive relationships and promoted ongoing learning connections in these schools.

The authenticity and caring attitudes of principals and teachers made students feel valued. The working relationships within the schools built upon a foundation of honesty, respect, and open communication among teachers and with parents and students. Commitment, pride, and feelings of trust with colleagues and between the teachers and the principal sustained school improvement and created a culture of risk taking and learning with and from one another. The pride that these professionals held was created by the good work they were doing.

Table 8.1 Core values identified for principal(s) and teacher(s).

Agreement of Values	Principals	Teachers
	Authenticity	Authenticity
	Caring	Caring
	Commitment	
	Cooperation	
	Empathy	
		Fairness
	Honesty/Transparency	Honesty
		Humility
		Noncomplacency
	Respect [mutual]	Respect [mutual]
	Openness/Open Door	Openness/Open Door
		Risk-Taking
	Positive (attitude)	Positive (attitude)
	Pragmaticism	
	Pride	Pride
	Trust	Sharing/Trust

Importantly, many low-performing schools, often serving students of poverty and color, had been largely ignored prior to No Child Left Behind. This federal legislation enacted in 2001 was intended to hold schools accountable for students' learning gains. Suffice to say that most educators could identify precisely where these schools were located; yet, they expected students to fail state tests, and these were not schools most educators wanted to teach or lead.

After the passage of NCLB, with new accountability sanctions and rewards, these low-performing schools were made visible. Accountability for demonstrating progress in student learning became a reason for deep structural changes to occur in these schools (e.g., turnaround leadership). Suddenly, an overabundance of scholarship on the effects of poverty on learning appeared, but an earlier book became pivotal in understanding the effects of poverty. This book, *A Framework for Understanding Poverty,* was written by Ruby Payne (1998).

Although criticized for providing stereotypes that exemplified the effects of poverty, this book became an overnight success and a resource guide for many principals seeking to understand the effects of poverty on learning. The reason we think it was such a success is that the book laid bare the assumptions of white, middle-class privilege—the elephant in the living room—which was the gold standard against which students were assessed. However, this book was highly criticized for reifying certain stereotypes that further marginalized students of poverty and color.

Our collective learning from the high- and low-performing, high-poverty elementary schools of color points to the intersection of poverty with race and how educators' values interact with the social and cultural capital students bring to school. The three studies conducted told a story, with the first one showing us how the attitudes, beliefs, and values within these lower performing schools contributed to their ongoing failure. The second study identifies high-performing and high-poverty schools with demographics similar to those of the 10 low-performing schools, but it shows how educators sustained high achievement with the same populations through a learning partnership that built organizational efficacy. The third study identified a set of core beliefs and values rooted in a learning partnership and in a strong climate and culture that supported the students' backgrounds. This third study identified the core values that these educators say added to this supportive culture and their success.

PART III: U.S. POLICY OF NO CHILD LEFT BEHIND— STILL ACTING LOCALLY!

The national policy of No Child Left Behind (NCLB) serves as a backdrop to what the federal government acknowledges is a serious problem in American schools—the achievement gap. Although NCLB may be a poor example of how a country should go about addressing injustices, inequities, and discriminations, the implications of NCLB—both good and bad—are on the public's radar screen because this law is up for reauthorization and what will be changed is yet to be decided. The public's awareness of the "achievement gap" that persists along socio-economic and racial and ethnic lines fails to ask about the national values that underpin this gap—when will these be addressed?

Corresponding to this idea of the "achievement gap" is the notion of *vulnerability*. What can we do to lessen one's vulnerability? How can we reach out to someone in need of a helping hand or acknowledge that where we are coming from is valued? According to the Web site for NCLB, four pillars provide the foundation for this legislation. These four pillars are stronger accountability for results, more freedom for states and communities to demonstrate these results, the employment of proven education methods, and the provision of more choices for parents (http://www.ed.gov/nclb/landing.jhtml).

To elaborate, the first pillar encourages states to be more accountable for closing the achievement gap and to ensure that all students, including those who are disadvantaged, achieve academic proficiency. Schools failing to make adequate yearly progress with subgroups (i.e., disadvantaged students) must provide tutoring or after-school assistance (http://www.ed.gov/nclb/landing.jhtml).

The second pillar, more "freedom for states and communities," provides states and school districts with "unprecedented flexibility" in how they use federal funds, allowing states to exercise their prerogatives in identifying priorities for where and how to make investments for increased student learning.

The third pillar, using "proven educational methods," stresses improving practices from research that have demonstrated results—research described as meeting the requirements of rigorous scientific study. Significantly, this particular pillar generates much debate among researchers regarding what constitutes "rigorous scientific research." (For example, NCLB favors a particular approach to reading that endorses a certain method of scholarship over another, even discrediting work of some reading scholars.) (http://www.ed.gov/nclb/landing .jhtml)

Finally, the fourth pillar of NCLB is "more choice for parents." Notably, parents in low-performing schools have options to transfer their children to higher-performing schools if the school fails to meet state standards for two consecutive years.

> Students from low-income families in schools that fail to meet state standards for at least three years are eligible to receive supplemental educational services, including tutoring, after-school services, and summer school. Also, students who attend a persistently dangerous school or are the victim of a violent crime while in their school have the option to attend a safe school within their district (http://www.ed.gov/nclb/landing .jhtml).

Within the last couple of years, Margaret Spellings, the secretary of education, has approved growth models that are being piloted in eight states: Alaska, Arizona, Arkansas, Delaware, Florida, North Carolina, Ohio, and Tennessee. She clearly acknowledges that the "growth model is a way for states already raising achievement . . . to strengthen accountability" (http://www.ed.gov/nclb/landing.jhtml). Spellings confirms different measures for individual student growth plans but stresses that the commitment must begin with disaggregating data for the different subgroups (e.g., white, black, Hispanic, students with disabilities, limited English proficient) to close the achievement gap and demonstrate that every student will be reading at grade level by 2014.

Ever since the enactment of NCLB in 2001, there have been both proponents and opponents of this legislation. From our collective experiences, we can see differences in how states chose varied routes to hold schools accountable—routes that could be deconstructed for their inherent beliefs about power. For example, in Florida, the language used to designate a failing school is aligned with school grades. An "F" means that the school has not achieved the state's criteria—referred to in the *A-Plus Plan*. Equally confusing with the passage of NCLB is the fact that a school can attain a grade of an "A" but fail to meet adequate yearly progress (AYP) as defined by NCLB because some subgroups failed to meet the expected increases for AYP. Thus, some states did not align their criteria tightly to the federal criteria. Clearly, the best of both worlds in Florida, as in other states with their own state accountability plans, would be for a school to be both an "A" school and make AYP. The fact that Florida chose to punish schools that served a disproportionate number of students of color, were economically disadvantaged, and had significant numbers of students who are English language learners, demonstrates its use of "power over" certain subgroups by state legislators. Yet, there are schools making a difference!

In contrast, some states, with more rigorous requirements than those in NCLB, might fail the state's measure for accountability but make national AYP. What constitutes a "good" school? Several states, such as Connecticut, believe that schools not making the grade need extra resources and help. If they are not performing, then the state must assist. In Florida, the state punishes low performance! Parents are left confused. How could a school make an "A" but fail to make AYP? Even more disconcerting is how parents, teachers, and administrators in Florida began to self-identify with their schools' grades. For example, when parents point out where their children attend schools, or when teachers state where they teach, or when leaders share where they are administrators, statements such as "I am at an 'A' school" follow. Notably absent are parents, students, and teachers who self-identify themselves as coming from "F" schools. As one administrator told researchers, these students already know they come from "F" families and "F" lives, so what difference does it make if they come from "F" schools?

Proponents of standards-based reform (SBR) argue that the conceptual underpinning for NCLB is

> the expansion of the moral community, embodied in expanded federal and state authority that began with *Brown v. Board of Education* (1954)[4] and continued through the state education finance suits. Standards-based reformers aspire toward an educational system in which students' educational opportunities and levels of educational attainment will not vary according to where they live, and achievement gaps between advantaged and disadvantaged groups will disappear. (McDermott, 2007, 84)

According to the SBR model, states that set low performance standards will be pushed by the centralized system of accountability of NCLB to level the playing field and increase their attention to both equity and excellence (Scheurich and Skrla, 2001). But not all scholars or school leaders view state standards and the passage of NCLB in the same way, or even see these two areas as positive school reforms. Those in opposition to NCLB argue that this is once again a scenario of blaming the victim (McDermott, 2007).

Rather than addressing the deeper cultural beliefs, policy, economic funding, and political issues which contribute to poverty (the haves versus the have-nots and racist policies), NCLB blames both students of color and from poverty for the achievement gap, and it points the finger at educators in these schools for not doing enough to reverse the trends. What is not addressed is how prejudices and biases, rooted in deeper social and structural arrangements, remain unchallenged in NCLB. Nor is there a mention of the lack of access to resources and opportunities, which have systematically worked against certain groups in our society.

Some educators are left to wonder whether the focus on the "achievement gap" further discriminates against students of color and poverty, holding them once again to an unwritten, white, middle-class value system and leaving existing societal norms unchallenged. How can this continue, when the country is becoming increasingly multicultural? Don't we all share some culpability in this?

Simultaneously, educators have begun to question the narrowing of the school's curriculum to "pass the test," particularly in low-performing schools. What are the effects of these practices over time on students' being able to think critically and creatively? How will these educational practices contribute to our country's future economic viability? To our students' becoming global citizens? To developing students with empathy and an ethic for living?

PART IV: LESSONS FOR PRINCIPALS

This last part of the chapter uses the patchwork quilt metaphor of bringing together global perspectives, research conducted, and the controversy surrounding NCLB to share what lessons can be learned about responding locally and globally to issues surrounding poverty and race.

We start out with a poem written by one of our colleagues who is a person of color.

Diversity
Diversity
Is not about numbers
It is about perspectives.
The presence and valuing of different views
The subconscious, automatic assumption that
The presence of divergent thought is inherently good
For all of us
Making us—and our institutions—stronger, smarter and more human(e).
If we have to talk about diversity
In terms of numbers, demographics, and boxes checked on the EEO[5] form
We still don't have it.
Diversity is about dismantling White Privilege
AKA[6] hegemony, supremacy
That has gripped institutions for centuries.
We cannot afford to mistake as "diversity"
Schemes that live up to the letter but not the spirit of Affirmative Action plans
Dressing up White Privilege in a different cast of characters.

Diversity
When an institution can be proud of it
Is when we don't have to mention the word at all,
Not in our mission statements, nor our strategic plans.
It should be normal; the natural result of standard operating procedures.
But if standard operating procedures stifle debate
Or confuse one's obligation to provide alternative perspectives
With insubordination, bullying, not knowing one's place,
Or if the diversity resulting from strategic hiring practices yields sameness of
    thought,
Status quo, business as usual,
Then diversity has not been achieved
No matter how colorful the parade of skin tones might be.

Dilys Schoorman
Associate Professor, Florida Atlantic University
April 2006

In this poem, we could substitute "EEO" with "NCLB." Mandating changes of mind and heart must be something that we seek to do because it is the right thing to do—and actions must follow! That is why this poem struck a chord. Next, we address lessons learned from three perspectives: global, local, and national policy.

Lessons for Global Perspectives

- The use of ethnographies, novels, biographies, autobiographies, and accounts such as the one from Desmond Tutu, with works from economists, political scientists, and policy makers can enable us to study poverty and race from an interdisciplinary perspective and provide students with a rich array of sources to help them understand more global perspectives about these issues.

- Patterns of extreme poverty in countries and continents faced with the most serious problems can become part of the school's curriculum. What is being done to ease poverty? Why should we care? What are the implications of not addressing poverty and racism?

- Countries that have more resources have a responsibility to assist others. Why might this be true?

- Poverty and racism affect all of us, everywhere around the world.

- Context influences perspectives about race and poverty.

- Values influence the way that people interpret race and poverty.

- Solutions to poverty and racism are not within current paradigms for thinking how to solve problems.

- Sustainability leadership needs to be defined and examined.

Lessons from Local Perspectives

- Personal experiences can help us understand and identify injustices, discriminations, and inequities that can be addressed in schools. Students and others need to be able to tell their stories.

- National policy may not be addressing the underlying issues that underpin negative practices and the institutional practices that foster prejudices against people of poverty and color.

- Students can participate actively in their communities to address issues around race and poverty.

- The goals of an education today must go beyond basic literacy and numeracy to prepare global citizens.

- Leaders promote compassionate leadership that creates a culture of caring and an ethic of living that can sustain improvements in student achievement.

Lessons from National Policy

- Poverty and racism are linked to bigger issues of social justice, equity, and ending discrimination.

- National policies cannot mandate what matters. There needs to be a mental shift followed by a change in the actions of people to show that they understand what to do differently.

- It is difficult to disagree with policies that state actions such as "no child left behind."

- Educators must collect their own data and be knowledgeable about their own practice to speak with authority and as professionals.

SUMMARY

Compassion is different from caring, but is in addition to it. Compassion is about making connections with others to make a difference. It is about activism and a desire to alleviate suffering. Compassion is inextricably connected to how educators' values interact with how they work with students of poverty and different races and ethnic groups to open up access to learning.

The dominator culture "over" certain groups of people continues to be challenged, most often by the groups of people being discriminated against. Invisible practices under the dominator paradigm fail to come to light without a partnership power lens to reveal the social injustices. Principals' values, beliefs, and attitudes can perpetuate inequities and disparities of marginalized groups within the dominator power perspective (i.e., men over women, whites over blacks, haves over have-nots). Or, you can widen your lens and acknowledge a shift in consciousness through your beliefs and actions that create opportunities for student learning for students of poverty and color. Furthermore, you can acknowledge what these students and their communities have, not what they lack.

Without getting involved and understanding local issues, it is difficult to see how you can become concerned about global issues. This is not an either/or. Responding to local and global issues of poverty and race require that you be involved at the local level. Only then can you begin to compare and contrast how different social and cultural values impact how racism and poverty play out on the local and more global stages.

The difficulty of addressing these issues requires the use of a partnership model of power that shares leadership and accountability for outcomes. Change is not a linear process but a process that starts out with a purpose to transform lives, that creates processes that distribute control over decisions to the people that are impacted, and that looks to those with the problems for the solutions. Small investments can make a big difference!

NOTES

1. By "teaching to the tests," educators are offering a curriculum that is based on students' passing the state standards-based criterion-referenced tests.
2. Florida recently started to measure science. One of the complaints by educators is that the focus in schools has been on the basics of reading and math to the exclusion of science and social studies. The arts have also been disregarded in many of the lower-performing schools with a focus exclusively on reading and math to raise school test scores.
3. The study was funded by the Annenberg Foundation.
4. *Brown v. Board of Education* (1954) established the fact that "separate" was not equal in segregated schools, mostly in the South.
5. Abbreviation for Equal Employment Opportunity.
6. AKA means "also known as."

Part 3

Tools to Facilitate New Prototypes of Schooling

Part III offers ways to implement the lessons from *living on the edge of chaos* and *quantum strategic thinking* within new power relationships. The purpose is to provide practical tools for guiding an organization's adaptation over time to changing conditions. Emphasis is placed on strategies, processes, and systems that are interdependent with all other systems. These practical tools will enable leaders to fashion prototypes of schooling through benchmarking and the case study methods.

Chapter 9, Taking Stock of Your Organization: Benchmarking, Evaluation, and Accountability, explores processes to improve the performance systems of work. This chapter emphasizes the role of information and new ways of thinking about evaluation processes and accountability regulations for organizational development. Drawing on quality management and understanding the uses of benchmarking processes promotes better organizational decision making. Find out what benchmarking is and is not, how it works, and the difference between benchmarking and performance appraisal systems.

Chapter 10, Building a New Dynamic through Social Networks, is the new challenge for school leaders and other professional educators. If we are to prepare students as global citizens while in school, educators who are responsible for their development will necessarily acquire their own professional networks. Building energy for change today comes through dense and dynamic networks that are engaged in both local and global activity while educators work on important projects. Social networks are able to achieve new kinds of success because of the resources and perspectives that emerge naturally. The International School Connection is a prototype example of a global learning network that is focusing on developing students as global citizens.

Chapter 11, Digital Cultures for Learning in a Global Age, discusses how digital cultures are fast becoming the norm in twenty-first century work places. The challenge for educators is to fashion digital cultures as a norm within schools every day, for every student. Technology is no longer considered separate from routine school work, but rather an integral part of its learning environment. This challenge requires a revolution in the concept of schooling, the resources that are available to facilitate learning, and the student engagement processes as educators work together on common goals with both local and global partners. Case examples are provided for clues about the importance and integration of technology into a school's culture of learning.

Chapter 12, The Strategic Dance of Life, offers ways to study an organization's growth and adaptation over time. The *case study technique* is introduced as a framework for gathering information within the organization as it currently exists by using multiple data sources and directing the energy of members for continuous improvement. Five steps provide a method to use multiple information systems to guide planning and decision-making processes.

Examples of case studies demonstrate the power of this method of information gathering. Using multiple sets of information for answering pressing questions about organizational life and its effects holds promise for more defensible and reliable decision making in organizations about their future directions and strategic intents.

9

Taking Stock of Your Organization: Benchmarking, Evaluation, and Accountability

Organizations today face major challenges in transforming their current practices into ones that are more responsive than ever to the customer without sacrificing their ability to meet accountability requirements and other legal standards. Leaders and workers often talk about the catch-22 that emerges for them when the goals of accountability are so time-consuming and yet often out of touch with the larger mission. A choice must be made either to use the regulations of accountability as a guide for organizational development or to develop organizational programs that simultaneously meet customer needs and accountability requirements.

Leaders are faced with a huge challenge if they want to develop learning organizations. To be involved in a learning organization requires that information be central to decision making and that evaluation be used to provide such information. Similarly, questions are formulated with an orientation to continuous improvement rather than to performance compliance. What can leaders do? Is it possible to develop effective continuous improvement processes based on strong evaluation techniques and benchmarking, while still fulfilling and exceeding the expectations of accountability?

We suggest that it is possible. What is required is a recognition of the role that philosophy plays in framing our perceptions and decisions. The accountability regulations of the past, along with compliance monitoring, are grounded in a positivist framework. The accountability trends of the future (results-based accountability), along with the evaluation techniques and practices of *fourth generation,* are grounded in the philosophy of social constructivism. The philosophical choice is critical, for each leads to a different path and to different outcomes.

The literature on *benchmarking* has grown tremendously in the last couple of years. Books exist not only about the *how-to's* of the process but also about lessons and experiences drawn from seasoned benchmarkers that can assist those just embarking on the field. The rapid growth of this movement in business speaks to how well it helps leaders shift out of a Newtonian compliance orientation to systems thinking and continuous improvement as a way of life.

Information is key to organizational growth. Wheatley (1992) suggests that it is the lifeblood of the organization. Without information, leaders and workers will not have a sense of how well they are doing or where they are going. The learning organization is grounded in the fundamental notion that to learn requires knowledge (Senge, 1990). Knowledge comes from information, to which everyone needs access. The key for leaders today is learning how to think differently about information so that it provides workers with knowledge to inform decisions and to grow.

Preskill and Torres (1999) suggest that for organizations to learn, they must recognize the role of evaluation as the heart of what drives learning. No longer will agencies merely collect administrative information (grades, attendance, days in school, volume of medical treatment) for reporting purposes, but they will also examine information regularly to locate trends and patterns. Leaders and workers will raise questions about the significance of the data as it relates to the goals of the organization.

Recently, a hospital conducted an evaluation of a unit that, data indicated, was performing worse than three other units. What started as an exploration of process led to important information about a problem in the larger system. The evaluation was conducted using a social constructivist, qualitative methodology. It revealed that the service delivery in the low-performing unit was the same as in the other three. The problem was not in the unit but in the communication systems between the hospital staff and the unit and between the unit administrators and the workers.

An exploratory approach to accessing information enabled leaders to understand the breadth and scope of the problem. Traditional evaluations would have ignored the important information as a result of the methods, and evaluators would have concluded that relative to the other units the low-performing unit was no different. The evaluation would most likely not have revealed information to uncover the basis of the problem. For leaders to use information to stimulate learning, the right type of data must be provided and the right kinds of processes must be used to generate the information. This lies at the heart of using evaluations to stimulate organizational learning.

This chapter focuses on the key arenas in which information has been used in the past and sheds light on how it needs to be rethought in the very same context so that organizational learning will occur. Accountability will not fade away, but the information that is used to *address* accountability—and the ways in which the information is used beyond meeting the status quo—is stimulated by the freedom and flexibility found in learning organizations.

It is very safe to say that the need for evaluations will always exist. However, the types of organizational evaluations that have been conducted in the past to fulfill a bureaucratic obligation need not be the only methods of evaluation today. Similarly, external experts are not the only people who can assess quality. Learning organizations value information that helps them improve their programs and services. Evaluations generate information. The natural thing is for the evaluations to be structured in such a way that they inform learning.

A historical review of accountability and evaluation illustrates the philosophical shifts that are beginning to occur. The opportunities for incorporating accountability and evaluation into the learning organization now exist. It will take the leaders who understand the philosophical choices to nurture the growth of the learning organization.

Following an examination of accountability and evaluation constructs, this chapter begins to explore the process and function of benchmarking as a broader resource for organizational decision making, a process that can be vital to the learning organization. In the following chapter, details of a benchmarking system we developed provide a framework for evaluating organizational progress beyond the limitations of accountability, which fulfills responsibilities to stakeholders.

We now examine different philosophical orientations to guide our discussion. Throughout this book, we talk about Newtonian physics, quantum physics, chaos theory, systems, theory, quality management, and bureaucratic theory. Each of these constructs is generated from certain assumptions about truth and knowledge. These very same assumptions have been at the core of our development as members of society, students in school, workers in agencies, and organizational leaders. Rarely do we take stock of our philosophical orientations. That, however, must change, for different choices have different implications and outcomes.

To lead the learning organization, administrators must understand the different philosophies converging at the crossroads where they now stand. To respond to accountability differently, leaders must have knowledge about those differences. Similarly, to use evaluation differently, leaders must understand their options. Two philosophical orientations are provided as a backdrop for making choices. The discussion does not encompass all philosophies since that goes beyond the scope of this book. Our purpose is to raise awareness about different ways of thinking and knowing and the different outcomes they foster for accountability, evaluation, and client need.

PHILOSOPHICAL CHOICES

Structuralism and Logical Positivism

Structuralism and modernity have become equated with a top-down, hierarchical worldview (Piaget, 1970) in which a particular institution and persons determine programs, services, and policies for the good of the whole. Structures are created by a few for the good of many. It is the responsibility of all players in this paradigm to maintain the highest levels of governance to control forces in the system and to recognize the internal integration of the system and its orientation to attaining the stated goals (Parsons, 1966). *Logical positivism* is the empirical label applied to this period in history, which reflects the orientation in Newtonian physics. For our purposes, the structuralist orientation has existed in schools and government for the last century. Accordingly, the federal government determines the policies and programs for all schools nationwide and leaves the states and schools responsible for meeting the federal requirements.

Social Constructivism

Social constructivism emerged in reaction to the logical positivist notions of truth and objectivity. Social constructivists argue that truth is contextualized and that the world is subjective (Lincoln, 1990). Meaning is based on the perceptions people arrive at when they experience a phenomenon (Geertz, 1973). Meaning is based on the collective perception that emerges when people share and learn from one another.

The application of this paradigm reshapes the way in which leaders and workers perceive their roles. Instead of searching for meaning from a place of objectivity, meaning is derived through collective investigation and dialogue about a particular issue or phenomenon. Information is seen as relative to a broader context rather than controllable and isolated. For leaders, this means that employees need to be involved in the acquisition and sharing of information to contribute to decisions and to meet strategic goals.

This brief discussion provides an orientation for thinking about response patterns and developing practices and behaviors. The structuralist period is aligned to Newtonian physics. For leaders to develop learning organizations, they will need to shift their philosophical orientation to social constructivism. As you read through the next sections of the chapter, consider your typical responses to accountability and evaluation. Are they structuralist in nature or social constructivist? If you answer structuralist, think about what you need to do differently to shift to a social constructivist way of thinking.

ACCOUNTABILITY: MOVING FROM COMPLIANCE MONITORING TO BENCHMARKING CHANGE

The accountability movement has guided public organizational life for decades (Wynne, 1972). Newmann, King, and Ridon (1997) state that accountability has been a relationship between a "steward or provider of a good or service and a patron or agent with the power to reward, punish, or replace the provider."

Its primary role has been to hold organizations responsible to public dollars that were spent on the delivery of services and goods. The original accountability model was designed in the scientific rationalist movement, in which efficiency was the primary goal. If the same service could be delivered for less money, then changes were made toward that end. Information was used to make decisions that were guided by economics rather than by changing customer needs.

The limitations for organizations caused by traditional accountability practices have led to new models that value a systems approach to the delivery of programs and services. In mental health, the focus is shifting to an examination of the multiple-service agencies that contribute to the success of children with special needs (Hernandez, Hodges, and Cascardi, 1998). In like manner, Darling-Hammond (1992) writes about the need to link the design of teacher-training programs to the requirements of professional accountability so that the criteria for success make sense. She further warns that hidden within is the opportunity for organizations to "shrink" their missions for the sake of accountability. In other words, the greater goals of the organization often are sacrificed for the good of accountability. The challenge for leaders today is to speak out and protect their organizational missions.

Newmann, King, and Ridon (1997) present a theory of accountability that should forewarn all leaders about how to detect accountability practices that have the potential to send their learning organizations into decline. There are four parts: (1) information about the organization's performance; (2) standards for judging the quality or degree of success of organizational performance; (3) significant consequences to the organization for its success or failure in meeting specified standards; and (4) an agent of constituency that receives information on organizational performance, judges the extent to which standards have been met, and distributes rewards and sanctions (43).

The concern with Newmann's theory from a learning organization standpoint is that it misses the mark on the potential to learn and stretch beyond what is known about a phenomenon. The concept of reward and sanction suggests that organizations achieve their goals once they demonstrate capacity and receive an award. Learning organizations never assume they have met a goal. Instead, they look for ways to improve their systems of work in a changing environment.

Results-Based Accountability

One form of accountability that holds promise for leaders as they move beyond the structural functionalist strongholds of bureaucracy is *results-based accountability,* a growing movement that calls for linking outcomes to process. Hernandez, Hodges, and Cascardi (1998) write that human services should be accountable for achieving measurable outcomes rather than continuing to focus on technical compliance with rules or on simple demonstrations of service need. To achieve this goal, organizations must rethink the information that is collected so that it is linked to program goals. Too often, information is used for compliance reporting, as in the case of a budget-allocation model, rather than for understanding whether programs and services make a difference (Hernandez, Hodges, and Cascardi, 1998; Burchard and Schaefer, 1992, as noted in Hernandez, Hodges, and Cascardi).

For programs and agencies to be appropriately accountable, they must develop information systems that provide usable data, implement feedback loops for continuous improvement, and link process to outcome. Results-based accountability, although in its infancy, has the potential to dramatically alter the way in which social services deliver programs of care and education to their constituents. According to Horsch (1996), new flexibility emerges with outcome-based accountability that "offers challenges not only in the articulation of goals and measurable results but also in the areas of service integration, governance and authority, and resource allocation."

The opportunities afforded agencies that develop results-based accountability processes are numerous and model the principles of the learning organization and emergent leadership. Stakeholders and program providers have opportunities to build a shared vision of program goals and strategies. They can learn to think creatively about problem solutions and move to a holistic mode of thinking about program development. Stakeholders share in dialogue about programs and outcomes and develop data collection and analysis systems to inform their decision making (Horsch, 1996).

Similarly, results-based accountability is grounded in information, which is needed to investigate the ways in which customer needs are being met. The links between results-based accountability and continuous improvement are growing. The emphasis on linking information throughout the system enables leaders and workers to build a holistic picture of how things are working in their organization. Linking information on process and output provides comprehensive information for building responsive systems to meet and exceed the changing needs of clients.

To enhance the continuous improvement process requires effective evaluation systems for accessing and analyzing information. We turn now to a historical exploration of evaluation models that have shaped our past practices and continue to give guidance to our current and future directions. There has been a paradigm shift in the field of evaluation from Newtonian physics to social constructivism, which enables leaders to think differently about the role of evaluation and the methods used to gather and assess information. No longer does information have to be bound by controllable conditions or external judges. New evaluation methods have the capacity to examine more complex problems and involve the organizational members as experts.

EVALUATION: MOVING FROM EXTERNAL JUDGMENT TO CONTINUOUS IMPROVEMENT

With the growing awareness that our social institutions need to be reshaped, assessment procedures must change as well (Linn, 1994). It is no longer enough to test students and assume that their achievement scores reflect the effectiveness of a curriculum or teaching. For evaluation to serve a meaningful function for development, it must be viewed as an integrating tool to examine the interconnected dimensions of the organization systems that influence student outcomes. This change represents a shift from structuralism to social constructivism.

In past years, evaluation was a programmatically driven activity designed to determine success or failure of implemented problem solutions or program changes (Guba and Lincoln, 1989). Rarely were evaluation practices integrated into the overall organizational development plan. Consequently, decisions for organizational improvement were developed around single, isolated events, which perpetuated a fragmented orientation to organizational growth.

Evaluation has been given many meanings and uses over the years, each of which, according to Guba and Lincoln (1989) and Borg and Gall (1989), have served well the needs of policy and have placed value in the external judge. Popham (1988) refers to evaluation as "a formal appraisal of the quality of educational phenomena" (7). Borg and Gall (1989) write that "evaluation is the process of making judgments about the merit, value, or worth of programs" (742). Evaluation research, write Rossi and Freeman (1989), is "the systematic application of social research procedures for assessing the conceptualization, design and implementation, and utility of programs" (5).

In the traditional model, an external consultant conducts an evaluation within parameters set by consultants who measure the effectiveness of organizational programs in response to policy. Guba and Lincoln (1989) argue that these definitions arose from a scientifically oriented process within the positivist paradigm (believing in an external, absolute measurable truth), in which evaluation is seen primarily as a technical process of inquiry by an external consultant. Rarely, they would add, are the internal members of an organization engaged in the evaluation process itself.

A historical examination of the paradigms in evaluation is offered to better understand the impact of philosophy on the type of information that is obtained through evaluation. We start our exploration from the practices that are most akin to logical positivism and Newtonian physics and move to those that are socially constructivist in nature. We do not wish to suggest that the positivist models are obsolete or out of date. The information is designed to raise awareness about the myriad options and their functions that exist for gathering information today. A careful understanding of evaluation is essential for leadership of the future.

Table 9.1   Models of evaluation.

Model	Focus	Paradigm
Formative Evaluation	Assessment of program toward goals while program is in progress	Positivism
Summative Evaluation	Assesses the effects or results of a program	Positivism
CIPP Model	Examines context, input, process, and product	Positivism
Stake's Countenance Model	Evaluates program prior to, during, and after implementation based on an emergent exploration	Postpositivism—bridge to social constructivism
Fourth Generation Evaluation	Focuses on the emergent nature of information and ideas, the constructed nature of knowledge, and the holistic context of reality	Social constructivist

Recognizing and selecting the paradigms most applicable to the type of information sought are critical.

We start with a table that presents the different periods and aligns them with the different philosophical paradigms (Table 9.1). The continuum ranges from the formative summative model (Scriven, 1973) to the *fourth generation evaluation* of Guba and Lincoln (1989).

Evaluation Models

Evaluation models over the years have taken many forms. Borg and Gall (1989) note that their methodology and epistemology can categorize such models. Quantitative evaluation models are built on the positivist notion of an objective measure, experimental control, and statistical data analysis. The models emphasize "a concern for determining what is generally true and worthwhile about the program being evaluated, rather than a concern for the individual case and idiosyncratic phenomena" (759). This philosophical underpinning, they continue, is limiting because it does not provide information about why a program does or does not work. Quantitative models emphasize the existence of a set of predetermined measurement criteria, an external judge, and a fixed goal.

Formative-Summative Evaluation

The most popular quantitative model has been Scriven's *formative-summative* model (Kaufman and Thomas, 1980; Rossi and Freeman, 1989). *Formative evaluation is* the "assessment of programs toward the identified goals while the program is still in progress" (Kaufman and Thomas, 1980, 111). The evaluation takes place during the program implementation and seeks answers to the following questions: *Does the program seem to be working as originally planned? Are all components of the program functioning effectively?* The framework for such assessment is an externally defined set of criteria (the program goals).

A limitation of this model is that there is a fixed goal and an assumption that change or interventions are static, occurring at a particulate point in time. New theories of program development are holding that organizational development (programs, services, and processes) is dynamic and constantly changing as new information becomes available (Fullan and Miles, 1992). Given this, it is necessary to extend the formative model to ask a third question: *Does everyone still agree upon the goal?*

The quality and systems theory literature suggests that goal setting and achievement assume a continuum of reshaping until needs are met. Rather than asking whether the goal is important, the question is raised, *Is our goal on target for meeting customer needs, given the information at this time?* The twist is slight, but it is consistent with distinctions between the judgmental model of the past and the new fourth generation evaluation model and benchmarking (Guba and Lincoln, 1989; McNair and Leibfried, 1992).

The *summative model* measures the effects or results of a program, and the evaluation is conducted at the program's conclusion (Kaufman and Thomas, 1980). Information is sought to answer the following questions: *Did the program make a difference? Did the program* fulfill *the identified needs and objectives? Are the students performing at the level specified in the goal statements?* Like the formative model, the summative model assumes a static goal and does not seek information about how well the program impacted the outcomes.

The *CIPP (context, input, process, product) model,* developed by Stufflebeam and Guba (1971), addresses several of the limitations with the formative and summative model. Accordingly, evaluation is defined as "the process of delineating, obtaining, and providing information useful for judging decision alternatives" (115). Contained in the definition is the framework for evaluation (Kaufman and Thomas, 1980): delineating information, obtaining data, and providing useful information to the decision maker. The CIPP model contains four components: context, input, process, and product. The model involves the evaluator as a team member with the decision makers for the planning and execution of the evaluation. This emphasis begins to bridge the gap between external judge and internal worker.

Another model, *Stake's countenance model* (Stake, 1967), introduced qualitative influences to the traditional quantitative designs, although it maintained the use of judgment as a major function of the evaluator. This model focuses on decisions that are made during the evaluation, which revolve around three phases of program development: antecedent, transaction, and outcome. During the antecedent phase, attention is given to the environmental conditions that have the potential to impact program outcomes. In the transaction phase, attention is paid to the effectiveness of the program while being implemented. The outcome phase examines the effects of the program after its completion. The evaluation involves both judgment and description (Kaufman and Thomas, 1980). Description is given to the program intentions and observations of its enactment. Judgment is given to the worth of the program by a set of established criteria, either absolute or comparative.

The strength of the model (Kaufman and Thomas, 1980) is that it "forces the evaluator to describe the events, activities, and conditions that exist before, during, and after the implementation of a program. This description will provide a wealth of information about both the intentions of the program developers and on-site observations of what actually occurred during each of the three phases" (124).

Borg and Gall (1989) refer to this model as "responsive evaluation," in which the focus is on the concerns and issues affecting the stakeholders. This is reflected in the antecedent phase, in which environmental conditions are identified that may influence the evaluation. Inherent in this model is the emphasis placed on emergent design, that is, the evaluation is shaped as new information is obtained. Unlike previous models, the evaluation protocol and criteria are not predefined. They emerge through the exploration of the issues and the stakeholders that affect and are affected by the program.

The introduction of Stake's model opened doors for the development of a new paradigm in educational evaluation. With an emphasis on issues and stakeholders, value is given to the needs, perspectives, and positions of organizational members relating to a program or service. Limited, however, is the involvement of all members in the organization as evaluative participants; and, further, an emphasis is given to the situatedness of the program within the larger whole of the schooling organization.

Fourth Generation Evaluation

Qualitative models are geared toward social constructivism and are based on the premise that the perspectives of the judges guide the worth of a program. Qualitative designs recognize the influences of environmental issues and build them into the design by valuing the subjective nature of the program designers and evaluators. Additionally, emphasis is placed on description as well as judgment. The major shift from quantitative to qualitative evaluation models occurred when Guba and Lincoln (1989) began talking about *fourth generation evaluation.*

Guba and Lincoln describe three other generations prior to the fourth generation. The first is called *measurement,* the testing of students and also the measuring of efficiency with the scientific management model of school design. During this generation, students were seen as raw goods to be processed in the school following the scientific management model (Borg and Gall, 1989; Guba and Lincoln, 1989; Kaufman and Thomas, 1980; Popham, 1988; Rossi and Freeman, 1989).

Guba and Lincoln (1989) refer to the second generation as *description.* This generation focused on identifying strengths and weaknesses of programs according to an established set of criteria. Measurement became a tool with which to collect data and then describe the findings. The third generation of evaluation they refer to as *judgment,* in which the purpose of an evaluator was to judge program effectiveness, thereby defining its worth.

Fourth generation evaluation is best characterized as an ongoing process of negotiation that involves all players in an organization and extends the notion of *emergent design* (Guba and Lincoln, 1989). Emergent designs, or fourth generation designs, socially construct an appropriate path for given information unique to the setting. This builds upon Stake's model and extends the definitions of description and judgment to reframe the evaluation paradigm. There are six properties that describe fourth generation evaluation:

1. Descriptions are not of a true state of affairs; they "represent meaningful constructions that individual actors or groups of actors form to 'make sense' of the situations in which they find themselves."

2. "It recognizes that the constructions through which people make sense of their situations are in a very major way shaped by the values of the constructors."

3. "It suggests that these constructions are inextricably linked to the particular physical, psychological, social, and cultural contexts within which they formed and to which they refer."

4. The "emergent form of evaluation recognized that evaluations can be shaped to enfranchise or disenfranchise stakeholder groups in a variety of ways."

5. "It suggests that evaluation must have an action orientation that defines a course to be followed, stimulates involved stakeholders to follow it, and generates and preserves their commitment to do so."

6. "Fourth generation evaluation insists that inasmuch as an evaluation involves humans, it is incumbent on the evaluator to interact with those humans in a manner respecting their dignity, their integrity, and their privacy" (8–11).

Fourth generation evaluation, to be effective, must (1) develop an evaluative process that recognizes the constructed nature of reality and as such the different values and situatedness of stakeholders; (2) recognize the holistic context in which a program and evaluation are defined and implemented; and (3) be fully participative of all stakeholders (Guba and Lincoln, 1989).

Guba and Lincoln raised some awareness for the evaluation community about who is the evaluator and have extended the doors on this field once again. For the learning organization, this is good news as they strive to incorporate a constructivist model of decision making and knowledge development. There are still, however, some limitations that need to be acknowledged.

Emphasis is still given to evaluating *programs* at a single level rather than evaluating the *organization* as a set of interconnected functions, processes, and work units. The literature on benchmarking addresses the need for expanding the role of evaluation in organizations to embrace not only the constructivist nature of reality as suggested by Guba and Lincoln but also the systems theory approach and quality management focus on student success and satisfaction.

Evaluation and the Learning Organization

As we traverse the history of evaluation, we can see that the focus has changed over time, calling into question who is the evaluator and what is evaluation. Much of the change resulted from a shift in epistemology from positivism to constructivism. Similarly, the value in learning together and from one another stimulated changes in the way that evaluation information is used for decision making and strategic planning.

Preskill and Torres (1999) state that these changes will impact the way people do work: Multidisciplinary teams will become the norm; innovation and diversity will be nurtured; professional cultures of support will be encouraged; and peer relationships will be valued. A major influence, they contend, will be the changing role of evaluation. Rather than focus on the rationalist approach to evaluation inquiry,[1] evaluative inquiry can become an integral part of daily life to help organizations develop, shape, and maintain effective programs and services. Evaluative inquiry "cannot only be the means of accumulating information for decision making and action but it [can] also be equally concerned with questioning and debating the value of what we do in organizations" (xix).

Learning organizations require value-laden evaluation that looks at process and outcome and their relation to organizational goals. The needs of the customer must be a key part of the formula, driving up the complexities of the evaluation itself. The people inside the organization must become a part of the evaluation team if the information is to be useful to the goals and mission. Failure to do so could result in information that is irrelevant to the program mission or so out of sync with the values and mission of its members that it is rendered obsolete.

Leaders need to take stock in their evaluations and rethink their approach to gathering information. The changes in evaluation that are taking place can free leaders to go beyond the traditional rigors of evaluation that were limited by sample size and available data and to support those processes that are designed to answer critical questions about needs that stem from a systems perspective.

Preskill and Torres[1] define the rationalist approach to evaluation inquiry as one that "assumes that the organization is an independent actor in its environment, that there is only one answer to the question, that everyone thinks rationally on behalf of the organization and will arrive at the same conclusion, and that full implementation follows every discovery of the one best strategy. This approach also focused on individual learning and short-term solutions . . . " (xix).

The challenge for leaders is to rethink the role of evaluation in the context of accountability and continuous improvement. By expanding the philosophical orientations to social constructivism, leaders expand the possibility of questions to be asked. No longer do agencies have to rely on external experts to collect and synthesize the information. The workers inside the organization, closest to the information, carry out the evaluations. The information that is generated is used for a host of functions, including accountability, knowledge development, and continuous improvement.

We turn now to a presentation of benchmarking to bring full circle the role of accountability and evaluation in the learning organization. Benchmarking is a process for examining organizational practices relative to best practices. Those higher standards of excellence exceed past requirements of accountability and help organizations continue growing beyond the status quo.

BENCHMARKING GROWTH

The role of evaluation in organizations is central to seeking information to inform decision making. However, the past and current models of evaluation seem to focus on a point-in-time question or process rather than on a continuous improvement effort. That is not to say that evaluation and continuous improvement are mutually exclusive. On the contrary, they are very interconnected and often one in the same. The difference lies more in the value and orientations of the distinct practices. On the one hand, evaluation focused on answering a fairly simple question: *Was the intervention successful? Benchmarking* focuses on answering the questions: *What are we doing? How are we doing it? Could we be doing it better?*

Several years ago, we began to explore the processes of benchmarking as part of the development of the Educational Quality Benchmark System. What we learned from our investigations and what we have developed over time, we think, are powerful for organizations today. There are many challenges facing leaders, many of which we have already highlighted. There are a number of how-to training programs on organizational development in the marketplace that leaders can tap into. The problem with them, from our perspective, is that they often place the consultant in the role of expert and fail to help organizations build their own expertise.

So much of what we like about benchmarking is that it is a concrete process that builds on the fundamental philosophy that supports social constructivism and systems theory. That is, people in the organization are in the best position to set goals, build strategies, and ask themselves how they think they are doing. Benchmarking also enables the development of another critical function in organizations: *self-reflection* (*self* can be the worker, the team, or the organization). For agencies to move into learning organizations, workers must learn to step back and take a look at where they are in relation to where they want to be. We call this *organizational reflection.* The heart of the learning often takes place in the reflective space.

How many times have you gone through a big project or a major move unaware of what you were experiencing or how well you were doing? It was not until you stepped back from the situation that you began to see the results of your efforts. Most of us, if not all, have grown up with sayings such as *stop and smell the roses,* or *in hindsight . . . ,* or *looking back. . . .* The process of continuous improvement (of which benchmarking is a part) is built on the premise that we need to stop and take a look around periodically to survey what we are doing. If we wait too long, we find ourselves saying things like *if only . . .* or *in hindsight. . . .*

The practice of benchmarking started years ago and was used regularly in the field of engineering (Camp, 1989). Surveyors who surveyed the land would mark a point on a tree and call that the benchmark. They used the benchmark as a reference point against which to measure everything else. The process of benchmarking has expanded into additional fields and is a common practice in business today. Leaders focus on an area of their organization that needs improvement and identify competitors who are successful in that particular area. They study the competitor's process and use it as the benchmark (the reference point) for their own improvement.

Organizations can establish benchmarking processes that emulate and fulfill performance-monitoring needs, or they can move beyond to focus on continuous improvement. We use benchmarking relative to the latter as a process to stimulate organizational learning, reflection, problem identification, problem solution, and continuous improvement. We encourage organizations to constantly "explore new options." Performance monitoring is an outdated practice of holding constant decisions that were made at one point in time. Organizations that learn and grow are dynamic and never static. To assume that one could *monitor* success relative to a static notion of excellence is reserved for another book by different authors. We challenge you to explore benchmarking as a way to develop your learning organization within a dynamic and constantly changing environment.

Concepts

Benchmarking as initially defined is the process of measuring organizational growth and development against industry best standards (Camp, 1989; Watson, 1993). As both a process and a tool, benchmarking provides important changes for organizational development that within the framework of systems theory hold promise for schools to rethink the ways in which they use evaluation information.

Camp (1989) states that benchmarking identifies processes, practices, and methods that establish and perpetuate the function of the organization. In the past, assessment focused on programs and services, ignoring the processes for achieving the outcomes (Spendolini, 1992). It was later recognized that the process an organization uses to conceptualize, produce, and market goods and services is a key to understanding the differences between successful businesses and less successful ones (Camp, 1989; McNair and Leibfried, 1992).

According to Camp (1989), benchmarking can benefit a company in the following ways:

- It enables the best practices from any industry to be creatively incorporated into the processes of the benchmarked function.

- It can provide stimulation and motivation to the professionals whose creativity is required to perform and implement benchmarking findings.

- Benchmarking breaks down ingrained reluctance of operations to change.

- Benchmarking may also identify a technological breakthrough that would not have been recognized or applied.

Camp (1989) suggests that the search must focus on industry best practices rather than on a competing agency. By examining the characteristics that advance an organization, business leaders are better able to implement changes beyond the program level to a broader conceptual level.

Camp (1989) defines what benchmarking is not. He states that "benchmarking is not a mechanism for determining resource reduction; it is not a program; it is not a cookbook process; nor is it a fad" (14). It is, however, a discovery process and learning experience; an ongoing management process that requires constant updating; and a business strategy for assisting managers in "identifying practices that can be adapted to build winning, credible, defensible plans and strategies and complement new initiatives to achieve the highest performance goals" (15).

In a review of the literature on benchmarking, Spendolini (1992) examined 49 definitions and found the following commonalties, which he used to create his working definition: a (1) continuous (2) systemic (3) process for (4) evaluating the (5) products, (6) services, and (7) work processes (of organizations) that are (8) recognized as (9) representing the (10) best practices (11) for time purposes of organizational improvement. The emphasis in Spendolini's work is on learning, rather than on competitive edge. Benchmarking, he submits, is another form of professional development and organizational growth, which connects to implications within the learning organization: "organizations need to step outside themselves and scrutinize their internal view of the world. This is done when one exposes one's own thinking and makes that thinking open to the influence of others" (16). Within this context, benchmarking becomes a tool for guiding people through the process of looking to the outside for ideas and looking internally from a different perspective at current practices.

Why Benchmark and What to Benchmark?

Benchmarking provides an organization with information about customer needs, effective goals, productivity, competitive advantages and disadvantages, and industry best practices (Camp, 1989; McNair and Leibfried, 1992). It is useful for strategic planning; forecasting; developing new ideas, products, and services; and for goal setting. As a change management tool, benchmarking enables organizations to improve upon existing performance in an objective, measurable way.

Several organizational elements have been identified in the literature as appropriate to benchmark. They include products and services, work processes, support functions, organizational performance, strategy (Spendolini, 1992), roles, and effectiveness and efficiency (McNair and Leibfried, 1992).

Types of Benchmarking

Benchmarking is a point of reference at different levels in organizational change and development to assess improved processes, services, and outcomes for increased customer satisfaction. There are three types of benchmarking: (1) strategic planning benchmarking, (2) process benchmarking, and (3) results benchmarking. (1) *Strategic planning* benchmarking is used as a method of comparing current organizational results against world-class standards of excellence. This method is a framework for planning and designing better quality services. (2) *Process* benchmarking gathers data and compares a procedure that the organization is interested in improving. The use of process benchmarking involves one organization studying and adopting the procedures of a well-designed process from another organization. (3) *Results* benchmarking is used to improve the outcomes of the organization by referencing world-class standards, such as the Education Quality Benchmark System (EQBS) for self-assessment and organizational-assessment purposes. Results benchmarking is used to gather pre and post data to measure "adequate progress" in relation to specified outcomes. In results benchmarking, then, there is an overall evaluation system in place for the organization. All three of these benchmarking methods are used to improve the organizational outcomes that impact customer success and satisfaction.

Four types of benchmarking processes are discussed in the literature (Camp, 1995; Spendolini, 1992): (1) internal, (2) competitive, (3) functional, and (4) generic. *Internal* benchmarking is the process of comparing similar operations within the organization. *Competitive* benchmarking involves comparing internal processes, products, and services with those of direct competitors. *Functional* benchmarking is a comparison to similar companies outside the industry. *Generic* benchmarking is a comparison of work processes to others' work processes that are identified as exemplary.

Watson (1993) identifies five generations of benchmarking, each one of which provides a different focus for organizational development: (1) reverse engineering, (2) competitive benchmarking, (3) process benchmarking, (4) strategic benchmarking, and (5) global benchmarking. *Reverse engineering* involved product comparison with competitors, focusing on the technical makeup of the product or service. *Competitive benchmarking* introduced product analysis to examine the capacities of the products and services. *Process benchmarking* shifted the comparison from industry competitors to businesses outside the industry, postulating that more information is attainable when the barriers to competition of industry are removed. *Strategic benchmarking* is known as a "systemic process for evaluating alternatives, implementing strategies, and improving performance by understanding and adapting successful strategies from external partners" Watson (1993) (8). The newest form of benchmarking, *global benchmarking,* emphasizes global comparisons that recognize the influence of cultural patterns and trade relations on business success.

Benchmark Modes

Camp (1995) outlines a five-phase model of benchmarking, which includes (1) planning, (2) analysis, (3) integration, (4) action, and (5) maturity. In the *planning* stage, it is decided what to benchmark and whom to benchmark, and an action plan is developed. In the *analysis* phase, performance gaps are identified and future performance levels are established. In the *integration* phase, findings from the assessment are disseminated and goals are refined. The *action* stage involves implementing new practices that were generated from the benchmark findings, which are presumed to advance the organization. *Maturity* is the phase in which continual process improvement occurs.

Spendolini (1992) provides a similar model, involving five stages: (1) determine what to benchmark, (2) form a benchmarking team, (3) identify benchmark partners, (4) collect and analyze benchmarking information, and (5) take action.

This particular model, unlike most others, is presented in a circular design, indicating the ongoing continual improvement process that underlies the heart of benchmarking. It is not enough to engage in a linear process of measurement and goal refinement. Best practices are established in an ongoing manner as new information is collected regularly and incorporated in the decision-making and program-development process.

Qualitative versus Quantitative Benchmarks

For years, traditional measurements in business have been number oriented, stemming primarily from profit margins and cost bases. Recent trends in organizational improvement have recognized its limitations, for it does not provide significant information about the qualitative characteristics of process (McNair and Leibfried, 1992). To balance this, benchmarking has developed around both quantitative and qualitative methods.

Quantitative benchmarks focus on operating or products characteristics and can reflect internal process performance (McNair and Leibfried, 1992). These measures examine productivity, product quality, and delivery rates. Such information is obviously critical for business leaders. Quantitative information, however, is not without its limitations. Organizational development through quantitative analysis tends to place emphasis on doing whatever is necessary to meet goals rather than on understanding why the goals and the tasks are necessary.

Qualitative benchmarks are organizational elements unidentifiable through a quantitative focus (McNair and Leibfried, 1992). Accordingly, qualitative benchmarks (components within an organization) are critical about the organization's ability to be responsive to industry and stakeholder needs. Common qualitative benchmarks include product complexity, organizational capacity, customer satisfaction, marketing and work processes, and paperwork processes. Defining mechanisms for both types of information is now recognized as critical to successful organizational development from a holistic perspective.

The benchmarking process expands the tool base for schools to engage in systemic organizational assessment by providing a mechanism in which to examine qualitative components of the organization, such as customer satisfaction, human resource development, and strategic planning. The value of benchmarking as a unique internal measure of success lies in its emphasis on continual improvement, information systems, employee involvement, and strategic planning. With the use of benchmarking, schools have a tool for guiding organizational development out of the bureaucratic model and into systems theory designs.

One area in organizational life (and the heart of benchmarking) that is often ignored is the development of effective information systems. We have talked considerably in this chapter about the processes in organizations that require information. Those processes are only as good as the information that is available. Leaders need to understand the value of information, as well as some of the bumps that lie in the road ahead as they begin to build information systems. In the next and last section of this chapter, we provide a broad examination of information systems and illustrate some of the ways in which they have been developed and some of the problems that have occurred along the way. Information systems are a complex entity and are at the heart of organizational learning.

INFORMATION SYSTEMS FOR BENCHMARKING

Burch and Grudnitski (1986) define information as "data that have been put into a meaningful and useful context and communicated to a recipient who uses it to make decisions" (3). There are many forms of information, including text documents, visual images, computer databases, audiotapes, and conversations. The ways in which we obtain and receive the information vary as well. We read magazines, watch the news, read quarterly and annual reports, surf the Internet, engage in conversations, attend lectures, and read books; the list goes on.

The challenge for today's organizations is to determine the type of information collected and the form of dissemination, accessibility, and processing. Agencies have at their disposals numerous sources of critical information, including student grades and attendance, promotion rates, teacher training, feedback from seminars, and comparisons to other schools. The problem is that much of this information is not perceived to be very useful in making program improvement decisions. The information, once used to comply with state accountability, needs to be reconceptualized as indicators of organizational success. Not all data are limited to compliance monitoring.

One of the authors recently conducted a research study (which could be seen as a learning organization evaluation) to examine the relationship between work culture and student achievement. Using existing data from an instrument on work culture development and a separate report on student achievement, she was able to link information by school to answer her question. What she found was that there is a statistically significant relationship between work culture and student achievement. What this means for schools is that one way to enhance student learning and achievement is to focus on the functions of work (visionary leadership, strategic planning, human resource development, systems thinking and action, quality services, and customer satisfaction). Schools that tend to their work norms, behaviors, programs, and service create a learning context that helps students succeed. More detailed study findings are given in the next chapter. It is used here to illustrate how organizations can take existing information and link it together to address new, often more complex, questions.

Organizations need to take inventory of their data and think creatively about how to link it both within their agency and across agencies. Linked information is the key to studying how organizational inputs are contributing to meeting customer needs.

A children's mental health project (Hernandez, Hodges, and Cuscardi, 1998) is built around a results-based accountability model and relies heavily on information to guide learning and change. The premise is based on a systems-of-care model that portends that people's outcomes are affected by a variety of forces. For example, children with special needs are influenced by social workers, teachers, and, at times, law enforcement. Successful outcomes may depend on the influence of all these forces. To understand the outcome requires information to be gathered and linked between the different agencies.

Information can be a powerful tool if used effectively. Development of information systems and pathways takes considerable care. In the early 1990s, a social service system in Florida set out to develop an administrative data system (capturing information on clients, such as hospital records) to record information on the clients that were being served by the system's providers. The data system was conceptualized at the state level and implemented locally. Considerable information was to be captured about the people served by the system (their age, race, gender, incoming level of care need, treatment plan, and outcomes). The invention of the system was needed and carefully constructed. The use of the system, however, fell short.

We found this out when one of the authors and a colleague tried to use the data to study the effects of a program model on the clients, which is a growing use of secondary administrative data in health services research. The data were inconsistent between providing agencies. What one person recorded in field A was different from that of the next recorder. In a qualitative investigation, we uncovered that caseworkers at the provider level did not have enough information to understand either the usefulness of the data or the meaning behind certain data fields.

One result of our investigation was that a statewide data committee was formed, facilitated by the state department lead agency. The mission of the group is to make necessary revisions to the data system to better meet today's information needs and also to address the pragmatic issues of implementing the data records at the local level. The members are state agency leaders, providers, and university staff who work with administrative data sets.

The challenge for social service agencies to build effective information systems is complex. First, leaders need to work together with staff to explore, understand, modify, and implement effective information sources for their purposes. Second, all parties need to be in agreement about the power of the information or else it will continue to be perceived as a paperwork burden for frontline workers. Third, the information needs to be linked to program goals *and* outcomes. Fourth, all sources of information need to be examined to determine whether there are ways to streamline what is captured and reduce unnecessary paperwork. In the age of information technology, we run the high risk of information overload. Teachers are testament to this today. Ask teachers anywhere, and you will hear that one of their greatest sources of frustration is the amount of paperwork

(Snyder, Acker-Hocevar, and Snyder, 1994a). The same is true for social workers, doctors, nurses, correction officers, probation officers, and the rest of those who work in social service positions.

Many books and programs in the marketplace address building effective information systems, the details of which go beyond the scope of this chapter. The message that we want to convey is that information is powerful but that it needs to be carefully cultivated and constantly reviewed and that personnel in agencies need to learn how to work with it and benefit from it. The need for information is great, but it has to be the kind of information that connects to program goals and is understood by its users and its builders.

The process of benchmarking is just that: a process. To carry out the process, people and organizations need access to a variety of information that will help them understand what is going on in the organization and how well they meet customer need. Leaders must give special attention to this otherwise underused aspect of organizational leadership to facilitate the learning organization.

SUMMARY

Building the learning organization takes the right philosophical frame for gathering information. It takes a commitment to information and knowledge development, as well as to meeting customer need. The practices that have guided public social organizations to date most likely will continue for some time and may get even more intense. Leaders and workers will always be held accountable to their constituents, which is not a bad thing. Furthermore, this kind of accountability lies at the heart of the learning organization. The difference is the way in which leaders approach accountability and information systems.

The challenge for leaders is to examine the link between accountability, evaluation, and continuous improvement through benchmarking. Practices that are grounded in the constructivist philosophy can enhance organizational success and exceed government and customer need. In so doing, leaders must confront the all too common catch-22 and develop strategies for incorporating accountability and evaluation techniques into models of continuous improvement.

NOTES

1. Preskill and Torres define the rationalist approach to evaluation inquiry as one that "assumes that the organization is an independent actor in its environment, that there is only one answer to the question, that everyone thinks rationally on behalf of the organization and will arrive at the same conclusion, and that full implementation follows every discovery of the one best strategy. This approach also focused on individual learning and short-term solutions . . ." (xix).

10

Building a New Dynamic through Social Networks

The growing focus on accountability and student achievement in most nations poses difficulties for educators who want to develop learning spaces that not only focus on academic knowledge but on social development as well. Moreover, educators and schools are drowning in bureaucratic mandates that more often than not replace creativity and stimulation with norms and standards. While there is nothing wrong with the principles that underlie accountability, educators need to find ways to work within the frameworks to also promote the love of learning and stimulate creativity.

This chapter underscores the importance of social networks for learning to help principals and teachers create schools in which youth are engaged in their own development for lifelong learning and global citizenship. Moreover, networks can serve professional development, through which educators can give rise to a new dialogue in education that is not merely about governmental mandates, but that has more to do with the purpose of education: to help youth develop knowledge, skills, and social competencies so they can contribute to humanity and society through living and work. Social networks create connections through which ideas are shared and knowledge is socially constructed. They are based on the premise that knowledge is what transforms groups and society, not structures and bureaucracies. We believe the concept of social networks holds great promise for advancing a new dialogue in education and promoting the future generations.

Several years ago, in a movie called *Pay It Forward,* based on the book by Catherine Ryan Hyde (1999), a teacher challenged each of his students to find a way to make a difference in the world that could be put into action. The main character, a young boy, develops a system that he calls "pay it forward" in which each person should do one good thing for three people, and those three persons should do a good deed for three more persons, and so forth. As the good deeds multiply, the number of persons who are positively touched by human difference increases. The movie focuses on the exponential power of human caring for making a difference in the world when we each reach out and touch one another.

Just yesterday I was reminded of this movie as I stood in line to pay for a ticket to park my car in town. A man came up to me and said, "You can have mine, it still has some time left and I don't need it." Caught off guard, I stared at the man, not quite understanding what he was saying. He then asked me how long would I be in the store shopping. I estimated 15 minutes. He gave me his ticket and said, "You have other things to use your money for," and left. I proceeded to my car with thoughts of the movie in my head and wondering: How can I pay this nice gesture forward? I looked at the time left on the ticket: "Expires 12:41." That appeared to be plenty of time for me, as it was only 12:10 and I estimated being in the store for only about 15 minutes. I placed the ticket on my dashboard and went to the store. When I returned, I looked at the clock: 12:41. How did that man know I would need a ticket to 12:41? I still am trying to figure out how I can pay it forward!

The movie *Pay It Forward* points out the importance of our social connections and the power of networking for transformation. Each time we make a connection, we impact others as well as ourselves. My personal exchange, while not related to what is going on in schools today, does strike a chord in the daily reminder that simple gestures stimulate us into action, which has the potential to facilitate change. When we establish connections and build on them, we are naturally building a network of energy that has the potential to transform. Social network theorists (Mohrman, Tenkasi, and Mohrman, 2003; Stephenson, 2005; Tenkasi and Chesmore, 2003) contend that it is through our connections with others that we learn and give rise to new knowledge. This is a provocative notion in relation to learning in a global age when we consider that most students are still learning in their own environments about other cultures, rather than connecting with other cultures to learn together. Meanwhile, there is talk daily about the need to find ways to solve global issues and bring peace to the world. Perhaps building networks of learners around the world, for youth and adults, is a part of the equation. As Russell (1998) suggests, it is through our human relationships that we "wake up" to create peace in accelerating times. If our connections are based on an ethic of care and mutual appreciation, our collective actions can have far-reaching consequences for societal change, as well as return to education to one of its primary purposes: social and human development.

When we consider the conditions of our global society, we see the need even more to place human social development front and center in education. The promises of technology and global advancement to bring greater equality to the world have not panned out. Capra (2002) points out that global capitalism is "harming the biosphere and the human way of life in ways that may soon become irreversible" (146). Castells (2000) argues that while globalization held a promise to decrease poverty and increase equality across nations, the reverse has happened. Rather than bringing together humanity, it has exacerbated social exclusion. This is the result, primarily, of an economic model of globalization, which has been shaped by corporate and national networks that are based on growing profits. Needed are counterforce networks, composed of social institutions and citizens, to create new directions in caring for humanity that address social justice and equality.

Society has "seduced us—in effect hypnotized us—into a set of false assumptions about what it is that we really want, and how to go about achieving it" (Russell, 1998, xii). For example, the heavy focus by governments to "produce" youth who have high achievement scores as a sign of success creates the false assumption that it is academics that matter for success in life. Moreover, their rhetoric leads to policies that promote a kind of education that focuses more on rote learning than creativity and knowledge development. Contrast this with a less audible message by such nongovernmental organizations as UNESCO in which the focus is on the importance of preparing youth for living and working in a global society with such competencies as networking, entrepreneurship, leadership, creativity, digital literacy, and the like. The media are strong and often aligned with the messages of governments, causing educators to focus on achievement rather than on social growth and development. As Cogan (1998) reminds us, this assumption is lacking, for we are also reminded daily of the global conditions of poverty, degradation of the environment, and violence, and to resolve these concerns requires a pedagogy of care that focuses on values for peace, humanity, and the environment. If schools continue to focus on academics and follow a pedagogical principle that schools have the knowledge for children and youth to acquire, how then will future generations be prepared to work together in harmony to generate knowledge for solutions to global problems?

In this chapter we explore ways in which educators can expand their learning environments by connecting youth and their schools in social learning networks around the world. As an example, we examine a model from the International School Connection that represents the ways in which schools can share information to build a global ethic of care through programming. The purpose is to be a part of the knowledge development that promotes solutions to world problems. We are not suggesting that educators ignore the structures or policies in which they work, but rather that they see the benefits of connecting youth and schools in a dynamic social learning network. Accordingly, we first explore what it means to develop an "engaged pedagogy," which reinforces the importance of education for societal development and transformation. Second, we examine key characteristics of networks that are powerful and important in order to stimulate learning and to connect schools globally. Third, we share an example of what happens when schools engage in a social network to leverage change in education and society. In this example, we also illustrate ways in which your schools can engage in social networks for learning.

EDUCATION FOR ENGAGED GLOBAL CITIZENSHIP

For years, it has been the responsibility of education to prepare citizens with both academic knowledge and opportunities for social development within the context of a single nation. As we enter the era of globalization, in which "the planet and family are facing an unprecedented set of challenges including the globalization of the economy . . . rapidly changing technology . . . loss of a sense of community and shared belief in the common good . . . and large scale migration" (Cogan, 1998, 1), it is time to rethink the role of education for preparing citizens on a global scale. Furthermore, rising rates of unemployment, illiteracy, student dropouts, community violence, and people disengaged from a cohesive sense of connection and purpose are taking a toll on our local, national, and global communities.

The question posed by Cogan (1998) is "how does one respond to these challenges both as a member of a particular nation-state as well as a member of a global community in a manner that is thoughtful, active, personal and yet with a commitment to the common good?" (1). The answer is not a simple one, but it does require a shift in the focus of education from preparing citizens for a single nation to a global community of nations. It requires an emphasis on characteristics of the global citizen including a sense of identity, responsibility to shared obligations, a degree of interest in public affairs, and an acceptance of basic societal values (Cogan, 1998).

The Commission on International Education states that "while education is an ongoing process of improving knowledge and skills, it is also—perhaps primarily—an exceptional means of bringing about personal development and building relationships among individuals groups, and nations" (Delors, 1998, 14). Through education, we as a global community have the opportunity to work with people of all cultures to ensure that as we move to a market-oriented focus on life, we do not lose a sense of connection to community and cultural heritage, nor lose our moral, social, and family values. For the children of the future, it is essential to keep these core components of life at the forefront of their human development. Failure to do so will result in a future lacking in humanitarian values and sense of community connectedness.

Recently, the International Commission on Education for the Twenty-first Century developed four pillars of learning that they believe are at the heart of education. They are learning to know, learning to do, learning to live together, and learning to be (Delors, 1998). Traditional schooling has focused primarily on learning to know. Yet for students to develop within the twenty-first century, they will have to know how to learn, how to live and work with people from different cultures, and how to be members of a humanitarian village. To meet this challenge, schools will have to embrace new forms of teaching and learning that are facilitated by a new kind of school leader. Additionally, students, teachers, and leaders will need to work closely with people of different cultures to solve world problems and with local businesses and agencies to address the needs of the local community.

The "knowledge society" is upon us, according to global policy, and it is shaping the ways in which we communicate, define borders, define knowledge, define citizenship, and shape our social institutions (Information Society Commission, 2002; UNESCO, 2002). No longer are we focused on production and efficiency, as in the industrial era. Instead we are focused on lifelong learning, active citizenship, and the knowledge worker (Field, 2000; Naval, Print, and Veldhuis, 2002). Our future development rests on our ability as citizens to develop a new kind of awareness and knowledge about living in the world today (Pink, 2005). We are no longer limited to local realities, but we now must understand our cultural heritage in relation to a larger community of nations and people. As such, we need to rethink our educational institutions to prepare us for living in the knowledge society.

Given that the responsibility of educational institutions has been to promote learning and knowledge development, a natural question arises about what knowledge is in the global age. The "knowledge society" is a big concept driven mostly by technological and economic thinking (Mokyr, 2002), and now people are beginning to question what it means in relation to human and social relations and learning (Mason, 1998; Naval, Print, and Veldhuis, 2002). Further, many are questioning whether the knowledge society is shaped for the common good or for the benefit of big business. Are we repeating the crisis in Brazil that Freire wrote about in his landmark book, *Pedagogy of the Oppressed* (1968), or are we truly in a new century of school and community development led by the notion of networks (Castells, 1996) and collaboration in a democratic society?

For decades, educators such as Paulo Freire (1970), Maxine Greene (1988), and Bell Hooks (1994) have promoted the notion that education is about freedom and emancipation. They suggest that giving voice and creating space for students, teachers, and educators to engage in reflection and dialogue about society and social values is a primary task of education. Freire (1970) long ago suggested that pedagogy can empower people to move beyond conditions of oppression and control. Together, in reflection and dialogue, the oppressed can liberate themselves. He states that "no one liberates himself by his own efforts alone, neither is he liberated by others" (53). This message has a double meaning in a global age, for at one level it reminds us of the importance of education for self-empowerment and emancipation, and at another level it urges us to *engage in community* as a way to transform current conditions.

Maxine Greene (1988) argues the need to develop education as a public space in which youth give meaning to freedom in order to actively engage in shaping society, rather than accepting external control, demands, and structures as an objective reality. The current political systems of control, both culturally and institutionally, have perpetuated a negative effect on freedom whereby we have come to accept such things as accountability and high stakes testing as *the* reality for what is important to education. Greene contends that such a view is

> antithetical to . . . education for freedom. They are antithetical because they alienate persons from their own landscapes, because they impose a fallacious completeness on what is perceived. Instead of reaching out, along with others, toward open possibilities in experience, individuals in all groups accept existing structures as givens. They may try to make use of them or escape them or move around them or make a mockery of them; but they feel themselves in a way doomed to see them as objective "realities," impervious to transformation, hopelessly there. To objectify in this fashion, to separate oneself as 'subject' from an independently existent "object," is to sacrifice possibility of becoming the author of one's world; and the consciousness of authorship has to do with the consciousness of freedom. (1988, 22)

More and more we see that the institution of education is being objectified by government controls, and now additionally with international politics. Educators are spinning by the minute to respond to new rhetoric about the "future citizen" (knowledge worker), and the need to reinvent the curriculum and classroom learning. Unfortunately, the rhetoric and policies are changing so rapidly that educators are forced to bypass the pedagogical reflection and planning necessary to develop healthy learning environments in favor of developing responses to the "rhetoric of the month." Bell Hooks (1994) talks about "engaged pedagogy" as necessary to emancipate teaching for social action and transformation. Her work communicates the importance of seeing oneself as subject rather than object, thereby empowering the self to engage in transformation and to question oppression and injustice. This concept of empowering ourselves to engage in shaping life, rather than accepting the status quo, is of central importance to education in a global age. It has implications for both teaching and learning, as educators and students engage together in their community to reflect on the social condition.

Hooks' concept of *empowerment through the subjectivity of self* is an important feature of a larger argument for educational development in a global age that is framed within a metaphor of community. Considering education as freedom within a global framework draws added value from the social networks and communities of collaboration that are building internationally. These networks are powerful silos for voice that can spread the impact of an engaged pedagogy from individuals to community. The global stage provides us with channels to help youth develop competencies for success in the global age as well as to empower them to participate in shaping a global ethic of care in dialogue with others around the world. In the next section we explore aspects of social network theory, to better understand the ways in which social networks can be used as a learning forum, as well as how the form creates natural spaces for knowledge development globally.

Social Networks for Learning and Knowledge Development

In the late 1990s, the need to change educational structures and programming to prepare youth for global living became more commonly understood, yet we continue to seek ways to respond. The rise of the network society was well under way, and technology was integrating into our daily lives. Over time we have come to understand more and more the importance of networks and their role in shaping new learning spaces built on collaboration and the social construction of knowledge. We suggest as well that social networks can be used by educators to expand the ways in which youth can both develop skills for living and working in a global age and engage in a global ethic of care. In Chapter 1 we introduced some basic theoretical concepts of social networks and their potential for advancing education in a global society. In this chapter we focus on how social networks can be applied in and across schools to engage youth in learning together with others across cultures and build a global ethic of care in the process. Because networks are structures that emerge and take shape from the persons and connections within the network, we want to highlight three central characteristics that are important for building social networks for learning. They are the concept of connections, dynamics, and structures. We highlight these three to point out the emerging nature of networks in order that you, as an educator, will see your role as facilitator of connections in which information can be shared, rather than transmitted as knowledge to students in a traditional educational structure based on passive learning.

Connections

Social network analysis is a process of understanding the connections between sets of people connected by social relationships (Garton et al., 1999). Social network analysts seek to

> Describe networks of relations as fully as possible, tease out the prominent patterns in such networks, trace the flow of information through them, and discover what effects these relations and networks have on people and organizations. They treat the description of relational patterns as interesting in its own rights—for example, is there a core and periphery?—and examine how involvement in such social networks helps to explain the behavior attitudes or network members,—for example, do peripheral people send more email and do they feel more involved." (76)

Connectors or connections are central to any network: Without them there is no network (Barabási, 2003; Buchanan, 2002; Watts, 2003). Connectors in human networks are the "who" that share the "what" with one another. The "what" in this case are resources, which can be in the form of information, ideas, experiences, or perspectives. As people share resources (exchange ideas), new knowledge emerges through the transaction. The more people who are engaged and the more ideas that are shared, the more complex the network becomes. Stephenson (2005) claims that relationships are the basis of any knowledge exchange and that building trust in our relationship that enables us to build powerful networks that sustain development. When we think about traditional learning theory, it is typical for the teacher to possess the knowledge and the student to acquire it through different activities. In network theory, knowledge development is assumed to take place through the social exchange of ideas, perspectives, and experience. This view of knowledge development is also beginning to have a stronger presence in learning theory today with the development of technology in education. Sorensen and Tackle (2002) state that collaborative learning is a process through which people build knowledge together. Lave and Wenger (1991) suggest that it is within a community of learning that a common curriculum is shaped, which naturally engages members of the community in practice. This is contrary to the non-community-based model of education in which students are objects of learning rather than the creators of learning. Social networks then are not only a form or structure for resource sharing; they reflect a human system of knowledge development, which we believe is powerful for engaging youth in building a global ethic of care. Through social networks, youth and educators have the possibility to share different perspectives and experiences across cultures through which they can shape knowledge globally. While most curricula focus on learning about world cultures and problems from a distance, social networks place youth in a global community to learn together through which they become the curriculum and enhance their own learning.

Dynamics

A second characteristic of networks is the dynamic that emerges from connections. Early theories about networks assumed that networks were static structures that did not develop. As Watts (2003) states, later findings disproved this notion:

> The crux of the matter is that in the past, networks have been viewed as objects of pure structure whose properties are fixed in time. Neither of these assumptions could be further from the truth. First, real networks

represent populations of individual components that are actually do-ing something—generating power, sending data, or even making deci-sions. Although the structure of the relationships between a network's components is interesting, it is important principally because it affects either their individual behavior or the behavior of the systems as a whole. Second, networks are dynamic objects not just because things happen in networked systems, but because the networks themselves are evolving and changing in time, driven by the activities or decisions of those very components. In the connected age, therefore, what happens and how it happens depend on the network. (28)

Watts suggests that a particular dynamic and energy are shaped by the con-nections within a network and what happens around the network. The kinds of connections thus become important for generating a certain kind of energy. In the world today, we have a variety of networks, including economic, political, business, and social. Not all the networks generate a positive energy or dynamic, as we are reminded daily. For example, the environment is deeply affected by our human network use of gasoline and electricity around the world. While we may not have understood our actions in relation to one another years ago, today we are aware that each of us is a part of the network impacting our environment, and it is we who need to change our actions to alter the dynamics of global warming. We cannot do this in isolation; required is a collective understanding as well as a collective exchange of information and ideas about what we can do differently. We are all beginning to understand this clearly through the work of Al Gore and the global network he is building around environmentalism. It was the dynamics of the connections associated with Al Gore and his recent movie, *An Inconvenient Truth,* that the dialogue got louder and the actions stronger around the world to participate in shaping new conditions for the environment. Today, not only can we watch the film or read the book, but we also can participate in global forums to be a part of shaping the knowledge about how to care for our global environment.

The concept of dynamics within and on networks is important for education when we think about learning and knowledge development. In networks, the knowledge is generated through a growing dynamic that takes place between the connections within the network structure. In most schools, the learning takes place in relation to textbooks and teacher-developed activities with predetermined tasks that often do not involve for creativity and innovation among youth. Even in those schools where group learning is used, the potential for a dynamic to build is limited by the curriculum and the teacher-led activities. What we can learn from network theory is that when knowledge is shaped in exchange with others, there is a synchrony (energy) that naturally stimulates curiosity, commitment, problem solving, creative thinking, self-direction, and knowledge development. When we consider learning and competencies necessary for life in a global age, it is natural to ask, What would happen to learning and global development if students were able to experience the dynamics generated from cross-cultural social networks in schools? Many students already know the answer to this, for they live in global social networks in their spare time. We suggest that there is much to gain from social network learning for stimulating energy in schools and communities and for preparing youth for global living. As Watts pointed out, what happens in the world depends on the dynamics in the networks and the dynamics on the network. In other words, the extent to which education can make a difference in the world depends largely on the kinds of networks in which educators and youth are engaged and the kinds of things about which they are engaged.

Structures

One of the assumptions that we have lived with for years is that "structures" are necessary to determine how work gets done, who does the work, and who connects to whom. The question that we need to ask today is "what kind of structure?" What network theorists have found is that it is not the formal structure of a hierarchy that is most reflective of how work gets done, but rather the structure of a network: in other words, who knows whom, and who is connecting with whom to get work done. While this may seem trivial to the context of learning in schools, we must remind ourselves that schools are preparing youth for working in a global, networked society. Thus it becomes important to understand both how networks function and how they can be applied in schools to promote competencies necessary for the global society. Stephenson (2005) points out that while organizations and governments have focused on the formal hierarchy for years to guide change and development, it is in the network structures where rapid transformation takes place through connections, nodes, and hubs. Moreover, she suggests, structures are not what drive change: "The real power of an organization exists in the structure of a human network, not in the architecture of command and control superimposed on it" (Stephenson, 2005, 245). Network analysts have found that more often than not people seeking information turn to someone they know rather than to a formal source. Moreover, whom you know has a significant impact on what you come to know. If social networks, as Stephenson points out, are spaces in which information transforms into knowledge, then the kind of information that is available and the persons who process it become critical.

When we consider the challenges facing our world, including famine, poverty, disease, and the like, it becomes important to understand where our information does come from and who is a part of the networks that are deciding what information is shared. Earlier we mentioned that the promises of the Network Society (to create equality across all nations through the sharing and access of information) were not realized. We still live in a society in which certain people are part of the networks of global knowledge development and others are outside. What then can education do to not only promote but also shape alternative networks to expand the kind of knowledge that is being shared and open the connections across nations so that more people share in the knowledge transformation? The hierarchical structures of government, although important, do not allow for rapid change. It is the social networks that hold promise for bringing about sustainable growth and development that addresses global issues that plague us all.

Catherine Ryan Hind understood this when she wrote the book *Pay It Forward.* Today, her abstract idea is a global network connecting people in action to make a difference in the world. Al Gore also understood that it would take networking to raise the volume on the discussion about global warming and stimulate change worldwide through a new dynamic of awareness and care. Youth today are also engaged in their own social networks of a variety of kinds through cyberworlds in which they generate relationships, share information and ideas, and build projects together on their own initiative. Unfortunately, many of these same students are too often told to leave their social networks behind when entering the school in order to honor the hierarchy of learning on which schools are based. One needs to ask, "Can schools compete with the energy that is experienced in social networks, or are schools losing their students to other connections?" Later, in the chapter on digital culture, we suggest that schools are losing young people and that this loss reflects a missed opportunity for schools to open their teaching and curriculum.

What would happen if schools organized learning around network connections facilitating cross-cultural learning centers for youth and educators to work together on common global problems? How might this kind of network learning facilitate the promotion of key competencies for youth's success in a global society? How might network learning structures promote engagement in learning that captures energy and excitement of youth? These are questions that we hope will be explored in your schools. In the global age, in which we are collectively challenged to find solutions to social and human conditions of global warming, violence and terrorism, famine, and poverty (to name a few), educators have an opportunity to create learning spaces that engage youth in these very questions together around the world. Through social networks, youth and educators have the power to shape new knowledge and a global community of care, which recognizes among other things the need for peace and human rights. Embracing a "pedagogy of engagement" through social networks creates space for dialogue and collaboration, which give voice to youth to make a difference in society. Together, educators and youth "pay forward" to help create a difference in the future of the global community and bring balance to the domination of bureaucratic programming on schools and knowledge development.

THE INTERNATIONAL SCHOOL CONNECTION: ENGAGED COMMUNITY

In this section of the chapter we present an example of how the International School Connection network fosters a global community of learning among educators and school districts to address the question, "What can schools do to make a difference in the world?" In this example, members of the network represent educators from around the world, including Spain, Finland, Sweden, Canada, Russia, China, Singapore, the United States, Colombia, Venezuela, and Norway. They are connected by a common purpose: to find new ways to develop learning for youth that engage them in knowledge development about global issues. Collectively, they contribute to a global dialogue for social action.

Integral questions of the ISC network are, "What can schools do to make a difference in the world?" and "What does it mean to be a global learning center?" At the 2005 ISC Annual Summit in Madrid, Spain, an interesting picture began to emerge from the presentations of members in the ISC global educational network. There appears to be no single, best response to global development, no meta-narrative, as we are often seduced into believing by political rhetoric. What emerged was a realization that the new story of schooling will never be complete, for the conditions of society and education are always changing. This is what Watts (2003) meant when he said that it is important to understand both what is happening in the network as well as on the network. Within the ISC network are the members who are engaged in developing schools as learning centers. What is happening "on the network" is contingent about changes in local and global forces, which cause the educators to respond in relation to the new conditions and information.

Model 10.1 illustrates members of the ISC network who were present at the 2005 Madrid summit. Among them were educators representing schools whose development efforts focused on such things as anti-racism, futures education, brain-based learning, education for a sustainable future, and learning technologies. Also present were non-school-based educators, who represented perspectives from theory about learning and school development. The model reflects members of the international network community who contribute ideas, experience, and approaches to global education with the common purpose to seek ways to connect schooling with the preparation of youth for global social development. The two circles represent the common place for connection and the arrows represent the different contributions that are made by the members of the network to the common interest. Together, the contributions stimulate a dynamic and knowledge about global educational development. Moreover, they illustrate the importance and power of social networks within education for advancing society.

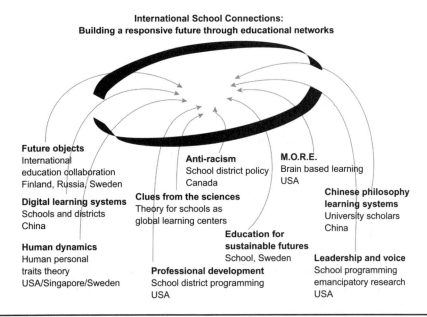

Model 10.1 Educational social network model for global development.

The Education Networks Model illustrates members' contributions to the ISC that created energy for knowledge sharing and development. No one of the contributions has the power by itself to bring about deep sustainable change globally, but in connection with other contributions the dynamic stimulates new structures, synchrony, and knowledge that have the potential to transform. What is also of interest in this model is that the contributions representing nodes in a network each reflect a unique set of knowledge, experience, and competencies that address pieces of global development. For example, digital learning systems in China focus on how technology can promote learning. It also seeks to understand the ideological balance and meeting place between Eastern and Western philosophical principles as a way to encourage sustainable peace worldwide. Anti-Racism in Canada provides the network members with an ideology about multiculturalism, as well as experience with whole school development and curriculum development in which there are persons with diverse backgrounds. Their work also serves as a micro system to the larger global system of diverse nations.

Because networks are open systems, it is important to recognize that each of the ISC network members is also engaged in other networks that focus on different issues. Each of those connections naturally contributes to the ISC network, extending the knowledge and resource sharing possible. Moreover, when members of the ISC network engage in their other networks, they naturally bring with them the ISC, in effect linking the different networks around the world. Let's take a look in detail at what is happening in some of these members' schools to understand better how the dynamics within and on the network are stimulating new knowledge about how schools can make a difference in the world.

In Ottawa, Canada, there has been a focus on cultural diversity for many years through programming that uses international languages as a central part of the educational community, curriculum, and pedagogy, which gives recognition and respect to the cultural heritage of its students and families and also provides a greater sense of emotional and psychological stability for students. Within the last two years the Ottawa-Carlton School Board has extended the focus on language and multiculturalism to antiracism and globalization, recognizing the importance of caring about the global human condition and the multicultural tapestry of the world (OCDSB, Report #06-151, 2006). Through a variety of local programs, student and faculty ambassadors, curriculum criteria, and faculty training, educators are hoping to contribute to positive change in the social and cultural dynamics of their communities. Further, through international networks and partnership programs, the school board is working with schools in other countries to develop programs addressing antiracism. The word is spreading, and the dialogue is changing as educators are engaging themselves in self-reflection and awareness about their role in addressing imbalances in human equity and diversity.

In Florida, school leaders and university researchers are working in partnership with a school district once plagued by social stigmas for the high rate of poverty and number of minority representatives in the community to reverse the trend and transform the story that is told. Caught in the vicious discourse about the failure of persons in poverty or from minority backgrounds, the school district is demonstrating a counter picture through research and programming. Touchton and Acker-Hocevar (2005) report in their study of this school that contextual leadership shaped a new "belief in making a difference through understanding and applying systems theory that integrates values of community to listening and giving voice to the community, teachers, and students" (25). A positive outcome of these efforts was more than improved grades: It also led to the "democratization of the school" through shared visioning, cooperation, and making connections to needed resources. The efforts of the schools, their communities, and the researchers helped to "address the institutionalized practices that ameliorate injustices, inequities, and discriminations" (26). This case example from Florida has now, more than ever, global implications. As the population demographics of many countries become more heterogeneous with globalization, educators experienced in working with a homogeneous student body are forced to develop programs that address multiculturalism and diversity, and consequently they have much to gain from the experience of this school and its community.

In Sweden, Gripenskolan is focused on education and sustainable development, which includes embracing care for human rights and social justice.

The school has been engaged in learning projects and teacher exchanges with schools in the Baltic states through a grant from UNESCO in 1989. Since that time they have developed other projects in Tanzania and Kilimanjaro, which begin with a course at their school in "knowledge about developing countries." At the 2005 ISC summit, the principal reported an example of a book the school uses, called *The Voices That Never Become Silent: Thoughts about Democracy and Other Important Matters*. The book is a collection of poems and reflections written by students at the school after visiting one of the Holocaust concentration camps during an international project, which has much to offer a global dialogue on education and social development. In 2005, the principal of Gripen High School was named educational representative of Sweden to the United Nations' 10-year program on sustainability. His local and regional efforts have led to an even larger engagement at the global level as a voice for engaging education in caring about the global condition. Through the ISC network, the principal is serving a key role in helping engage larger numbers of educators from around the globe in dialogue and programming related to sustainable development. This work is naturally connected to the development work in Ottawa that focused on antiracism and expands the discourse on educational involvement in global development.

In another project, 10 schools in Helsinki, Espoo, and Kerava, Finland, and Sochi, Russia, extended their several years' partnership on science education to a build a program focusing on futures education, which was coordinated by the Helsinki University Institute for Technology and Lifelong Learning. The project grew out of a common interest to keep alive the cross-national partnerships and stimulate continued dialogue and learning on the future development of youth and society. Futures education is based on a concern for developing skills and awareness in youth that prepare them for engaging in the future society (UNESCO, 2002). Futures education focuses on pedagogical and didactical development that promotes among other things "global and human-centered issues such as peace, human rights, development, multiculturalism, and environmental degradation" (Särkijärvi, 1999). Together schools from the two countries work on their own development of futures education, and through their participation in other educational networks are able to spread their knowledge and experience, adding to the broader dialogue on education and global development. The concepts in the futures education project have been paramount in informing and shaping the development of the ISC mission and vision.

As a last example within the context of this chapter, we would like to turn to the East and highlight the power of networking for opening the ISC Global Network to collective learning between Eastern and Western philosophy. Professor Xinmin Sang (2005) from Nanjing University sees a vital need for connecting schools and educators in global partnerships. The technological revolution, he argues, has opened doors for learning between the East and the West, creating possibilities for shaping harmony around the globe. He reminds us that there is much knowledge and wisdom from Eastern philosophy, as there is from Western perspectives, and together these reflect the yin and yang of life: the balance of life forces. Within the context of this philosophical perspective, Sang (2005) argues that technology and global networks will play an important role in liberating the human spirit. He states,

> With the popularization of modern educational technology, high technology will play an increasingly important role in education, and completely transform the old educational model, an inefficient labor-intensive model based on lectures and cramming methods. It will converge school education, home education, and social education, and realize a multi-level development and reasonable configuration of human and material resources. Only in this way can teachers' productivity and teachers and students' creativity be liberated. Only in this way can educational modernization be truly realized. (4)

Sang suggests that technology is a means by which educators and students can create new spaces globally that not only reach the intellectual development of youth, but that also bring people together socially to liberate creativity and the human spirit. He reminds us of the importance in connecting mind, body, and spirit.

Each of the highlighted examples is situated within its own cultural context, reflecting educational development that is responsive to a local or regional situation. At the same time, they also reflect different dimensions of the global social challenge to bring about peace and human dignity. Within a social network, then, their contributions become even more significant as the global differences are diminishing. The dynamics of the structure (based on membership connections) are one piece of the picture, while the dynamics of the conditions around the network (global forces) are another. The variety of contributions by members of the ISC international network demonstrates how change is complex and requires the contributions of a global community of educational leaders. In singular, each of these efforts is commendable. In combination they reflect the importance and power of collaboration, as all persons engaged in the network learn from and with one another, impacting changes in their local conditions at a more rapid rate, with far-reaching consequences for global action.

CONCLUSIONS

The school programs and projects highlighted in this chapter are not unique. There are, and have been, many schools around the globe that address multiculturalism, diversity, environmental issues, and democracy challenges. What is unique to the stories highlighted here is their connection within a larger global social network. These educators have joined together, along with others, in a global community of practice to share information and shape knowledge collectively about learning and education in the global age. Moreover, students in the schools in Spain, Canada, the United States, China, and Sweden are working with one another on common projects in a context of globalization. They are learning not only with one another, but also from one another, building their global competencies as well as a collective knowledge about what is important in the world today. Through their connections in school they have a greater potential to affect change in the future as they build dynamic networks of action and knowledge development. Together, in a community of practice, they give voice to a new discourse on education that has the potential to emancipate the human and environmental conditions on a global scale.

Engaging in social learning networks does not require great changes in the school. It does require that educators see the value of learning in collaboration with others and that network learning is more than international connections. Engaging in a social learning network often starts with examining what international connections and partnerships already exist within the school and asks, "How can we develop the connection to stimulate learning in global social networks?" This can require that teachers set students in the center of the networks and let the dynamics build around their connections naturally. The natural excitement that we feel when learning about others is often all that is needed to start a conversation. It is up to the school to develop the conditions for connections by creating space in the curricula and classroom to integrate the learning networks with the daily work of schools. Taking a look inside your school today will most likely reveal that a number of international exchanges are already taking place, which can naturally serve as a starting place to build learning networks. As well, there are emerging networks around the world, such as the International School Connection, that provide a system and structure for schools interested in global education.

Often we hear educators say that networks are interesting but that they take too much time and that they cost money. While aspects of this are true, one needs to also ask what kinds of resources exist to support a network, and what kinds of resources do the networks themselves generate. There are many financial programs for international exchange, for example, which can be used to start a contact through which teachers and students identify a common interest and begin to work on a project together. Through the use of technology, as we point out in the chapter on digital culture, students are able to work across cultures without the added costs of travel. Ultimately, we suggest that the financial cost of not engaging youth in social networks is a high price to pay for the future of the global society. Through the use of global social networks, schools can become a counterforce to the heavy emphasis on student achievement as a measure of school success by creating spaces for learning that address global competency development and engage youth in knowledge development and transformation. Moreover, social network learning can help youth develop an ethic of care that contributes to reshaping the imbalance caused by global capitalism; and replace it with an ethic of care (Noddings, 1991, 2002) through which youth come to care about, not just care for, the world. In this sense, education, through youth, can pay it forward.

11

Digital Cultures for Learning in a Global Age

As an adult living in a technological age, I find myself in something of a dilemma. As a participant in organizational and social life that uses e-mail and text messaging (SMS), my life is certainly technologically oriented. But I feel like something of an outsider to a developing generation that has been born into and thoroughly baptized into a digital age. Technological immersion is the norm, access to information is increasing rapidly, the amount of information to which one needs to respond daily is at times overwhelming, and social networking is understood without even being discussed. While I recognize that my perspective predominantly represents life in the developed countries, the rate at which rural and underdeveloped communities around the world are gaining access is increasing daily. I observe these phenomena from the outside as an adult, as well as experience them from the inside, both culturally and organizationally, as e-mail and SMS communication (text messaging through mobile telephones) are increasingly institutionalized. As an educator interested in creating learning spaces for youth that are both stimulating and contribute to the development of society, I am continually pressed with the question: *Why are we not learning from youth and integrating the digital culture in the school today?*

Research has shown for many years that keeping students stimulated in schools is tough. While the majority of youth succeed in school systems around the world, there remains a substantial number of youth who drop out for many reasons, among them boredom. Survey results of students in 400 high schools in the United States show that 89 percent of respondents said that school itself was somewhat or very boring (Shaw, 2004). Studies in adolescence and truancy, report *understimulation* as one of the key variables to student dropout (Bridgeland, Dilulio, and Morison, 2006). Getting kids to school is often not the problem; keeping them there is. Compare this to a rapidly growing cyberculture in which youth are engaged daily in online activities with friends locally and globally. In fact, parents in many countries are now concerned with the amount of time students spend online (reflecting among other things family disengagement).

Studies in Sweden report that each week 88 percent of Swedish youth ages 15–20 are actively engaged in a cyber community, and this number is growing (Johansson, 2004). Among the activities of engagement are homepages, chat, podcasts, and e-mail.

While studies are still examining the motivation for online behavior, initial findings suggest that the opportunity to create one's own identity and explore life with others is enticing. The ability to fantasize and to develop questions of interest in dialogue empowers youth to take command of their own social relations and knowledge development. Similar cyber communities exist in other countries as well, including China, India, and South Korea, and their function is on the rise. One study reports that in India, youth are using the Internet to worship, linking technology and religion (Majumder, 2007). The Web site serves as a host for religious services, making the practice of prayer and meditation more accessible to people who don't have time or access to large cities.

An even more encompassing recent development is Second Life, which is a 3D online digital world, "imagined, created and owned by its residents" (www .secondlife.com). In December 2006, Second Life reported that 3,568,651 residents participate in that digital world, which is characterized by new "creations," a marketplace, social networking, and a cyberdollar (Linden dollars) for economic transactions. BusinessWeek Online (May 1, 2006) reported that Second Life, once characterized as a game, is really more akin to an alternative world, and as such "real-world" businesses are exploring questions about how a virtual system can "provide a template for getting work done, from training and collaboration to product design and marketing" (Businessweek Online cover story, May 1, 2006).

Considering this social networking reality of life outside the school, in which youth are actively and captivatingly engaged (in creation, exploration, self-empowerment, and identity development), we begin to see that youth have both the motivation and the skills to initiate and sustain connections and learn together with others. What can schools do to adapt their learning environments, systems, and curricula to build on the energy and opportunities of youth culture today that is already connected to societal development? We speculate that if we continue to develop schools only in relation to a model that focuses on academic or vocational achievement, we will lose more and more kids to cyberland. One could certainly argue that cyberland has the potential to serve as a new community for those who don't like school. In fact new research studies are examining the phenomenon of cyberland to better understand what motivates youth (Näslundh, 2003, 2005).

This chapter examines a conceptual model called the digital culture model (Snyder, 2005, 2006) and its implications for learning in a global age. The model was conceptualized after years of research on technology in education, through which we came to understand that it is no longer sufficient to discuss technology as a learning object. The integration of technology in human learning systems is impacting communication, pedagogy, and organizational systems, which necessarily alters the conditions of the learning environment, as well as social values and knowledge development.

We begin by exploring the concept of the digital culture from a conceptual perspective drawing on cultural theory, constructivist theory, and the concept of sensemaking. Second, we examine the digital culture model and discuss implications for educational practice suggesting the need for educators to embrace the technological revolution to build a digital culture for learning. Third, we explore an example of the way in which the digital culture is beginning to emerge in a school partnership between two middle schools in the United States and China. The intent in this chapter is to raise awareness and stimulate dialogue among educators about the need to see technology integrated with pedagogy, communication, and organizational systems. While considerable research has addressed dimensions of technology in learning and societal development, educational systems have yet to develop a holistic model that integrates all four components (technology, communication, pedagogy, and organizational systems). We suggest that this is a missed opportunity not only for schools, but also for engaging youth in lifelong learning.

DIGITAL CULTURE: A CONCEPTUAL FRAMEWORK

The concept of the digital culture emerged from a five-year study of an international social learning network for educators (Snyder, 2005, 2006), in which a void was identified in the discussions and development of technology in education. Traditionally within the field of education, research has focused primarily on technology as a learning device, exploring developments in didactics and learning theory as it relates to classroom or online learning. While these contributions have been significant for expanding views about knowledge development and the importance of social dynamics in the learning environment, they have not addressed the development of social behaviors, norms, and values that cultural theorists suggest are being altered through interactions with technology.

To a culture theorist studying schools, it became evident that the focus of technology in education was too limited to achieve certain stated goals in educational policy that call for schools to prepare youth with skills and knowledge for working in the global knowledge society, among which include an orientation to life-long learning, active citizenship, networking, entrepreneurship, and communication skills for understanding others (Field, 2000; Naval, Print, and Veldhuis, 2002). Furthermore, the growing social development of youth in cyberspace communities, such as MySpace and Facebook, potentially reinforces a divide between schooling and society as youth are creating alternative sources of connection and stimulation for learning and social networking that appear to mirror the very characteristics of living and working in the twenty-first century. Seeing both the void and the growing divide raises questions about what schools can do to embrace a digital culture of learning that does not see technology as secondary to learning, but rather a co-creator in the learning environment to promote both academic and social development.

Technology has taken on an integrated and integrating role in our social-human systems, which leads to new values, norms, and symbol systems that transcend the culture of nations and social groups (Lull, 2000). The digital culture is a reframing of the relationship between technology and humans, suggesting both dimensions are interchangeably subject and object within a cultural manifestation. This concept is embedded in cultural theory, which posits that culture is the shared values, assumptions, beliefs, rules, and social practices that give rise to meaning and identity (Geertz, 1973; Lull, 2000; Schein, 1985). With reference to this definition, we suggest that technology has become an integrated part of our human communication system, and as such it is a member of the process for shaping meaning. Given the increasing global connection for learning and living today (Castells, 2000; Snyder and Acker-Hocevar, 2000), we need to ask ourselves in what ways are our perceptions, behaviors, values, and norms being shaped through our interactions with technology, and what are the implications when we consider technology in education that is based on a social-cultural perspective of learning? Furthermore, what are the implications for education in the development of citizenship?

To understand this more fully, we turn to the constructivist concept (Berger, 1966) of sense-making and Weick's (1995) concept of sensemaking (intentionally spelled differently) as they both describe processes in which we, as humans, give meaning to identity, events, experiences, and encounters. Both concepts have elements that are relevant to understanding digital culture. Constructivist theory posits that we co-create our realities together, as we share and react to our perceptions and experience in response to situations. Through this co-construction we give meaning to our realities, resulting in common language, symbols, values, behaviors, norms, and understanding. As learners, we make sense out of our world by analyzing and synthesizing our experiences in an attempt to give meaning. The elements that contribute to our sense-making process are those parts of an event or experience with and through which we interact and act. In contemporary society, technology and media have become a part of this social interaction process.

Weick's (1995) *theory of sensemaking* suggests that we are confronted by ambiguity and uncertainty in our daily encounters about which we must make sense. Through a series of stages that are characterized by "identity, social, retrospective, ongoing, enactment, and cues and plausibility" (17), we give meaning to events and experiences, which become the process of sensemaking. This is distinct from understanding, interpreting, or attributing, as those require a certain predetermined knowledge or framework in which to place information. The uniqueness of sensemaking then is that it takes place over time in response to patterns of experience, rather than in response to a predetermined knowledge framework. This theory has direct application to the digital culture, as we encounter daily ambiguities and uncertainties in our communication with and through technology that create the need for us to make sense out of our experiences. The ambiguities and uncertainties are stimulated by a variety of factors that characterize life in a digital culture today: technology, rapid information intake and synthesis, flexible and dynamic communities of exchange, asynchronous exchange, the broadening of perspective and experience with the expansion of our social communities.

Referring to social constructivist theory and Weick's notion of sensemaking, we can identify three key elements that are central to the digital culture argument. The first is that we give meaning to experience, events, and encounters socially. In a growing world of connectivity and social networks, we are connecting with a greater number of people across communities and cultures, expanding the type of encounter and experience in which we engage, as well as the persons with whom we shape meaning. This has the potential to impact the kind of reality that we co-construct, as our social groups expand.

The second element is that social construction takes place by interacting with one another and our surroundings. As technology is central to human interaction today, it necessarily becomes a part of the act of communicating and influences perceptions and behaviors. Studies from Reeves and Nass (1996) support this claim. They found that we treat computers like real people and places, suggesting that the way in which we receive a message is influenced by our relationship to the technology. For example, a negative attitude toward computers will affect the receiving of a message sent through the computer, no matter the sender. The presence of technology in human communication is thus changing our perceptions and behaviors, through which we socially construct a digital culture of meaning.

The third element relates to Weick's notion of ambiguity and uncertainty. As the tools of technology advance, our acts of communication are met with ambiguity and uncertainty, causing us to ask new questions about how we can understand one another. The old frameworks for understanding human communication, based on knowing how to interpret nonverbal and verbal cues, are no longer helpful in many of our exchanges, which are characterized by text-based messages and asynchronous exchange. We are now faced with the ambiguities and uncertainties of how to interpret one another, placing us in a space of what Weick calls sensemaking.

When we consider Weick's (1995) concept of sensemaking and constructivist theory in the context of our use of technology in human interaction, it is possible to see the way in which digital media not only are integrated into our daily lives, but also have become a layer in our culture and in the meaning-making process. In an earlier paper Snyder (2005) suggested:

> No longer are we living in an era where "online communication" is a separate phenomenon from our daily lives. It now permeates our organizational walls and human systems to create a digital culture, which is reflected by the integration of technology in everyday life such that our human systems of interaction and work transpire in a physical and virtual space interchangeably. (Snyder, 2005, 7)

The message is that the placement of technology in our lives and its role in connecting humans also contributes to the process of shaping meaning. This is in contrast to the technological determinist theory (Chandler, 1995), which suggests that technology drives development, and that we, as humans, do not participate in shaping its purpose or function in society. Contrary to this view, we suggest that not only do we shape our realities through interaction with our surrounding context, but that elements, such as technology, also take on new meaning and become a part of the culture, shaping it and being shaped by it. In an earlier work, Snyder (2005) argued that McLuhan's (1964) notion that the "medium is the message" is powerful, albeit unidirectional: It omits the interaction that now exists between humans and technology through which we communicate. Radio and television (as in McLuhan's examples) address a unidirectional relationship of sending and receiving, in which case meaning making takes place in a separate act disengaged from the technology. In contrast, with the current advances in communication technology, today's media have become a part of the sense-making equation, thus calling for an interactive perspective (Denzin, 1992), rather than a deterministic view.

Using culture theory as a lens, we can illustrate ways in which the presence of technology in our human communication systems is altering our behaviors, challenging social norms and expectations, and contributing to the development of our perceptions. As a cultural dimension, technology has taken on a value-laden symbol and role as connector. Those who are "connected" are perceived differently from those who are not. We see this perception of connectedness both at the global level and at the human user level. At the global level, the spread of communication technology was initially hailed as a potential stimulus for bringing about greater equity among nations and cultures around the world (Castells, 1996). Many countries within the European Union developed a 10-year plan to provide connectivity to every household and community in EU countries. Ten years later, such plans have brought about considerable change, as many more persons and cultures are connected. Yet there still remain areas and whole countries (e.g., villages in China, Sweden, Russia, and Africa) where connectivity is nonexistent. Consequently, the world is witnessing a new set of inequities, economically and socially, brought about by the quest and promises of connectivity (Capra, 2002; Castells, 2000; Friedman, 2005).

At the institutional level the value of connection has led to new assumptions and codes of conduct in both human communication as well as work production. In the initial years of technology in the workplace, value was given to our "ability to use" technology; today the value is on "us as users." Not only are we expected to know how to use a computer and the appropriate software, it is anticipated in many settings and countries that we are comfortable communicating through e-mail and virtual platforms, and accessing and working with information storage and sharing systems. The assumption is that technology is no longer an external tool to our human interactions but an integrated dimension of working and living in the twenty-first century.

On the one hand, the value of connection is opening new models of work and knowledge development that build on and promote network formation across nations, industries, and economies. On the other hand, it is amputating our ability to be fully present in many of our human exchanges, both in formal settings and in informal social settings of family life. In places of business and schools, for example, the presence of the telephone is so common that we don't even blink twice when our meetings are interrupted by a telephone call or when students SMS their friends (we can be frustrated, but not surprised). In organizations where wireless connections are made possible, many people take their computers to meetings and remain connected online while they also engage in the face-to-face meeting. In addition, for those working in virtual organizations, it is not uncommon to answer a stationary phone while participating in a Webcast meeting.

In the context of family, Bakardjieva (2005) found that computers are altering family dynamics and parenting in dramatic ways. With access to "everything" through the Internet, youth are spending more time online than with family. They are still at home, yet absent from family connections. The impact of our connections through technology is great now, for it both extends us and amputates us. The ability to get work done anywhere and to stay connected energizes us for action. For those on the outside of the connection, however, a perception can develop about how they are valued by others, reinforcing technology over human, which impacts our perceptions, social dynamics, and emotions.

Another phenomena is "information overload," which is leading to new retreat behaviors and task overload for others. With the 24/7 exchange of information, instant messaging, and e-mails, finding time to complete intended tasks is difficult as the definition of work shifts focus to "reading and replying to e-mail" or "answering the mobile telephone." In some cases, people are taking it upon themselves to develop new work habits, either setting aside a specific time to respond to e-mail or phone calls or just ignoring e-mails altogether because they take too much time away from the intended work. The emerging codes of conduct are not yet institutionalized, and as such are shaping peoples' perceptions of information and one another. Human communication and sensemaking is influenced as some people "turn off," while others sit waiting.

The speed of connection and information exchange also contributes to changing perceptions, behaviors, and expectations. We have developed a social dynamic in which we often assume that a person will respond to us immediately, as we have become so ingrained in the "instant response" capability of technology. As technology and human action become integrated, we no longer associate "instantaneous" with the technology, but rather with the human act of communication. When the response isn't immediate or as anticipated, we often begin to speculate why. Sometimes we speculate falsely, causing us to think or take action based on false information or assumptions. We perceive that because people have the technology at their disposal, they should be available for open communication "when we need them." Our changing perception alters social dynamics, as well as the communication exchange that shapes sensemaking.

Among youth the need to be connected is high, and it is problematic as technology adds to stress and addiction with the need to always be available. Newspapers in Sweden (where of the rate of mobile telephone use is one of the highest in the world) report an increase in adolescent stress caused by youth sleeping with their telephones turned on so they don't miss calls in the middle of the night. During school time they stay connected with friends through SMS. An Australian study (Australian Youth Facts and Stats, 2005) reported that more than one-third of Australians age 14–24 said they cannot live without a mobile phone. And Lonkila (2004) found that mobile phones are increasing our connectivity and the strength of our social networks, "impacting the very nature of sociability" (59). Whether it is the computer and connections to the Internet or the mobile telephone, our need to be connected and available 24/7 has become a norm and value in our global society.

As a last example, we would like to address power, which is a complex phenomenon in any social culture. How it is shaped, defined, and used can be different from group to group, resulting in very different cultures. Within a digital culture, emerging perceptions of power result from a number of factors, including our personal relationship to technology (Reeves and Nass, 1996), our perceptions of the written word (Ramberg, 1996), and how digital communications are used to include or exclude members of a work or social environment (Castells, 2000). These elements add a new dimension to existing power structures in some cases, and in others they give rise to new perceptions of power bases and, consequently, to the ways in which communication is mediated by technology. Studies (Reeves and Nass, 1996) have shown that technology itself has a perceived power, and that those who use it, or even have access to it, obtain a kind of power over others in some organizational settings. In this case it can matter who is sending, as well who isn't sending. Further, it can matter who is included and who is excluded. In some organizations and social groups, for example, e-mail can be used to privilege the senders, giving them a perceived power. This can be achieved by sending e-mails to only a few, creating an "in" group and an "out" group. Power can thus also be perceived by the way in which the digital dialogue takes shape. If only a few recipients of a group e-mail respond and continue to engage in the dialogue, for example, they build a power base that eventually can exclude those who don't participate. In such a case, it becomes critical to understand the reasons why only certain people respond: time, role, expectations, or knowledge. Digital communication has the power to reinforce existing power structures or invite collaboration.

In addition to our own relationship to technology, perceptions of power are affected by how we perceive the written word (Reeves and Nass, 1996). When we receive an e-mail, we perceive the text and the computer to be *the* communicator. In order to see the sender (and hold in perspective the power of the message), we are required to envision or fantasize beyond the text and the technology to the person. It is in this space that we often stop short of the fantasizing and relegate the text and computer to a higher position in the communication than the sender. Depending on our relationship to text and technology, as Reeves and Nass (1996) suggest, our perception is altered and so is our sensemaking, for it is often our actions with technology that we hold first and foremost. In an era when knowledge development is perceived as social and networking is more and more the structure for working, living, and learning, new questions arise about the need for a holistic understanding that integrates technology in the sensemaking and knowledge development process. Seen once as an external tool, technology is now an integrated artifact in our cultures and a part of our processes of shaping meaning, perceptions, behaviors, norms, and values.

So what does this have to do with education? We believe there are two primary dimensions to consider, and they relate to the pedagogical and sociological responsibility and context of schooling. A number of questions are raised about the pedagogical practices in schools because of changes in society as they relate to a higher value placed on knowledge development and human capital. The ability to network and be entrepreneurial are raising questions about the pedagogical practices in schools for citizenship preparation. Moreover, the need for a digital literacy in which one can use technology for communication and work reinforces not only the technological know-how, but also an awareness and social responsibility to using technology to promote human equity and sustainable societal development. While advances in technology have opened the door for the kinds of changes we are witnessing in society, it is the social dimension that becomes so critical for schools to consider. In particular, it calls upon education to play a role in helping to develop citizens with the skills necessary to interact in a global and local context.

The premise of the digital culture is that we as a society, including our social institutions, have a responsibility to understand the process of sensemaking in general, as this becomes a more complex phenomenon in a multicultural land-scape. As our human connections are conducted more and more with and through technology, we need to understand what is happening to our perceptions, norms, values, behaviors, and customs as these all relate to the ways in which we shape meaning. For schools the challenge is how to embrace a digital culture that cares for both the pedagogical task of education, as well as the social development of citizenry, which includes an understanding of the implications for knowledge development and sense making. Through the digital culture, then, education can contribute to both a pedagogical and sociological development, which I refer to as "peda-socio" transformation.

THE DIGITAL CULTURE AS A PEDAGOGICAL REVOLUTION IN THE TWENTY-FIRST CENTURY

In an attempt to articulate the need for change in education, a number of key competencies for success in life and the workforce have been developed. Rychen and Salganik (2003) categorized the key competencies for successful life and a well-functioning society into three broad areas: (1) interacting in social hetero-geneous groups, (2) acting autonomously, and (3) using tools interactively. The European Commission on Education (2004) refers to the knowledge worker, who has skills in networking, entrepreneurship, lifelong learning, and active citizen-ship. Thomas Friedman's (2005) metaphor that the world is flat suggests workers need to be prepared for a new business model built on insourcing, outsourcing, networking, collaboration, and open sourcing and digital living. Also emerging are concerns about human caring and social engagement, which have led to a plethora of arguments for developing skills in dialogue, collaboration, apprecia-tive inquiry, caring, and spirituality (Bohm, 1996, 2004; Brown and Isaacs, 2005; Nodding, 1991, 2002; Russell, 1998; Wells and Claxton, 2002). In 2004, the European Commission on Education identified eight key competencies that should underpin education in the twenty-first century, of which "digital compe-tence" is one. The commission's report states that "ICT (information communi-cation technology) skills comprise the use of multi-media technology to retrieve, assess, store, produce, present and exchange information, and communicate and participate in networks via the Internet" (22). Included in the equation now is the social dimension, reflecting a pedagogical shift from individual learning to a social-cultural model (Claxton, 2002; Wells and Claxton, 2002).

The stimulus for the above competencies and focus on networking and life-long learning stems from advances in technology and changes in organizational, economic, and national systems. In 1996 Manuel Castells (1996) awakened us to the concept that we were "living in the network society." His basic message was that the growth in technology would create possibilities for people to connect within and across cultures, anticipating advances in democracy, solidarity, and peace around the world. While later observations (Castells, 2000) have shown that this has not happened yet, the network society did lead to the expansion and significance of social networks in shaping global transformation. Capra (2002) states, "In the information age, networking has emerged as a critical form of organization in all sections of society. Dominant social functions are increasingly organized around networks, and participation in these networks is a critical source of power" (149). With the use of the Internet, blogs, FAQ pages, and chat, videoconferencing, and asynchronous conferencing systems, we have raised the ante on the power of social networks for global transformation through knowledge exchange. As we mentioned in the beginning of this chapter, many youth already understand this as witnessed by the high numbers of youth engaged in Internet-based communication daily around the world. In education, building a digital culture for learning naturally engages educators and youth in global communities of practice based on collaborative learning practices (Soresen and Tackle, 2002; Wenger et al. 2002), through which youth and teachers develop the curriculum together around common issues and concerns. In this sense, technology opens new spaces for learning rather than merely providing a tool for acquiring information from the Internet.

Contrast this with the dominant pedagogical model still found in most schools. There is a vast divide between K–12 education and preparation for living, working, and lifelong learning. Recent studies examining technology in schools (Fredriksson et al., 2006) demonstrate that most innovations related to ICT in schools have not influenced pedagogical or school development. The dominant pedagogical model, based on individual psychology, has yet to be replaced with a pedagogy based on sociocultural theory. It is not until we come to higher education and professional development that we witness learning models that reflect the social context of living and work today. In fact, the majority of research on learning communities and online learning has been conducted at the college and university level.

So what then can educators do to respond? Four key components are shown in Model 11.1, which frames a platform for lifelong learning by integrating technology, pedagogy, communication, and organizational systems. The premise is that by integrating the four, rather than holding them as separate aspects of education, learning can become a dynamic process in which youth are engaged in social networks and communities of practice, shaping their own knowledge in relation and response to society and the workforce. At the heart of the interaction is the digital culture of sensemaking that emerges through human interactions with one another in the presence of technology. For example, technology is used for communication and learning (pedagogy), which impacts the role of the student, the teacher, and views of knowledge and learning. Technology is developed to meet learning needs and capacities, which extend both human communication

Model 11.1   The digital culture.

and technology. The organization of learning and the educational institution in relation to scheduling, resource allocation, use of space, teaching models, and the organization of the curriculum are all impacted.

Table 11.1 is a linear reflection of the Digital Culture model to identify common elements that are found in each of the four dimensions of a digital culture in schools. Column 1 identifies aspects of technology that need to be considered in relation to the other three columns, and vice versa. For example, developing technology in schools requires a focus on the instructional design of Web-based learning materials, as well as identification of the types of media that will be used to support learning. Often the discussions about technology relate to the technique that is required to use a tool, rather than what kind of pedagogy should be supported by the technology or how the technology influences the pedagogy. Meanwhile, discussions about pedagogy (teaching and learning) focus on what is knowledge, how can knowledge be achieved, and what kind of materials should be used for learning, as well what kinds of didactical approaches should be used to promote learning. The digital culture suggests that these discussions should take place in dialogue with one another to inform how technology is applied to support a pedagogy within the school.

Continuing to the right in Table 11.1 is the column on communication. In face-to-face classrooms, questions about communication are often assumed with

Table 11.1   Factors that underlie the pedagogical dimensions of the digital culture.

Technology	Pedagogy	Communication	Organizational Systems
• instructional design • media tools • course administration	• learning theory • communities of practices • teacher-learner role • power • learning styles • mentoring	• language • group dynamics identity • role • text and visual communication • time	• information management • leadership • legal relationships • communication • norms and protocol • information sharing

the conversation about didactics. This, however, is changing with the use of media and ICT in learning. Using media requires us to think differently about communication, as we can no longer rely on the nonverbal cues available to us in a face-to-face exchange. Moreover, as mentioned earlier in this section, the human dynamics of communication are altered with technology. The column on communication thus identifies new aspects of the communication that need to be considered when integrating technology into learning to create a digital culture. The final column represents the organizational systems that are used to support schools and learning and that need to be reconsidered in relation to a digital culture. The use of technology for learning networks places new demands on classroom organization, time, assignments, norms, and behaviors, often requiring a re-assignment of resources to support changes in the learning environment. In a digital culture, each of these elements is part of the system of learning and sensemaking in a global age.

What does this model mean in practice, and how does it reflect something different from what already exists in schools? We suggest the difference in many cases (where technology already exists) has to do with the perceived relationship between the teacher as knower and the student as knowledge creator, as well as the way in which we give meaning. As we presented in the first part of the chapter, if meaning making and knowledge are socially constructed, and if meaning is shaped in context, then it is important to consider the conditions of learning in a technological age, as well as the implications for communication that impacts our sensemaking. It also has to do with the ways in which schools see the interrelationship between pedagogical ideology, resources, organizational structure, and technology to create learning spaces that reflect the real world and integrate it to build learning environments that stimulate youth and help them develop competencies for life in a global age.

Most research shows that while technology is in many of the schools, the traditional ways of perceiving knowledge development as acquisition rather than creation remain. Moreover, teachers change their curriculum or teaching methods by adding technology in the classroom, but the school as a whole does not transform its learning environment when the work of a classroom teacher is not connected to the organizational structures and pedagogical ideology of the school.

Meanwhile, youth are using technology and building social learning networks in their spare time. They recognize the interconnectedness of social connections, technology, learning, and communication. This, we suggest, is an underused resource to inform school development. Consequently, schools risk the possibility that their inaction keeps separate competence development and preparation for life and work in a global age from academic subject knowledge, rendering schooling an outdated institution as more and more students turn to cyberworlds. Naturally we begin to wonder whether this is a fate schools need to accept or whether there is something they can do about it.

We suggest that elements already within many schools can be further developed in relation to the digital culture model. Take as a starting point the fact that many youth spend their evenings online, in chat forums, interacting with blogs and making their own podcasts, and so forth. Their world in many ways reflects a global learning context through technology, which is used to form social learning networks for knowledge development. What could happen to learning environments in schools if they engaged the cyberworld of youth in the classroom? Encourage young people to build their own social networks of learning in the school and across schools, through which they work together to develop a collective curriculum. The work of the teacher then is not to decide what and how students should learn, but rather to facilitate learning and growth in relation to a social curriculum, focusing on issues of democracy, ethics, values, reading, writing, math, and so forth. Further, teachers have an opportunity to help facilitate awareness among youth about how the digital culture in which they are engaged shapes their perceptions, norms, behaviors, and expectations of one another as a way to develop citizenship. The basics of schooling need not change; the question is, from where does the curriculum develop and what role do students have in the development process?

A CASE EXAMPLE: GLOBAL LEARNING

The partnership between Pasco County Middle School in Florida (www.pascoglobal.com) and Shuren Junior High School in Nanjing, China, (www.shurenxz@163.com—in Chinese) is an example of two schools building digital cultures of learning. Their work started in 2006 during the annual ISC Global Summit when an assistant principal (Laurie Johnson), a language teacher (Josh Borders), and the technology specialist (Steve Zoni) from Pasco Middle School discussed the possibilities for transforming learning and schooling through technology. They met a principal (Zanbao Wang) from the Nanjing high school affiliated with Nanjing Normal University and agreed to connect the Middle School (Shuren) in Nanjing China. They also agreed that the digital culture would become the initial tool for learning. The Florida team returned to their school and invited teachers to work with them on the project, which now includes teachers from geography, math, science, language arts, technology, and media, as well as an exceptional student education specialist, the principal, and the assistant principal. Together this team works with partners in the school, the community (including parents), and their partners in Nanjing.

The first connections between the groups of students took place through Skype, which is an Internet-based telephone system with video cameras. Skype enables students to meet one another while sitting in their own schools. This initial connection led to other projects between the schools. The topics began around a culture theme, sharing cultures and experiences from Chinese and American perspectives. Planning was conducted by a teaching team of teachers and students from both of the schools, using Skype. Students then prepared their own lesson plans, using a combination of technologies. Students now are divided into learning teams and have a variety of subjects in which they are responsible for teaching to one another. The two schools use a combination of technology, which is supported in partnership with a college in Florida. All of the work by the students is made available on a Web site at each of the schools, including blogs, student Web pages, photos, and streaming video.

American students participating in the videoconference in February 2007 had this to say about their learning experience:

> . . . by using this web cam we can discuss a lot more information in just a short amount of time. During our web meeting we gave two lessons, one on the everyday life of an average American teenager, and the other was the history and Geography of Dade City. It is also where you can get to know people like we did. Those who taught the lessons were a few students from our class. Those were the presenters that explained each topic. If anybody had questions they were the ones to answer it. Everyone else in the class put together the lessons for the presenters to make the lesson better and easy to understand. It was choppy but we all learned a lot from this experience. The technology we used was a computer, camera for feedback, projector, microphone, Internet, software, and speakers. Also the Chinese students had to have the same exact technology for this project to work. (http://www.pascoglobal.com/projects.htm)

From two of the blog entries, students from the journalism team wrote about their preparation for a lesson to their Chinese partner students:

> "Today in GLC our class was busy working on our NASA Podcast which we will be showing the Chinese in one of our soon to come conferences. Learning team one and some of our other learning teams are recording their synopsis."—student A GLC Blog. entry date November 9, 2007.

> "Today in GLC Mrs. Brock came in and talked to the boys about the Powerpoint they will be presenting at the fashion show on Sunday. The girls stayded in mrs Borders room and continued working on their NASA podcasts. Team 1 finished recording and began putting transitions. As for the other teams they started on their transitions for each picture and made sure everyone was in the right place. All the teams are doing great and we are all looking forward to the fashion show Sunday afternoon." —Student B GLC Blog. entry date November 15, 2007.

The connection started simply with the sharing of culture between students from America and China using technology. According to participants, including teachers, students, and school administrators, the connection has been so stimulating that the focus is growing and the content is connecting to other subjects as well. In an interview reported in the *St. Petersburg Times* newspaper in Florida (Pace, 2007), "Assistant Principal Laurie Johnson said, 'The program excites students because they lead it, with students writing lessons to share with the Chinese students, as well as developing and creating Web sites, blogs and photo pages.'" Moreover, "'It brought passion into the classroom,' Johnson said. 'They can't wait for the next teleconference.'" (http://www.sptimes .com/2007/04/14/Pasco/Learning_together_th.shtml)

One key learning from the exchange has been the importance of language, not only for the daily connections, but also for understanding culture. As part of the work with language development, a group of students from Pasco was able to travel to their partner school in Nanjing to teach conversational English as part of the Chinese goal to prepare youth to compete in the global economy. Moreover, the trip took place as China was preparing to greet the world at the Beijing Olympic Games in 2008, which added a dimension to the learning context for youth to develop their curriculum in relation to a real-world situation. In preparation for the trip, the staff and students developed a lesson plan that integrated storytelling, drama, and student mentoring as part of their pedagogical approach. In addition, they generated podcasts and blogs to spread their learning together to other schools around the world.

This trip reinforced the importance of language development for cultural exchange to better prepare students for the global economy. According to Jeff Morganstein, (coordinator of world languages in Pasco County Schools), instructors are now planning to teach Mandarin Chinese to their students starting in the 2008–2009 school year. There is also talk about expanding the program to include agriculture and geography. Josh Borders, a teacher at Pasco Middle School, "said that while it's great the students are learning about China, the main focus is to teach them how to communicate across cultures to prepare them for a global work force" (Pace, online edition, April 14, 2007).

Exploring this example in relation to the digital culture model we see evidence of the ways in which the school has opened up the learning environment by integrating technology, communication, pedagogy, and organizational systems. Turning first to technology, several different technological tools were employed, including podcasts, Web sites, blogs, Skype, and a videoconference system. Each one of these technologies, and in particular, Skype and the videoconference, required students to become aware of how they communicated and what they communicated to each other in Florida and to their student partners in China. Given the language barrier, students also naturally focused on the impact of English as a second language for sharing ideas and experiences.

Pedagogical discussions were also present from the beginning of the partnership as teachers asked what their role was and what the role of students was. Seeing the importance of engaging students in the teaching and learning, teachers provided students with guidance in how to use the technology, as well as how to develop a lesson plan and teach a class. Moreover, the use of podcasts and blogs as learning materials altered the dynamics of the "classroom," placing students in nontraditional learning spaces in both their local community and during the U.S. students' visit to China. The pedagogy changed from one in which students passively followed a teacher's instructions to one in which students self-directed the curriculum development with teachers in a supporting role.

Supporting the digital culture also required that the administration support changes in the school's curriculum and pedagogy. Moreover, it required the administrators to allocate resources differently, which in this case example meant that the community (parents, businesses, and colleges) offered support through funding and participation in the student learning. Saint Leo University supplied the videoconference system for Florida schools. Parents of students in both countries participated by telling stories of their own work and conducting demonstrations as part of the culture exchange. While these changes and others occurred at the school level, district leaders began to understand that sustaining a digital culture for global learning requires the vision and goals for schools to be supported by the leadership of the school system as well. Consequently, the Pasco School District is developing a districtwide plan to prepare all students to be global citizens. In China, the schools in Nanjing already have the support of their local educational governing bodies to develop global partnerships for global citizenship.

The Pasco-Nanjing example illustrates ways in which digital cultures of learning can open learning spaces to prepare youth with the competencies necessary for living and working in a global society. Students in this example are working across cultures, connecting their school subjects to real-life situations, and engaging in problem-based learning. Moreover, they are developing an active citizenship and multicultural awareness by their exchange of culture and language. Their reliance on technology develops a digital literacy in which technology as a tool is not the only focus; learning how it can be used to support human communication becomes central. Students, teachers, and schools are networking and collaborating, which is having an impact on the local and the global. The integration of technology in learning naturally expands the pedagogical practices and engages youth in a social construction of knowledge and self-directed learning.

CONCLUSIONS

In this chapter we have put forth a thesis that the role of technology in education is broader than a vehicle to access information or send an e-mail to a pen pal. Technology creates for us the possibility to communicate with one another and learn in collaborative communities, which impacts not only what we are learning, but also how we learn. Even more, the integrated place of technology in our communication naturally shapes a culture of understanding, behaviors, and norms that impact the way in which we connect, as well as what we determine to be important in our relationships. This cultural aspect has a role in the social construction of learning that impacts students, teachers, and the organizational support systems of schools. Understanding the interconnectedness of technology, communication, pedagogy, and organizational systems opens doors for schools to build a digital culture of learning in which students actively participate in shaping learning and curriculum development and naturally develop academic and social competencies for living and working in a global age.

The current use of technology shows little innovation, reflecting a sense that if we just put a computer in the classroom, schools have somehow integrated technology into education. Yet as we look to what is happening among youth connections through technology outside of school we come to understand that this is not the case. A few years ago a school principal said to me, "Our students are living in another world than we as adults. It is our job as educators to learn from them about how to develop the future school." His words came in the late 1990s before virtual communities were popular among youth, yet he was able to see that what kids were doing already with technology was far more advanced than how educators were thinking. In many ways this divide has only continued to grow, and now researchers are beginning to study the phenomenon of the cyberworld hoping to understand more about motivational theory to engage kids in schools. As their after-school world expands rapidly with social connections and whole new virtual worlds of identity and meeting places, schools fall further behind in their ability to capture the attention of youth. It is in this space that we believe schools have both an opportunity and a responsibility. The opportunity arises from the possibility to build learning environments based on the social, communication, and technological aspects found in society today. The responsibility relates to developing awareness about the impact on sensemaking in a digital culture.

With the growing challenge and public demand for schools to foster future citizens in the information age, educators have a natural context in which to expand and transform their knowledge and understanding of the relationship between humans and technology from a variety of perspectives. Building a digital culture in schools implies that educators use multimedia to facilitate learning in a social context, in which youth are networked interculturally and the global community informs the curriculum. Youth of today need to learn in a context that mirrors the society they already know so well, which is based on connections, networking, rapid rates of information at high volumes, and a changing cultural landscape. Moreover, educators who see themselves as members of the digital culture, interconnected in their own social networks of learning and knowledge development, can ensure a pedagogy that is responsive to changing societal conditions. The digital culture is one in which we are all members, connected in a variety of communities of practice (Wenger, et al., 2002) shaping society and culture.

Such a pedagogical shift recognizes the integration of technology in our lives and its impact on our human connections and learning. Shaping a digital culture of learning in the global age is about more than technological innovations in schools. It is about creating a working culture in which staff and students engage in shaping their own learning and social development. Borrowing from the fields of culture and communication studies, we are reminded that as learners we are not just students in a classroom following a curriculum. We are members of a larger culture that becomes our curriculum. As we engage with one another in active exchange, we give meaning to a collective space. Using media and technologies contributes to our communication, giving rise to new knowledge to shape a global ecumene. Educators have the possibility to take the next step and support the development of schools as living systems, not just bureaucratic institutions. As living systems, composed of cultures and networks, schools can adapt their learning environments to respond to changes in society and prepare youth for lifelong learning and living in a global age.

12

The Strategic Dance of Life

Improving the quality of programs and services and the pilots of new initiatives requires fresh perspectives for the organizational-development process. Within the *bureaucratic model,* workers typically are told what and how to do it and are assessed on the extent to which they perform their assigned tasks. Employees, both professionals and trade workers, have little voice or power in decisions about their work, except in the details of daily activity. Within the *systems model,* however, workers function as partners in shaping and refining their work systems and services and in assessing the quality of effects on those being served. While few organizations operate any longer within a purely bureaucratic model, a fully developed, system-oriented one is still quite rare.

The purpose of this chapter is to provide a systemic approach, which we call *the strategic dance of life,* to guide transformation initiatives. Developing institutions as responsive systems requires us to shift our attention from policy compliance to life issues, for social institutions serve communities to advance the quality of life for its members. The choices that leaders make in the strategic dance, both in its planning, living, and assessment, determine the quality of adaptation to the needs of those being served; ultimately, those choices influence the quality of life. Improving life and the outcomes of work are the focus, rather than any plan.

The first part of the chapter explores the changing nature of *assessment* as examined in light of systems theory and the nature of change and stability in an organization's journey. Rather than information serving to present a rosy picture, as in the traditional annual report, information can highlight successes and also point out critical areas for further development. The focus of the second part of the chapter is the *case study technique* (CST), which is a five-stage structure for gathering multiple forms of quantitative and qualitative information. The CST is a tool for continuous management and facilitation of the *strategic living system* (SLS) for responding to conditions, processes, and effects to guide the organization systemically toward its vision. The SLS is a practical tool that stimulates a broad examination of current policies and work systems, for it combines essential professional dialogue with systemic thinking, decision making, and action in areas that matter. The model is based on the practices that have evolved over time in the Pasco County School District in Florida, and in our work with educators around the world.

Our discussion assumes that a vision of the organization is based upon a broad perspective of possible futures for the customers being served. Information, planning, living, and assessment serve the vision and together form the operational process for achieving the organization's mission. We have observed that when planning and assessment are independent functions, work tends to remain traditionally unexamined and virtually unchanged. When planning and assessment are linked together dynamically, they function as a balance for the improvement and transformation journey, the organizational yin and yang. In this sense, a growing organization thrives on information for guiding the course of change.

ASSESSMENT AND THE STRATEGIC DANCE

Principals in our 28-school study, when asked about their schools' monitoring and assessment systems, shared their discomfort with the weakest link in the school-improvement chain: *assessment. Assessing for compliance* (bureaucratic model) and *assessing for trends and effects* (systems model) require different philosophical orientations and approaches to institutional improvement. Creating a dynamic assessment system for advancing a vision is a major leadership challenge. If information is the vital link for developing the future, then assessment for development needs to become central to new initiatives.

It is clear to us that fresh perspectives are needed on assessment to enable school leaders to grasp the yin and yang dynamic of the strategic dance: facilitating simultaneous strategic planning and strategic assessment. Being tough about collaborative planning as a response to changing conditions, combined with clarity about the organization's vision, moves the organization forward and in the right direction. Unless new practices and their effects are assessed on the improvement journey, the organization is likely to make no significant advances; it merely shifts to new activity and new efforts.

The increasing complexity of institutional life and the profound changes that are influencing its every dimension are precipitating a crisis in management thinking. *We are at a major turning point in how we view schools and other institutions and their evolution over time. A mindshift is required if we are to transform education systems for a global age of living, rather than an industrial one.* Narrow perceptions of organizational reality, which grow out of ambitions to control systems of work, are inadequate in dealing with the complex problems of our time. The emerging incongruities and inconsistencies we work with daily cannot be understood with fragmentation mind-sets, outdated conceptual models, or an emphasis on irrelevant variables. We need to understand more about *the strategic dance of life* in institutions.

Toward Wholeness

The prevailing paradigm in organizations has been to dominate and control parts of systems and their operation through data that provide statistical information, which is presumed to offer some relative truth. The assumption has been that statistical information provides a degree of truth about the condition of parts in the system, which often reinforces dysfunctional fragmentation of those very systems being examined. How the parts function interdependently to make the system work remains unanswered within the traditional assessment paradigm and remains a challenge for administrators in any kind of agency or organization. *The question of how well systems operate together as a whole matters in the long run, which is a departure from analyzing the existence of certain static characteristics and features.*

Nature does not show us isolated elements at any time; rather, it shows us a complicated web of relations between the parts of a whole (e.g., growth of a child, growth of a forest). This web of relationships in a school, for example, between learning and its conditions, context, programs and services, and their effects, needs to become the focus of our attention in analyzing schools rather than the effectiveness of isolated and independent programs and services. What is learned by studying independent program features and their effects is often useless. It is the interrelationships of program, contexts, and conditions that matter most. In a sense, we are shifting our focus *from isolated objects* (programs, services, structures, and their delivery) *to dynamic connections* (processes, integration, dynamics, and their effects on customers).

When the school, for example, is viewed as a machine-like system, it is assumed that parts add up to a whole: seven periods a day of instruction; independent curriculum and instruction; graded classes and isolated services. Leaders perceive that the machine's maintenance over time evolves through a linear chain of cause and effect, and the breakdown of any part in the system is based on a single cause. This fragmented model of schooling has been the basis for planning and assessing school-improvement efforts in the last 50 years. However, if we consider the school as a living and growing dynamical system, its emergence over time is based on an integrated and rapid response to changes in the environment. Continuous self-organization and renewal, with the adaptation of programs, structures, and processes characterize the school's or district's development process. Learning and schooling are both bundles of phenomena, which need to be analyzed as a whole, for it is in the wholeness that they can be understood.

Schools as self-renewing systems need information from multiple sources and in large doses to guide the continuous improvement process of maintenance and creativity. Schools/teams/teachers/other professionals have the ability to adapt to changing conditions if they are given useful information; this is what needs to be studied by leaders: *the adaptation process and its effects.*

As a school progresses naturally in its own evolutionary response to challenges, it is important to recognize the balance that exists within the self-organization process. *Self-maintenance and self-transformation are the yang and yin of growth,* and they function together within a dynamic/stable environment (things will not get out of hand!). *Maintenance* (the yang) is concerned with self-renewal, healing, homeostasis, and adaptation; *transformation* (the yin) involves learning, development, evolution, and creation (Capra, 1982). Creating new structures and behaviors will lead to an unfolding of complexity and to a creative reaching out beyond itself—a fundamental property of life for a natural system.

Maintenance and transformation, the yin and yang of the organization's dance of life, though considered to be a stable emergence process, are also dynamic, continual, interdependent, and unfluctuating. Healthy systems are flexible and have many options for interacting with and responding to their environment. Therefore, the process of a school's emergence or *evolution is dynamic and yet stable as the strategic dance of life unfolds.* Can a leader influence that which is natural? Yes! As a part of the school's natural system, leaders continuously influence decisions about the school's natural change process, giving shape and direction to the quality of the dance and to its interactions and effects upon students—to its very life as a human social system.

The Case Study Technique

In the last few decades, qualitative research has emerged within a naturalistic paradigm to study the emergence processes and dynamics in natural organizations, from native tribes in the Amazon to classroom life in schools around the world. In pursuit of knowledge about how natural social systems function, researchers have come to recognize the limitations of using quantitative approaches alone for establishing truth, for statistics yield little that is open for interpretation and understanding of the complex life in organizations. While statistics yield critical information about trends and patterns, the findings offer little that is useful in guiding decision making for renewing or changing practices. Hence, qualitative methods, linked at times with quantitative methods, provide vital clues about the nature and dynamics of relationships between and among variables.

The *case study technique (CST)* is introduced as a management assessment tool, which helps leaders to determine *how things are progressing* in relation to goals, to emerging challenges, and to specific projects and innovations. The CST represents a way of thinking about the organization's emergence and about the quality of information that is used to guide the organization into its next phase of emergence. Built upon the foundations of qualitative research, the CST is relatively simple in concept and in execution. It requires *a question* about how well something is working and *three sources of data* (at least) to provide reliable information for discussion. The *outcome of the query* may lead to a new plan of action or to a modification of the planning dimension in the strategic dance.

If we had settled for quantitative data in our 28-school study, we would have learned only which schools were higher- and which were lower-involvement schools; we would not have understood what contributes to those conditions. Neither would we have had the perspectives of teachers who work in different kinds of schools, nor how principals think about building collaborative systems over time in varying contexts to influence student success patterns. To help us understand school change over time, the quantitative and qualitative data combination was necessary. Quantitative data helped us to sort schools into higher- and lower-involvement patterns, while the teachers' written responses to questions and the principals' verbal stories informed us about the human dynamics and complexities in each school.

Our 28-school study provides a good example of the case study technique. The research question was *What does the change process look like from a systems perspective over time and across schools that are found in different contexts and in different conditions?* Three data sources were:

1. *Administration of the School Work Culture Profile* to all the teachers in 28 schools ($n = 1235$) to generate relative teacher involvement levels in shaping the school's improvement

2. *Interviews of the 28 principals* to obtain perspectives on school development challenges over time

3. *Open-ended questionnaires to all teachers* to solicit reactions to their school's change process, the nature of their involvement, and the challenges of schools today

From these three data sources we were able to determine the kinds of challenges that principals face in building collaborative work systems to improve the success rates of students and the perspectives of teachers at various stages in the school's emergence. These three data sources helped us identify the new trends and patterns we share throughout this book.

Let us now consider the nature of qualitative inquiry. What is the *case study?* Denzin and Lincoln (1994) define it as "multimethod in focus, involving an interpretive, naturalistic approach to its subject matters. . . . Researchers study things in their natural setting, attempting to make sense of or interpret phenomena in terms of the meanings people bring to them. . . . It involves the studied use and collection of a variety of empirical materials: case study, personal experience, introspective, life story, interview, observational, historical, interactional, and visual texts that describe routine and problematic moments and meanings in individuals' lives."

The case study technique is a way of assessing systemically what is occurring within a school. It involves a five-step process that has evolved from our work over the years and that has become a way of thinking for many school leaders:

1. Design the study.

2. Collect at least three kinds of information.

3. Analyze the data within and across each data set.

4. Interpret the data analysis in light of existing knowledge.

5. Determine the answer to the study's question and its implications for further action.

These five steps provide a reliable *snapshot* of *what is happening now* in the school or district and its effects as they relate to a particular phenomenon. The focus is on the *now* rather than on the past or future; it answers the question, *What is going on now, and what are its effects?*

Step 1: Designing the Case Study

The case study technique can be used for answering questions about the nature of current practice and its effects. Examples of questions that can be asked follow:

- How are cooperative learning processes working?

- How does the parent-involvement program affect the school?

- How does the interdisciplinary curriculum pilot facilitate student success?

- How does the peer-coaching program affect teaching?

- What can be learned from the nongraded pilot?

- What effect does team teaching have on teachers and on students?

- What are the effects of the school's partnership with the local social agencies?

- What are parent responses to the new reporting system for students?

Whatever the management question and its effects are, the practice of gathering and analyzing three data sources will yield reliable information for decision-making purposes. The important first step is to articulate a question for the study, keeping the question broad enough for data to be useful and specific enough to learn something important for guiding the school's or district's natural emergence process. After using the case study technique several times, the best kinds of research questions (not too broad and not too narrow) for a case study become apparent.

After the case study question has been identified, the next decision is to identify the data sources that will be most helpful in answering the case question. We have worked with five general categories of data: (1) surveys, (2) interviews, (3) documents, (4) observations, and (5) focus groups. The objective is to determine at least three different sources of data. The principle of three-data sets offers considerable flexibility. For example, a data-gathering decision might include (1) interviews from three role groups; or (2) interviews among selected members of one role group, multiple documents, and surveys of another role group. Or, one data source from each category might be more suitable to the situation. The concept is to use at least three data sources to answer the case study question reliably. In the research literature, the concept of using three data sources for formulating conclusions is referred to as *triangulation.* Hence, the concept of at least three data sources helps establish reliability for the impression that is drawn about *how things are now progressing.*

If only one data source is used, the conclusions are likely to be slanted and unrepresentative of the complete story and the actions. If all three data sources yield the same information, such as "the cooperative learning structures are helping more students to succeed," then the conclusion is rather simple and the leaders can proceed to the next step in its development with confidence either to refine or expand practice. If, on the other hand, three data sources produce different information, the findings become a new intellectual question to be addressed. Consider these findings:

1. Most students are happy to work with their friends in a cooperative learning environment.

2. Teachers are fearful that they cannot control the progress of each student.

3. An analysis of test data suggests that cooperative learning is working especially well with the brighter students, but many of the slower learners feel ungrounded.

The management challenge is one of further analysis or data gathering. In the example, the answer to the question of *how cooperative learning is progressing* is complex and might lead to refining the work with slower learners, altering the systems of cooperative work, and launching more training programs for teachers with follow-up coaching. Whichever the conclusion to the study, the multiple sources of information provide a more reliable picture for guiding a school's or district's journey.

Step 2: Collecting Information

The choice of which kinds of data to collect for a case study relates to the purpose of a specific case study and to perceptions about which kinds of information will provide the most valuable insights. Each of the five data categories yields perspectives that are different and that provide relative truths about the question being pursued. Following are options for consideration in planning for data collection.

A. Survey Data

The purpose of a survey is to determine the perceptions of many people on various dimensions of a topic, yielding degrees of perspectives. For a case study, there are two kinds of surveys to consider: (1) *a validated instrument designed for broad use* that is related to the case study question and (2) *an instrument that is designed specifically for the purposes of a particular study.* For example, in the 28-school study, the *School Work Culture Profile* (Snyder, 1988c) was administered to the total faculties of the schools, yielding reliable information about planning, development, and assessment patterns found in higher- and lower-involvement schools, Because the instrument had been tested continuously since 1988 for its reliability and validity and for its factor structures, we had confidence in the information it yielded for our study.

When an instrument is designed for a specific case study, there are two factors to consider: (1) the validity and importance of the items that are generated and (2) the clarity of the items as they are written. A rule of thumb is to conduct a simple review of the literature on a given subject, such as cooperative learning or school planning systems, and write the items for the instrument based on the themes and patterns that are found in the literature review. Too often, survey instruments are developed without a firm foundation in the current research literature and the inquiries that are made merely reinforce traditional practices. The function of a survey is to conduct an inquiry using state-of-the-art concepts. To design anything short of a literature-based survey instrument is a waste of time, for the survey will assess practice in relation to untested truths. One function of an instrument's content is to advance thinking about the quality of a new initiative and its operation.

The construction of a survey instrument can be rather simple and follow general guidelines. First, consider all the major dimensions of the topic under study. For example, a study of cooperative learning might include dimensions such as student-grouping strategies, group training, leadership training, group planning, and assessment strategies. From these five general dimensions, which are drawn from reviewed literature, several statements for each theme area can be written to become the items in the survey. As a general rule, consider from 10 to 20 statements for a survey instrument.

After the items have been written, invite reactions from a few people about the items' *importance* and *clarity*. Feedback is vital to improving the quality of the survey items. Often, an item will ask about several concepts and the responses to such questions will be problematic. When changes have been made to the survey, after several field tests and revisions, and it is perceived that the items are ready for broad use, the scoring dimensions are then designed. The *agree–disagree continuum* or the *always–never continuum* is most typical and employs a five-point scale known as the Likert format. The middle of five choices can be labeled *sometimes, not important,* or *don't know.* Prepare the instrument with simple directions for responding, and list each item with the range of choices for response and procedures for marking the choice. Pilot the instrument before broad use to make certain that the choice of responses in the scale corresponds with the wording in the items. After any necessary modifications, the survey is ready for administration.

B. Interview Questions

Interviews on a topic yield perspectives that extend beyond survey questions and offer additional insights into the dynamics of the case being studied. Interview questions (or, protocol) are prepared using the same dimensions of the literature on a given topic, such as the five dimensions of cooperative learning. The first consideration is the role group to be interviewed. *Will they be the same persons as those surveyed?* If so, then the interview questions will need to be different from those in the survey and address issues, perspectives, and practices that are not included in the survey. If those persons who are interviewed represent a different role group from those surveyed, the interview questions can be drawn from the survey instrument. In this case, the same questions would be asked in two different ways from two different role groups and would yield different perspectives.

There are several approaches to conducting the interview: structured, semistructured, or unstructured. In the *structured interview,* each question is asked in the order in which it appears on the interview protocol and the interviewer is in control of the direction of the responses to questions. The structured interview is especially useful for quality control purposes when several different interviewers conduct the interviews. The *semistructured interview* allows for a more natural flow of conversation and often yields more potentially useful information. In this case, the questions are all addressed but the order in which they are asked depends on the natural flow of the interview itself. A response to one question might lead quite naturally into one question more than another. The natural emergence of the interview guides the order in which the questions are asked, and the questions themselves are likely to function as concepts to be addressed rather than specifically worded questions. The *unstructured interview* has a focus, such as cooperative learning, but has only general issues to be addressed. The unstructured interview is useful when it is unclear what the questions might be. It is most commonly used for the case study, however, for there is a content, which is the structure, and the natural unfolding of the interview directs the order in which the content is pursued.

Data may be hand recorded or gathered on an audio or video recorder. We have found that recorded notes alone are relatively useless because, in taking notes during an interview, the person doing the recording naturally filters out most of what is being said, using current values about what probably will be trends and patterns. It is best to record the interview on an audio recorder and then either have the data transcribed for analysis or listen to the recording in search of text-driven themes. The totality of the verbatim interview is searched for themes and patterns.

C. Documents

Analyzing existing documents offers perspectives on the intentions or to the lack of intentions that relate to the case question. Documents offer clues about the topic, either intended or not. After the specific documents are identified, an analysis protocol that outlines the features of the topic to examine is prepared. The documents are not analyzed in general but in relation to the topic under study. For example, if cooperative learning is the case study focus, the documents will be analyzed for evidence that might exist regarding the planning, funding, development, implementation, and assessment of cooperative learning practices.

The document analysis protocol contains dimensions that focus the analysis task (e.g., cooperative learning dimensions), and the observations are recorded from the documents in relation to the major question and to the multiple dimensions of that focus. It may be that selected documents reveal little about the topic, which is important information for the researcher. Or, extensive evidence of intended outcomes may exist, which may or may not reflect work in progress. The overall case study question provides the general guide to the analysis of documents. Documents that may be of use might include annual school plans, newsletters to parents, annual school reports, minutes of meetings, team plans, evaluation reports, achievement or survey data, and communications to and from the school.

D. Observations

Observations of meetings or events provide information about the life of the school's or district's interaction system—its life! If *observation* is selected as a source of data, it answers the question, *What events might be observed to offer insights into the dynamics and content of work that relate to the overall case study question?* Observations might be made of school planning sessions, school leadership council meetings, teaching team meetings, ad hoc committee meetings, parent work sessions or meetings, interactions within the classrooms, special meetings, and student events. After specific observations have been decided, the observation protocol is determined in relation to the topic of the case study.

In the case of cooperative learning, the observations might include a team planning meeting or students who are working in cooperative groups. The protocol might include questions about student readiness for the group task, student placement in groups, the sharing of student responsibilities for group work, assistance by the teacher(s), students working on cooperative projects, assessment of group work, and so on. The protocol provides a focus for the observation. Data are recorded on a tape recorder, on a video recorder, or in handwritten notes. The question driving the observation is *What evidence is there . . . of cooperative learning?* For classroom observations, the questions might relate to the processes being used in a cooperative learning activity and their effects. In a teaching team meeting, the observation might focus on both the content of dialogue about cooperative learning and the strategies for continuing or improving its practice. The data that are recorded relate to the observation protocol (dimensions of cooperative learning) and to the observed behaviors and relationships in the interaction system.

E. Focus Groups

Recently new in data-gathering methods is the focus group, which is a group interview of 5 to 10 persons. A few discussion questions, identified by the researcher, relate to the challenges and conditions in which cooperative learning practices exist, for example. The group is asked to discuss one question at a time, while the leader of the focus group records on an easel pad key ideas that are being offered. The dynamics of a group and the dialogue that ensues typically lead to new understandings of issues that relate to the case study question. While individuals initially have their own perspectives, which can be addressed in interviews, the focus group achieves another purpose. Individual perspectives, when shared in a group discussion, cause ideas to grow and new perspectives to emerge from the dialogue. These new understandings can be instructive to the focus group members themselves, while they become important perspectives on an issue for the purpose of the case study.

While the focus group is simple in design, it is important that the process be managed well so that the event yields the anticipated information. The leader (e.g., the person who is conducting the case study) identifies 6 to 10 members for the focus group. Three or four questions are asked of the group, with time to discuss each. Guidelines are presented for participating in the focus group, such as *Discuss the questions that are given to the* group and *Seek to derive some group understanding of the situation and its complexity.* While the group discusses each question, the leader records the key ideas on chart paper or audio and video recordings and asks further questions for amplification or interpretation. The recorded ideas from the focus group activity become new data for the case study.

Step 3. Data Analysis

After the data have been gathered, the next task is to analyze each data set. It may be that the first set of data is gathered and analyzed before the next data set is gathered. What is learned from the first data set may be a useful guide to define the focus and emphasis of the second and third data sets. In other words, a decision may be made to encourage an evolution of the study by gathering and analyzing one data set before designing and gathering the next. There are two choices then: (1) to gather all the data before analyzing any data set or (2) to gather one set of data at a time and analyze it prior to gathering the next data set. Decisions are made based on what the leader perceives will yield the most valid and reliable information to answer the study's overall question.

Analyzing survey data requires that all responses be either tallied and quantified to determine the average or the percentage rating of all items, or analyzed for common themes and patterns. If a survey instrument is administered to different groups, the data are analyzed for each group and then across groups. The survey is quantifiable data in a case study and provides numerical perspectives on various dimensions of the study. For example, 85 percent of teachers *surveyed* may believe that cooperative learning systems will help more students to succeed but perceive that students need more training and coaching in working together toward a common purpose. An analysis of *observation data* from classroom events might suggest that students lack understanding and skills for working collaboratively, and an analysis of student *interview data* might highlight the skills that are needed. It is important that survey findings are viewed as a form of relative truth and general perceptions, for the survey instrument itself may not be asking the best questions about the study focus or the wording of the items may be confusing or irrelevant. Thus, it is important to understand that the survey data provides one of several perspectives in the case study and the other data sources illuminate the trends observed in survey data.

Transcripts from the interviews are analyzed for themes and patterns. Each interview text is analyzed, with major themes identified as they relate to the case study question; then the themes are identified across the interview transcripts. Each transcript may yield the same themes and patterns, and there may be a general agreement about responses to the interview questions. More typically, however, different themes are found across the interviews, with conflicting or different perspectives or themes emerging as indicators of complexity in the organization's life. The data analysis task is to identify the themes and patterns both within and across the interview data sets and to determine in general terms the extent of agreement and disagreement.

Document data also are analyzed in terms of themes and patterns, or big ideas, that are prevalent in the data. One kind of data may be the lack of any data about the topic in the documents; there may be other evidence that the documents offer confusing or conflicting data. Whatever the documents contain is information of some sort that relates to the question of the case study. For example, planning documents may yield information about training for teachers in cooperative learning principles; or cooperative learning pilots throughout the school may be a school goal, with significant budgetary and parental support documented. Whatever evidence or lack of it exists, as it relates to the case study question, becomes the themes and patterns from the document analysis.

Observation data are analyzed to determine themes and patterns from the observed event, as they relate to the question driving the case study. Typically, observation data are in the form of notes made on observed events, although at times checklist protocols are developed around a certain topic for the observer to tally events and record impressions. The observer in a cooperative learning setting may notice that group leaders assume responsibility for most of the work and pay little attention to their peers who are not engaged, or are minimally engaged, in the work. When asked, neither group leader nor members may care about the imbalance of work responsibility; it may be that group leaders have few skills for ensuring that work is shared equally and according to a plan for everyone's involvement. Themes and patterns become apparent in the data analysis phase of the study, and the observer will naturally perceive the ways in which the observation themes reinforce or refute those found in other data sets. The linking of findings from all data sets occurs naturally in the data analysis phase and provides the beginning for data interpretation.

Analysis of *focus group data is* similar to the analysis of documents and observation data. Ideas recorded on chart paper are analyzed for themes and patterns, which provide perspectives from a group and their collective and emergent thinking about an issue. Themes may reinforce and extend the meaning of other data that are gathered, or they may provide perspectives on contradictions. The data analysis phase of the case study is one of searching for patterns in the data that provide perspectives on the question under examination.

Step 4. Interpreting the Data

The greatest intellectual challenge in conducting a case study is found in the interpretation of multiple sets of data. What does it mean when all data sets point in the same direction? Consider the conclusion: *Students appear to need more training in basic elements of working in groups.* If teachers know what is needed to enable cooperative learning systems to function better, and if the observation of students and interviews with team leaders point to the same finding, then the interpretation is somewhat clear. The literature tells as that students will perform in cooperative learning structures only to the extent of their knowledge and skills. The case study yields support for further teacher training and coaching in cooperative learning systems and strategies.

What if the data derived from different data sets point to general confusion about an issue? This condition creates a problem-solving context, one in which more data may be needed or a greater understanding is needed of the literature on a given topic. One might interpret student leaders doing all the work as dominance and control on the part of student leaders. Or, with an understanding of productive groups, it may be clear that student leaders lack knowledge and skills for engaging everyone in the tasks. It may also mean that teachers lack knowledge in designing student accountability systems within a group context or the skills for coaching student leaders in their tasks.

A basic guideline for interpreting the data is to identify the themes and patterns within each data set and across data sets and then interpret the findings through multiple frameworks found in related literature. For understanding how useful current cooperative learning operations are, the data might be interpreted through the various lenses. *Group theory* tells us that the most productive groups function around planned activities that include all members equally. *Leadership theory* today suggests that the best leaders have a vision for their organization and the skills for helping the unit evolve toward that end. *Motivation theory* for workers today emphasizes worker involvement and empowerment to pursue tasks for the organization. *Coaching theory* assumes that workers benefit from feedback that enables them to be more successful in their work. While each theoretical framework for interpretation might be different, if we trust in the interdependence of knowledge any current and related principles are likely to further the school emergence process within student learning groups, for example, to teaching teams or to the school as a unit.

Step 5. Answering the Case Study Question

The fifth and final phase of the case study technique is answering the overall question. What was learned and what are the implications for next steps in the emergence of the organization? The answer is derived from a blending of the data that are gathered and analyzed and the literature that is used in the interpretation. A critical dimension in answering the question is the use of current knowledge to formulate the conclusion. It is easy to use outdated lenses or knowledge bases in the conclusion, which only perpetuates the problem.

The challenge is to identify new knowledge that will enlighten the process of data interpretation and formulating conclusions. For example, understanding current cooperative learning conditions along with an understanding of systems theory would suggest creating an interdependence among learning teams. This idea strengthens the interdependence of learning units and reinforces common goals for all groups and the contributions each group makes to the learning of the entire class. Another concept from systems theory is that of building strong connection systems, that is, forging communications within groups and across groups through sharing and coaching and building the strong connection within the classroom and then within small student work teams.

Next are the decisions for action. The literature not only enlightens the analysis process, but it also provides direction for action. For example, the decision to institutionalize cooperative learning might include the following:

1. Training and coaching student leaders in team leadership

2. Training teachers in a system of student accountability for group work contexts

3. Training teachers in interdependent work teams in the classroom

4. Training teachers in multiple ways to build a strong connection system in the classroom that emphasizes communications

The next steps in the decision-making process include (1) expected outcomes, (2) key activities (clusters of) and (3) resources to advance the process, (4) responsibilities of the professional staff, and (5) a timeline of activities. The intention of the improvement initiative is critical to the decisions that follow, for the objectives determine which activities will be planned. For each activity (all the dimensions of work that are needed), the responsibilities need to be assigned, the resources identified that exist or might be available, and the time line outlined within which this work will occur. We have learned over the years, which chaos theory confirms, that action plans are primarily big ideas to guide, but not control, action for the emergence of the next phase for the organization. Surprises will occur, and changes in the environment will dictate that plans be altered as the work unfolds. It is important to remain open to the changing environment and respond as needed as the plan unfolds. The next-step action plan is a concept for what will happen next in development and a framework within which changes will be made.

A CASE STUDY EXAMPLE: THE DYNAMICS OF WORK CULTURES IN HIGH- AND LOW-ACHIEVING SCHOOLS

In a research study by Darlene Bruner (1997), a group of three elementary schools that scored low on state achievement tests was studied and compared with three schools that scored high on the same tests. This particular case study is more comprehensive and more extensive than is typical when examining a single organization. It is offered here to illustrate the power of multiple forms of data and also to reinforce the strength and importance of connections and interdependencies in quality work cultures. Hence, the report reinforces the case study method and also documents the influence of quality-like work cultures on an organization's performance. In this case study, several elementary schools are examined in search of connections between quality work cultures and student performance. (The information that follows was prepared by Bruner for a presentation at the University of South Florida in November 1997.)

The case study technique was the framework for data gathering and analysis with this question governing each phase of the study: *What are the differences found in work cultures between schools with high and those with low levels of student achievement as measured on state tests?* Schools with similar levels of socioeconomic status were selected for the study.

Data Reports

Five sets of data were gathered in each school:

1. The *Education Quality Benchmark System* was administered to the total staff of each school [survey].

2. The School Work Culture Profile was administered to each school [survey].

3. The principals at each school were *interviewed.*

4. *School-improvement documents* from each school were analyzed.

5. *Observations* were made in each school.

1. *EQBS data:* The responses were tabulated for each school and clustered into two groups for comparison: higher student achievement and lower student achievement. The data reveal that *schools with higher levels of student achievement had significantly higher scores on the EQBS than schools with lower levels of student achievement.* The EQBS scores were grouped into developmental categories, which ranged from 1 to 4: bureaucratic system, awareness, transition, and transformation. Table 12.1 reports the percentage of responses in each category of development by school type (high achievement, low achievement).

Table 12.2 reports the range of categories in which the numbers fell. Differences in range category were found to be statistically significant.

Table 12.1 EQBS levels of development by high- and low-achievement schools.

EQBS	Bureaucratic System	Awareness	Transition	Transformation
Low-Achievement Schools	3.1%	23.1%	58.5%	15.4%
High-Achievement Schools	8.9%	15.2%	43.0%	32.9%

Table 12.2 Mean statistics for the EQBS by high- and low-achievement schools.

Performance Areas	High-Achievement Schools	Low-Achievement Schools
Visionary Leadership	Transition	Transition
Strategic Planning	Transition	Awareness
Systems Thinking	Transition	Awareness
Information Systems	Transition	Awareness
Resource Development	Transition	Awareness
Programs & Services	Transition	Awareness/Transition
Customer Satisfaction	Transition	Awareness

2. *SWCP data:* The SWCP was administered to the total staff of each school. The scores were analyzed by school and then grouped into the same categories of schools as the EQBS data: *higher-achievement schools and lower-achievement schools.* The percentages of responses by group are shown in Table 12.3, which reports a significant difference between the work cultures found in each group of schools. The lower-achievement schools had primarily *moderately developed school work cultures,* while the higher-achievement schools had primarily *highly developed school work cultures.*

3. *Interview data:* The principals of each school in the study were interviewed to seek their perspectives on the seven dimensions of a quality culture as identified in the EQBS: *visionary leadership, strategic planning, systems thinking and action, information systems, human resource development, quality services and programs, and customer success and satisfaction.* There were striking differences in the ways that principals from the lower-achieving schools perceived life in the schools from those in higher-achieving schools.

In the *lower-achieving schools,* communications appeared to be fragmented and were limited by the school's traditional structures of work. Principals focused their attention on the school's environment and training the staff. There appeared to be no vision that related to students or to school goals, and the activities mentioned were not linked to any particular mission. Bruner had the sense that these principals saw themselves as managers over the change process rather than as participants in discovering alternative solutions to school challenges.

Table 12.3 SWCP levels of development by school groups.

SWCP	Requiring Development	Moderately Developed	Highly Developed
Low-Achievement Schools	1.5%	60.0%	38.5%
High-Achievement Schools	6.3%	26.6%	67.1%

Principals in *higher-achieving schools* reported a vision of *communities of learners,* where everyone was involved in learning. The vision centered on life-long learning and continuous growth for all members of the school community. These leaders had a sense of purpose and direction. Their focus was on student achievement and success, and the activities were directed to this end. Their talk throughout the interview related to the school's improvement plan. Principals reported that the staff were engaged in problem solving, planning, and analyzing conditions in collaborative and productive ways.

4. *Document data:* In the *lower-achievement schools,* little evidence was found in documents of involving or communicating with parents, and the focus was on teacher work rather than student learning. Conformity and compliance were themes found in the documents, and plans were segmented rather than connected to goals or a mission. The fragmented programs and services seemed to be connected with low student success patterns.

In the *higher-achievement schools,* communications systems and data analysis processes were in place. There was evidence of a commitment to continuous improvement that centered on student success, and all school activity appeared to be directed to that end. School-improvement plans reflected work cultures that were moving toward systems thinking and action (collaboration and involvement, recognition, and activities aligned with goals) and focus on customer.

5. *Observation data:* Bruner sought information on impressions of the schools she observed: school building and grounds, reception of visitors to the campus, reception by the teachers and principals, and overall climate of the school.

In the *lower-achievement schools,* the office staff were reserved with the researcher. Teachers were restrained in sharing their perspectives during the meetings, and, in fact, teachers volunteered little information. The school atmosphere in one school was tense and uncomfortable for the visitor.

In the *higher-achievement schools,* the atmosphere was relaxed, yet business-like, and friendly. The researcher was greeted warmly by the office staff, who volunteered to assist her in making the contacts she sought. In her meetings with teachers, there was a sense of camaraderie, with laughter and jokes a common occurrence. Interviews with the principals were comfortable, and there was a sense of wanting to cooperate in the study.

Data Triangulation

When analyzed across data sets, clear distinctions appeared in the work culture patterns of the high-achievement schools and the low-achievement schools. Bruner found several themes and has reported the data across sets in the following clusters: *focus, leadership, work processes, results orientation, and involvement/responsiveness.* The comparison of work patterns in the high- and low-achievement schools is found in Table 12.4.

Table 12.4   Work patterns in low- and high-achievement schools.

High-Achievement Schools	Low-Achievement Schools
Focus	
Goals guide process	Events guide process
Strategies for implementing goals	Strategies for implementing goals
Improve student performance	Focus on teacher performance
Student centered	The school vision focuses on changing the school environment
Vision for a community of learners	
Effectiveness	Efficiency
Leadership	
Talk about goals	Little talk of goals
Establish direction for change	Plan for predictable outcomes
Align people to accomplish goals	Establish structures for goal
Not bounded by political, bureaucratic, or resource barriers	Bound by political, bureaucratic, and resource barriers
Personally examine individual student data	Review collective student data
Involved in professional growth activities	Provide growth options for others
Recognize and encourage innovation	Recognize some innovations
Empower teachers as leaders and trainers	Encourages teachers as leaders and trainers
Work Processes	
Schoolwide implementation of strategies to improve student learning	Limited new strategies to improve student learning
Teaching teams work to meet the needs of students	Teachers work in isolation
Limited principal involvement with staff	Visible administrative participation in classroom activities
Classroom activities explore alternative methods of instruction	Train teachers in standardized instructional methods
Results Orientation	
Begin programs with the end in mind	List activities rather than desired results
Goals drive training, implementation, and resources	Circumstances drive training
Professionals search for solutions to problems	Implementation and resources
	Deviations from plans are limited
Monitor student performance in a variety of ways throughout the year	Teacher performance monitored
Revise action plans on student data and circumstances	Actions revised based on events

Continued

Table 12.4 *Continued.*

High-Achievement Schools	Low-Achievement Schools
Involvement/Responsiveness	
Required committees are in place	Required committees are in place
Membership on school committees is encouraged	Representative membership on committees
Home-school communications are successful	Lack of effective school-home communication
A variety of data are used to monitor and revise actions	Various forms of student data are gathered and analyzed
Professional growth related to student needs	Professional growth related to teacher interests

To summarize her findings, Bruner made several summary conclusions about the differences between high- and low-achievement schools. Commitment in high-achievement schools centers on students' achieving success, whereas in low-achievement schools the emphasis is on mandates. In high-achievement schools, teachers tend to look for solutions to problems, whereas in low-achievement schools the tendency is to blame external factors. In high-achievement schools, principals promote professional growth, whereas in low-achievement schools monitoring teacher performance is the focus. Schools with higher student achievement have a common vision, a lively communication system, participation of everyone, high expectations of students and staff, and an atmosphere of continuous improvement. In conclusion, Bruner notes that schools that have more quality-like cultures of work develop more effective school-wide responses to the changing needs of students, and this emphasis results in greater levels of student success.

The purpose of gathering and analyzing information is to provide a reliable perspective on current conditions, which then informs planners for the next phase of development. In the next section, we offer a strategic planning system that illuminates the complexity of moving an organization forward.

Strategic Planning

An organization's growth and virtual survival depend on the quality of information gathered about the changing environment and the effects of its programs and services on customers being served. A case study tends to produce considerable amounts of information that are a rich resource when analyzed and used to improve the quality of services and programs. In his book, *The Rise and Fall of Strategic Planning* (1994), Henry Mintzberg raises important questions about the nature of strategy and planning within an organization's culture and political dynamics. His message is that strategy making is a process of planning, one of vision and especially learning. Over the last few decades, strategic planning has gone through many phases, from a logical and linear control of work to the continuous intellectual engagement of the organization in achieving the strategic advantage of the moment and over time. Mintzburg suggests that it is time to settle on a set of balanced roles for planning, plans, and planners in organizations. He mentions some planning themes found in the literature:

1. Planning is future thinking.

2. Planning is controlling the future.

3. Planning is decision making.

4. Planning is integrated decision making.

5. Planning is a formalized procedure to produce an articulated result in the form of an integrated system of decisions.

Several themes about strategy are also identified in Mintzburg's work (1994): (1) strategy is a plan; (2) strategy is also a pattern; (3) strategy is position; and (4) strategy is perspective, an organization's way of doing things. Gomer's (1976) studies from Sweden led to conclusions about formal planning: It lends some evaluative support to problem-solving activities related to a crisis but does not provide early warning or otherwise make the organization more sensitive to environmental changes. *Planning emerged from his study as a lagging system,* more concerned with the output from strategy making than the input to it. Thus, while planners were of help in dealing with a crisis, planning, as conventionally conceived, was not. It seems to have rather little use as a method for problem solving, and in the end its contribution is relatively insignificant.

Mintzburg (1994) observes that a strategy is formulated to direct energies in a certain direction; momentum is the desired result. The more clearly the strategy is articulated, the more deeply embedded it becomes in both the habits of the organization and the minds of its people. Planning is fundamentally a conservative process; it conserves the basic orientation of the organization within existing categories. Planning may promote change but only within the context of the organization's overall orientation. Planning works best when the broad outlines of a strategy are already in place, not when significant strategic change is required from the process itself. Planned change is incremental, generic, and oriented to the short term.

Creativity, by definition, rearranges established categories (Mintzburg, 1994), whereas planning preserves them. Planning is useful for managing the business that already exists and is helpful for looking backward rather than forward; creativity requires an act of faith. George Steiner once acknowledged (Mintzburg, 1994) the inflexibility of planning: Plans are commitments and thus they limit choice, which is a profound limitation. Organizations must function not only *with strategy* but also *during periods of strategy, when the world is changing in ways not yet understood.* There is a tendency to close on strategies prematurely, to skip past the creative but uncomfortable stage of inventing new models or strategies. Management cannot turn to conventional planning practice when faced with uncertain conditions.

Planning generally garners its greatest support when conditions are relatively stable, and it has setbacks when conditions change unpredictably. Planning works best when it extrapolates the present or deals with incremental change within the existing strategic perspective. It deals less well with unstable, unpredictable situations or quantum change in the organization. Planning is so orientated to stability, so obsessed with having everything under control, that any perturbation at all sets off a wave of panic and perceptions of turbulence. Turbulence often is change that cannot be handled through planning processes. We are conditioned to think about planning as controlling unpredictability, when in fact planning needs to be responsive to unpredictable shifts. Planning systems often create a sense of turbulence (when we cannot stick to our plan), when in fact humans have great capacities to flow with shifting currents. Our planning systems need to expect discontinuities and facilitate adaptations to changing conditions.

Mintzburg (1994) argues that a visionary approach to planning is a more flexible way to deal with an uncertain world. Vision sets the broad outline of a strategy while leaving the detail to be worked out, so that when the unexpected happens the organization can adapt and learn. Hence, the sense of turbulence may be a signal of an inflexible planning and operation system, rather than the ability of the organization to learn and adapt to changing conditions.

If the research has taught us anything, it is that strategy formation is a fundamentally dynamic process. It proceeds at its own pace through a form of learning. Strategy formation is interference, for it tends to occur irregularly and unexpectedly, upsetting stable patterns because of unanticipated discontinuities. New ideas do not originate according to a timetable. The strategic window, notes Mintzburg (1994), is a brief time that an organization may have to exploit a fleeting opportunity.

Scenario building has become a strategist's tool, for if you cannot predict the future, then by speculating upon a variety of possible futures you might hit on the right one. Building scenarios of possible futures stimulates inquiry and strategic thinking. Once scenarios have been built, several options exist:

1. Bet on the most probable one.

2. Bet on the best one for the organization.

3. Hedge so as to get satisfactory results no matter which one results.

4. Preserve flexibility.

5. Exert influence to make the most desirable scenario a reality.

Shifting managerial worldviews in the process of building scenarios enables an organization to deal more effectively with crises when they occur. Strategies are a product of a worldview. When a worldview changes, managers need to share some common views of the new world for strategy building.

Organizations engage in formal planning not to create strategies but to program the strategies they already have, that is, to formally elaborate and operationalize their consequences. Schlechty (1997) poses several questions to educators: *What business are we in, and what business do we want to be in? What products do we have that might respond to needs, and what new products or services need to be developed?* The aim of schooling, he asserts, is an educated citizenry, but the core business of schooling is engaging students in work that results in their learning what they need to learn to be *viewed as well educated* in society. The requirement now is for education to prepare ordinary citizens to construct new knowledge and products based on existing knowledge. It is no longer sufficient for students to be informed and critical consumers of knowledge constructed by others.

A Strategic Living System

Mary Giella, Karolyn Snyder, and Robert Anderson (1999) have developed a strategic planning system that has as its centerpiece for school districts and for schools *what students need for success in a global village.* The model presented in Figure 12.1 and the strategic living guidelines that follow were developed for a training system for school districts and school leaders who are responsible for district development. The concepts and ideas are grounded in systems and chaos theories and reflect what Pasco County learned over the past decade in its school district transformation process.

Based on systems thinking, all parts of the system (refer to figure) are interdependent and function as a unit to influence student success patterns. This approach reflects less about strategic planning and more about strategic living, as Victor Pinedo proposes (2004). He argues that strategic living is an orientation to daily work that is driven by core values, a vision and mission, and a few big ideas. By living strategically, educators can respond to rapidly changing conditions, and become more nimble and flexible as they take advantage of emerging dynamics and their opportunities.

The centerpiece of this model addresses the district's and schools' vision for students within a changing global environment. What are the generic capacities for young people that will drive all district instructional and learning activity? School districts and schools engage in a series of analysis questions to determine the fit between their vision for students and the policies and practices that govern work (1). Based on their analysis of policy, leaders entertain questions about the changes that need to be made to the curriculum, school structures and processes,

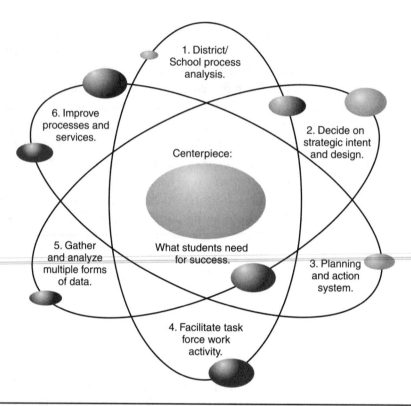

Figure 12.1   A strategic living system.

assessment systems, and so on (2). Big changes are identified and become strategic goals that are followed by a structure for work. A steering committee and its task forces, which represent all units, role groups, and schools within the district, work on the strategic plan to study and refashion district work systems (3). The planning and action system guides work activity that relates to the vision for students and the major systems of work that need renovation or development; the work is facilitated by a steering committee (4). The research division of the school district or a task force engages in information gathering, with modifications of the case study method used continuously to inform planners and decision makers (5). Services and processes that require improvement are identified and developed (6).

In this strategic living system, six interdependent dimensions collectively influence *what students need for success:*

1. District/school process analysis.

2. Decide on strategic intent and design.

3. Planning and action system.

4. Facilitate task force work activity.

5. Gather and analyze multiple forms of data.

6. Improve processes and services.

We encourage you to develop a strategic mission for moving your school or school district forward as a responsive system to the communities being served.

Centerpiece

What do we want young people to be able to do (the vision) within a context of a changing global environment? What are the generic capacities for young people's development that are to drive all work activity in the school or school district? Identify the core competencies for success in life (such as the workplace competencies and foundation skills presented in the SCANS report in 1992: *use of resources, interpersonal skills, information, systems, and technology with the basic skills of reading, writing, and math:* creative *and critical thinking: and personal qualities of responsibility and integrity).*

District/School Process Analysis

Use the following *analysis questions* as a guide for analyzing the current policies and systems that govern work in the school or school district:

1. *Review school board policies governing curriculum, instruction, assessment, instructional materials, and student progression.* Do they facilitate student success as described in your organizational vision and mission statements?

2. *Review the way teachers and leaders are selected.* Are the selection processes consistent with the type of employees needed to provide student success as described in your vision and mission statements? List the strengths and weaknesses.

3. *Review the staff development systems that are provided to the staff.* Are they consistent with what the staff needs to stimulate student success as described in the vision and mission statements?

4. *Are budgeting, purchasing, facility, school transportation, and school food services focused on the needs of schools?* Are they consistent with what is needed to provide for students as described in the vision and mission statements? List the strengths and weaknesses.

5. *Are student support services consistent with what is needed to provide for student success* as described in the vision and mission statements? List the strengths and weaknesses.

6. *Are parental, community, and business support directed at student success* as described in the vision and mission statements? List the strengths and weaknesses.

7. *Are educational linkages (preschool, community colleges, colleges, and universities) connected to student success* as described in the vision and mission statements? List the strengths and weaknesses.

Based on your analysis of current conditions, continue your strategic dialogue and planning. Discuss the changes you want to make in light of your analysis of current policies and the organization's vision and mission statements.

Decide on Strategic Intent and Design

Based on your analysis of school and school district processes, policies, and systems, what changes need to be made in the following areas?

- Curriculum

- Assessment

- Materials

- School structures

- School processes

- Service development and integration

- Human resource development

- School board policies

- Facility design and redesign

Planning and Action System

Coordinate all activity to ensure that progress is being made. Leaders convene regularly to report, discuss, and solve problems. Pep rallies are held to reinforce the vision, which involves the community. The process of development remains open continuously so that progress is realized and so that antagonists cannot get a foothold and delay or destroy progress. Decide the following:

- Names of task forces

- Responsibilities assigned to each task force

Facilitate Task Force Work Activity

Make the changes that you perceive are important to the system of work, and create an organizational structure to provide the context of work. How do we organize ourselves to work on it all? A steering committee? Task forces? Sub-task forces? In Pasco County, the steering committee was responsible for the following work:

1. Ensure that the vision is addressed in all task forces.

2. Ensure that the plans within each major division are consistent with one another and move the system forward toward the vision.

3. Convene task forces to celebrate their work and progress.

Design your organization's structure for strategic activity that reframes all the systems of work around the vision and mission statements for students. Provide a major purpose for each work task force and sub-task force. What is the infrastructure that will support the strategic ideas leading to the vision and mission statements?

Gather and Analyze Multiple Forms of Data

The research division of the school district or a task force in a school gathers information on a need-to-know basis, which is long term, for each task force. In addition, a case study plan is created to study continuous progress in improving the systems of work and institutional policies toward the vision and mission statements. Consideration is given to information that is gathered from surveys, interviews, document analysis, observation, and focus groups. Information is gathered from sources both inside and outside the organization, such as state, national, and local test information. Be proactive about the use of information. Address the question of how the information will be used in the planning process:

1. What is the case study *question* driving the study?

2. Whom will you *survey* and about what?

3. Whom will you *interview* and about what?

4. What *documents* will you analyze?

5. What events or work processes will you *observe?*

6. Whom will you convene for a *focus group* (a group interview)?

Improve Processes and Services

Based on the analysis of the data gathered, what are the themes and patterns you found? What are your strategies for improving the work plans? After you have examined dimensions of the deep culture in your organization, it will become clear that plans for improvement are in order.

Continue to Analyze the Conditions

Organize work, facilitate progress, and make adjustments to the systems, structures, and processes. Respond to changing conditions and opportunities that are in keeping with the mission and vision, which may alter the course set out in plans. And consider how the work and its effects will be reviewed periodically to ensure that the vision and big ideas continue to drive work?

The *case study technique* is a tool for listening to and identifying the deep trends in the natural environment of a school or school district, and it can be enhanced or redirected. The kind of information gathered in a case study tells about the current life force in an organization and can become a new source of disequilibrium for stimulating new kinds of responses. *This is emergence leadership.* A *strategic living system* is a useful guide to action over time within the complex environment of schools and school districts. The yin of planning and the yang of assessment provide healthy parameters for guiding an organization's systemic transformation and continuous development over time. *Continue forever this strategic dance of life!*

Part 4

Thriving at the Edge of Chaos

This part offers perspectives on essential elements of designing and sustaining schools as learning organizations in this global age of living. Developing the school as a learning organization begins with a shared vision, mission, and goals for a new era of schooling, and it is realized by building teams and task forces within the school also as learning organizations. The digital culture of work will replace the teacher-dominant feature of schooling in the last century, and enable professionals and students to engage in qualitatively different kinds of learning experiences and their outcomes because of the rich resources and human community outside the school door. New professional capacities are required for leading sustainable development initiatives as schools adapt to the conditions of work in this global age. The stories of pioneer principals and teachers are shared at the end of this book, and provide important clues for what is possible as leaders imagine new schooling futures for their community.

Chapter 13, Developing Work Teams as Learning Communities, explains how teams provide the energy for work and learning within the larger organization. Teams working together can transform learning results for students and enable educators to share knowledge and improve their practices over time. Work teams are the building blocks for vital organizational development. The literature on work teams today represents much of what was learned about group dynamics and processes in decades past. The team version of the *Education Quality Benchmark System* provides leaders with a frame for developing strong temporary and permanent teams, as well as networks and partnerships. Emphasis is given on how teams use benchmarking to develop their continuous learning and growth. Case examples are offered that feature a school in Sweden that has 14 international partnerships, most of which are connected to specific school programs.

Chapter 14, Leading Schools as Global Learning Centers, is the education challenge for the twenty-first century. To be successful, educators need a new mindset, new knowledge, and new skills for building all kinds of communities of work, both within the school facility and beyond to other parts of the local community, nation, and global community. New leadership capacities are offered for leading sustainable school development initiatives, which are in contrast to the command and control orientation of the last century. Perhaps the most important feature of this book is the stories that are told by school leaders who are pioneers, those who are exploring the global landscape and adjusting school learning to new conditions. These stories illustrate possibilities that exist now for reshaping schooling for a new era of human living.

13

Developing Work Teams as Learning Communities

Teams have become pervasive as the unit of work for transforming all kinds of organizations. High-performing companies have learned the power of teamwork for advancing their organizations toward their visions and missions. Price Waterhouse (1996) reported that by 1994, 68 percent of the Fortune 500 companies were using *self-managed teams* that assumed responsibility and accountability for their productivity. Self-managed teams give employees control over everything from work schedules to hiring and firing, to performing their work, and to learning about and guiding all dimensions of their naturally complex work environment (Maeroff, 1993).

A major change in the work culture of responsive organizations is the development and empowerment of work teams. The range of teams includes *primary work units,* which in schools or districts are interdisciplinary and cross-grade or cross-functional teams. In addition to primary work units, new dynamic structures have evolved in recent decades in response to changes and complexities in the environment. *Ad hoc groups* within organizations enable new project teams to add value to the entire organization. *Networks* enable role-alike groups across institutions to work together informally to share information and resources and to pursue the evolution of new concepts and practices within a particular environment. *Partnerships* are different from networks in that professionals from different role groups and across different kinds of agencies and institutions pursue a common cause or goal. To understand the natural evolution of this spectrum of work teams, chaos and complexity theories offer fresh perspectives for exploring what Begun (1994) says is the 95 percent of organizational life that we have avoided until now because it has been too dark, murky, and intimidating.

To make the shift from individuals to teams of professionals, high-performing leaders have shed their function as the director of work in favor of a connector of resources. Leaders everywhere are becoming facilitators of empowered work groups who solve the organization's emerging challenges while addressing its central functions. So central and successful is this shift from individuals to work teams in organizational development, it seems likely that, until teams become the focus for school and district accountability, they will continue to merely refine and alter independent services and produce only minor improvements. The connections within and across teams generate the necessary energy to stimulate major renovations in the systems of work.

Work teams can achieve major breakthroughs for the organization when they embrace systems thinking as a way of life. By developing and empowering work teams, school leaders are preparing professionals to stimulate the organization's emergence as a world-class social enterprise. If we are intent upon inventing more vital forms of schooling, we should cease toleration and support of isolation in any form. Principals and district leaders who understand the vital function of work teams help to develop their teams' capacities to respond quickly and flexibly to shifts in the environment.

Schools and school districts simply are too complex today for a few leaders to direct and control all the work. Kauffman's (1995) biological concept of *patching* is helpful in understanding the utility of work teams in responding to changes in the environment. A *patch* in biology is a cluster of cells that provides a unique function for a larger cell system. A cluster of patches, because of its small size, is able to create solutions that would never evolve from the larger, more cumbersome system. Kauffman observes that in biology a multiple *patch system* has the flexibility and leverage to solve multiple problems for a growing system. A crazy quilt of adjacent patches can find ways to easily alter conditions because of the coevolving dynamic found within a self-organizing system (253). Breaking large systems into patches allows the patches literally to coevolve with one another, for a move of any one patch alters the other patches (258). An adaptive move by one patch virtually changes the fitness and reforms the fitness landscape or energy landscape of adjacent patches (256).

If a problem is complex and full of conflicting constraints, breaking the system into patches so each patch can optimize enables all patches to coevolve. When the system is broken into well-chosen patches, each adapts for its own benefit, as well as for the whole lattice of patches (Kauffman, 1995, 262). No central control is needed, for properly chosen patches work selfishly to achieve coordination with other patches. The principle is this: Small patches are able to move toward chaos (the place where natural systems are the most dynamic and alive), whereas large patches freeze into poor compromises (264). A one-patch system is stuck forever. Kauffman claims that when properly pared into the right-sized patches, complex problems can be rapidly brought to fruitful compromise solutions (266).

For the last several decades, we have worked with principals in the development of their school teams. We have observed a natural evolution in their development, progressing from a level where people ask permission to work together to a level of accountability for the results of their work. In this evolution, we observe teams necessarily shifting their orientation from compliance to invention, from low connections of members to highly integrated levels of coinvolvement, and from working together within a school to link across schools, districts, and other agencies or associations.

The first part of this chapter reports on trends in teams as learning communities. Emphasis is given to building responsive work teams and developing high levels of work group competence, which are characteristics of self-managed teams. The work of leaders is critical to maturing learning communities, and their new roles are examined. The voice of professional workers is the key for launching development initiatives, and so we present the teachers' voice from our 28-school study. In the second part of the chapter, emphasis is given to the Team Quality Profile (TQP) as a tool for developing learning communities. Essential concepts that guide team growth are offered within the TQP framework, and the effects of high levels of integration of the work culture are reported to illustrate the difference that quality cultures create in a school's performance. The new work of team leaders and school leaders is examined within the TQP development frame, with examples offered from two world-class schools in Sweden. Our intention is to provide fresh perspectives on the work of school and team leaders in developing increasingly responsive schools and for building high-performing and empowered teams that are integrated into the school's priorities. This is the central task of leadership for building responsive learning communities.

TRENDS ON TEAMS AS LEARNING COMMUNITIES

Building Responsive Work Teams

The concept of working alone has virtually disappeared from the work environment, for isolation and its disconnection from energy sources and from life itself virtually promote decline. Teamwork, however, has great potential for strengthening the organization's connection and energy systems within and across work teams and also across organizations, agencies, and professional groups. Leaders who merely respond to isolated crises by themselves fail to invigorate the work culture and keep things moving forward. When considering the laws of physics, it becomes clear that no transformative capacity can be built within an organization by continuing the practices of fragmentation. Building a cohesive, integrated system of work enables self-generated energy to drive the work culture toward a common vision and mission.

The management challenge in developing a learning community is to build the district's or school's energy and connection system so that it thrives *on the edge of chaos*. As Tom Gaul reported when he was superintendent of schools in Sarasota County, Florida, "I have noticed that those high schools that respond best to their students are those that live near the edge of chaos. They understand the nonlinear nature of creativity and the organic processes of change within the school environment." In a similar spirit, John Fitzgerald, when he was a principal in the Ottawa/Carlton School Board near Ottawa, Canada, told us, "Developing a responsive professional staff requires that I function as the head cheerleader, keeping the energy up and moving the school in the right direction to promote student success. It's chaos, and it works!"

Because of the known power of connections in work teams, leaders are shedding the long-cherished preoccupation with individual workers as the unit for development and appraisal and instead are shifting their focus to work teams of professionals. To overcome our traditions and training to work alone, teams need knowledge and skills for working together. They need to know, for example, how to learn from information of all kinds as they improve programs. To foster school and classroom emergence as learning communities, school leaders who think and act systemically are a natural resource to their work teams. They herald the school's vision, facilitate development, and empower teams *to do whatever it takes* to help more students succeed in school and in life. Not only is the interdependence of work teams a feature of systems thinking in organizations, but it is also a cornerstone of quality organizations today. Shilliff and Motiska (1992) observe that a totally integrated quality work culture incorporates teamwork across organizational lines, which requires a change in individual attitudes, beliefs, ideas, work objectives, and relationships for all role groups.

Developing High Levels of Work Group Competence

Learning to work in teams requires new sets of assumptions about work and about the value of others' ideas. We have observed that schools that embrace a systemic approach soon develop high-performing, cross-functional, specialized teams with multidisciplinary knowledge and skills. In pursuit of new capacities, teachers are becoming equipped with knowledge for co-creating new systems and processes of work. The habits of isolation are not easily shed, however, as Price Waterhouse (1996) found from a nationwide poll. People with poor communication skills do not perform well in teams. In addition, problems emerge on teams when some members fail to work hard, are just plain difficult, or are unwilling to tackle tough issues. Common problems on work teams in their national study included:

- People who were assigned inappropriate tasks

- Inadequate commitment to the work objectives

- Inadequate and inappropriate training

- Unrealistic management expectations

- Indecisiveness

Becoming an expert in specific knowledge and skills is imperative for working in cross-functional teams, which are lightly structured systems of interconnections that Peters (1992) calls *spiderweb organizations.* An aspect of the adult learning process for teams is framing and reframing issues and concepts together through continuously experimenting, crossing boundaries, and integrating the perspectives of others (Brooks, 1994). Guiding teams in their learning process is similar to coaching and cheerleading; it involves assessing team skills and helping them to use knowledge in addressing the complexity and challenges of their work (Shonk, 1992).

Characteristics of Self-Managed Teams

In recent years, a strategy for managing complexity is the self-managed team, which has the potential for responding to actual shifts in the environment of schooling. Kanter (1989) projects that organizations are likely to be run by self-managed teams in the future, for workers and managers will succeed only if they find ways to invest in learning and development, lead change efforts, and somehow add value. The project teams of the future, according to Peters (1992), will neither squash individualism nor blunt specialization; individual contributions will be more important than ever. Becoming expert will be imperative for work, which will encompass interdisciplinary functions within the organization (154).

So powerful is the concepts of teams and their self-management, that people are finding ways to work together collaboratively across continents and time zones. One of the most recent examples of self-managed enterprises is the evolution of Wikipedia, the online open encyclopedia that is developed and managed by those who participate in its evolution. Tapscott and Williams, in their 2007 publication of *Wikinomics: How Mass Collaboration Changes Everything,* predict that the metaphor of an army marching in lockstep to tightly arranged military music belongs to yesterday's workplace. The workplace of the future will be more like a jazz ensemble, where musicians improvise creatively around an agreed upon key, melody, and tempo. Employees are developing their own self-organized interconnections and forming cross-functional teams that are capable of interacting as a global, local, and real-time workforce.

In *The Distributed Mind,* authors Fisher and Fisher (1998) pursue the challenge of achieving high team performance through collective intelligence and knowledge. To begin, teams will shed words in their work vocabulary that are mechanical, such as *steer, jump-start, retool, redesign, reengineer, structure, organize, drive,* and *mechanism.* As they pursue their tasks naturally, searching for shifting patterns and appropriate responses, teams will begin to use organic words such as *nourish, nurture, grow, evolve, prune, educate, adapt, cultivate,* and *organisms.* Viewing teams within an organic context, the authors compare workers in the industrial age and those in the information age. Here are several comparisons (119):

Industrial Age	Information Age
Hierarchy of people	Hierarchy of purpose
Division of labor	Integration of specialists
Rules and regulations	Resources and task boundaries
Mandates	Communications
Chain of command	Flow of information
Jobs	Missions
Control emphasis	Innovation emphasis

We found from our 28-school study that *higher-involvement work cultures* are more capable of responding to changing conditions than lower-involvement cultures. It is through interdependent work teams that the school's strong connection system is built. Isolated content-based departments in high schools typically are minibureaucracies, as are many grade-level teams in elementary schools. The tradition of bureaucratic teams is to function in isolation from other teams and from the school's overall direction focus. They tend to be oriented to stated policy and curriculum rather than to the varying needs of their students. Within systems-oriented schools, we found that work teams have become multidisciplinary and multigraded at all levels, and their members work interdependently within and across teams to provide a comprehensive and holistic program for all students. In all high schools in our 28-school study, nongraded structures are gradually replacing the strict graded curriculum and classrooms of the past, for as teachers pursue the natural condition and rhythm of their students' lives, novel structures and programs quite naturally emerge.

Self-directed work teams are groups of five to eight persons who are empowered to manage their own daily work within formal, rather permanent structures (Wellins, Byham, and Wilson, 1991). Systems-oriented teams are interdependent and are charged with continually improving their processes, products, and services. Highly developed teams not only handle their job responsibilities, but they also plan and schedule their own work, make decisions about new initiatives, take action to solve problems, manage their own budgets, decide on their own professional-development needs, and share leadership responsibilities. Trust is a function of the partnership that exists between members and across levels of employees, where team playing, not rivalry, is the norm.

A feature of high-performing teams is their attention to the quality and direction of their work as a unit of influence (Shilliff and Motiska, 1992). The team leader provides support, guidance, and direction to quality improvement efforts. Cooperative team interaction fosters communication and innovation, and enhances the team's capacity to respond to chaos and complexity with skill and confidence. By being empowered, teams quite naturally maintain an atmosphere of cooperation and commitment as they pursue the mission of the organization and their own unit goals (Miller and Krumm, 1992).

However, high-performing teams do not emerge naturally within the school context if they are left alone. The traditions of isolation are still so strong that the pull to work alone is a socialized tendency. For self-managed teams to emerge, leaders spend their priority energy, as well as time and resources, to facilitate team growth toward self-management and accountability. The struggle over the previous decade, according to the principals in our 28-school study, was for teaming to become a work norm in schools. It is clear from principals' stories that isolation in all dimensions of a school's program and services will continue unless the interdependence of work teams is a top priority for the school's leaders. With continuous nurturing, the traditions of isolation eventually can be overcome, for as teams become successful in designing new programs and solving problems, they learn how to thrive on natural doses of chaos.

For those who value adapting to changing conditions, the traditions of *power over* workers eventually will be replaced by *power to*. Power distribution and new definitions of power play a vital role in the productivity of teams. Wheatley (1992) defines power in organizations as the capacity that is generated by relationships. Power is energy that flows through the organization and cannot be confined to levels and functions; it is the quality of relationships (connections) that gives power its charge. Brooks (1994) found there to be an explicit link between the distribution of formal power to individual team members and the collective outcome of producing useful new knowledge. In her research, Brooks inquired about why some teams learn and others do not. She observed that the effects of formal power distribution, along with organizational structures and policies, influence a team's learning process. Both team and individual learning occur in a team, she concluded, when it is facilitated by an atmosphere of collaboration and when team leaders show concern for each member's participation. Different degrees of power on a team are critical levers that affect team performance. Equal power among team members is a key to team success for controlling their own time, movement, and work.

The New Work of Leaders

Leaders in organizations are no longer the caretakers of order, but rather are facilitators of disorder; their function is to stir things up, keep the pot boiling, and look for disturbances that challenge and disrupt the equilibrium (Wheatley, 1992). The focus for this work in the organization, we believe, is work teams. Rather than controlling for how teams perform, leaders are learning to shape the organization through a vision, powerful ideas, conceptual models, and development opportunities that nurture self-organization within teams. Kanter (1995) predicts that survivors in the years ahead will be managers and workers who are oriented toward projects, succeed when they invest in learning and development, lead change initiatives, and add value to the organization. In facilitating life *at the edge of chaos,* leaders build within teams a tolerance for ambiguity, build confidence in taking risks, question the value of historical performance, support renegades, redesign information systems, and rebuild trust through dialogue (Nadler et al., 1995). Gunter (1995) urges managers who are building a learning organization to use instability to innovate, for bounded instability creates the future as responses are made to fluctuations in the environment.

The challenges that leaders face have escalated everywhere. To achieve high performance as an organization, leaders will necessarily become adept at balancing conflicting demands while continuously transforming the culture of work. As superintendents and principals face tougher demands for student performance on state standardized tests, with increasingly stiffer punishment for school failures, the challenge of preparing students for success in a global village taxes their imagination as well as their moral fiber. How do we manage these paradoxes and contradictions? Price Waterhouse (1996) argues that managers in the decades ahead will acknowledge and overcome this current chaos and complexity, not with formulas or rigid policies but by working flexibly and with uncommon intelligence, that is, by managing the paradox itself.

The greatest challenge we have observed over the years, as principals shift from *bureaucratic* to *systems thinking,* is letting go of assumptions about control as a viable strategy for building the organization. By replacing control with the development of empowered work teams that progress toward a common vision and several big ideas, quantum leaps will be realized. Toward this direction, teams require new knowledge and skills for understanding and developing their own natural work environments and for making adaptations to the chaos and complexity they experience. And, contrary to our traditions, open debate among team members and new opportunities for exploration enable teachers to self-organize in their teams around emerging conditions, needs, and opportunities.

The message of this chapter is that the work of *emergence leadership* for building learning communities centers on developing highly responsive and empowered cross-functional teams over time. In so doing, the organization moves quite naturally *to the edge of chaos,* which is the place of greatest creativity, adaptation, and responsiveness to changing conditions. A team organization offers the best chance for making sense of an institution's social complexity, for within the actual team learning environment (a patch), teachers can constantly examine the growth of students being served and make creative adaptations.

Without top leadership as the champion of self-directed and empowered teams, the potential of teams to contribute in fresh ways to the organization's emergence is limited, if not insignificant (Ryan, 1992). The success of teams is directly related to the ability and willingness of top-level leaders to cope with broad-scale change and to fundamentally alter the organization's power structure.

BENCHMARKING TEAM GROWTH

The Team Quality Profile

To assist teams in their own development and to provide school leaders with useful information to assist team growth, the EQBS has been adapted for team benchmarking purposes. All seven dimensions of the EQBS are found in the team version and give direction for improvement efforts: *team visionary leadership, team strategic planning, team systems thinking, team information systems, team human resource development, team quality services and programs,* and *team customer success and satisfaction.*

In the *awareness stage* of the team's growth, work continues primarily according to traditions and policy guidelines and team members explore ways to work together. In this learning stage, the focus is on program improvements and professional development, with the beneficiaries being the students and administrators and other teams they may serve. The team leader makes policy decisions and responds to requests for information that relates to policy, while other team members engage in routine work. Individual team members may explore the utility of new practices or concepts in their own individual work. Team decisions are made together, under the direction of the team leader, but the work itself is typically performed by individuals with the work being divided according to a common plan. The improvement focus generally centers on routine practices and programs, with an efficiency orientation.

In the *transition stage,* the team begins to consider going beyond *planning together* and actually *works* together to explore issues, while designing new programs to work together with students. More examples of cross-grade and interdisciplinary programs have evolved by now, with an interest in exploring the potential that exists with the integration of functions and student age groups. This transition time is critical in forming mental models for integration as the team plans, observes, assesses, and reflects upon innovative strategies. The collective knowledge about how groups work and the skills for shared decision making and learning become critical to the success of teams. It is at this stage that teams either proceed into interdependent structures and services or retreat into a *planning only* form of teaming. The middle stage is one in which teams begin to get a sense of their own collective power and future and of *emergence* as a phenomenon. In the process, they are coming to understand their pivotal role as learners and enablers.

In the *transformation stage,* the team no longer questions the utility of coinvolvement and interdisciplinary activity. When teams become convinced of their power to build their own connections for their students, the teams' focus centers on shedding outdated work patterns, taking greater risks, and often venturing further into unknown futures that have potential and promise. This stage *at the edge of chaos* is where the team is the most dynamic, creative, and alive, and the most capable of responding well to the greatest complexities and contradictions it faces. Now that coinvolvement is a way of life, the team centers its attention on taking greater risks to take the toughest challenges and to learn from other world-class teams.

Standards for High-Performing Teams

Let us now consider benchmarks for work teams that are based on the Education Quality Benchmark System (EQBS). World-class practices such as these can guide team growth and stimulate major breakthroughs in services and programs.

Visionary Leadership.   A team shapes its vision around the conditions of its students (or other customers) and also the school's social, political, and educational environment. The question of vision relates to the population of students being served, their duration in the team's program, and the team's central purpose. The vision also guides the team's development and delivery of all programs and services and becomes a key element in team assessment. In a sense, the vision is the meter for self-organization on the team and directs the purpose and quality of professional-development activity.

Strategic Planning.   The team's plan includes more than its instructional programs; it addresses the team's vision and mission, along with strategies for delivering responsive programs and services. The strategic plan includes a vision of what students need to become for success in a global village, which provides the umbrella for daily planning, work activity, and assessment, all of which emerge dynamically as the team progresses toward its goals and team vision. The team's strategic plan links with the school's plan and addresses the challenges and development initiatives that are anticipated. Included in the plan will be goals, programs, resources, responsibilities, and time line, which functions as a general guide while team members work with emerging conditions, forces, and connections.

Systems Thinking.   Initially, team members may all perform the same functions, which follow a plan developed by the team. As teams develop greater comfort with teaming and understanding of the power of interdependence, members will shift their emphasis from all doing the same thing to each member carrying a different responsibility that supports the team vision and plan. Differentiation relates to responsibilities as well as to the various dimensions of working together that make the program function well. The energy that results from interdependent learning is like a dance, which always amazes teams, for it is continuous interdependence that enables teams to break from traditions and to give shape to the future in fresh new ways.

Information Systems.   A challenge for teams is to determine the kinds of quantitative and qualitative data that will provide clues about trends and effects from programs and services. The tendency, throughout the organization and research literature, is to use a combination of both, for quantitative data provides overall trend information and qualitative data helps teams interpret quantitative data that provides direction for improvement or change. Because teams function within a larger system, it is important to gather information from customers who are both internal and external (students, parents, social agencies, and businesses). In addition, attention needs to be given to those who provide services to the team (special services in a school; district curriculum and support departments; other teams at the school; professional organizations). Sharing and exchanging information broadly is another function of work teams, for information is the lifeblood between customer and supplier groups and provides the connections for the continued emergence of the team.

Human Resource Development.   A team will become as competent as its collective knowledge and skills. High-performing teams are learning communities who study information about their context and who anticipate what new knowledge will help them to be more responsive. To achieve autonomy in their emergence, teams need funds to manage their own professional development as it relates to their overall purpose, needs, and specific improvement goals. An autonomous team is one that has the authority to make decisions about improving its function in the organization and about its professional development priorities, which may include training, seminars, conferences, visitations, peer coaching, study groups, and the analysis of its innovations and implications.

Quality Services.   Teams provide programs and services to meet obligations for the organizations serving the needs of special populations. Routinely, high-performing teams learn about the effects of their programs and services to determine their relative value and also to point to next steps in the team's emergence and utility for the organization. Learning about the quality of services is somewhat different from learning about effects of those same services (information systems). The team needs to learn continuously from students and other service providers and from other customers about reactions to the design and delivery of particular services. Reactions to service quality questions guide future design work.

Customer Success and Satisfaction.   Data gathered from students themselves (or other work team customers) or from parents and the community provide information about the relative value of the services being offered. Major trends that are identified from the data provide additional information for team planning. Data on team performance reveal trends of success and satisfaction for all customer groups to which the high-performing team responds in its continuous improvement efforts. In our conversations with principals and with team leaders recently, it has become apparent that teaming has now become an accepted feature in schools. Yet, there is little training available for team members to learn basic skills and knowledge about working in groups. Neither are there benchmarks that describe the function of highly developed teams and the stages of development along the way. We expect that the Team Quality Profile (TQP) will be useful as a benchmarking tool.

Quality Work Cultures Make a Difference

Bishop (1997) conducted a study of schools that documents the differences that exist between highly integrated systems of work and those that are more traditional. She examined the relationship between the organizational culture of four elementary schools and their referral rates for exceptional student education programs. From the administration of the EQBS, she learned that high-referral-rate schools had significantly lower scores than the low-referral-rate schools. See Figure 13.1 for the actual trend information.

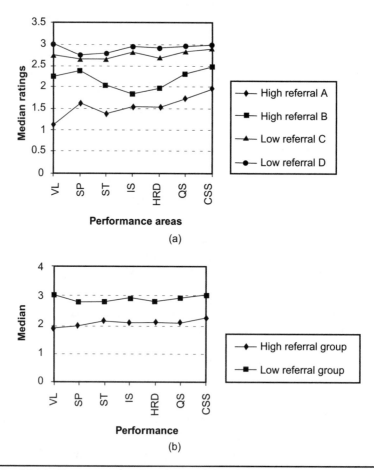

Figure 13.1   (a) Median scores for the phase of development for each performance area and result area for each school. (b) Median for referral groups.

Bishop gathered additional information from interviews with school leaders at various levels, from examining documents such as school improvement plans and referral information, from observations of life in classrooms in all schools, and from focus groups with selected teachers at each school site. When she triangulated the data across all data sets (see Table 13.1), she noticed striking differences in the ways teachers function in the high- and low-referral-rate schools.

In summary, Bishop found that teachers in more highly developed work cultures had evolved many ways of thinking and acting together; they had many options for working with students. As a result, they perceived it to be their professional responsibility to care for all their students. A highly developed system of alternatives had evolved for the team of teachers for working with exceptional students, whereas teachers in the lower-developed work cultures continued to function essentially in isolation and, as a result, had few options for working

Table 13.1 Triangulated information on high- and low-referral-rate schools.

Low-Referral-Rate Schools	High-Referral-Rate Schools
Visionary Leadership	
Local needs guide change that is guided by a vision and school mission.	Policy and public opinion guide change initiatives and processes.
Strategic Planning	
Teachers and administrators develop the school plan together, in relation to a vision and mission.	External forces influence the content of plans, where teacher involvement is limited.
Systems Thinking and Action	
Cooperation, teaming, and networking are the work norm.	Collaboration in any form is very limited.
Information Systems	
Feedback is gathered from various sources and is discussed within systems of open communication.	Feedback is gathered from district surveys, and administration controls access to the information.
Human Resource Development	
Professional development options are guided by emerging staff needs and where teachers help one another.	Educational trends influence the professional development options that are provided.
Quality Services and Programs	
Everyone on the staff participates in making changes to programs to help more students succeed.	Improvements are made by a few, which are used by many faculty.
Customer Success and Satisfaction	
Groups of teachers identify and solve problems with student success.	Few professionals are involved in making improvements to meet student needs.

with students who fell out of the normal range. These teachers felt greater pressure to comply with policy and regulations concerning the curriculum delivery, and, in a drive for their class to function at acceptable levels on state tests, they referred many students to exceptional student education programs. We see that the power of connections enhances teacher repertoires for addressing complexity. The quality of connections and integrated services makes the differences in the professional outcomes of work.

THE NEW WORK OF SCHOOL LEADERS

The development of work teams is the work for the team leader and the school's leadership team. The team leader is the boundary manager, a liaison with the administration, and a representative of the team on all central organizing committees. While representing the best interests of the team, team leaders scan the environment for adjustments that need to be made to teamwork. Team leaders who function within a systems view of organizations are not directors but facilitators of team growth. The team leader observes and analyzes conditions and needs continuously.

The team quality profile provides a mental model for benchmarking development over time. *Visionary leadership for team customers* becomes the primary focus for the team's growth. The vision is shared and shaped together by all members of the team as they explore their challenges and opportunities. The team leader's *strategic plan* emphasizes a personal strategy for facilitating the team's growth, which might center on responsibilities of team members or training and coaching needs. *Systems thinking* guides the team leader in considering how to balance the talents, skills, and interests of team members with the needs and priorities of the team within the context of the organization's conditions. The goal is to build interdependency among members in the planning, delivery, and assessment of their collective work.

Information systems become important in guiding team leader planning for continuous improvement, using information from others in the schools and from team members, students, parents, and other partners. Information provides a guide for team dialogue about their programs and services and leads to decisions that evolve from the team itself. *Human resource development* is the key to team improvement; listening to and observing members work, combined with other information, enables the team leader to anticipate development needs and search for opportunities. *Quality services* are identified through data gathering from clients (students and others) and relate to the services that the team leader provides for the team and its work patterns. Hence, one source of data for determining quality is team members themselves. *Customer success and satisfaction* is the key to making adjustments to the team's operations, and so a constant reading of the effects of programs on students (or others) is the barometer for the team learning. A distinction of team leaders within a systems orientation is their facilitation of the team's performance, which plays out within an environment of collaboration and consensus. Hence, the team leader plays a vital function in supervising and facilitating the team's learning and its evolution.

During an extended visit to Sweden, one day was spent with a multiaged primary-aged learning community in the Kyrkmons School in Sundsvall, under the leadership of Bodil Gidlund. The team leader, Christina Norlin, is responsible for five teachers and two-and-a-half aides and leisure-time helpers (before, during, and after school care). This team had been working together for five years and had developed a culture of work beyond anything we had seen previously. It was difficult to determine what subjects were being taught as well as the responsibilities of the teachers and students at any given time. Students each had a plan and a portfolio, which they eagerly shared when we inquired about their tasks. And, there was no disruption of class by any students during the day; all the students seemed to be working on things that were important to them. It was a dance of life!

The team's facility was a small, old school building that had recently been renovated. Six traditional classrooms were replaced with eight rooms of varying shapes and sizes, with lots of glass and open doorways between rooms. There were curtains and plants everywhere, as well as rugs and comfortable furniture. The students and their teachers moved in and about the spaces all day, working on the next sets of multiple tasks. We observed not a single behavior problem all day, for every student was working according to a special plan; some tasks were individual and others were group tasks. At the end of the day, the team leader and the teachers shared brief comments about how they made decisions together. These are a few features of their thinking:

1. A *clear vision of success for each child* and for the group drives all work and emphasizes helping students to be successful in living and learning.

2. *Specific strategic plans for the year and the month* provide the backdrop for weekly and daily plans and adjustment. These plans are guided by national curriculum guidelines and the needs of their students.

3. Students and teachers are organized into continuously changing groups that are multiaged. Exceptional needs students are integrated into the life of the team.

4. Information is gathered continuously from a wide range of sources and is used to work with parents and to adjust plans.

5. Their own budget enables them to plan for their professional development and to purchase resources for the learning community.

6. Programs are modified routinely to adjust activity to the changing student needs and conditions.

7. The success patterns of students are monitored daily to ensure their continued growth, challenge, and success.

About a year later, the team was visited again for a more formal interview. Our purpose was to learn more about how they think about their professional responsibilities with students, parents, their principal, and one another. Following are a few of the stories they shared. They are reported here within the TQP framework:

Visionary Leadership

Our vision is to teach children the basics and get them at least up to the fifth-grade class during their three years with us. We help them to find knowledge on their own, to be motivated to grow and discover for their own sake, to behave, to work together and help each other, and also to have fun in school.

Strategic Planning

The children, teachers, and parents all plan together. We each know all the parents, and so any one of us can talk to any parent about their child. We develop plans for the basics of reading, writing, speaking, and mathematics. In the old days, we used to think of planning the second-grade and the third-grade curriculum. We have a Swedish curriculum that helps us to develop our own curriculum now, which is for three years. We have themes for a whole year; last year it was the earth and the big bang theory, and this year it is water. All subjects are integrated around the theme, while we are building skills for success in life. We meet with the children and find out what they want to learn. Then we meet together as a team and plan for the month, and then for each week as we go along. We don't have specific time schedules or responsibilities. We have been together as a team for a long time and have worked together with all the children on an integrated curriculum; we just know what needs to happen next. It all just evolves; it is a process that has a life of its own. It is organic and requires that we each know how each other thinks and makes decisions.

Systems Thinking and Action

First, we needed to change our building of six regular classrooms, with walls between them, into a collection of spaces that would have certain functions and in which everyone could work and feel at home. Because we spend so much time here with the children, we wanted to create a home atmosphere. Our principal gave us some money for the renovation. We had some walls removed, others replaced by glass, smaller spaces and larger spaces, a kitchen, a library, and a work space for us that felt like home. We got our spouses to help us paint the rooms; we made curtains, bought furniture to fit a variety of needs, and created a home for us all. The children treat this facility like a home, and we all learn how to live together in it. We make rules with the children for how to live together and tell them the price of things when they break. We have developed a kind of organization for children and adults, but the structure is very fluid all day long, as we make adjustments in the program.

Information Systems

We ask students in every program what they are good at and what they want to learn next. We talk with parents all the time, encouraging them to drop in our school whenever they can for a visit. We have no grades now, but rather ask students and their parents to assess what they are learning and how well they are doing. We have formal conferences with parents and students twice a year. For every program or project we ask the children what they think about the experience, what was good, or what could be improved. We discuss the students' reactions with them and make plans for the next program. We also talk with parents and solicit their reactions all the time. Our principal visits our team once a week. She often sits down and asks students for their reactions and for what they have learned. Twice a year the principal also has a planning and evaluation meeting with us, talking over every part of our work with children.

Human Resource Development

We are given money for our own professional development and for our program development. We visit other schools, attend workshops, listen to lectures, take computer courses, read books and articles, and discuss these with each other. We are always learning new things to help us with our children.

Quality Services and Programs

We have five years to get our children ready for the National Swedish test. We work with them continuously to reach that level. But we focus primarily on the tools that students will use in life: how to find things, where to look for information, how to assess how well you are learning. We constantly ask children if they are happy and if they are satisfied with what they are learning. We want to build internal motivation to learn and to grow for their own sake and not that of their parents or teachers.

Student Success and Satisfaction

About 98 percent of our students are successful and satisfied with their experiences with us. There are several special needs students who receive special help. We talk with the next teachers, after their three years with us, to give them the information so the special needs students will continue to grow. We watch students learn to use the tools, learn to find information, to plan for their own work, to be flexible, to take responsibility, and show confidence with other people. They learn to be flexible in this atmosphere, where we are training them to behave and not to be afraid, and to know that there are different perspectives.

The New Work of Principals

It is possible for teams to evolve and improve the quality of services to their students in isolation from other factors in the school's environment. However, when teams become the focus of administrative development activity, quantum leaps are made in the team's performance and also in its effect on the entire school. The work of administration shifts in a systems-orientated school from individual faculty and staff to the work of teams working with and through team leaders. The principal's task in facilitating groups is different from that of a team leader in scope but essentially the same in the quality of assistance and support to teams. Teams will thrive in schools that are driven by a vision of success for their student populations and where the strategic plan and the school's structures and processes are guided by that vision. In addition, when work teams become the building block of the school's renovation and when school leaders focus their primary attention on team development, miracles happen quickly and often.

The school leader's concern in developing teams lies in the system of permanent and ad hoc teams and their growing interdependence and effects on the school's performance. The energy that comes from the natural connections within and across teams generates continuous supplies of energy to sustain the school's continuous journey of transformation. Thus, the collective needs of work teams become a tapestry in the making at any moment in time. The goal is to stimulate life *at the edge of chaos,* which happens over time and because of success and recognition.

The TPQ can become a useful mental model for guiding team development throughout the school. The *vision* relates to the future performance capacities of each team, given their function in the organization and their potential for the clients they serve. The principal's *strategic plan* translates the vision of high-performing teams into action, a plan that reflects the goals of each work team and leadership strategies for enhancing their growth. *Systems thinking* becomes a reality in the integration and interdependence of teams, which strengthens the connection system. Integration can be fostered by school leaders through sharing sessions, celebrations, problem-solving meetings, observations and coaching, and through numerous communications structures.

The school leader *gathers information* routinely on how well each team is doing, learns from teams themselves, and then listens to students, parents, and other professionals who are connected with a team. In considering *human resource development of teams,* principals scan the environment constantly for learning options and listen to the deep structures of work to identify those that may come from within the team. Consideration of *quality services* relates both to those that are provided by each team, using team data. The quality of supervisory services can be determined by feedback from teams. The *customers* in this situation are both the clients of each team and trend data on all teams. The teams themselves are also customers of the administration, and so the performance trends and work culture of each team become a barometer for determining the quality of supervisory services.

When we visited Kyrkmons School the second time, we asked Bodil Gudlund how she thinks about developing her six multiaged teaching teams. Here are her responses as organized around the EQBS framework:

> My vision is for the school to be part of the community, a place where everyone can come and learn, and a place that works with the community in its celebrations and its growth. I want this place to be fun for children and for those who work here. To begin our planning each year, we start with a celebration event of singing together with our children. Then I share with the children and teachers what I believe about the pupils getting involved in and responsible for their work and about connecting with our community and parents. Afterward the teachers meet and we decide on what we want to work on for the year, and one of the areas relates to team development. Teams develop their own plans with their children and parents and decide how to work together.
>
> We use systems thinking in designing our organization of three minischools, each with two multiaged teams. The team leaders meet with me every week, and we often meet as an entire faculty for an evening of reflection and planning. We talk about our pupils at all levels and their comfort throughout their years in our school. It is important that the teachers come together to discuss how we can improve our services to children. I visit the teams and often watch them work. We also have some task forces that are working on problems for the whole school.
>
> I gather information all the time by visiting the teams regularly. They tell me how things are working and what help they want. I am concerned with the learning atmosphere for children, as well as the climate of work for the teaching team. My questions all relate to the challenges they face,

the freedom they need, the ideas they are working on, the ways they trust each other, special dynamics, debates, conflicts, risks, and how they use time. I also talk with the students during my visits to ask them about their learning and their satisfaction.

To help my staff to develop their professional capacities, I have hired a consultant to meet with teams regularly to listen to them, have them talk about their goals, and freely discuss things that are important to them. This is an additional resource to the team from my regular work with team leaders and visits to the teams and their pupils. Several times a year, I meet with the team leaders outside school at a nice place, and we talk over what is happening in our school. I also take them with me to seminars, for I want them to feel appreciated for what they are doing and to stretch their thinking as well.

Every team talks with students regularly in a series we have called *boys and girls chat* to find out how the school's programs are working for them and to get their ideas for improving the school. We want to know how well satisfied they are. Every week they sit together and have talks about how things are going and things they think are important to discuss. Sometimes they talk about conflicts with grown-ups, about life in general, about sexuality, and about other problems they may be facing. We also talk about what they want to become as grown-ups. It is important to me that our school become a place where pupils feel successful and a place that is providing them with the right learning environment.

BECOMING WORLD CLASS

The rising complexity of school life prompts teams to respond in new ways for meeting the changing needs of students. If schools are to survive as social agencies, teams will become the building blocks, for they will self-organize around their emerging needs, challenges, and resources. Principals and team leaders together will learn to facilitate teams that thrive on chaos and live near its edge routinely. Let us see how the six lessons for *living on the edge of chaos* affect a team.

(1) To develop the capacity for disequilibrium as a way of life, teams will develop strong listening systems for scanning the environment and learning about shifting social, political, and educational winds that affect their work. (2) Teams who learn from their journey know well the function of disequilibrium in their growth and know how to explore difficult situations and take advantage of complexity and change. (3) The most dynamic teams are learning how to build strong coalitions with other teams, with parents and the business community, and with teams in other schools and even in other countries. Vital teams, who understand their own power and potential, also perceive that they will become as responsive

as their connection system. (4) Teams will engineer their own strategic dance of planning and assessment as they self-organize around their challenges. (5) Those teams who have had experiences with new programs have learned the value of piloting new ideas and working on their improvement before launching whole-scale change. They promote pilots, not only of individual new elements, but also of clusters of new features, in order to learn about their collective effects. (6) High-performing teams know that to move quickly and to be responsive they must shed practices and work habits that no longer serve a purpose, and so they celebrate naturally the dance of life and death.

In Nordvik, Sweden, the *Naturalgymnasium* (Nature high school), under the direction of Birger Jonsson, has become a model for the Swedish government for environmental schools. This school offers six programs, which they call branches of nature and environmental care: agriculture, forestry, horticulture with landscaping, aquaculture with water and fish management, horsekeeping, and animal care for pets and zoo animals. Principals and teachers work continuously with local and global communities to create the best programs in the world for their students. The school has formed a partnership with Terra College in The Netherlands in which teachers and students send information and drawings over the World Wide Web. The goal is for Dutch and Swedish students to perform practical landscaping tasks.

Two innovations have triggered the school's rise to prominence. The first is the working partnerships that its leaders, students, and teachers have formed with schools in Hungary, The Netherlands, and Russia. Visitors from these foreign schools are on site regularly to share their experiences and to learn about new systems for their own school, while students and faculty members of the Swedish school visit their international partners routinely to learn program-specific knowledge and skills. A linkage system with similar schools in other countries has triggered new work patterns and programs that set this school apart from others.

The second unique feature of the Nordvik environmental school is its involvement of the business community in assessing its students' performance. Major industries and environmental agencies are routinely involved in assessing the quality of student work, using industry standards to measure adequate progress. This form of benchmarking has triggered significant improvements and has also forged working relationships with their community.

The Nordvik School has developed one of the most extensive systems for benchmarking its programs anywhere in the world. This school is *world class* in every sense of the word. In a speech that Principal Birger Jonsson delivered in 1998 to a conference in Tampa, Florida, he shared that an important feature of his job is to identify world-class programs around the world and link the programs in his school to those. Over time, the nature of school partnerships has evolved and today includes a range of involvement and impact on the school. Today the school's 14 partnerships with schools in countries other than Sweden include principal contact, teacher contact, student contact, student exchange, teacher and student exchange, mutual student projects, school leadership seminars, courses that are offered from his school in other countries for credit, and other country courses that are offered to his students for credit. The partnerships are typically program specific, where teachers and students link for common purposes. Consider the partnerships listed in Table 13.2.

Developing world-class schools requires a support system from school districts that revolves around what young people will need for success in the global village and the internal capacity to build connections with the local and global environments to guide innovation and development. As in the case of Nordvik, the school has its mission of preparing youth for a global village within six programs. It is within these programs that the international partnerships are formed and function systemically to stimulate the emergence of the school as a unit. Becoming world class also requires leaders who understand connection building and who believe in the power of faculty and students connecting continuously with the real world of work and community, both locally and globally. The term *glocal* was invented recently in the Leadership Development Department at the University of South Florida as professors explored the nature of school development within a global context, such as Nordvik. The work of the school must simultaneously become local and global in its connections, its work, and its assessment and continuous improvement.

Table 13.2 Nature high school in Nordvik, Sweden.

Finland	Gardening program
Norway	Forestry Fishbreeding
Estonia (2 schools)	Agriculture Culture, helping rebuild a school for Swedish-speaking adults
Hungary (4 schools)	Forestry Water management Horsery Gardening Hunting and wildlife care
The Netherlands	Landscaping
Belgium	Forestry
Scotland	Agriculture Fishing Hunting
Australia	Agriculture
Russia	Cultural
United States	Forestry

TEAM QUALITY PROFILE

A diagnostic instrument that teams use to assess how well members work interdependently to provide services, the *Team Quality Profile* generates information for a team to benchmark its own development as it responds to changing conditions and needs.

Directions

This profile is designed to help you assess the quality features of your work team as they are illustrated in the following model and its categories. Read each statement on the following pages, and select the number that most closely reflects your perceptions of how your team now functions. After you have analyzed your current practices and have shared these among your team members, together you can plan for improvements and benchmark your progress over time.

5 = always; 4 = often; 3 = sometimes; 2 = seldom; 1 = never

Area 1. Visionary Leadership: *A vision of long-term customer needs and expectations affects time direction for improvement in team services.*

_____ 1.1 The team's vision of success reflects the complexity of conditions today.

_____ 1.2 The team's vision evolves over time in relation to the organization's priorities, global trends, and customer perspectives.

_____ 1.3 The team pursues promising ideas and practices to improve its services.

_____ 1.4 The team aligns its services and programs to its vision.

_____ 1.5 The team supports continuous innovation and breakthrough thinking.

Area 2. Strategic Planning: *The team's work plan links its vision and emerging needs to strategies for improving services.*

_____ 2.1 The needs of customers are continually assessed.

_____ 2.2 Data are used consistently as a basis for adjusting plans to needs.

_____ 2.3 World-class standards guide the quality of team work.

_____ 2.4 Resources are actively sought and linked to the strategic plan.

_____ 2.5 Customers contribute to the team's planning process.

Area 3.   Systems Thinking and Action: *The team's services are interdependent with other services to improve quality.*

_____ 3.1 Collaboration within the team is a way of life.

_____ 3.2 Strong connections are built with other teams to improve services.

_____ 3.3 Strong connections are built with the community to improve services.

_____ 3.4 The team creates new work systems for adapting to needs.

_____ 3.5 Piloting is a strategy used for testing new ideas.

Area 4.   Information Systems: *Information systems are created to study changing conditions, customer needs, and the effects of services.*

_____ 4.1 The team generates customer data continuously for improving its services.

_____ 4.2 The team gathers multiple sources of information to study effects of its services.

_____ 4.3 The team creates data storage and retrieval systems to guide its work over time.

_____ 4.4 The team perceives that the complexity of life today creates opportunities for development.

_____ 4.5 Communications networks exist for exchanging information.

Area 5.   Human Resource Development: *A professional-development system enhances the team's ability to respond to emerging needs.*

_____ 5.1 The team is a learning community in which knowledge influences the quality of work.

_____ 5.2 The team seeks training opportunities to improve the quality of its work.

_____ 5.3 Team members coach and mentor each other to improve performance.

_____ 5.4 The team's work culture improves the health, safety, and job satisfaction of its members.

_____ 5.5 The team is optimistic about meeting and exceeding customer needs today.

Area 6. Quality Services: *The team's processes, programs, services, and interventions meet and exceed customer needs and expectations.*

_____ 6.1 Data confirm that the team's services meet or exceed the changing needs of its customer groups.

_____ 6.2 Connections with customer groups influence the quality of team services.

_____ 6.3 Barriers to progress are routinely identified, altered, and/or eliminated.

_____ 6.4 Practices are eliminated when they no longer meet needs.

_____ 6.5 Practices are continuously enhanced to meet needs more effectively.

Area 7. Customer Success and Satisfaction: *Customer data are gathered regularly to assess the extent to which needs are being met and to improve team services.*

_____ 7.1 Trends of success and satisfaction are documented for all customer groups.

_____ 7.2 The team responds quickly to emerging needs and challenges.

_____ 7.3 The team demonstrates a commitment to meeting the changing needs of its customers.

_____ 7.4 Customer perspectives are reflected in improved services.

_____ 7.5 The team benchmarks its progress over time in meeting customer needs.

PERSONAL ANALYSIS WORKSHEET

Work Team: _____   **Organization:** _____

Task 1: Calculate Your Performance Category Score

For each of the seven work categories in the profile, add the numbers in your response column and divide by the number of performance statements (5).

Visionary Leadership:

Strategic Planning:

Systems Thinking & Action:

Information Systems:

Human Resource Development:

Quality Services:

Customer Success & Satisfaction:

Task 2: Graph Your Team Quality Profile

Draw a bar graph of your score for each performance area to visually represent the personal assessment of your team's practices. A score of 5.0 is ideal.

5.0							
4.0							
3.0							
2.0							
1.0							
	Visionary Leadership	Strategic Planning	Systems Thinking	Information Systems	Human Resource Development	Quality Services	Customer Success & Satisfaction

Task 3: Identify Patterns to Maintain and/or Develop

Analyze your *Team Quality Profile* and identify the areas of team strength, as well as those areas for development. What do you perceive are the next steps in building a quality team that meets and exceeds your customers' requirements?

Strengths

Areas to Develop

Suggestions

TEAM ANALYSIS WORKSHEET

Work Team: _____   **Organization:** _____

Task 1: Calculate Your Performance Category Score

For each of the seven work categories in the profile, add the team member scores for each category, and then divide the total by the number of team members.

Visionary Leadership:

Strategic Planning:

Systems Thinking & Action:

Information Systems:

Human Resource Development:

Quality Services:

Customer Success & Satisfaction:

Task 2: Graph Your Team Quality Profile

Draw a bar graph of your score for each performance area to develop a visual representation of your assessment of practices. A score of 5.0 is ideal.

	Visionary Leadership	Strategic Planning	Systems Thinking	Information Systems	Human Resource Development	Quality Services	Customer Success & Satisfaction
5.0							
4.0							
3.0							
2.0							
1.0							

Task 3: Identify Patterns to Maintain and/or Develop

Analyze your *Team Quality Profile* and identify the areas of team strength, as well as those areas for development. What do you perceive are the next steps in building a quality team that meets and exceeds your customers' requirements?

Strengths

Areas to Develop

Suggestions

14

Leading Schools as Global Learning Centers

In this last chapter we hope to stimulate your thinking about what it will take to become an inspirational leader in these times of great transition. How will you help move schools onto a global platform or uplift existing international features of school life to become the centerpiece for all school learning? Preparing youth for the great transformations we have shared causes us to examine our assumptions about schooling, for surely its purpose, the programs offered to students, and the learning systems that nurture their growth will change. To function as citizens and professionals, we are continuously learning how to use new technologies and new protocols to meet requirements, meeting the daily demands of the job while facing the changing conditions in our communities.

How can we add another big challenge to our overflowing sets of responsibilities: shaping schools as global learning centers? Daniel Pink (2004) says it best: "We need *a whole new mind,* one that blends both analytical and synthesis functions as we work on the big picture." An intellectual dance is what it's all about as we juggle the realities of daily life and keep our head high to catch the winds of change to which we must respond. This dance somehow connects with our sense of worth and a passion to make a difference, for there are educational leaders on every continent who are breaking new ground every day to reshape the purpose and processes of schooling to fit these times.

The job of twenty-first-century leaders is to find the future and take their people to it, which requires us to keep an eye on the big picture of life and ask the question continuously and relentlessly: *For what kind of life are we preparing our students?* Victor Pineda (2004), in his book *Tsunami: Organizations Capable of Prospering in Tidal Waves,* observes that in these rapidly changing times, survival will require deep cultural and structural transformation. Leaders play a critical role, he argues, in providing the purpose for setting a new direction, which is guided by clear personal beliefs and values. A leader helps the staff co-create the pathway to that new future, while they learn how to grow together as the new forms of schooling unfold.

We now perceive that leading schools into the global age will require a revolution of the mind, a fundamental shifting of priorities, purpose, processes, and outcomes. We hope that the ideas shared in this book have prompted new insights about both the challenges and the strategies for creating a collective *mindshift,* which is the task of an educational leader today. As in every era of great transformation in human history, people rise to the occasion and study, explore options, and learn from the features of the new era. In time, every profession develops its own way of equipping its people with the new knowledge and skills needed to be successful. For educational leaders today, there are few if any degree programs or training programs that prepare educational leaders for the global era of schooling. Yet bright and committed educational leaders are likely to be successful when following the principles found in systems, chaos, and complexity theories. You will read stories in this chapter of many pioneers we have met in the past few years as they shift their schools to a global platform. Some of these leaders are successful in stepping out to find the global future of schooling without necessarily knowing how. They just begin with a connection or an opportunity and let the energy lead them on a continuing journey of surprise and exploration. It is often a relentless pursuit.

In each story that is shared in this chapter we see evidence of our new theory of change in action. There is confirming evidence in these stories and many more, that *Living on the Edge of Chaos* is a useful mind map for a leader's quest. In essence we find that leaders who understand "living on the edge" have observable traits; they: (1) *respond to environment changes* (whether they are new state mandates for schools or emerging careers for which students need preparation); (2) *build disequilibrium* for the staff and parents over time with information that is continuous and persistent; (3) *network* with numerous groups of people to dialogue, share, and build energy for the tasks ahead; (4) *foster self-organization* by creating new plans, work teams, responsive systems of work, and partnerships that are local, national, and global; (5) *expect new prototypes of schooling to evolve* that are adaptations to changing conditions in which people develop more powerful programs and services; and (6) *celebrate the dance of life and death* by acknowledging progress for a new era of schooling.

In January 2006 an opportunity emerged to help design a training program that built upon the chaos theory of change and set the stage for shaping schools for the global age of living. The first story in this chapter is once again about Pasco County School District and how it is leading the quest to prepare its school and district leaders for sustainable futures. The events that happened led to the creation of a new training program that is grounded in our new theory of organizational change, *Living on the Edge of Chaos,* and it also incorporates the global transformations of our times and the digital environment in which educators now work. What follows is the 2006–2007 Pasco County School District story, which we offer as an inspiration for school districts everywhere who will one day ask how to prepare their leaders for a global era of schooling. This story identifies new leadership thinking and new capacities to build the vision and action communities that will foster change over time.

PART I. LEADERSHIP CAPACITIES FOR SUSTAINABLE SCHOOL DEVELOPMENT: THE LATEST DEVELOPMENT IN THE PASCO COUNTY STORY

The new story had its start about a decade ago when educational leaders began sharing with Karolyn Snyder the impact that *Managing Productive Schools (MPS) Training* (Snyder, 1988) had on their careers. MPS training, they shared, provided the knowledge foundation and skills to work systemically and to build collaborative work cultures to achieve goals. In brief, *MPS training was a systemic approach to school development that centered on building collaborative work cultures around school improvement goals, staff development systems, responsive learning programs within multi-age and continuous progress structures, and assessment of outcomes and the impact on student performance.* Learning about Snyder's involvement in the International School Connection, many educators in Tampa Bay asked her to bring back the MPS training program and update it for the global/information/digital age. After two years of pressure and some resistance on Snyder's part, she returned to the training business. It happened when someone unexpectedly reported to a large gathering that she might consider redesigning MPS training for the modern era.

The leader of a new unit in Pasco County School District, leadership development, was in the audience that evening: Max Ramos, who was a former principal and an original MPS trainer for the school district. Ramos reported that during the past year he had been unsuccessful in finding a training program that was built on systems thinking and that addressed global and digital challenges. As Ramos told the story, the current top school district leaders, who had all participated in MPS training, years ago perceived that a new training initiative was needed to maintain the cherished values of the school district and to prepare new leaders in the fund of knowledge and skills that enabled Pasco County to achieve its mark of excellence. Because of rapid population growth in Pasco County over several decades, many school and district leaders were new to the district.

By the end of the conversation, Snyder set a date with Ramos to explore what Pasco County was seeking in a new training program. A development team of five was organized: *Karolyn Snyder,* who created MPS training and is currently the president of the International School Connection; *Elaine Sullivan,* who is the ISC vice president for Youth Leadership and School Development; and three Pasco County district leaders: *Max Ramos,* leadership development; *David Scanga*, research and measurement; and *Marti Meacher,* professional development. This team worked for five months to analyze MPS training elements and synthesize the new challenges for school and district leaders. Eventually a training design emerged to enable Snyder to create the training materials for a 10-day program that is now titled *Leadership for Sustainable Development (LSSD).*

The LSSD program provides a systemic orientation to school development, which today functions within a global context and digital culture. The first edition of this book *(Living on the Edge of Chaos: Leading Schools into the Global Age)* is the major resource for the new training program pilot groups. Participant manuals that were created by Karolyn Snyder supplied additional resource materials for each of the 10 training days.

Key capacities for leading sustainable development in education institutions.

1. Develop a vision for development by continuously studying the local, national, and global context for living and learning, and by building a strong personal network system to support development.

2. Engage staff and community members in gathering information for setting organizational goals and for living strategically.

3. Design and facilitate the organization's work system of internal task forces and learning communities, and foster external partnerships and networks.

4. Design and build a high performing organizational energy system for learning, living, working, and succeeding.

5. Lead the organization's continuous development process toward the vision by living strategically and being accountable.

Table 14.1 provides an overview of the training program knowledge and skill bases that function as a whole unit of experience to prepare educators for living on the edge of chaos and stimulating continuous development.

Table 14.1 LSSD knowledge and skills.

Summary: LSSD Knowledge & Skills

A. Getting Ready for Schooling in a Global Age

Knowledge:	Skills:
Global Trends	Trend Analysis; Leverage Point
Systems & Chaos Theories of Change	Analysis
Networking Science	Delphi-Dialogue Technique
Sustainable Development	Building a Learning Community
	Continuous Vision Building

B. Gathering Information for School Goals and Plans

Knowledge:	Skills:
Case Study Method	Conducting a Case Study
Strategic Living, Planning, & Working	Leading the Delphi-Dialogue
	Technique

C. Organizing & Leading the School's Work System

Knowledge:	Skills:
Permanent & Ad Hoc Work Groups	School Network Analysis
Partnerships & Networks	Designing & Leading the Work
Learning Community Organization &	System
Networking	Benchmarking the Learning
	Community Systems

D. Designing & Leading the Learning System

Knowledge:	Skills:
High Performing Professional Systems	Develop a collective vision & core
Mentoring & Social Networks	values for the Student Learning
The School's Digital Culture	System
Poverty & Minority Populations	Benchmark the Professional Learning
	System

E. Leading Strategically & Accountably

Knowledge:	Skills:
Frameworks for Benchmarking in a	Identify indicators of progress in a
Global Age	global age

"What I now know about leading sustainable development in a global age": Individual Presentations

What Happened to those in the First Two Pilot Training Groups?

On the tenth day of LSSD training, participants shared their story of learning during the one year LSSD training program in which they reported on projects they created, and highlighted their major learnings. In analyzing the reports of about 50 leaders from the two cohorts that have graduated, several themes emerged. Most reports were made in teams that crossed school age levels and district leaders, which represent the natural connections that leaders made during the training period. Most projects were undertaken by a team of school and district leaders. Some teams conducted extensive case studies to examine a school problem and create a new process or system to respond to what was learned. Other teams studied districtwide questions or problem areas, and designed new programs to address needs. One school created a partnership with a school in China, which is shared in Chapter 11. And four members of the original pilot group began training their own cadres, revisiting LSSD concepts and skills.

As their stories unfolded, most participants highlighted *networking* as a new capacity for leading in these complex times. Learning teams crossed school and district boundaries to pursue common projects that mattered. The second and third cohorts are networking with each other outside the training context, and with those in the first pilot cohort as well. District problems are addressed by teams of school and district leaders who are learning to build new study and action teams. What ideas were most important to their work now? Everyone talked about becoming comfortable with the chaos that emerged from facing new information, and from the dialogue communities they were building with their new process skills. Learning about disequilibrium and its useful function in moving organizations forward was a surprise for most, as they reported delight in seeing its magic move people to new places of understanding and development. The power of networks was the biggest surprise for many leaders, for they now have a life strategy for garnering resources and energy for the tasks ahead. Technology experimentation was evident in all presentations as leaders met the challenge to present information in new and more powerful formats.

When we began training trainers for the LSSD training program, we were working with people we had journeyed with for decades. They were all seasoned and gifted educational leaders and trainers. The trainer training experience began with a few questions: The first was: *What are the central ideas from the sciences that are personally important to you?* Here are their responses:

Big Ideas from the Sciences *(Systems, Chaos, and Complexity)*

- The power of connections, both strong and weak.

- The power of disequilibrium—everyone needs to understand the need for change.

- Natural systems are always reforming from feedback both from inside and outside the schools.

- Complex adaptive systems respond to and act as a system.

- Information and data are drivers of change in the system. Teachers need to know this. Leaders need to know this.

- Information creates disequilibrium and stimulates the best and most long-lasting kind of change.

A second question was raised: *What are the global trends that need to influence school development today?* Here are their responses:

Big Ideas for the Global Context of Schooling
(Globalization, Networking, and Technology)

1. The global arena is the new context of school leadership, for it provides perspective on new work and literacy skills that are needed today.

2. The challenge is to lead teaching and learning for today's students.

3. It is important to build a community that believes in reflection and continual learning.

4. Reform is not it; rather, developing the future, which is emergent, is the work of educators.

5. Synergy comes from building community.

6. Networking provides information, and it contributes to the direction of development.

7. Strength in relationships makes networks strong.

8. Building trust relationships makes a difference.

9. The networks of others provide additional resources for development

10. Networks provide leverage.

11. We're on the world stage now.

12. New communication technologies provide new kinds of learning opportunities.

While the first pilot group was in training, another pilot group was launched with two leaders from the first pilot group as trainers. Elaine Sullivan created the LSSD trainer manuals from observing the first pilot, with Snyder as trainer.

The trainer manuals provided the trainers with resources for their work with new cohorts of school and district leaders. John Mann, who trained more school and district leaders in the 25-day MPS program than anyone except Snyder, became one of the first trained trainers of LSSD, along with David Scanga, who was on the design team for LSSD (and now the Director of Elementary Schools). A third cohort soon began with two additional trainers: Larry Albano, an original MPS trainer and a recently retired exemplary principal, and Jeff Morgenstein, who is the coordinator of foreign languages for Pasco County. The visionary leader Max Ramos retired after completing the LSSD training pilot, in which the design team all participated, and John Mann was appointed the new director of leadership development. Pasco County is planning for four more cohorts to begin training in 2007–2008. Master trainers Max Ramos, John Mann, and Larry Albano will apprentice other school or district leaders as trainers.

During the second and third pilots, several observations were made that led to the creation of a second year of training for LSSD. First, leaders come to understand their new challenge of preparing students as global citizens during the schooling years clearly near the end of the program. And, only a few began to link with schools in other parts of the world. It became clear that Year 1 provided participants with a new mental model of schooling, along with current knowledge and skills for building a vision community in their organizations, but it did not facilitate development with networking or global partnership building. A second year of LSSD is being designed now for leaders to continue developing greater capacity with the new skills and to begin reaching out to other school leaders around the world. The theme for year two is building our own professional network,

During year two, participants will develop greater competence with the knowledge and skills from year one LSSD training while they focus on developing their local, national, and international professional network. In the process, they will engage in a partnership venture with a school or district across the world, work with their own learning community in training, and live within the digital culture of activity and resources to foster an orientation to a global perspective on school development and student success. The Global Learning Center Benchmarks will become the foundation for their development projects. In the process of preparing for this new two-year program, the district's technology department is creating new work and communications systems in the digital environment, video clips are being created to support training, and the Leadership Department's website is being created to foster continuous reinforcement for the knowledge and skills taught, and the stories of success as they emerge. John Mann is exploring the school district's many human and technology resources to fashion a state-of-the-art context for leadership development with LSSD.

In essence, the refined two-year training design will feature both a local and global social networking culture, along with the creation of a digital culture to redesign school programs that prepare students as global citizens. Participants will be nurtured and coached while being responsible for producing significant outcomes to their learning from the LSSD experience. Rather than considering training as 10 actual training days, with practice assignments, the two years will become a performance outcome learning period along with demonstrated competence for year one, and demonstrated international project outcomes for year two. In the process the role of the trainer becomes more than delivering days of training, and becomes a trainer, coach, and facilitator in the competency development process.

A major insight from this pilot project is the vital role the school district plays in expecting and supporting the learning and outcomes from training. Under the strong leadership of Superintendent Heather Fiorentino and her exceptionally cohesive top leadership team, the stage has been set for school and district leaders to perform at high levels in the LSSD training and influence the quality of work in their schools or district units. The school district's vision and mission statement are undergoing changes now as its leaders consider the new expectation of preparing students for global and local living and working. With a vision and mission to prepare students for global living and a strategic plan to follow each year, the agenda becomes a guide for school and district development. When the district's expectations support the global agenda for schools, all kinds of support emerges for the journey. And with a clear intent to shift to a global focus, it will be more difficult to sabotage projects that move in this direction. With a vision for a global future of schooling, knowledge to create new prototypes, tools to facilitate collaborative ventures, and models for designing learning systems for all, leaders are likely to build sustainable education systems over time. With guidelines for shaping schools as Global Learning Centers, the direction of school improvement has new targets that will continuously reinforce the direction for school and district development initiatives.

PART II: STORIES ABOUT LEADING SCHOOLS ONTO THE GLOBAL STAGE

As schools began to use the Global Learning Center (GLC) benchmarks, a wide range of approaches surfaced. In this section are the stories of five schools and their journey to connect students with people and projects around the world. The stories begin with the power of one teacher in a school in China who linked students to global leaders and many other schools around the world. A school in the United States tells of the beginning phases of virtual partnership with schools in China, Singapore, and the Republic of Georgia, using a Weboffice environment for communication. A model school in Sweden tells its story about the impact of global learning on their students as its leaders connected with the

United Nation's Sustainability Program. A Blue Ribbon School in the United States creates professional development connections with schools in Spain and China, and in the process it becomes a global training center that features its research and best-practices-based approach to teaching and learning. One of the top middle/high schools in China shares examples of how it engages students in international competitions and global partnerships, and its special role in hosting international events. And, finally, we share the story of a secondary school in Canada that is the *first school in the world* to become a certified ISC Global Learning Center School. Samples of the global activity for each GLC benchmark are shared to provide guidance and inspiration.

Global Connections in One Classroom— Zhixin Elementary School in Shaoguan, China

In Shaoguan, China, John Wu, the linguistic and cultural communications and ICT (Information and Communications Technology) project coordinator, sought ways to bring the world to his students. His belief was expressed this way: *If the motion of a butterfly's wing has the power to create a storm the size of a hurricane in another state* (a chaos theory principle), *then certainly collaboration between children of every race has the potential to make our world a much better place.* The specific purposes were to build global connections through projects with these goals:

- To familiarize children with technology

- To practice the use of authentic English

- To encourage global collaboration

- To improve each country's image by creating friendships with children and educators around the world

Wu began by connecting his children with a school in Texas through a pen pal program in 1994. Building on the continuing success of this project and emerging technology, in 1999 he began e-mail projects with schools in the United States, Canada, Australia, and South Africa. By 2001 his students were working on many projects with their peers around the world. In 2002 he participated in a face-to-face celebration with students from a school in Rhode Island, which was supported by a visit from former president Bill Clinton. A U.N. peace pole was dedicated at Zhixin School to commemorate the peaceful connections the students had made with others around the world. By 2006 the international school connection projects had been extended to schools in Israel, Japan, and Spain. Connecting with people around the world had become a key element in the curriculum.

Today Wu is responsible for the international projects for all schools in Shaoguan. He also writes a column for a national e-journal in China sharing the newest developments in connecting students around the world. His is a story of an educator who made a profound difference in the lives of children in one school. Many of us have shared his story in presentations around the world, inspiring others to begin the journey of connecting students on the global stage.

Connecting Students in a Weboffice Environment: A. J. Ferrell Middle Magnet School of International Studies—Tampa, Florida

As the original middle magnet school in the Hillsborough County School District in central Florida (eighth largest school district in the United States), Ferrell Middle Magnet School featured technology to attract students from around the district. Because most schools by 2004 had become equipped with technology, A. J. Ferrell was faced with a challenge of finding a new specialization. After exploring options, the faculty expertise in technology was married with "international studies," and the school was renamed the Center for Language Exploration and Global Communications. Over the next year, the faculty and staff created a slogan that embodied what they hoped the school would become for its students: "Gateway to the World." The art teacher created a logo to help brand and illustrate the school's new focus. A number of symbolic initiatives announced the new global orientation: (1) A local artist was commissioned to create murals of world landmarks in the school's media center, (2) clocks displaying times in major cities around the world were installed in the main office, (3) signs labeling common areas and objects were erected to depict their names in several languages, (4) international flags were displayed around the campus, and (5) a group of students penned the "Global Citizenship Pledge," which is posted throughout the campus:

As a responsible Global Citizen,
I will volunteer to make the world a better place.
I will respect that everyone is different and accept their way of life.
I will communicate with other citizens of the world to
create a friendlier environment.
I will represent my school, my community and
my country in a positive way.

As the school's environment began to reflect the new global theme, the staff found ways to integrate an international perspective with their major units of study. A language lab was built, and the computers were equipped with Rosetta Stone software. Beginning in 2006, students were able to study Chinese, Japanese, Portuguese, Hindi, and Latin through this elective. In 2007, a yearlong program in Mandarin Chinese elective was launched, gaining the attention of local media. Ferrell was the first middle school in the district to teach Chinese. In that same year, Arabic was added for interested students.

In time teachers and students made connections with partners across the country and around the world so that classrooms would be *without walls*. Three projects that evolved from these early explorations were: (1) Students from a school in Brazil exchanged gifts celebrating their culture with Ferrell's seventh graders; (2) geography students participated in a postcard exchange with students in Australia, the United Kingdom, and the Dominican Republic; and (3) relationships were fostered with other global partners to enable Ferrell students to become citizens of the world.

Then, as part of an International School Connection (ISC) seminar in Tampa during the fall of 2005, the school's lead teacher, Lisa Cobb, witnessed a demonstration of an interactive videoconferencing program called HomeMeeting, which was given by Professor Kai Sung from Taiwan. Cobb envisioned that the Weboffice environment could provide new opportunities for students and faculty to connect with other schools around the world. The school decided to use a portion of its grant money to purchase a site license for HomeMeeting.

At the same time, Cobb registered Ferrell School with the ISC to become a partner with other schools around the world, expecting to connect with new schools through HomeMeeting. To begin, sixth graders designed a project with students in Beijing 101 Middle School in Beijing, China, working with Lydia Li, who teaches English. Through countless e-mails and two online planning sessions, teachers and students in both schools decided to share parts of their national cultures with each other. Ferrell students planned their lessons about famous figures from either American history or pop culture. Each student chose a project, researched that person's life, and created a period costume. The students in Beijing planned to share stories of their most popular holidays and festivals. They created live demonstrations in the web-office environment to coincide with their content, such as the art of paper cutting and even how to make dumplings. Chinese and American students also shared songs, which were sung in English by Chinese students.

Finally, the night of the HomeMeeting presentations arrived. To accommodate the 12-hour time difference between the two schools, Ferrell faculty and staff welcomed the participating sixth graders and their families back to the school at 7:00 P.M. on a Friday. Meanwhile, the faculty and 100 participating students at Beijing Middle 101 returned to their campus at 7:00 A.M. on Saturday. The meeting and presentations were a great success and were covered by the *Tampa Tribune.* A clip from the videoconference is featured on the school's Web site (http://www1.sdhc.k12.fl.us/~ferrell.mid/).

Near the end of that first HomeMeeting event, Ferrell's sixth graders were introduced to three of the Beijing students who were planning to visit Tampa to attend the 2006 ISC Global Summit. Two weeks later, these students, with their Principal Guo Han and teacher Li Fang, flew from Beijing to participate in the summit and also to visit Ferrell's campus, which was part of the school tours offered during the summit. When they entered the classroom holding Ferrell students who had participated in the HomeMeeting event, the energy became charged! The Ferrell students' new friends brought pen pal letters and gifts from others in Beijing. They answered questions and showed the American students how to write their names using Chinese characters.

The Beijing students and educators also visited such classes as the Mandarin Chinese elective and experimented with the Rosetta Stone software in Ferrell's language lab. The representatives from Beijing Middle 101 presented the Ferrell faculty with a beautiful banner marking the beginning of their partnership. The top of the banner is inscribed, "Friendship Forever." Anyone witnessing the exchange between the American and Chinese students would agree that this is the case. The chance to have these children from very different backgrounds in the same room was a life-changing experience for everyone. Beijing Middle and Ferrell Middle teachers continue to correspond about projects for the coming year.

Since the first HomeMeeting event with Beijing 101 Middle School, Ferrell has conducted HomeMeetings with students in the Republic of Georgia and in Singapore's Cedar Primary School. Cobb and a teacher from Cedar Primary identified students for a planning meeting in the HomeMeeting Weboffice. In between the planning session and actual presentation, students blogged about their plans on a Web site set up by the school in Singapore. This helped create a more immediate connection between the two groups of students. The first project between the schools included PowerPoint presentations and videos from each site so that students could explore the similarities and differences between each other's communities and schools. Each school's part of the presentation concluded with a question and answer session to enhance understanding and relationship building. (Former Cedar Elementary School Principal Shirley Ho-Woo is now sharing the school's partnership story and the ISC's global learning network with educators around Southeast Asia.)

The A. J. Ferrell relationship with the ISC offered many other opportunities to connect with students and educators from other countries, such as: (1) To host a China seminar for area schools, featuring Professors Xinmin Sang and Shuhua Li from Nanjing University in Nanjing, China, along with four Nanjing University students; (2) Ferrell hosted a visit by principals from private schools in Spain to observe Ferrell's international initiatives; and (3) Lisa Cobb and the Ferrell principal, Charles Dixon, participated in a Tampa Bay–area meeting for a delegation from Wuxi, China, that sought information about the ISC and its schools. During that meeting and dinner Cobb shared the stories about International Student Connections and linked live with Lydia Li in Beijing through HomeMeeting; (4) Cobb made a presentation about their international school connections and demonstrated the Weboffice environment at a national convention in the United

States; and (5) at the 2007 ISC Global Summit hosted by Beijing 101 Middle School, Cobb and Li gave a presentation on their student projects in HomeMeeting, inspiring other Summit participants to find ways to connect their students for learning projects using virtual environments. Also, the teacher from Cedar Elementary School in Singapore sent a video to share their part of the story during this seminar. A new plan is unfolding to create a story-sharing project between their students. The beat goes on! A. J. Ferrell has submitted a portfolio to the ISC for consideration as a certified GLC school.

Becoming a Global Learning and Training Center: Independent Day School—Corbett Campus (IDS), Tampa, Florida

After becoming headmaster of a private school in Tampa, Joyce Burick Swarzman, a former college professor and the director of an award-winning teacher training program called SCATT (Sun Coast Area Teacher Training), set out to create a continuous learning environment for the school's faculty to advance the success of its students. Although Independent Day School Corbett Campus (IDS) is a private school, it has a public purpose. Swarzman's A+ Action Approach to Leadership and Change model guided the design of new programs and systems of learning, which included: (1) model the models, (2) proceed purposefully, (3) embrace the vision, (4) build leadership capacity in teams and networks, (5) adopt "presence," (6) develop a lifelong learning mentality, and (7) persevere and persist.

Eventually a cluster of basic training programs became important to their pursuit of the A+ Challenge, which evolved into an integrated system of teaching and learning, called the MORE Approach (More Options for Results in Education). Seven clusters include the following: 1) child-centered vision, 2) appreciating the uniqueness of the learning, 3) motivational strategies to increase time on task, 4) creating dignity and respect, 5) teacher presence, making connections, 6) learning community, and 7) curriculum development. (Debbie Happy Cohen, 2003) (For more information, details about the MORE Approach are found in the Appendix.)

The school soon became known for its success in creating a world-class teaching and learning environment, and it emerged as a major teacher-training center for schools in Florida. In time, teachers from both private and public schools in the United States and many countries around the world attended training sessions at IDS, and also came to the campus to work with IDS teachers. Local teacher-training institutions learned about the high quality of teaching and learning at IDS, and its teachers soon were training teacher interns. Some teachers taught with Swarzman in a program at St. Petersburg College to prepare the next generation of teachers. This school, which is on its journey to greatness, has become not only a great school for its students, but also a training site for both preservice and in-service teacher preparation programs.

What is the MORE Approach? The model integrates learning strategies to nurture children and provide a safe and caring environment, which is built through communication skills, relationship skills, motivation, and an emphasis on promoting pupils' self-esteem. Time is invested each week to develop highly skilled teachers in cutting-edge strategies, in which an "Olympic mentality" drives the work of everyone. The MORE Approach is used to create a brain-friendly environment to accelerate the learning process.

The school staff wrote a book to tell their story, *It's all about Kids* (Cohen, 2003), which has been translated into Spanish (2007) and Chinese (2007). In 2004 IDS was recognized as a Blue Ribbon School by the U.S. Department of Education. The learning environment exhibited excellent results because of the training, high expectations, and dedication of the IDS staff. Independent Day School–Corbett Campus was also named during 2007 as an International Baccalaureate (IB) Middle School Years Program school. Teachers participated in extensive training and worked diligently to create even greater influence on learning patterns.

When Swarzman learned about the International School Connection (ISC) and its mission, it seemed that becoming a global school might take her staff and students to new levels of excellence. Swarzman purchased a HomeMeeting license and software and began to connect with ISC members, especially in Spain. There followed a strong partnership with Luis Perez Martinez, who directs *Global Learning,* an initiative designed to strengthen the private schools of Spain; he is also the ISC Hub Coordinator in Spain. Swarzman began working with one school at a time for weeklong seminars and classroom demonstrations about how the MORE Approach can enhance learning for all teachers and students. This movement with Spanish schools is growing, and Spanish teachers are coming to Florida as interns for various periods of time at IDS.

Many international guests were brought to the campus over several years, during which time IDS also hosted events that were sponsored by the ISC for the Tampa Bay area. Creating a global learning environment in the school eventually became a conscious choice for teachers, and in time a tipping point was reached. Almost overnight all teaching teams were integrating global learning activities into the curriculum. Having already achieved the IB honor, IDS teachers and leaders began working to become an ISC Global Learning Center School, and are preparing their portfolio now to be certified as a global learning center. Skype and HomeMeeting technologies are used regularly to connect students and teachers with their partner schools in other countries. In addition, groups of teachers and their principals come from Spain and China to study for short periods of time to learn the MORE Approach with IDS teachers. In November 2007 two IDS teachers worked with MORE-trained schools in Spain to advance their learning, which was a professional honor for the selected IDS teachers.

In 2006/2007 students from Nanjing University spent four months at IDS, teaching Chinese and also interning with the ISC by giving seminars to schools in the Tampa Bay area with their sponsors, Professors Xinmin Sang and Shuhua Li. The four students (Jun Liang, Rain Guo, Vanessa Yang, and Jie Yan) have all returned to China and now communicate regularly with students at IDS, using many forms of technology. In October 2007 IDS sent many of its teachers and students to Beijing to participate in the first ISC Global Youth Summit, which was co-directed by Linda Boza, a leader of IDS's Middle School. The Nanjing Four, as they came to be called, helped prepare IDS students and staff, using technology to communicate from China to Florida.

The IDS story will continue to emerge as a sustainable development school because of the leadership of the school's headmaster and other school leaders, and the continuous training and high levels of caring and proficiency of the teachers (http://www.idsyes.com).

A Make-a-Difference School: Gripenskolan in Nyköping, Sweden

"Gripenskolan—for your future" has been the motto for a long time for this upper secondary school in Nyköping, Sweden. Under the former leadership of Principal Hans Forsberg, the school emphasized the health and personal well-being of people everywhere, as well as protecting the natural environment. The campus of Gripenskolan holds six upper secondary programs or units, with a total of 1,000 students. These units provide education in natural and social science, various techniques such as ICT and construction/design, house building, electricity/electronics/automation, motor vehicle techniques, a variety of handicraft, and individually adapted programs for those students with specific needs.

In the first edition of this book, we reported on Gripenskolan's science project on the health of the Baltic Sea, working with students in other countries that bordered the sea. Now read what has happened to this school since that initial project.

To promote a school focus on sustainable development while continuously raising the quality of education, Hans Forsberg launched an initiative that connected Gripenskolan with the United Nations sustainability project. The U.N. World Summit on Sustainable Development, held in Johannesburg in 2002, proposed that all future development efforts cover three dimensions of sustainability: economic, social, and ecological. All governments of the world are to take their full responsibility and cooperate in securing a sustainable development for the future for mankind and for the environment. The world summit stressed that education is of crucial significance to make sustainable development possible.

The U.N. General Assembly thus proclaimed the period 2005–2014 a decade for Education for Sustainable Development (http://www.un.org/esa/sustdev/mgroups/success/success.htm). The U.N. sustainability challenge provides the framework for much of the school's activity now to *make a difference.*

Gripenskolan has a tradition of working with environmental issues, particularly concerning water. The school was involved for many years in the Baltic Sea Project, a UNESCO-based network with schools in nine countries around the Baltic Sea. The objective was to increase awareness of environmental problems, exchange information, and suggest strategies for action to protect the environment. Gripenskolan was awarded the Water School of the Year as a result of outstanding student performance during many years of the national Junior Water Prize competition, which has since become an international program. Every year students of Gripenskolan invite younger children from the compulsory schools in town for water experiments and mini lectures and workshops at Gripenskolan. Senior students of Gripenskolan also make regular visits to junior schools and give lessons on environmental issues. On an island in the archipelago, Gripenskolan runs a nature school involved in extensive environmental studies in close cooperation with students ranging from primary up to secondary and university levels.

Students in the house-building/painting program spent many weeks restoring an orphanage in Moscow, Russia, repainting, redecorating, repairing, and supplying it with medical help, hygiene articles, eyeglasses, clothes, and toys, as well as raising money for tuition. The orphanage recently became identified as the best, and so Gripenskolan directed its focus to another orphanage in Saratov, which is a major city on the Volga River. Funds for these other projects have been collected through Gripen Helps, the school's annual one-day odd-jobs project, as well as through external sponsors and a parent association.

For some years, students of Gripenskolan's natural science and social science programs have supported 12 upper secondary schools in Tanzania with laboratory equipment for science studies, as well as computers. Funds have been raised through Gripen Helps and through financial contributions from Swedish national agencies and private companies. Within the framework of Gripenskolan's locally designed course, Developing Countries, some students traveled to Tanzania each year to learn about living conditions, especially of children and women; health; HIV/AIDS; education; employment; culture; environmental problems; and access to fresh water. Students express their findings in scientific reports and project essays, and they are often invited to lecture about their experience and results. For several years, graduates from Gripenskolan have returned to work as volunteers in Tanzania. Having completed this project of giving "help for self-reliance," Gripenskolan has now made connections with South Africa and recently sent 16 students and three teachers there on a study tour. Contacts are also being established with a poor orphanage in Venezuela.

These examples show how staff and students at Gripenskolan go from words to action to promote a focus on sustainable development in education and to strengthen international understanding, knowledge, attitudes, and values. Likewise, support is given to every student to take personal responsibility and action to become a global citizen who contributes to a better world. This school is making a difference for others in the world, and for its own students in the process.

Developing World Class Students— Beijing 101 Middle/High School, Beijing, China

In Beijing 101 Middle School's more than 60-year history, its high school graduates have became major leaders in all sectors of Chinese society. Today its rich tradition continues under the leadership of its entrepreneurial principal, Guo Han, and assistant principal Tao Wang. The school is both a middle school and a high school of 4000 students, who are selected from the general population of China. It is recognized as one of the top 10 middle and senior high schools in China. The school is led with democratic management, and the teaching staff is engaged in continuous professional development to perform at the very top levels in their profession. Recently an educational reform-oriented spirit was created around the theme Non-Compromised Aggressiveness, Unselfish Dedication to Education, and Scientific Spirit of Realism and Innovation. In that spirit, Guo Han continually searches the globe for ways in which her students can excel and compete against the best in the world in a wide range of specializations. While there are many great features of this school to learn about, you are urged to visit the school's Web site, http://www.beijing101.com. A few of the school's international activities are shared here for inspiration about the many ways in which students can connect on the global stage during middle and high school.

1. In November 2007, a 600-student delegation from Japan visited Beijing 101 School, where students enjoyed many activities together and planned an exchange program.

2. Students attended a 2006 summer camp in the United Kingdom.

3. A Russian winter camp of students visited Beijing 101 School, where students gave traditional performances for each other. The students also made dumplings together as the teachers introduced the history of cooking dumplings in China.

4. A 16-person delegation from Beijing 101 visited their friendship school in Sindelfingen, Germany, in October 2007.

5. The Olympic Youth Camp, as an important component of the 2008 Beijing Olympic Games, will be hosted by Beijing 101,

with the theme Youth for Future. Young people from more than 200 countries will be housed at Beijing 101 High School for the Olympic Youth Camp.

6. Student Zhong Yuechen participated in the Intel International Contest of Science and Engineering, in which young scientists were honored by the Lincoln Asteroid Lab at Massachusetts Institute of Technology. An asteroid was named after Zhong Yuechen after this event.

7. In 2005, Zhong Yuechen won the Second Rank Award and the reward of $1500 in the 57th Intel International Science and Engineering Competition Prix, which is held in the United States.

8. Two packages of Tomato Seeds in Space were delivered to Beijing Municipal Commission of Education as a gift from NASA. Beijing 101 High School was chosen for the experimental breeding of the tomato seeds.

9. Senior student Yan Xin participated in the European Union Youth Scientists Contest held in Valencia, Spain. The event was designed to attract young people to the science and technology industry.

10. Barry Marshall, who won 2005 Nobel Prize in Physiology or Medicine, visited Beijing 101 High School and gave a lecture on the Significance of Scientific Discovery for Human Life.

11. In 2005, Beijing 101 High School won the Innovation Award for Education Promoting Sustainable Development, which is a project of UNESCO.

12. The Golden Sail Symphony Orchestra of Beijing 101 High School has won honors in Beijing, throughout China, and on the international stage. The 100-plus members have performed in many countries, such as Germany, France, Italy, Austria, Japan, Singapore, and Russia. In 2003, they performed in several cities in France.

13. In 2005, 140 members of the Golden Sail Symphony Orchestra went to Europe to perform in Germany, Austria, and Italy, and they were invited to attend the thirty-fourth International Youth & Music Festival at Vienna Golden Hall. They won first prize!

14. The Beijing International Youth Art Week was hosted at Beijing 101 Middle School in 2006 for more than 500 students from all over the world.

15. The Golden Sail Symphony Orchestra was invited by the Ministry of Education of China to participate in a festival at Moscow University, where they played *Festival Sinfonia* by Shostakovich, a famous Soviet composer.

16. Student Liu Fei won the gold medal in the long jump and the bronze medal in the 110-meter-hurdle race in the 2007 International Championship of High School Students, which was held in Bordeaux, France.

17. Student Diao Jie won the gold medal in the 200-meter race, and another student, Song Hao, won the silver medal in the high jump during the fortieth International Youth Athletic Meeting in Thailand in August 2006.

18. The International School Connection's Annual Global Summit was hosted by Beijing 101 in October 2007. Many school connections were made with principals from around the world.

19. The school sends delegations to schools all over the world. In fact, each agreement is signed after a period of working out ideas of global education and international experience. Those schools are from America, Germany, Austria, and Canada, and so on, and the school will have some more friendship schools from the United Kingdom, Ireland, and South Africa.

20. An online debate was held among four schools from four places in China: Hong Kong, Shanghai, Chongqing, and Beijing. The students had a topic that they debated simultaneously. A teacher from the school had an online class for students in Hong Kong. It was a big success.

21. Finally, school symphony orchestras from America, Japan, and Australia have come to the school with the aim of art exchange and learning from each other.

The beat goes on for this prize-winning global school, for it is on the move to become one of the best middle high schools in the world. The school scans the globe continuously for opportunities to connect students with others to develop projects or to compete in competitions. To achieve both of these goals, students must excel in their academics and also have the self-confidence to outperform their peers around the world. And other projects require cooperation and an entrepreneurial spirit to achieve something in common. Both sets of personal capacities are needed to succeed in the world today.

The First Certified ISC Global Learning Center School: A. Y. Jackson Secondary School, Ottawa, Canada

In a ceremony during the 2007 ISC Global Summit in Beijing, A.Y. Jackson Secondary School was recognized as the *first in the world* to become certified as an ISC Global Learning Center school. This event followed a presentation by seven students, two teachers, and the principal, Martin Kleiman, on their GLC portfolio. Their achievement recognized the impact of the school's global activities over five years to prepare its students as global citizens and broaden their understanding of the world and its challenges.

How did it all begin? In an interview with Martin Kleiman, he reported that the school of about 900 students is located in a high-tech area of Ottawa, where the student body is multicultural because of the large second-generation community of Canadians from all over the world. The global focus began with students giving to their community through activities such as raising funds for soldiers coming home from Afghanistan, sponsoring one child through the Diabetes Association, building a food cupboard for the poor, and raising funds for local charities while using the local newspaper to promote their cause. A club on global caring grew into various courses for credit and a program of international studies. Now students write and produce five editions of a newspaper on their many local and global activities.

With lots of globally oriented activity continuing to emerge, Kleiman began to ponder how it all could fit together for the school. When he and Cathy Belanger connected with John Fitzgerald, an officer in the ISC, and Constantine Ioannou, a member of the ISC leadership team, he learned about the new ISC benchmarks for schools seeking to become Global Learning Centers. Kleiman was excited about the organization of the benchmarks and how they might help his school to focus its global activity and develop some guiding principles for development. The school staff and students then considered what they were doing globally in relation to these benchmarks, and realized they were working on an important frontier for schools all around the world.

Over several years, the ISC Ottawa hub generated indicators for each benchmark, a project in which A. Y. Jackson leaders and teachers invested time and energy. The indicators have been shared with others in the ISC Global Network schools, continually being refined because of collective learning. The indicators are a useful set of ideas for developing global school features, as well as for documenting success. Both the benchmarks and indicators were used by A.Y. Jackson staff and students in preparing their portfolio and are now used in other schools in the ISC network as guides for developing the benchmark capacities.

In the 2006 ISC Global Summit, held in Tampa, Florida, A.Y. Jackson was awarded the distinction of being the first school in the world to apply for certification as an ISC GLC school. A year later, at the ISC Beijing Summit, following A.Y. Jackson's second portfolio submission, which addressed ISC recommendations from the first portfolio effort, the school's application was accepted for a full three-year certification as a Global Learning Center.

Since the 2006 ISC award, staff and student involvement in international activity has increased, with nearly one-third of the staff meeting regularly in the International Studies Committee. Kleiman had more than 100 international flags purchased and hung in a central gathering place in the school. Students thanked Kleiman, saying they felt recognized for the heritage. Each teacher adopted a flag to stimulate learning and class discussions. This recognition of the multicultural mix of the community was the launching pad for the global learning culture that has emerged. Kleiman anticipates that the global foundation for the school's culture is now sustainable, for students initiate the projects, seek faculty support, and raise the funds necessary for their success. The student-led project life of the school has had a positive effect, for there are fewer school dropouts now and fewer students repeating grade 12.

A.Y. Jackson's students and staff piloted the use of Global Learning Center Benchmarks and their indicators to prepare an e-portfolio to the ISC leadership team. The school's portfolio was built around the benchmarks and indicators and then submitted to the ISC leadership team. A site visit was made by John Fitzgerald and Elaine Sullivan to observe the school in operation and to interview students, teachers, and leaders. Their portfolio can be viewed on the school's Web site, http://www.ayj.ca/documents/isc/newsletters/Beyond%20Our%20Walls. pdf.

In the ISC's portfolio review, A.Y. Jackson was recognized for many factors that together created a culture of caring and learning about the world:

> There is a genuine focus on caring about human issues and challenges, both locally and globally. Student activities emerge naturally in response to the need for action. The school and its community are successful in raising funds for its many global projects. . . . The generosity . . . is pervasive. Internalized caring about individuals and the human challenges and issues at large will be the bedrock of what defines the school community of A.Y. Jackson.

The aim of the school is "to equip today's students with skills to live and work in an increasingly global society with a greater understanding of the knowledge and values necessary to be citizens of the world." (*Beyond our Walls,* newsletter: A.Y. Jackson).

The ISC Portfolio Review indicates that the strategic plan is emerging from the school's guiding principles, values, and core purpose that integrate the GLC benchmarks. The school's strategic leadership, vision, and purpose are in alignment to create a sound future for global learning. Classroom teachers and activity sponsors are modeling how to connect the GLC benchmarks to the curriculum standards and learning activities.

The school's e-portfolio is filled with evidence that global learning permeates school life. Using the benchmarks as guides, the following samples illustrate the range of global initiatives that exist, both with the local community of Kanata in Ottawa, and from connections and partnerships around the world.

Benchmark 1: The Curriculum Reflects Global Forces

- The International Studies Program promotes global citizenship through a wide range of learning experiences, and awards a special certificate of achievement at graduation.

- Students attended workshops presented by international organizations.

- Students attended a National Youth Debate on Darfur.

- Students studied about apartheid and the Soweto uprisings and how the youth of South Africa came of age and took the front line in the fight for freedom.

- A summer conference promotes understanding of the political, economic, and social aspects of global interactions.

- Global events are integrated into daily classes in physical education, science, English, world issues, and business.

Benchmark 2: A School Vision and Plan Connects Students with the Global Community

- The school's aim is *to equip today's students with skills to live and work in an increasingly open society with a greater understanding of the knowledge and values necessary to be a citizen of the world.*

- A new goal exists to continue developing A. Y. Jackson as a Global Learning Center.

- The school aims to raise the profile of its multicultural programs.

- The International Studies Committee created a data collection system for the school's global activity for its archives, promotions, contacts, liaisons and partnerships, curriculum connections, field trips, exchanges, and fundraising initiatives.

Benchmark 3: Educators Participate in Professional Development in a Globally Networked Environment

- Two teachers and the principal participated in the 2006 ISC Annual Global Summit in Tampa, Florida.

- Six students, two teachers, and the principal attended the 2007 ISC Annual Summit in Beijing, China, which sponsored the first global youth leadership program.

- The staff development program centers on becoming global professionals.

- Professionals communicate with other professionals around the world using technology to promote global learning activity for students.

- The staff locates international resources in the community to enhance global initiatives.

Benchmark 4: Partnerships with Global Businesses Enhance the School's Development

- School sponsorships include Dell Canada, Scotiabank, and Kanata Toyota, which paid for students to attend a Global Youth Leaders Conference, including a laptop for each student.

- Students found support for sponsoring an exchange with students in northern Canada: the First Air and Air Inuit Partnership.

- Students found resources for providing a haven for displaced northern Ontario students.

Benchmark 5: Students Demonstrate High Levels of Academic Achievement

- The Isis Officer Ethno-cultural Equity Award was awarded to A.Y. Jackson in 2002 and 2006, and again in 2007.

- A. Y. Jackson students demonstrated in 2005–2006 and in 2006–2007 achievement patterns that were all above the school district levels, as well as above the Ontario levels in reading, writing, and math.

- The A.Y. team won third place in the regional Junior Achievement business competition in 2005.

- The school's jazz band won the gold at the Kiwanis Music Festival in 2005.

- Students won over $240,000 in university entrance scholarships in 2006.

- At the 2006 graduation, 26 French Immersion certificates, 59 Ontario Scholar's certificates, and 17 Ontario Scholar's certificates with business concentrations were awarded.

Benchmark 6: Current Knowledge about Learning Guides Student Activity

- A school partnership with Colegio Juan de Lanuzi in Spain promotes student exchanges each year to both campuses to learn about life in each country and their unique contributions.

- Students learn and teach each other games from many cultures around the world.

- The school demonstrates a culture of caring for one another, for their community, their nation, and for life around the world.

- The school models a dynamic and positive learning community that supports innovation, student initiation, and participation in shaping the curriculum with various global projects.

- An inquiry approach to learning permeates school life and students work in teams to explore the options and opportunities.

- Respect and dignity is an earmark of student projects to make a difference.

Benchmark 7: International Projects Are Included in the Curriculum

- The former ambassador to the United Nations spoke to the class on world issues, where the students also presented miniseminars on various world issues.

- Students visited World War I and II sites in Belgium and France to learn about the history of Canada and its connection with other parts of the world during those moments in history.

- Students have pen pals in Nairobi, Kenya, through the Ubuntu pen pal club.

- Current events are addressed in many classrooms, focusing on climate change, sustainable development, the changing world economy, security, and conflict resolution.

- Students organize a global celebration event each year for the community.

Benchmark 8: Students Develop Global Workforce Capacities, Including Technology

- Students participated in World Issues Day at Carleton University.

- Students helped to organize the e-portfolio for the ISC to become a Certified Global Learning Center.

- The GLC e-portfolio was developed by students for posting on the school's Web site.

- Students created an e-newsletter on their global activity.

Benchmark 9: Students use Democratic Decision-making Processes

- Students worked with faculty to prepare for certification as a GLC school.

- Students planned for the school's presentation at the ISC Global Summit in Beijing.

- Students initiate projects that require continuous democratic decision making, organization, resources, and assessment.

Benchmark 10: Students Care about the Global Community and its Sustainability

- Students raised funds for World Vision through the Sports Marathon.

- Funds were raised to sponsor two girls to attend Lwak High School in Kenya.

- Students raise funds to support troops overseas.

- Students organized two clinics to raise 75 units of blood for the Red Cross.

- Students organized an annual food and toy drive from their international business class.

- Funds were raised to sponsor a nine-year-old girl in El Salvador and for UNICEF, the Humane Society, and Houses for Haiti.

- The school hosted the first national students from Kaschewan and Kangiqsualujuac regions of northern Canada.

For more information, check the school's Web site, http://www.ayj.ca, and learn all the ways that students and faculty live together to explore new global learning opportunities, and then shape each one together. Global learning has become a way of life for A.Y. Jackson's students and staff. (Contact John Fitzgerald, johnfitz1@sympatico.ca, for more information about the school certification process as a GLC school.)

CONCLUSION

Leaders with an orientation to *living on the edge of chaos* enjoy the confidence that comes from building disequilibrium to a tipping point and supporting self-organization to create a new and more responsive learning system for a global age. This is what Meyrtha and George Leetz have achieved on the Dutch island of Curacao. They conducted almost 30 World Café events for children and their families to talk about domestic violence. More than 30 projects have resulted from this important work, and the island's education systems, various ministries from the government, and the business community are now involved in creating solutions to the problems of domestic violence. They intend to build a strong and vital island nation by working together systemically! Building disequilibrium over time, with an intent to make a difference is the backbone of this story (http://www.5starcuracao.com). Curacao is now preparing to host the 2009 ISC Global Summit, which is being sponsored by the government, local business leaders, school districts, and non-profit organizations. This integrated community envisions that the ISC will promote the island's connection with others around the world and develop its capacity to prepare its next generations for global/local leadership.

By reaching out to one another across borders and regions of the world, let us learn together to survive, enjoy, and thrive on the *Edge of Chaos,* where significant change occurs. Let us listen and respond to environmental changes, build disequilibrium with information to a tipping point, network across all sectors of professional life to build energy for new approaches to schooling, foster self-organization among students, teachers, parents and the community, and from partnerships, and also expect that new prototypes of school life will emerge that are more responsive to students today and their learning requirements. In the end let us celebrate both the passing of outdated practices and the emergence of new life forms of schooling.

In the process let us develop friendships that cross borders and regions, cultures and languages, while we form school and district partnerships and build our networks of support to sustain continuous success. This journey is for the brave at heart and for those with a passion to do what is needed to make schooling relevant to the youth of today. This is our opportunity now, to become a global network of educators learning with one another to fashion a new story of schooling, one fit for this global age of living.

Appendix A

Global Learning Center Benchmarks: Examples from Many Schools around the World

Benchmark 1: The curriculum provides opportunities to learn about local and global forces that influence change. For example:

- The Futures Project in Europe permeates many school programs for all age groups and is designed to develop an awareness of emerging global trends (Finland).

- The content of one science project reflects the latest that is known about astronomy, within the context of online courses that are taught worldwide (Finland).

- A school has adopted environmental education and the Futures Project for all students (Sweden).

- Six nature programs are linked with local industries (Sweden).

- Students have received teachers and leaders in the school from many schools in Spain, the United States, and China (United States).

- Teachers in two schools meet on Skype to plan for student projects, which are then designed and produced by students (United States).

Benchmark 2: The school has a vision for a global future and plans to connect students with the global community and its dynamic forces. For example:

- Students in astronomy classes are involved in a project with the National Science Teachers Association, where they share data across borders. They also learn about different ways the Astronomy-with-a-stick Project is being used in classrooms, using stories and myths that students create (Finland).

- Students are assessed by local industries in their performance. They also take courses from schools in other countries (Sweden).

- The school is planning now to become an ISC Global Learning Center Benchmarked School (United States).

- A United Nations approach to school learning engages students in debates around major world challenges (China).

Benchmark 3: Educators participate in professional development activity in a global networked environment. For example:

- Teachers study the Futures Project literature about emerging global trends, then organize seminars with other teachers to share and explore these trends (Finland).

- The principal and teachers host visits of educators from other countries (Finland).

- The principals are members of the International School Connection and have hosted many international groups of educational leaders in their schools, along with seminars they organize with leaders in the school district and the National Education Agency (Finland).

- Two teachers visit a partner school in Luxemburg for one month. Six teachers from Luxemburg will then spend a month in our school and community (Finland).

- The principal participates in a job-shadowing program sponsored by the British Council, with a school in Glasgow (Finland).

- The principal is involved in an international planning team for the Comenius Project in Europe (Sweden).

- Next year our teachers will exchange with teachers from Iceland (Finland).

- Through active engagement with colleagues from other countries and with local industrial leaders, the role of teacher has been changed forever. Teachers are active facilitators of student capacity-building for specific careers (Sweden).

- Our school has hosted seminars, global conferences, and workshops for educators from Spain, China, the ISC Global Community, and the local urban area and region (United States).

- Principals in Katrineholm, Sweden, and Ottawa, Canada, exchanged teachers to live and work together as partners for one week in each other's homes and classrooms, first in Ottawa and then in Katrineholm.

Benchmark 4: Partnerships with local-global businesses enhance the direction of school development. For example:

- Students are responsible for developing employability capacities in their selected field. They work in the context of learning communities that develop goals and assign student responsibilities. They participate in the real work of their chosen industry (Sweden).

- Business leaders work with teachers to shape student learning in each program area, and then annually assess the quality of student work (Sweden).

- High school students explored ways to generate political and financial support for hosting the ISC First Youth Leadership Global Summit (China).

- The Ottawa School Board has partnerships and exchange programs with a number of school districts in China, South Korea, and Vietnam. Large numbers of teachers come to Ottawa to learn to speak and teach subjects in English (Canada).

- The school district has established in China "schools within schools" in which Canadian teachers offer Canadian high school credits in English to Chinese students.

Benchmark 5: The school has achieved high student performance results. For example:

- A school has received an award as a Blue Ribbon School from the Department of Education for its high levels of student performance (United States).

- Two schools in Helsinki are in the number one country in the world for its education, according to results from the PISA examination (Finland).

- One school's youth orchestra won first place in the 2006 world competition in Vienna (China).

Benchmark 6. Current knowledge about human learning guides learning activity. For example:

- The principal conducts weekly workshops about human learning in a brain-friendly learning environment. The professional development of teachers is continuous throughout the school year (United States).

- Teachers attend many conferences and workshops outside their school to add to their knowledge about human learning (United States).

- Students throughout the school understand the reasons why they experience certain learning activities, and they can explain to visitors those reasons, from a human learning perspective (United States).

- Teachers belong to networks of educators in their specialization, which influences the learning environment in schools (Finland).

- Teachers are linked together in virtual networks by the Chinese Ministry of Education for continuous learning as professionals through training, seminars, pilot programs, visiting each others' classrooms and talking about observations, reflection, and sharing (China).

Benchmark 7: International projects are included in local curriculum to promote global learning opportunities for all students. For example:

- The science project and the Futures Project involve most students in the school. This includes exchanges with students from Estonia, Sochi in Russia, Bolton in England, and Katrineholm in Sweden (Finland).

- Environment projects promote student interaction from schools in other countries in Europe (Finland).

- Our School Program Connections include the following (Sweden):

  - Gardening: Finland, Hungary
  - Forestry: Norway, Hungary, Belgium
  - Fish breeding: Norway
  - Agriculture: Estonia, Scotland, Australia
  - Culture: Estonia, Russia
  - Water management: Hungary
  - Equestrian activity: Hungary
  - Hunting and wildlife care: Hungary, Scotland
  - Landscaping: The Netherlands
  - Fishing: Scotland

- Students go to Kenya and take courses for credit in our school as it relates to studying about and working with local people to build communities in Kenya (Sweden).

- Students create friendships with children and educators around the world to improve our country's image (China).

Benchmark 8: Students are developing capacities for success in the evolving global workforce, which includes emerging technologies. For example:

- Students are actively engaged in learning projects with students from many other countries, using the Internet, DVDs, CDs, and videos (China).

- Through active selection, planning, working, and assessment, students are involved in preparing for a specific career in nature and environmental care (Sweden).

- Students make presentations at adult conferences on the results from their multinational research on real problems of the Baltic Sea (Sweden).

- Students in our school learn to use authentic English through storytelling, singing, drama, writing, and creating PowerPoint presentations (China).

- Students participate in projects with students in Israel, Japan, Spain, Belgium, the United Kingdom, and Argentina (China).

- Our students are pen pals with students in four cities in Texas (China).

- Students in Shaoguan participate in a Belgian project called Virtual Zoo, involving students around the world (China).

- Students in a middle school develop and manage their school's Global Learning Web site (United States).

Benchmark 9: Students learn about and use democratic decision-making processes, peace building strategies, and practices for ethnocultural equity. For example:

- All students each day help shape the work of their team on its tasks (Sweden).

- Student representatives from each program area form the school's governance council, which establishes and manages policies (Sweden).

- A delegation from Rhode Island dedicated a U.N. peace pole on our school campus (China).

- Students in high schools and middle schools from China and the United States are preparing a program for the first ISC Global Youth

Leadership Summit, working with the international ISC Youth Leadership Design Team.

- Students create learning opportunities for students in their partner schools (United States, Singapore, China).

- The World Voices Choir, which is formed by students in multicultural Ottawa High Schools, sing songs and rhythms in the languages found among their classmates (Canada).

Benchmark 10: Students demonstrate an orientation for caring about the global community and its sustainable environment. For example:

- Some students participate in exchange programs in project schools (Finland).

- Students travel to countries in Africa, where they have partnership projects to raise the level of living and learning conditions. For this the students receive course credit (Sweden).

- Our students help a school in Australia learn Mandarin with our letters to them and theirs to us (China).

- Our students sent a letter that was hand delivered to Belgium's King Albert II and Queen Paula. The king sent a letter back to our class (China).

- The Ottawa School Board has a well-established International Languages Department, which teaches more than 40 languages to students in credit and noncredit after-school and Saturday programs (Canada).

Appendix B

The MORE Approach

The MORE Approach was developed by Dr. Joyce Burick Swarzman, Headmaster of Independent Day School Corbett Campus, and her staff, in Tampa, Florida. The model is designed to include the various approaches to learning that the staff values and includes in their daily work with students. This same model is the foundation for teacher training that is conducted by Swarzman for schools in the southeastern United States, and throughout Spain. What follows are the seven strands to the MORE model. For additional information, go to www.idsyes.com.

Strand 1: **Appreciating the Uniqueness of the Learning** includes multiple and emotional intelligences, and various learning style indicators.

Strand 2: **Motivational Strategies to Increase Time on Task** includes a range of questioning techniques, signal systems for gaining whole group and work team attention, cooperative learning strategies, and brain activating processes.

Strand 3: **Creating Dignity and Respect** includes a variety of communication skills along with guidelines for acceptable behavior, with consequences for taking personal responsibility.

Strand 4: **Teacher/Student Presence—Making Connections** includes strategies for connecting and building rapport through body language, tone and words, along with reference to the habits of successful people.

Strand 5: A **Learning Community** organization includes group dynamics, multi-age classes, teamwork skills, processes for shared decision making, and key elements in high-performance learning systems.

Strand 6: **The Curriculum Framework** includes planning for high levels of student academic performance, such as the content, contextual factors, thematic approaches, curriculum mapping, and accountability.

Strand 7: **A Child-Centered Vision** includes what is now known about the growth process from neurobiologists, the power of an Olympic attitude, and a vision of high levels of achievement.

Appendix C

Training Clusters

Training Cluster A

Getting Ready for Sustainable School Development in a Global Age of Living

Day 1: Analyzing the Global Context of Schooling

Purpose: To develop an orientation to the global context & the purposes of schooling in a global age.

Knowledge Base

- Globalization Trends
- Global School Performance Trends
- Networking Science & Practice

Leadership Skills

- *Trend Analysis*
- *Building a learning community*
- *Mini-Delphi/Dialogue Technique*

Practice Assignments

- Trend Analysis
- Organizing a personal learning community
- Lead a Mini-Delphi/Dialogue Technique

Day 2: Developing a Systemic Orientation to School Development

Purpose: To envision a systemic & chaos approach to school development for a global age of living.

Knowledge Bases

- Systems, Chaos & Complexity Theories
- *The School Work Culture Profile:* SWCP

Leadership Skills

- *Leverage Point Analysis*
- *Personal vision for school development*

Practice Assignments

- Survey Staff, using the SWCP
- Lead a *Leverage Point Analysis*

Training Cluster B
Gathering Information for Setting Goals & Planning

Day 3: Conducting a Case Study to Prepare for Planning

Purpose: To acquire basic knowledge for conducting a school case study to provide information for setting school goals.

Knowledge Bases
- Case Study Method
- Case Study Examples
- Global Learning Center Benchmarks

Leadership Skills
- *Conducting a Case Study*

Practice Assignments
- Conduct a *Case Study* to prepare for planning & school development for a global age of living
- Conduct a Survey: *Global Learning Center Benchmark Analysis*

Day 4: School Development Goal Setting for a Global Age of Learning

Purpose: To develop skills to facilitate the Delphi/Dialogue Technique, a shared decision making tool to use information & identify school goals.

Knowledge Bases
- Strategic Living and Leading
- *The Delphi/Dialogue Technique*

Leadership Skills
- Leading the *Delphi/Dialogue Technique*

Practice Assignments

Lead a group in the *Delphi/Dialogue Technique* to use case study information & identify school development goals

Training Cluster C
Organizing & Leading the School's Work System

Day 5: Developing School-wide Professional Work Teams

Purpose: To create a management plan for the professional work system to achieve school goals.

Knowledge Bases
- Building communities of trust, involvement, & high performance
- Permanent & ad hoc work teams
- Partnerships & networks

Leadership Skills
- *Network Analysis* of a school organization
- *Designing the planning, action, reflection, adaptation work system*

Practice Tasks

Develop a Management Plan for creating a responsive work system

Day 6: Designing the Student Learning Community Organization

Purpose: To design the student learning system, and identify the leadership & management elements to foster growth.

Knowledge Bases
- Learning Community Organization
- Team Teaching & Career Academies
- Student Networks
- Student Learning Community Benchmarks

Leadership Skills
- *Benchmarking the student learning community system*
- Analysis of a school's learning system

Practice Tasks

Plan for strengthening, or developing, one student learning community

Training Cluster D
Designing & Leading the Learning System

Day 7: Leading the Professional Learning Community

Purpose: To design & lead a sustainable & job-imbedded professional learning community to support a vision & goals

Knowledge Bases

- Features of sustainable development
- High performing professional systems
- Co-mentoring & social networks

Leadership Skills

- Create benchmarks for a sustainable professional learning system

Practice Tasks

Use the *Professional Learning Community Benchmarks* to improve your organization's adult learning system

Day 8: Leading the Student Learning System

Purpose: To design the core elements of a student learning system for this global age of living

Knowledge Bases

- Strategic leadership for learning
- Poverty, minority, & immigration issues
- The School's Digital Culture

Leadership Skills

Develop a collective vision and core values for a student learning system in this global age

Practice Task

Develop a plan for advancing the student learning system & effects

Training Cluster E
Leading Strategically & Accountably

Day 9: Benchmarking Progress: Toward Students as Global Citizens

Purpose: To design & lead a system of continuous development toward preparing students as global citizens.

Knowledge Bases

- A Diagnostic Model of Change
- Analyzing Student Performance
- Systemic Quality Control & Assessment
- Leadership for Benchmarking Change

Leadership Skills

- Identify indicators of progress for school development in a global age
- Framework for benchmarking progress

Practice Task

Prepare a 10–15 minute media report on the personal effects from LSSD Training

Day 10: Personal Reports on the Effects of LSSD Training

Purpose: For Participants to report in a media presentation the effects of LSSD Training on themselves, their organizations, and their future plans to prepare students as active global citizens.

Bibliography

Acker, Joan. (1992). *Gendering Organizational Analysis.* Newbury Park, Calif.: Sage.

Acker-Hocevar, Michele. (November 1994). "The Content Validation of Standards, Outcomes, and Indicators for Organizational Development in Region IV of Florida." Dissertation, University of South Florida, Tampa.

Acker-Hocevar, Michele, and Marta Cruz-Janzen. (in press). "Principal Preparation Programs." *International Journal of Learning.*

Acker-Hocevar, Michele, and Debra Touchton. (2002c, Spring). "How Principals Level the Playing Field of Accountability in Florida's High-Poverty/Low-Performing Schools, Part I: The Intersection of High-Stakes Testing and Effects of Poverty of Teaching and Learning." *International Journal of Educational Reform, 11*(2), 106–124.

Acker-Hocevar, Michele, and Debra Touchton. (2002b, Summer). "How Principals Level the Playing Field of Accountability in Florida's High-Poverty/Low-Performing Schools, Part II: Building Organizational Capacity under the Auspices of Florida's A+ Plan." *International Journal of Educational Reform, 11*(3), 268–278.

Acker-Hocevar, Michele, and Debra Touchton. (2002a, Fall). "How Principals Level the Playing Field of Accountability in Florida's High-Poverty/Low-Performing Schools, Part III: Effects of High-Poverty Schools on Teacher Recruitment and Retention." *International Journal of Educational Reform, 11*(4), 334–346.

Acker-Hocevar, Michele, Marta Cruz-Janzen, and Cynthia Wilson. (January 2006). "International Congress for School Effectiveness and Improvement (ICSEI). Embracing Diversity: New Challenges for School Effectiveness and Improvement in a Global Learning Society." 19th Annual World ICSEI Congress, Fort Lauderdale, Florida.

Acker-Hocevar, Michele, Marta Cruz-Janzen, Cynthia Wilson, Perry Schoon, and David Walker. (2005/2006). "The Need to Reestablish Schools as Dynamic Positive Human Energy Systems That Are Non-Linear and Self-Organizing: The Learning Partnership Tree." *International Journal of Learning, 12*(10), 255–266.

Acker-Hocevar, Michele, and Patricia A. Bauch (Fall 1998). "Florida Awards Teachers' Perspectives on Empowerment and Their Involvement With Parents Under Recent School Reform Efforts." *Organization Theory Dialogue.* Organization Theory Special Interest Group, American Educational Research Association. Indiana University, Bloomington.

Acker-Hocevar, Michele, Patricia Bauch, and Barbara Berman. (1997). "Emerging Constructs of Power: Teacher Beliefs Embedded in Practice with Implications for School Leadership." *Educational Leadership and Administration, 9,* 21–32.

Acker-Hocevar, Michele, Roseanne MacGregor, and Debra Touchton. (April 1996)."The Problem with Power: Whose Definition? An Exploratory Study of 'Gendered Language' Differences on Personal and Organizational Factors of Power with US and Canadian

Teachers." Paper presentation, annual meeting of the American Educational Research Association, New York.

Acker-Hocevar, Michele, Debra Touchton, and Julie Zenz. (March 1995). "Perceived Power: Embedded Practices in Present Educational Structures." Presentation, annual meeting of Women and Power Conference, Middle Tennessee State University, Murfreesboro, Tenn.

Alvarez, Benjamin. (1998). "Life Cycle and Legacy of the Educational Reforms in Latin America and the Caribbean." *International Journal of Educational Reform, 7*(1) (January), 34–45.

American Education Research Association (AERA). Go to http://www.aera.net.

Anderson, Robert H. (1988). "Team Teaching: Quo Vadis?" *Florida ASCD Journal, 5,* 17–22.

Anderson, Robert H., and Barbara Nelson Pavan. (1993). *Nongradedness: Helping It to Happen.* Lancaster, Pa.: Technomic Press.

Apple, Michael. (1982) *Education and Power.* Boston: Routledge and Kegan Paul.

Barabási, Albert-Laszlo. (2003). *Linked: How Everything Is Connected to Everything Else and What It Means for Business, Science, and Everyday Life.* Auckland, New Zealand: Plume.

Barnard, Chester. (1964, originally published in 1938). *The Functions of the Executive.* Cambridge, Mass.: Harvard University Press.

Beavis, Allan K. (April 1995). "Towards a Social Theory of School Administrative Practice in a Complex, Chaotic, Quantum World." Paper presentation, American Educational Research Association, San Francisco.

Begun, James W. (December 1994). "Chaos and Complexity: Frontiers of Organization Science." *Journal of Management Inquiry 3*(4), 330–334.

Belenky, Mary Field, Blythe Clinchy, Nancy Goldberger, and Jill Tarule. (1986). *Women's Ways of Knowing: The Development of Self, Voice, and Mind.* New York: Basic Books.

Bennett, Nigel, and Alma Harris. (1997). "Hearing Truth from Power? Organisation Theory, School Effectiveness, and School Improvement." Paper presentation, annual meeting of the American Educational Research Association, Chicago.

Bennis, Warren, Jagdish Parikh, and Ronnie Lessem. (1994). *Beyond Leadership: Balancing Economics, Ethics and Ecology.* Cambridge, Mass.: Basil Blackwell.

Bently, R., and A. M. Rempel. (1980). *Purdue Teacher Opinionaire.* 2nd ed. Lafayette, Ind.: Purdue Research Foundation.

Bertalanffy, Ludwig von. (1968). *General System Theory: Foundations, Development, Applications.* Rev. ed. New York: George Braziller.

Bishop, Cheryl. (1997). *Relationship Between the Organizational Culture of Four Elementary Schools and the Referral Rates for Exceptional Student Education Programs.* Dissertation, University of South Florida, Tampa.

Bjorkman, Conny. (1996). *School Work Culture as a Platform for School Development: A Study of Two Swedish and Two Russian Schools.* Paper presentation, conference on Multicultural Education, Sochi, Russia.

———. (1997). *An Exchange of Experiences.* Sundsvall, Sweden: Mid-Sweden University Press.

———. (1998). "School Work Culture as a Platform for School Development." *Wingspan, 12*(1), 2–9.

———. (1998). Slutredovisning Av Projekten "Utveckling och anvandning av instrumentet SWCP och PBL." A report to Skolverket. Submitted by Brua at Mid-Sweden University. Ostersund, Sweden.

Blase, Jo. (1991). "The Micropolitical Perspective." In *The Politics of Life in Schools,* ed. Jo Blase, 1–18. Newbury Park, Calif: Corwin Press.

Blazey, Mark L. (2008). *Insights to Performance Excellence 2008: An Inside Look at the 2008 Baldrige Award Criteria,* Milwaukee, Wis.: ASQ Quality Press.

Blueprint 2000: Initial Recommendations for a System of School Improvement and Accountability. (1992). Tallahassee: The Florida Commission on Educational Reform and Accountability.

Bohm, David. (1995). *Wholeness and the Implicate Order.* New York: Routledge.

Borg, Walter R., and Meredith D. Gall. (1989). *Educational Research: An Introduction.* 5th ed. New York: Longman.

Bridgeland, J. M., J. Dilulio, and K. B. Morison. (March 2006). *The silent epidemic: Perspectives of high school dropouts.* A report of the Civic Enterprises in association with Peter D. Hart Research Associates for the Bill and Melinda Gates Foundation. Retrieved March 6, 2006, from http://www.civicenterprises.net/pdfs/thesilentepidemic3-06.pdf

Brooks, Ann K. (1994). "Power and the Production of Knowledge: Collective Team Learning in Work Organizations." *Human Resource Development Quarterly, 5*(3), 213–235.

Bruner, Darlene Y. (1997). *The Dynamics of Work Cultures of Low and High Performance Schools: A Case Study.* Doctoral dissertation, University of South Florida, Tampa.

Brunner, Cryss C. (1993). *By Power Defined: Women in the Superintendency.* Unpublished dissertation, University of Kansas.

Buchanan, Mark. (2002). *Nexus: Small Worlds and the Groundbreaking Theory of Networks.* New York: W. W. Norton & Company.

Buckley, W. (1967). *Sociology and Modern Systems Theory.* Englewood Cliffs, N.J.: Prentice-Hall.

Burch, John G., and Gary Grudnitski. (1986). *Information Systems: Theory and Practice.* New York: John Wiley and Sons.

Burchard, John D., and Mark Schaefer. (1992). "Improving Accountability in a Service Delivery Model in Children's Mental Health." *Clinical Psychology Review, 12,* 867–882.

Bush, George. (1992). *America 2000.* Washington, D.C.: U.S. Department of Education.

Callahan, Raymond E. (1962). *Education and the Cult of Efficiency.* Chicago: The University of Chicago Press.

Camp, Robert C. (1989). *Benchmarking: The Search for Industry Best Practices That Lead to Superior Performance.* Milwaukee, Wis.: ASQC Quality Press.

———. (1995). *Business Process Benchmarking: Finding and Implementing Best Practices.* Milwaukee, Wis.: ASQC Quality Press.

Capra, Fritjof. (1982). *The Turning Point: Sciences, Society, and the Rising Culture.* New York: Simon & Schuster, Bantam Books.

———. (1991). *The Tao of Physics.* 3rd ed. Boston: Shambhala.

———. (1994). "Systems Theory and the New Paradigm." In *Concepts in Critical Theory: Ecology,* ed. C. Merchant. Atlantic Highlands, N.J.: Humanities Press International.

———. (1996). *The Web of Life: A New Scientific Understanding of Living Systems.* New York: Anchor Books, Doubleday.

———. (2002). *The Hidden Connections: Integrating the Biological, Cognitive, and Social Dimensions of Life into a Science of Sustainability.* New York: Doubleday.

Carnegie Task Force on Teaching as a Profession. (1986). *A Nation Prepared: Teachers for the 21st Century.* New York: Carnegie Forum on Education and the Economy.

Castells, Manuel. (1996, 2000). *The Rise of the Network Society,* 2nd ed. Oxford: Blackwell.

———. (2000). "Information Technology and Global Capitalism." In W. Hutton and A. Giddens (eds). *Global Capitalism.* New York: The New York Press.

Casti, John L. (1995). *Complexification: Exploring a Paradoxical World Through the Science of Surprise.* New York: HarperPerennial.

Cherryholmes, Cleo H. (1988). *Power and Criticism: Poststructural Investigations in Education.* New York: Teachers College Press.

Clegg, Stewart. (1989). *Frameworks of Power.* London: Sage.

Cleland, David I., and William R. King. (1972). *Management: A Systems Approach.* New York: McGraw-Hill.

Clinchy, Evans. (December 1998). "The Educationally Challenged American School District." *Phi Delta Kappan, 80*(4), 272–277.

Cogan, John. (1998). "Citizenship Education for the 21st Century: Setting the Context." In *Citizenship for the 21st Century: An International Perspective on Education.* Cogan, John, and R. Derricott, ed. London: Kogan Page Limited.

Cohen, Debbie Happy. (2003). *It's All About Kids: Every Child Deserves a Teacher of the Year.* Tampa, FL: Bee Happy.

Coveney, Peter, and Roger Highfield. (1995). *Frontiers of Complexity: The Search for Order in a Chaotic World.* New York: Fawcett Columbine.

Crozier, Michael. (1964). *The Bureaucratic Phenomenon.* Chicago: University of Chicago Press, Phoenix Books.

Dalin, Per. (1995). *Skolutveckling, Praktik.* Stockholm: Liber Utbildning.

———. (January 1996). "Can Schools Learn? Preparing for the 21st Century." *NASSP Bulletin, 68,* 9–15.

Darling-Hammond, Linda. (1992). *Professional Practice Schools: Linking Teacher Education and School Reform.* New York: Teachers College Press.

Delors, Jacques. (1998). "Learning the Treasure Within." Report to UNESCO of the International Commission for Education for the Twenty-first Century. Paris: UNESCO.

Deming, W. Edwards. (1986). *Out of Crisis.* Cambridge, Mass.: Massachusetts Institute of Technology.

Denzin, Norman K., and Yvonna S. Lincoln, eds. (1994). *Handbook on Qualitative Research.* London: Sage.

Derrida, Jacque. (1976). *Of Grammatology.* Baltimore: Johns Hopkins Press.

DiMaggio, Paul, and Walter Powell. (1983). "The Iron Cage Revisited: Institutional Isomorphism and Collective Rationality in Organizational Fields." *American Sociological Review, 48,* 147–160.

Dubinskas, Frank A. (December 1994). "On the Edge of Chaos: A Metaphor for Transformative Change." *Journal of Management Inquiry, 3*(4), 355–365.

Dunlap, Diane, and Paul Goldman. (1991). "Rethinking Power in Schools." *Educational Administration Quarterly, 27*(1), 5–29.

Eisler, Riane. (1987). *The Chalice and the Blade: Our History, Our Future.* San Francisco: Harper & Row.

———. (1993). "The Challenge of Human Rights for All: What Can We Do?" In *The Years Ahead: Perils, Problems, and Promises,* ed. H. F. Didsbury, 99–115. Betheseda, Md.: World Futures Society.

———. (1995). "From Domination to Partnership: The Hidden Subtext in Organizational Change." *Training and Development, 49*(2), 32–39.

Engels, F. (1940). *Dialectics of Nature.* New York: International.

English, Fenwick W. (1992). *Educational Administration: The Human Science.* New York: HarperCollins.

Eratuuli, Matti, and Kauko Hamalainen. (1996). "Participants' Evaluation of a Specialist Training Programme for Principals." In *Improving Educational Management,* eds. Jaroslav Kalous and Fons van Wieringen. De Lier, the Netherlands: Academisch Boeken Centrum.

Eratuuli, Matti, and Christer Nylen. (1995). *The Improvement of School Leadership: Cooperation between Russian, Swedish, and Finnish Principals. Part 1: The Background, Context, and the Principals' Job Descriptions.* Helsinki: University of Helsinki.

European Commission. (November 2004). "Implementation of 'Education and Training 2010' Work Programme. Working Group B 'Key Competencies.'" *Key Competencies for Lifelong Learning: A European Reference Framework.*

Feigenbaum, Mitchell. (1990). "The Transition to Chaos." In *Chaos: The New Science,* ed. John Holte. Lanham, Md.: Gustavus Adolphus College, University Press of America.

Field, J. (2000). *Lifelong Learning and the New Educational Order.* Stroke on Trenton, UK: Trentham Books.

Fisher, Kimball, and Mareen Duncan Fisher. (1998). *The Distributed Mind: Achieving High Performance Through the Collective Intelligence of Knowledge Work Teams.* New York: American Management Association.

Fitzgerald, John. (1991). "Management Practices: A Case Study of Supervisors and Directors of Curriculum and Instruction in One School District." Unpublished dissertation, University of South Florida, Tampa.

Florida Department of Education. (1992a). *Blueprint 2000.* Tallahassee: The Florida Commission on Educational Reform and Accountability.

———. (1992b). *Guidelines for School Improvement.* Tallahassee, Fla.: The Commission on Educational Reform and Accountability.

Florida Office of Program Policy Analysis and Government Accountability (OPPAGA). (1997). *Improving Student Performance in High-Poverty Schools.* Tallahassee, Fla.: Author.

Foucault, Michel. (1984). *The Foucault Reader,* ed. Paul Rabinow. New York: Pantheon Books.

Freire, Paulo. (1970). *Pedagogy of the Oppressed.* New York: Herder and Herder.

———. (1973). *Pedagogy of the Oppressed.* New York: Continuum.

Friedman, Thomas L. (1999). *The Lexus and the Olive Tree: Understanding Globalization.* New York: Farrar, Straus, and Giroux.

———. (2006). *The World Is Flat: A Brief History of the Twenty-First Century.* New York: Farrar, Straus, and Giroux.

Fullan, Michael. (2006). *Turnaround Leadership.* San Francisco: Jossey-Bass.

Fullan, Michael G., and Mathew B. Miles. (June 1992). "Getting Reform Right: What Works and What Doesn't." *Phi Delta Kappan, 745*–752.

Garton, L., C. Hayhornthwaite, and B. Wellman. (1999). "Studying Online Social Networks." In Jones, S., ed. (1999). *Doing Internet Research: Critical Issues and Methods for Examining the Net.* Thousand Oaks, CA: Sage.

Garvin, David A. (1993). "Building a Learning Organization." *Harvard Business Review, 71*(4), 78–91.

Geertz, Clifford. (1973). *The Interpretation of Cultures.* New York: Basic Books.

Getzels, Jacob W., and Egon Guba. (Winter 1957). "Social Behavior and the Administrative Process." *School Review, 65,* 423–441.

Giella, Mary. (1996). *The Superintendent's Handbook.* New Florida Superintendents' Orientation Conference. Tallahassee: Florida Association of District School Superintendents.

Giella, Mary, Karolyn J. Snyder, and Robert H. Anderson. (1999). "A Strategic Planning System." In *Leadership for Systemic School District Transformation: A Professional Development Program.* Tampa: Pedamorphosis.

Giella, Mary, and Myndall Stanfill. (January 1996). "Concurrent School Transformation: Resolving the Dilemma." *NASSP Bulletin, 80,* 58–66.

Gilligan, Carol. (1982). *In a Different Voice: Psychological Theory and Women's Development.* Cambridge, Mass.: Harvard University Press.

Glasser, William. (1990). "The Quality School." *Educational Leadership, 71*(6), 425–435.

Gleick, James. (1987). *Chaos: Making a New Science.* New York: Penguin Books.

Gomer, H. (1976). "The Functions of Formal Planning in Response to Sudden Change in the environment." (Ph.D. paper), Graduate School of Business Administration, Harvard University.

Goodlad, John I., and Robert H. Anderson. (1959, 1963). *The Nongraded Elementary School.* New York: Harcourt, Brace & World.

Gore, Al. (2006). *An Inconvenient Truth: The Planetary Emergency of Global Warming and What We Can Do About It.* New York: Rodale.

Graham, Pauline. (1995). *Mary Parker Follett: Prophet* of *Management.* Boston: Harvard Business School Press.

Gramsci, Antonio. (1971). *Prison Notebooks.* New York: International.

Greene, M. (1988). *The Dialetic of Freedom.* New York: Teachers College Press.

Greenlee, Bobbie Jean. (1997). "A Study of the Internal Consistency Reliability and Criterion-Related Validity of the Education Quality Benchmark System." Doctoral dissertation, University of South Florida, Tampa.

Guba, Egon G., and Yvonna S. Lincoln. (1989). *Fourth Generation Evaluation.* Newbury Park, Calif.: Sage.

Gunter, Helen. (1995). "Jurassic Management: Chaos and Management Development in Educational Institutions." *Journal of Education Administration, 33*(4), 5–20.

Hamalainen, Kauko. (1994). *Capability Statement: Vantaa Institute for Continuing Education.* Helsinki: University of Helsinki.

Handy, Charles. (1994). *The Age of Paradox.* Boston, Mass.: Harvard Business School Press.

———. (1995a). *Beyond Certainty: The Changing Worlds of Organisations.* London: Hutchinson.

———. (1995b). *The Empty Raincoat: Making Sense of the Future.* Great Britain: Arrow Books Limited, Random House.

Hanushek, E., J. Kain, and S. Rivkin. (2004). Why Public Schools Lose Teachers. *Journal of Human Resources, 39*(2), 326–354.

Hargraves, Andy. (1994). *Changing Teachers, Changing Times: Teachers' Work Culture in the Postmodern Age.* New York: Teachers College Press.

Hart, Elvo Tevino. (1999). *Barefoot Heart: Stories of a Migrant Child.* Tempe, AZ: Bilingual Press.

Hawking, Stephen W. (1988). *A Brief History of Time: From the Big Bang to Black Holes.* New York: Bantam Books.

Heathers, Glen. (1972). "Overview of Innovations in Organization for Learning." *Interchange, 3,* 47–68.

Herbert, Nick. (1985). *Quantum Reality: Beyond the New Physics.* New York: Anchor Books, Doubleday.

Hernandez, Mario, Sharon Hodges, and Michelle Cascardi. (1998). "The Ecology of Outcomes: System Accountability in Children's Mental Health." *The Journal of Behavioral Health Services and Research, 25*(2), 136–150.

Hodgkinson, Harold. (September 1991). "Reform Versus Reality." *Phi Delta Kappan, 73,* 9–16.

Hofstede, Geert. (1984). *Culture's Consequences: International Differences in Work-Related Values.* Abridged edition. Beverly Hills: Sage.

Holte, John, ed. (1990). *Chaos: The New Science.* Lanham, Md.: Gustavus Adolphus College, University Press of America.

Hooks, B. (1994). *Teaching to Transgress: Education as the Practice of Freedom.* New York: Routledge.

———. (1995). *Killing Rage: Ending Racism.* New York: Henry Holt and Company.

Horsch, Karen. (1996). "Results-Based Accountability Systems: Opportunities and Challenges." *The Evaluation Exchange, 2*(1), 2–3.

Hurst, David K., and Brenda J. Zimmerman. (December 1994). "From Life Cycle to Ecocycle: A New Perspective on the Growth, Maturity, Destruction, and Renewal of Complex Systems." *Journal of Management Inquiry, 3*(4), 339–353.

Hyde, C. R. (1999). *Pay It Forward.* New York: Pocket Books.

Immegart, Glenn L., and Francis J. Pilecki. (1973). *An Introduction to Systems for the Educational Administrator.* Reading, Mass.: Addison-Wesley.

Imparato, Nicholas, and Oren Harare. (1994). *Jumping the Curve: Innovation and Strategic Choice in an Age of Transition.* San Francisco: Jossey-Bass.

Information Society Commission. (2002). *Building the Knowledge Society: Report to the Government.*

Ishikawa, Kaoru. (1985). (Translated by David J. Lee). *What Is Total Quality? The Japanese Way.* Englewood Cliffs, N.J.: Prentice-Hall.

Jaworski, Joseph. (1996). *Synchronicity: The Inner Path to Leadership.* San Francisco: Berrett-Koehler.

Johnson, Jonathan L., and Brian K. Burton. (December 1994). "Chaos and Complexity Theory for Management." *Journal of Management Inquiry, 3*(4), 327, 328.

Johnson, William L., Karolyn J. Snyder, Robert H. Anderson, and Annabelle Johnson. (1997). "Assessing School Work Culture." *Research in the Schools, 4,* 35–43. ERIC: ED 404339.

Juran, Joseph M. (1988). *Juran on Planning for Quality.* New York: The Free Press.

———. (1992). *Juran on Quality by Design.* New York: The Free Press.

Kanter, Rosabeth Moss. (1977). *Men and Women of the Corporation.* New York: Basic Books.

———. (1989). *When Giants Learn to Dance: Mastering the Challenges of Strategy, Management, and Careers in the 1990s.* New York: Simon & Schuster.

———. (1995). *World Class: Thriving Locally in the Global Economy.* New York: Simon & Schuster.

Kasler, Dirk. (1988). *Max Weber: An Introduction to His Life's Work.* Chicago: The University of Chicago Press.

Kast, Fremont E., and James E. Rosenzweig. (1979). *Organization and Management: A Systems and Contingency Approach.* 3rd ed. New York: McGraw Hill.

Kauffman, Stuart. (1995). *At Home in the Universe: The Search for Laws of Self-Organization and Complexity.* New York: Oxford University Press.

Kaufman, Roger, and Susan Thomas. (1980). *Evaluation Without Fear.* New York: New Viewpoints.

Kleiner, Art. (2003). "Karen Stephenson's Quantum Theory of Trust," *Strategy and Business, 29.*

Kosko, Bart. (1993). *Fuzzy Thinking and the New Logic.* London: Flamingo.

Lappe, Frances, Joseph Collins, Peter Russett, and Luis Esparza. (1998). *World Hunger: Twelve Myths.* New York, NY: Grove Press.

Lauwerier, Hans. (1987). *Fractals.* First published in the Netherlands by Aramithy Utigevers, Bloemendaalm. This English translation first published in the United States (1991). Oxford: Princeton University Press.

Lave, Jane, and Etienne Wenger. (1991). *Situated Learning: Legitimate Peripheral Participation.* Cambridge, UK: Cambridge University Press.

Learning for Tomorrow's World: First Results from PISA 2003. (2004). Paris: OECD.

Lennard, Earl J. (1993). "A Comparative Study of Shared Decision Making and Job Satisfaction Among Selected Secondary Vocational Education Teachers." Dissertation, University of South Florida, Tampa.

Lewin, Kurt. (1935). *A Dynamic Theory of Personality: Selected Papers.* Translated by Donald Adams and Karl Zener. New York: McGraw Hill.

———. (1951). *Field Theory in Social Science: Selected Theoretical Papers.* New York: Harper and Brothers.

Lewin, Roger. (1993). *Complexity: Living on the Edge of Chaos.* New York: Macmillan.

Li, Shuhua. (2004). *Scientific Spirit and Education in the Information Age: From Systems to Chaos.* (Only in Chinese). Guanzhou, China: Guangxi Press.

Lilenfeld, Robert. (1988). *The Rise and Fall of Systems Theory: An Ideological Analysis.* Malabar, Fla.: Robert E. Kreiger.

Limerick, David, and Bert Cunnington. (1993). *Managing the New Organization: A Blueprint for Networks and Strategic Alliances.* San Francisco: Jossey-Bass.

Lincoln, Yvonna S. (1990). "The Meaning of a Constructivist: A Remembrance of Transformations Past." In *The Paradigm Dialogue,* Egon Guba, 67–87. Newbury Park, Calif.: Sage.

Lindley, David. (1993). *The End of Physics: The Myth of a Unified Theory.* New York: Basic Books.

Linn, Robert. (1994). "Performance Assessment: Policy Premises & Technical Measurement Standards." *Educational Researcher, 23*(9) (December), 4–14.

Llamas, Jose Manuel Coronel. (July 1994). "The Process of Educational Reform in Spain: Where Is Don Quixote?" *International Journal of Educational Reform, 3*(3), 307–311.

Lomborg, Bjorn, ed. (2004). *Global Crises, Global Solutions.* Cambridge: Cambridge University Press.

Longenecker, Justin G. (1964). *Principles of Management and Organization Behavior.* 2nd ed. Columbus, Ohio: Charles E. Merrill.

Maeroff, Gene I. (March 1993). "Building Teams to Rebuild Schools." *Phi Delta Kappan, 74*(7), 512–519.

Mandelbrot, Benoit. (1990). "Fractals." In *Chaos: The New Science,* ed. John Holte. Manham, Md.: Gustavus Adophus College, University of America Press.

Martin, Joanne. (1992). *Cultures in Organizations: Three Perspectives.* New York: Oxford University Press.

Mason, R. (1998). *Globalizing Education: Trends and Applications.* New York: Routledge.

McDermott, Katherine. (2007). "'Expanding the Moral Community' or 'Blaming the Victim'? The politics of state education accountability policy." *American Education Research Journal, 44*(1), 77–111.

McLagan, Patricia, and Christo Nel. (1995). *The Age of Participation: New Governance for the Workplace and the World.* San Francisco: Berrett-Koehler.

McNair, C. J., and Kathleen Leibfried. (1992). *Benchmarking: A Tool for Continuous Improvement.* Essex Junction, Vt.: Oliver Wight Publications.

Merchant, C. Key. (1994). *Concepts in Critical Theory: Ecology.* Atlantic Highlands, N.J.: Humanities Press International.

Merrill, Harwood, ed. (1960, 1970). *Classics in Management.* American Management Association.

Miller, George L., and LaRue Krumm. (1992). *The Whats, Whys, and Hows of Quality Improvement: A Guidebook for Continuous Improvement.* Milwaukee, Wis.: ASQC Quality Press.

Mintzberg, Henry. (1994). *The Rise And Fall of Strategic Planning.* New York: Free Press.

Mirel, Jeffrey. (Fall 1994). "School Reform Unplugged: The Bensenville New American School Project." *American Education Research Journal, 31*(3), 481–518.

Mommsen, Wolfgang J. (1989). *The Political and Social Theory of Max Weber: Collected Essays.* Chicago: The University of Chicago Press.

Mokyr, J. (2002). "The Knowledge Society: Theoretical and Historical Underpinnings." Paper presented at the Ad Hoc Expert Group on Knowledge Systems, United Nations, New York. September 4–5.

Moran, Gabriel. (1996). *A Grammar of Responsibility.* New York: Crossroads.

Morgan, Colin, and Stephen Murgatroyd. (1994). *Total Quality Management in the Public Sector: An International Perspective.* Buckingham, UK: Open University Press.

Morgan, Gareth. (1997). *Images of Organizations.* Thousand Oaks, Calif.: Sage.

Morhman, S. A., R. V. Tenkasi, and A. M. Mohrman. (2003). "The Role of Networks in Fundamental Organizational Change." *The Journal of Applied Behavioral Science, 39*(3) (September), 301–323.

Mortenson, Greg, and David Oliver Relin. (2006). *Three Cups of Tea: One Man's Mission to Promote Peace . . . One School at a Time.* New York: Penguin Books.

Murgatroyd, Stephen, and Colin Morgan. (1993). *Total Quality Management and the School.* Buckingham, UK: Open University Press.

Nadler, David A., and Marc S. Gernstein. (1992). "Designing High-Performance Work Systems: Organizing People, Work, Technology, and Information." In *Organization Architecture,* eds. David Nalder, Marc Gerstein, and Robert Shaw, 110–133. San Francisco: Jossey-Bass.

Nadler, David A., Robert B. Shaw, A. Elise Walton, and Associates. (1995). *Discontinuous Change: Leading Organizational Transformation.* San Francisco: Jossey-Bass.

National Association of Secondary School Principals. (March 1996). "Breaking Ranks: Changing an American Institution: Prologue and Recommendations." *NASSP Bulletin, 80*(578), 54–67.

National Staff Development Council in cooperation with National Association of Secondary School Principals. (1995). *Standards for Staff Development.* Oxford, Ohio, and Restin, Va.: National Staff Development Council.

Naval, C., M. Print, and R. Veldhuis. (2002). "Education for Democratic Citizenship in the New Europe: Context and Reform." *European Journal of Education, 37*(2), 107–128.

Nemerowicz, Gloria, and Eugene Rosi. (1997). *Education for Leadership and Social Responsibility.* Washington DC.: Falmer Press.

Newmann, Fred M., Bruce M. King, and Mark Ridon. (1997). "Accountability and School Performance: Implications from Restructuring Schools." *Harvard Educational Review, 1,* 41–74.

Ngcongo, Rejoice P. (January 1994). "Conflict, Justice, and Problem Solving: Focus on South Africa." *International Journal of Educational Reform, 3*(1), 15–21.

No Child Left Behind. Retrieved December 6, 2007, from http://www.ed.gov/nclb/landing. jhtml.

Noddings, Nel. (1991). "Stories in Dialogue: Caring and Interpersonal Reason." In Witherell, Carol, and Nel Noddings. *Stories Lives Tell: Narrative and Dialogue in Education.* New York: Teachers College Press.

———. (1993). *Educating for Intelligent Belief or Unbelief.* New York: Teachers College Press, Columbia University.

———. (2002). *Starting at Home. Caring and Social Policy.* Berkeley: University of California.

Nonaka, Ikujiro, and Hiro Takeuchi. (1995). *The Knowledge-Creating Company: How Japanese Create the Dynamics of Innovation.* New York: Oxford University Press.

Norlin, Sture. (1996). "Systems Thinking for School Restructuring: A Cogwheel Model for School Development." Master's thesis, Institute of International Education, Stockholm University.

OECD. (2001). *Education at a Glance: OECD Indicators.* Paris: OECD

OECD. (2001). *Knowledge and Skills for Life: First Results from PISA 2000.* Paris: OECD.

Oshry, Barry. (1996). *Seeing Systems: Unlocking the Mysteries of Organizational Life.* San Francisco: Berrett-Koehler.

Parkinson, Ann. (1990). *An Examination of the Reliability & Factor Structure of the School Work Culture Profile.* Doctoral dissertation. University of South Florida, Tampa.

Parsons, Talcott. (1951). *The Social System.* New York: The Free Press.

———. (1966). *Structure and Process in Modern Societies.* Chicago: Free Press.

Pasco County 2001. (1993). Land O'Lakes, Fla.: Pasco County School Board.

Payne, Ruby. (1998). *A Framework for Understanding Poverty.* Baytown, Tex.: AhaProcess.

Pedler, Mike, John Burgoyne, and Tom Boydel. (1997). *The Learning Company: A Strategy for Sustainable Development.* New York: McGraw Hill.

Peitgen, Heinz-Otto. (1990). "The Causal Principle, Deterministic Laws, and Chaos." In *Chaos: The New Science,* ed. John Holte. Lanham, Md.: Gustavus Adolphus College, University Press of America.

Peters, Tom. (1992). *Liberation Management: Necessary Disorganization for the Nanosecond Nineties.* New York: Alfred A. Knopf.

Peters, Tom, and R. H. Waterman, Jr. (1982). *In Search of Excellence: Lessons from America's Best Run Companies.* New York: Harper & Row.

Piaget, Jean. (1970). *Structuralism.* New York: Basic Books.

Pinchot, Gifford, and Elizabeth Pinchot. (1993). *The End of Bureaucracy and the Rise of the Intelligent Organization.* San Francisco: Berrett-Koehler.

Pinedo, Victor. (2004). *Tsunami: Building Organizations Capable of Prospering in Tidal Waves.* Lincoln, NE: iUniverse.

Pink, Daniel H. (2005, 2006). *A Whole New Mind: Why Right-Brainers Will Rule the World.* New York: Penguin Press.

Poincare, Henri. (1892. Reprint, New York: Dover, 1962). *Methodes Nouvelles de la Mechanizue Celeste.* In *Foundations of Physics.* Paris: Gauthier Villars, 1990.

Poitier, Sidney. (2000). *The Measure of a Man: A Spiritual Autobiography.* San Francisco: Harper.

Popham, James W. (1988). *Educational Evaluation.* Englewood Cliffs, N.J.: Prentice Hall.

Preskill, Hallie H., and Rosalie Torres. (1999). *Evaluative Inquiry for Learning in Organizations.* Thousand Oaks, Calif.: Sage.

Preus, Betty. (October 1, 2007). "Educational Trends in China and the United States: Proverbial Pendulum or Potential for Balance?" *Phi Delta Kappan (89),* 2.

Price Waterhouse Change Integration Team. (1996). *The Paradox Principles: How High-Performance Companies Manage Chaos, Complexity and Contradiction to Achieve Superior Results.* Chicago: Irwin Professional.

Prigogine, Ilya. (1990). "Time, Dynamics, and Chaos: Integrating Poincare's 'Non-Integrable Systems.'" In *Chaos: The New Science,* ed. John Holte. Lanham, Md.: Gustavus Adolphus College, University Press of America.

Prigogine, Ilya, and Isabelle Stenger. (1984). *Order Out of Chaos: Man's Dialogue with Nature.* New York: Bantam Books.

Reich, Charles A. (1995). *Opposing the System.* New York: Crown.

Rhodes, Lewis. (1996). "Making Sense of (and with) TQM." In *Schools That Make Sense,* 18–23. Alexandria, Va.: American Association of School Administrators.

————. (April, 1997). "Connecting Leadership and Learning." Planning paper developed for the American Association of School Administrators, National Center for Connected Learning, Restin, Va.

Rossi, Peter H., and Howard E. Freeman. (1989). *Evaluation: A Systematic Approach.* Newbury Park, Calif.: Sage.

Rusch, Edith, and Catherine Marshall. (October 1997). "Gender Issues in Educational Administration Classrooms: The Confounding Questions, a Conversation Constructed from the Works of Rusch and Marshall." Handouts presented at the annual meeting of the University Council for Educational Administration, Orlando, Fla.

Russell, P. (1998). *Waking Up in Time: Finding Inner Peace in Times of Accelerating Change.* Novato, Calif.: Origin Press.

Ruthen, Russell. (January 1993). "Adapting to Complexity." *Scientific American,* 131–140.

Ryan, John M. (1992). *The Quality Team Concept in Total Quality Control.* Milwaukee, Wis.: ASQC Quality Press.

Sachs, Jeffrey D. (2005). *The End of Poverty: Economic Possibilities for Our Time.* New York: Penguin Press.

Sallach, David. (1974). "Class Domination and Ideological Hegemony." *Sociological Quarterly, 15,* 38–50.

Sang, Xinmin. (2006). "Present and Future Education in China: Technological Advancement, Globalization, and Educational Liberation." *Wingspan Journal, 16*(1), 27–30.

Sarason, Seymore. (1996). *How Schools Might Be Governed and Why.* New York: Teachers College Press.

Särkijärvi, A. (1999). "Do UNESCO Schools in Finland Prepare Their Students for the Future? A Study of Their School-Based Curriculums." Master's thesis. University of Helsinki, Department of Teacher Education.

Sarup, Madan. (1993). *Post-Structuralism and Postmodernism.* Athens: University of Georgia Press.

(SCANS) Secretary's Commission on Achieving Necessary Skills. (April 1992). *Learning a Living: A Blueprint for High Performance. A SCAN'S Report for America 2000. Part I.* Washington, D.C.: U.S. Department of Labor.

Schein, Edgar H. (1985). *Organizational Culture and Leadership.* San Francisco: Jossey-Bass.

Scheurich, Jim, and Linda Skrla. (2001). Continuing the Conversation on Equity and Accountability: Listening Appreciatively, Responding Responsibly. *Phi Delta Kappan, 83,* 322–326.

Schlechty, Phillip C. (1997). *Inventing Better Schools: An Action Plan for Educational Reform.* San Francisco: Jossey-Bass.

Schoorman, Dilys. (April 2006). Personal Correspondence to the Equal Employment Opportunity Committee (printed with permission).

Scott, Richard W. (1992). *Organizations, Rational, Natural, and Open Systems.* 3rd ed. Englewood Cliffs, N.J.: Prentice-Hall.

Scriven, Michael. (1973). "The methodology of evaluation." In Blaine R. Worther, and James R. Saunders. *Educational Evaluation: Theory & Practice.* Worthington, Ohio: C. A. Jones.

Seiling, Jane Galloway. (1997). *The Membership Organization: Achieving Top Performance Through New Workplace Community.* Palo Alto, Calif.: Davies Black.

Senge, Peter M. (1990). *The Fifth Discipline: The Art and Practice of the Learning Organization.* New York: Doubleday.

Senge, Peter M., and Colleen Lannon-Kim. (1991). "Recapturing the Spirit of the Learning Organization Through a Systems Approach." *The School Administrator, 48*(9), 8–13.

Shakeshaft, Carol. (1986). "A Female Organizational Culture." *Educational Horizons, 64*(3), 117–122.

Shaw, James. (2004). *Center for Youth Studies: Boredom.* Retrieved February 9, 2007, from http://roswellga.ourlittle.net/Boredom

Shilliff, Karl A., and Paul J. Motiska. (1992). *The Team Approach to Quality.* Milwaukee, Wis.: ASQC Quality Press.

Shonk, James H. (1992). *Team-Based Organizations: Developing a Successful Team Environment.* Homewood, Ill.: Business One Irwin.

Simon, Herbert A. (Winter 1946). "The Proverbs of Administration." *Public Administration Review, 6,* 53–67.

Sisodia, Raj, David B. Wolfe, and Jag Sheth. (2007). *Firms of Endearment: How World Class Companies Profit from Passion and Purpose.* Philadelphia: Wharton School of Business.

Snyder, Karolyn J. (1988a). *Competency Training for Managing Productive Schools.* San Diego: Harcourt Brace Jovanovich.

———. (1988). *Managing Productive Schools Trainer's Guides: Competencies 1, 2, 3, 4, 5, 6, 7, 8, 9, 10.* Tampa, FL: Managing Productive Schools.

———. (1988). *Managing Productive Schools Training Program: A Ten Module Series.* Tampa, FL: Managing Productive Schools.

Snyder, Karolyn J. (Fall 2005). "Leading Schools into the Global Age: The Challenge of our Times." *Wingspan Journal, 15*(1), 12–26.

Snyder, Karolyn J. (Fall 2006). "Schools Becoming Global Learning Centers: A Challenge and Opportunity for Our Times." *Wingspan Journal, 16*(1), 73–83.

Snyder, Karolyn J., and Mary Giella. (1988b). "Managing Productive District Programs: A Job Model for Instructional Supervisors." *Wingspan: The Pedamorphosis Conmmnunique, 4*(2) (December), 34–38.

———. (l988c) *School Work Culture Profile.* Tampa, Fla.: Managing Productive Schools Training Systems.

———. (1991). *Managing Productive Programs.* Tampa, Fla.: Managing Productive Schools Training Systems.

———, ed. (1994). "Welcome to the Quality Revolution." Theme issue of *Wingspan, 10*(1).

Snyder, Karolyn J., Michele Acker-Hocevar, and Kristen M. Snyder. (1994a). "Organizational Development in Transition: The Schooling Perspective." Paper presentation at the American Educational Research Association, ERIC EA 026 086.

———. (April l994b). "Typology for Principals of Learning Organizations Committed to Reframing Work Cultures." Paper presented at the American Educational Research Association Annual Program Conference, New Orleans. ERIC: ed 372469; EA 025941.

Snyder, Karolyn J., and Robert H. Anderson. (1986). *Managing Productive Schools: Toward an Ecology.* San Diego: Harcourt Brace Jovanovich.

Snyder, Karolyn J., John Fitzgerald, and Mary Giella. (1993). "Preparing School Districts for the 21st Century." *National Forum of Applied Educational Research, 6*(2), 16–22.

Snyder, Karolyn J., and Mary Giella. (1991). *Managing Productive Programs: A Training System for School District Leaders.* Tampa, Fla.: Managing Productive Schools Training Programs.

Snyder, Karolyn J., Kristen M. Snyder, and Michele Acker-Hocevar. (September 1995). "Chaos Theory as a Lens for Advancing Quality Schooling." Paper presentation at the Annual Conference for British Education, Management, and Administration Society. Oxford, England. ERIC: ED 413 630, EA 027 647.

Snyder, K. J., M. Acker-Hocevar, and K. Snyder. (2000). *Living on the Edge of Chaos: Leading Schools into the Global Age.* Milwaukee, Wis.: ASQ Quality Press.

Snyder, Kristen M. (1997). "A Construct Validation and Reliability Estimation of the Educational Quality Benchmark System." Doctoral dissertation, University of South Florida, Tampa.

Snyder, Kristen M., and Karolyn J. Snyder. (January 1996). "Developing Integrated Work Cultures: A Study on School Change." *NASSP Bulletin, 80,* 67–77.

Snyder, T. Richard. (2001). *The Protestant Ethic and the Spirit of Punishment,* Grand Rapids, Mich.: Eerdmans.

Sorensen, E. K., & E. S. Takle. (2002). "Collaborative Knowledge Building in Web-Based Learning: Assessing the Quality of Dialogue." *International Journal of E-learning, 1*(1), 28–32.

Spendolini, Michael J. (1992). *The Benchmarking Book.* New York: American Management Association.

Stake, Robert E. (1967). *American Education Research Association Monograph Series on Evaluation.* Chicago: Rand-McNally.

Stephenson, Karen. (2005). "Trafficking in Trust: The Art and Science of Human Knowledge Networks." In *Enlightened Power: How Women Are Transforming the Practice of Leadership,* ed. L. Coughlin, E. Wingard, and K. Hollihan. San Francisco: Jossey-Bass, 242–265.

Stewart, Vivian. (April 2007). "Becoming Citizens of the World." *Educational Leadership, 64*(7), 8–14.

Stiglitz, Joseph E. (2006). *Making Globalization Work.* New York: W. W. Norton & Company.

Strike, Kenneth A. (1993). "Professionalism, Democracy, and Discursive Communities: Normative Reflections on Restructuring." *American Educational Review Journal, 30*(2), 255–275.

Stufflebeam, Daniel L., and Egon Guba. (1971). *Educational Evaluation and Decision Making.* Itasca, Ill.: F. E. Peacock.

Sullivan, Elaine C. (Fall 2006). "The International School Connection: An Evolving School Development Platform for a Global Age." *Wingspan Journal, 16*(1), 66–73.

Swieringa, Joop, and Andre Wierdsma. (1992). *Becoming a Learning Organization: Beyond the Learning Curve.* New York: Addison-Wesley.

Tannen, Daniel. (1995). "The Power of Talk: Who Gets Heard and Why." *Harvard Business Review, 75*(5), 138–148.

Tapscott, Don, and Anthony D. Williams. (2007). *Wikinomics: How Mass Collaboration Changes Everything.* London: Portfolio.

Taylor, Frederick Winslow. (1912). *Shop Management.* New York: Harper and Brothers.

Tenkasi, R. V., and M. C. Chesmore. (2003). "Social Networks and Planned Organizational Change: The Impact of Strong Network Ties on Effective Change and Implementation and Use." *The Journal of Applied Behavioral Science, 39*(3) (September), 281–300.

Tilles, Seymour. (1963). "The Manager's Job: System's Approach." Reprinted (1970) in Chapter 12 in *Organization Theories,* ed. William P. Sexton. Columbus, Ohio: Charles E. Merrill.

Toffler, Alvin. (1990). *Powershift: Knowledge, Wealth, and Violence at the Edge of the 21st Century.* New York: Bantam Books.

Touchton, D., and M. Acker-Hocevar. (2005). Contextual Leadership: Responding to Issues of Social Justice and High-Risk Schools. Paper presentation at the University Council of Educational Administration. Nashville, Tenn. November 10–13.

Tutu, Desmond. (1999). *No Future Without Forgiveness.* New York: Doubleday.

UNESCO. (2002). *Learning to Be: A Holistic and Integrated Approach to Values Education for Human Development: Core Values and the Valuing Process for Developing Innovative Practices for Values Education Toward International Understanding and a Culture of Peace.* Bangkok: UNESCO Asia and Pacific Regional Bureau for Education.

———. (2003). "From the Information Society to Knowledge Societies." http://www.unesco.org/wsis.

University Council of Educational Administration (UCEA). http://www.ucea.org.

Useem, Michael, and Thomas A. Kochan. (1992). "Creating the Learning Organization." In *Transforming Organizations,* T. A. Kochan and M. Useem, eds., 391–406. New York: Oxford University Press.

Vaill, Peter B. (1996). *Learning as a Way of Being: Strategies for Survival in a World of Permanent White Water.* San Francisco: Jossey-Bass.

van Gigch, John P. (1978). *Applied General Systems Theory.* 2nd ed. New York: Harper & Row.

van Lakerveld, Jaap. (1997). "Schulautonomie in den Niederlanden." *Erziehung und Unterricht, Oestereichisches Paedogogische Zeitschrift, 3,* 219–225. Vienna, Austria: OBV Padagogischerverlag.

van Lakerveld, Jaap, and Peter Nentwig. (March 1996). "School-Based Inservice Education." *Educational Leadership, 53*(6), 68–71.

Walker, Allan, Vu Van Tao, and Dang Quoc Bao. (April 1996). "Education Renovation in Vietnam." *International Journal of Educational Reform, 5*(2), 140–145.

Wallenberg, Helena H. (1997). *The Welfare Renaissance: The New Swedish Model. Are We Educating for The Future?* Stockholm: Barn Academiem.

Wartenberg, Thomas E. (1990). *The Forms of Power: From Domination to Transformation.* Philadelphia: Temple University Press.

Watson, Gregory H. (1993). *Strategic Benchmarking: How to Rate Your Company's Performance Against the World's Best.* New York: John Wiley and Sons.

Watts, D. J. (2003). *Six Degrees: The Science of a Connected Age.* New York: W. W. Norton & Company.

Weber, Max. (1922). "Bureaucracy." In *Max Weber: Essays in Sociology,* eds. H. Gerth & C. W. Mills. Oxford: Oxford University Press.

———. (1924). "Legitimate Authority and Bureaucracy." In *Organization Theory: Selected Readings,* ed. D. S. Pugh. London: Penguin Books.

Weiss, Heather B., and Francine H. Jacobs. (1988). *Evaluating Family Programs.* New York: Aldine de Gruyter.

Welhage, Gary, G. Smith, and P. Lipham. (1992). "Restructuring Urban Schools: The New Futures Experience." *American Education Research Journal, 29*(1), 51–93.

Wellins, Richard S., William C. Byham, and Jeanne M. Wilson. (1991). *Empowered Teams: Creating Self-Directed Work Groups That Improve Quality, Productivity, and Participation.* San Francisco: Jossey-Bass.

Wheatley, Margaret J. (1992). *Leadership and the New Science: Learning about Organization from an Orderly Universe.* San Francisco: Berrett-Koehler.

Wheatley, Margaret J., and Myron Kellner-Rogers. (1996). *A Simpler Way.* San Francisco: Berrett-Koehler.

Wilson, Cynthia, David Walker, Marta Cruz-Janzen, Michele Acker-Hocevar, and Perry Schoon. (2005/2006). "A Systems Alignment Model for Examining School Practices: A Standards-Based Alignment Model." *International Journal of Learning, 12*(7), 303–310.

Wynne, E. (1972). *The Politics of School Accountability. Public Information About Schools.* Berkeley, Calif.: McCutchan.

Yunus, Muhammad. (2007). *Banker to the Poor: Micro-Lending and the Battle Against World Poverty.* New York: Public Affairs.

Young, Stanley, and Charles E. Summer. (1966). "The Management System and the Meaning of Organization." Reprinted (1970) in Chapter 13 in *Organization Theories,* ed. William P. Sexton. Columbus, Ohio: Charles E. Merrill.

Zohar, Danah. (1990). *The Quantum Self: Human Nature and Consciousness Defined by the New Physics.* New York: Quill/William Morrow.

Zukav, Gary. (1979). *The Dancing Wu Li Masters: An Overview of the New Physics.* New York: Quill/William Morrow.

Index

Functions of the Executive, The, 52
Fusion approach, 93
Fusion, 91–93
Fuzziness, 81
Fuzzy thinking, 81

G

Gains, John, 72
Gall, Meredith D., 165–166, 168–169, 319
Garton, L., 187, 321
Garvin, David A., 321
Gaul, Tom, 251
Geertz, Clifford, 162, 202, 321
General system theory (GST), 52–53
Gernstein, Marc S., 325
Getzels, Jacob W., 53, 321
Giddens, A., 319
Gidlund, Bodil, 263, 268
Giella, Mary, 63, 71, 75, 241, 321, 328
Gilligan, Carol, 126, 321
Glasser, William, 321
GLC. *See* Global Learning Center
Gleick, James, 62, 64–65, 322
Global citizenship, 184
Global community, challenges, 12–19
Global Dynamics, 7–9
Global Learning Center (GLC), 4, 25, 285
   benchmarks, 24–25, 299–303
Global learning, 23–27, 212–215
Global Organization Development, 24
Global Trends, 7–9
Global Youth Leadership Summit, 17
Goldberger, Nancy, 126, 318
Goldman Sachs Investment Bank, 8
Goldman, Paul, 110, 120, 320
Gomer, H., 322
Goodlad, John L., 322
Gore, Al, 17, 189, 191, 322
Graham, Pauline, 51, 322
Grameen Bank, 142–144
Gramsci, Antonio, 110, 113, 322
Gravitational interactions, 49
Greene, M., 185–186, 322

Greenlee, Bobbie Jean, 322
Gripenskolan, 292–294
Gripen Helps, 293
Group of 8G8, 8
Group theory, 232
Grudnitski, (1996), 177
Grudnitski, Gary, 319
GST. *See* general system theory
Guba, Egon, 53, 165–170, 321–322, 329
Gunter, Helen, 256, 322
Guo, Rain, 292

H

Hamalainen, Kauko, 320, 322
Han, Guo, 289, 294
Handy, Charles, 73–74, 322
Hanushek, E., 141, 322
Hargraves, Andy, 112, 322
Harris, Alma, 109, 318
Hart, Elvo Tevino, 138–139, 322
Hawking, Stephen W., 46, 49, 322
Hayhornthwaite, C., 187, 321
Heathers, Glen, 88, 322
Hegemony, 110
Helplessness, 141–142
Helsinki City Schools, 6
Heniksson, Lena, 86
Herbert, Nick, 31, 46–47, 322
Hernandez, Mario, 163–164, 178, 322
High-achieving schools, 233–246
Highfield, Roger, 66, 74, 320
High-performing schools, 144–149
High-performing teams, standards, 258
High-poverty schools, 144–149
High-referral rate schools, 261
Hillegas, 38
Hillsborough County School District, 69, 87, 287
Hodges, Sharon, 163–164, 178, 322
Hodgkinson, Harold, 43, 322
Hofstede, Geert, 322
Holte, John, 62, 66, 68, 74, 322
Homeschooling, 41
Hooks, B., 113, 185–186, 322
Hooshmand, 12

DATE DUE
